PARIS AND THE MUSICAL

Paris and the Musical explores how the famous city has been portrayed on stage and screen, investigates why the city has been of such importance to the genre and tracks how it has developed as a trope over the 20th and 21st centuries.

From global hits *An American in Paris, Gigi, Les Misérables, Moulin Rouge!* and *The Phantom of the Opera* to the less widely-known *Bless the Bride, Can-Can, Irma la Douce* and *Marguerite*, the French capital is a central character in an astounding number of Broadway, Hollywood and West End musicals. This collection of 18 essays combines cultural studies, sociology, musicology, art and adaptation theory, and gender studies to examine the envisioning and dramatisation of Paris, and its depiction as a place of romance, hedonism and libertinism or as 'the capital of the arts'.

The interdisciplinary nature of this collection renders it as a fascinating resource for a wide range of courses; it will be especially valuable for students and scholars of Musical Theatre and those interested in Theatre and Film History more generally.

Olaf Jubin is Professor of Musical Theatre and Media Studies at Regent's University London. He has written, co-written and co-edited several books on popular culture, including *British Musical Theatre since 1950, The Oxford Handbook of the British Musical* and the forthcoming *The Oxford Handbook of the Global Stage Musical*.

PARIS AND THE MUSICAL

The City of Light on Stage and Screen

Edited by Olaf Jubin

Routledge
Taylor & Francis Group

LONDON AND NEW YORK

First published 2021
by Routledge
2 Park Square, Milton Park, Abingdon, Oxon OX14 4RN

and by Routledge
52 Vanderbilt Avenue, New York, NY 10017

Routledge is an imprint of the Taylor & Francis Group, an informa business

British Library Cataloguing-in-Publication Data
A catalogue record for this book is available from the British Library

Library of Congress Cataloging-in-Publication Data
A catalog record for this book has been requested

ISBN: 978-1-138-61106-1 (hbk)
ISBN: 978-1-138-61109-2 (pbk)
ISBN: 978-0-429-46543-7 (ebk)

Typeset in Bembo
by Apex CoVantage, LLC

*For Anja P. Helm, the acclaimed graphic designer,
with thanks for nearly half a century of friendship
and that wonderful day in Paris in January 1987*

CONTENTS

ACKNOWLEDGEMENTS

Many thanks to Ben Piggott and Zoe Forbes at Routledge for their support, trust and expert guidance.

This volume is the outcome of collaboration at its most satisfying and joyous: the seventeen contributors delivered essays that made my job as editor not just easy, but thrilling. Thanks to all of you for joining me in this endeavour.

I would also like to express my gratitude to the individuals and photo agencies that gave permission for use of their images: Elizabeth Seal as well as Alamy Stock Photo, ArenaPal, Getty Images, the New York Public Library, Photofest NYC, Donald Cooper/Photostage and Shutterstock. In this context I wish to acknowledge the great work of the following photographers: Clive Barda, Richard Brodzeller, Len Cassingham, Denis de Marnay, Friedman – Abeles, Michael Le Poer Trench, Bob Marshak, Alastair Muir, Nigel Norrington, Johan Persson, George Rinhart, Bettina Strenske and Michael Ward.

I am eternally grateful to John Snelson, scholar and friend *extraordinaire*, who in addition to Chapter 11 also took on the essay on *Bless the Bride* at the shortest notice when the previously contracted author dropped out after the agreed deadline, claiming that there simply 'wasn't enough material' on the Ellis/Herbert musical to write about it. John has proved him gloriously wrong; I couldn't be happier with each of John's texts which demonstrate his impressive range of expertise on British musical theatre (among many other things).

I would like to thank Professor William Harris at Regent's University London for helping me arrange my work schedule to make room for this long-gestating project and my wonderful colleagues Leslie Viney, Phil Grey, Elena Hristova and Elif Toker-Turnalar, for their continuing support.

As always, my gratitude goes to my family, Helga, Britta, Oliver, Joshua and Amira Jubin as well as to Janet Fehler – where would I be without you?

Finally, this volume would not have been possible without Robert Gordon whose importance in my life cannot be overstated.

CONTRIBUTORS

Daniel Batchelder is a visiting assistant professor of musicology at the University of Cincinnati College-Conservatory of Music, where he teaches courses on musical theatre, film and music aesthetics. His primary research examines the dramatic and expressive functions of music and song in musicals with an emphasis on the animated musicals of the Walt Disney Studio. His review of the Master Score to *Snow White and the Seven Dwarfs* was awarded the Eva Judd O'Meara Award for best review in the journal *Notes*, while his 2018 dissertation *American Magic: Song, Animation, and Drama in Disney's Golden Age Musicals (1928–1942)* was awarded the Adel Heinrich Award for Achievement in Musicological Research. His forthcoming work will appear in *The Oxford Handbook of Children's Film* and *American Music*, and he is currently serving as guest editor for a special edition of the journal *American Music* on music and sound in Disney media.

Maya Cantu teaches on the Drama and Literature faculties at Bennington College and is the author of *American Cinderellas on the Broadway Musical Stage: Imagining the Working Girl from* Irene *to* Gypsy (Palgrave Macmillan, 2015). She serves as Dramaturgical Advisor for Off-Broadway's Mint Theater Company and as Editor of Book Reviews for *New England Theatre Journal*. Maya is the 2020 recipient of the American Theatre and Drama Society's Vera Mowry Roberts Research and Publication Award for her essay, 'Beyond the Rue Pigalle: Recovering Ada "Bricktop" Smith as "Muse", Mentor, and Maker of Transatlantic Musical Theatre', published in *Reframing the Musical: Race, Culture and Identity* (ed. Sarah Whitfield, Red Globe Press/Springer Nature Ltd., 2019).

Marguerite Chabrol is Professor of Film Studies at Université Paris 8 in France. Her research tackles intermediality in film, more specifically the relations between theatre and film in classical Hollywood cinema. She studied the transfers of straight plays between Broadway and Hollywood in *De Broadway à Hollywood* (CNRS

Editions, 2016) and Katharine Hepburn's stage and film career in *Katharine Hepburn: Paradoxes de la comédienne* (Presses universitaires de Rennes, 2019). She is currently interested in the musical and recently published a French critical edition of Jane Feuer, co-edited with Laurent Guido (*Mythologies du film musical*, Presses du Réel, 2016). She also co-edited with Pierre-Olivier Toulza *Star Turns in Hollywood Musicals* (Presses du Réel, 2017).

Clare Chandler is a senior lecturer in musical theatre at the University of Wolverhampton. She has previously worked at the Liverpool Institute for Performing Arts and Edge Hill University. Clare's research interests include the impact of technology on the development of contemporary musical theatre, feminism and musical theatre, and pedagogical practice and performer training. She has an MA in Musical Theatre from Goldsmiths University. Clare has worked as a dramaturg on *Em*, a new musical by Benjamin Till and directed the regional premiere of *Angry Birds the Musical* by Dougal Irvine in 2018.

Venita Datta is Professor of French Studies at Wellesley College (Massachusetts). The author of *Birth of a National Icon: The Literary Avant-Garde and the Origins of the Intellectual in France* (1999) and *Heroes and Legends of Fin-de-Siècle France: Gender, Politics, and National Identity* (2011), she is at work on a book on French-American rivalries at the *fin de siècle*. Recent articles include 'Buffalo Bill Goes to France: French-American Encounters at the Wild West Show, 1889–1905', *French Historical Studies* (2018) and 'Gilded Age' in Dominique Kalifa, ed. *Les noms d'époque: de Restauration à 'années de plomb'* (Gallimard, 2020). Datta is co-editor (with Elinor Accampo) of a special issue of *French Historical Studies* (2019) on 'Patriarchy, Protection, and Women's Agency in Modern France: Essays in Honor of Rachel G. Fuchs'. The past Chief Editor of H-France Forum, Datta is currently serving as its 19th- and 20th-Century History editor.

Julia Foulkes is a professor of history at The New School and the author of *A Place for Us: West Side Story and New York* (2016); *To the City: Urban Photographs of the New Deal* (2011); and *Modern Bodies: Dance and American Modernism from Martha Graham to Alvin Ailey* (2002). She curated the exhibition *Voice of My City: Jerome Robbins and New York* (New York Public Library for Performing Arts at Lincoln Center, 2018–19) and appeared in Netta Yerushalmy's *Paramodernities* (2018) as a writer/speaker on Bob Fosse. She is currently researching the rise of New York as a capital of culture in the 20th century.

Stefan Frey is a writer, broadcaster, lecturer, dramaturg and director. He was born on 1962 in Heilbronn, Germany and read theatre studies, art history and German literature at the University in Munich (MA 1989). In 1993, he obtained his doctorate with a thesis on Franz Lehár under the supervision of Prof. Dr. Dieter Borchmeyer in Heidelberg. He has worked as Assistant director at the Deutsche Schauspielhaus Hamburg, the LTT Tübingen and the Thüringer Landestheater

Rudolstadt, where he directed several productions. From 2004 to 2006, he was head of the Studio Theatre at the Institute for Theatre Studies at Munich University; since then he has worked there and at the University of Vienna as a lecturer. Since 2015, he is one of the hosts of the radio Broadcast *Operetten-Boulevard* (BR-Klassik). Frey has written many articles on operetta in academic and non-academic publications, radio features and books, including *Franz Lehár oder das schlechte Gewissen der leichten Musik* (1995); '*Was sagt Ihr zu diesem Erfolg*'. *Franz Lehár und die Unterhaltungsmusik des 20. Jahrhunderts* (1999); *Emmerich Kálmán – 'Unter Tränen lachen'* (2003; English translation: 2014); *Leo Fall. Spöttischer Rebell der Operette* (2010); '*Dem Volk zur Lust und zum Gedeihen'. 150 Jahre Gärtnerplatztheater* (2015) and *Franz Lehár. Der letzte Operettenkönig* (2020).

Michael G. Garber, PhD, is an interdisciplinary scholar and a specialist in Tin Pan Alley and the early-20th-century American musical. Currently he is a research fellow of the University of Winchester and University of London, Goldsmiths College. His work integrates the Diamond Method for the Arts (of psychiatrist Dr John Diamond) with academic pursuits, through his publications, international lecturing and teaching in fields as diverse as literature, education, anthropology, communications and the histories of film, media and all the lively arts. His book *My Melancholy Baby: The First Ballads of the Great American Songbook, 1902–1913* (University Press of Mississippi, 2021) focuses on ten songs that developed intimacy within the jazzy American popular song traditions of Tin Pan Alley and Broadway. Their complex and colourful histories demonstrate the collective nature of innovation. His articles are equally interdisciplinary, covering: reflexivity in Broadway lyrics; the ragtime, jazz and country-western traditions of nonsense syllable singing called 'eephing'; and the mode of tragicomedy in early Hollywood musicals. His current research includes: reception of movies and music; lullabying and story-time practices; images of the sad clown and torch singer; and a history of American women popular songwriters of the first half of the 20th century.

Robert Gordon is Professor of Theatre and Director of the Pinter Centre for Performance and Creative Writing at Goldsmiths, University of London, where in 2003 he introduced the first European MA in Musical Theatre for producers and writers. He is author of *The Purpose of Playing: Modern Acting Theory in Perspective* (2006), *Harold Pinter's Theatre of Power* (2012) and, with Olaf Jubin and Millie Taylor, *British Musical Theatre Since 1950* (2016). Edited collections include the *Oxford Handbook of Sondheim Studies* (2014) and, with Olaf Jubin, the *Oxford Handbook of the British Musical* (2016) as well as the *Oxford Handbook of the Global Stage Musical* (2021). Robert has worked internationally as an actor, director and playwright and is author of *Red Earth* (1985) and *Waterloo Road* (Young Vic Theatre, 1987). In 2012 he devised and co-directed *Pinter: In Other Rooms* for a tour of Eastern Europe and directed the European première of Kander and Ebb's *Steel Pier* at Na Zabradli in Brno, while his musical with Nick Hutson *Five Children and It*, received a professional workshop performance in 2015. He is currently engaged as a writer and actor of *Shylock Speaks*, which premiered in February 2020, and in 2018 introduced a BA in Musical Theatre at Goldsmiths.

Olaf Jubin is Professor of Musical Theatre and Media Studies at Regent's University London and Associate Lecturer on the MA in Musical Theatre at Goldsmiths, University of London. He gained his PhD from the Ruhr-Universität Bochum, Germany, and has written and co-edited several books on the mass media and musical theatre, including a study of the German dubbing and subtitling of Hollywood musicals and a comparative analysis of reviews of the musicals of Stephen Sondheim and Andrew Lloyd Webber. He is co-author of *British Musical Theatre since 1950* (Bloomsbury, 2016) and co-editor of the *Oxford Handbook of the British Musical* (OUP, 2016). In 2017, his monograph on *Into the Woods* appeared as part of the Routledge Fourth Wall series. He recently co-edited the *Oxford Handbook of the Global Stage Musical* (OUP, 2021) and is currently working on a book on the dramaturgy and lyrics of Tim Rice.

Raymond Knapp is Distinguished Professor of Musicology and Humanities at UCLA, where he serves as Academic Associate Dean for the Herb Alpert School of Music and Director of the Center for Musical Humanities. He has authored five books and co-edited two others, including *The American Musical and the Formation of National Identity* (2005; winner of the George Jean Nathan Award for Dramatic Criticism), *The American Musical and the Performance of Personal Identity* (2006), the *Oxford Handbook of the American Musical* (2011, with Mitchell Morris and Stacy Wolf), and *Making Light: Haydn, Musical Camp, and the Long Shadow of German Idealism* (2018). His published essays address a wide range of additional interests, including Beethoven, Wagner, Brahms, Tchaikovsky, Mahler, nationalism, musical allusion, music and identity, disability studies and film music.

Robert Lawson-Peebles worked at the Universities of Oxford, Princeton, Aberdeen, and finally Exeter, where he is now an honorary senior research fellow. He has been a Leverhulme emeritus fellow and was awarded a number of other fellowships, for instance from the Salzburg Seminar and the American Council of Learned Societies. He has published three books on the cultural history of the American environment, a history of earlier American Literature, and co-edited *Writing the Americas, 1480–1826* for the 2016 *Yearbook of English Studies*. He has written articles on subjects ranging from Sir Walter Raleigh to the relationship of ideology and the arts. His interest in transatlantic music led to *Approaches to the American Musical* (1996); contributions to the Oxford handbooks on Stephen Sondheim (2012), the British Musical (2016) and the Global Stage Musical (in press), and essays about 20th-century versions of *The Beggar's Opera* and about the reception of jazz in Britain.

Mitchell Morris is Professor and Chair of Musicology as well as Chair of LGBTQ Studies at UCLA. He has written and spoken on a wide variety of topics, including music, gender and sexuality; opera, musical theatre and film; and the musical culture of the last *fin de siècle*. He is a co-editor of the *Oxford Handbook of the American Musical* and the author of *The Persistence of Sentiment: Display and Feeling in Popular Music of the 1970s*. A working librettist, he has had works premiered in the United States and Mexico.

Stewart Nicholls is a director/choreographer, writer and lecturer. He is also the archivist for David Heneker, Julian Slade and George Posford, and has restored and directed/choreographed many works of British Musical Theatre including: *Popkiss* (Electric Theatre, Guildford, 1997), *Sail Away* (Rhoda McGaw Theatre, Woking, 1998), *A Girl Called Jo, Follow That Girl, Zip Goes a Million, Vanity Fair, Grab Me a Gondola, The Amazons, Ann Veronica* (all staged at Theatre Museum, Covent Garden, London between 2000 and 2005), *Gay's the Word* (Finborough Theatre, London, 2012 and revived at Jermyn Street Theatre, London, 2013), *Salad Days, The Biograph Girl* (both staged for London College of Music, 2013), and *Free as Air* (Finborough Theatre, London, 2014). Many of his productions have been recorded and released on CD, while his restoration of Noël Coward's *Sail Away* is published by Warner/Chappell Music. Over the past 20 years, Stewart has professionally directed and choreographed many musicals, new works, revivals, cabarets and pantomimes. In parallel with his professional career, Stewart is Programme Leader for the MA and MFA Musical Theatre course at the Guildford School of Acting/Surrey University.

Hannah Robbins is an assistant professor in popular music at the University of Nottingham in the UK. Her previous publications include chapters on queer reception to MGM's *The Wizard of Oz*, the studio's film adaptation of Cole Porter's *Kiss Me, Kate*, and an article about feminism and palatability in the stage version of Disney's *Frozen*. Hannah's first monograph *Kiss Me, Kate: the Life and Legacy of a Classic Musical Comedy* is due for publication with Oxford University Press in 2021. Her current research focuses on Cole Porter's screen musicals and the representation of Black creatives in the Broadway and Hollywood musical.

Florian J. Seubert works as Associate Lecturer in Music Theatre at Goldsmiths, University of London. He holds a BA in German and English Studies from Otto-Friedrich-University Bamberg and an MSt in Modern Languages from University of Oxford. He is currently working on a practice-based PhD that explores music theatre-making as inclusive practice. In addition to teaching theatre and performance, Florian works as writer-director and drama facilitator. His inclusive and innovative music theatre projects have been funded by the Arts Council England and Opera Holland Park among others (www.florianjseubert.co.uk).

John Snelson is a musicologist and cultural historian. He specialises in the lyric stage, especially 20th-century British musical theatre and its relationship to national identity, the subject of his PhD. His publications include *Andrew Lloyd Webber* (Yale

University Press, 2004) and chapters in *The Cambridge Companion to the Musical* (Cambridge University Press, 2002; revised for the 3rd edition, 2017), *The Oxford Handbook of the British Musical* (OUP, 2016), *Musical Theatre in Europe 1830–1945* (Brepols, 2017) and *The Oxford Handbook of the Global Stage Musical* (OUP, 2021). He was a member of the three-year international research network 'Screen Adaptations of *Le Fantôme de l'Opéra*: Routes of Cultural Transfer', funded by the Leverhulme Trust, and contributed to the volume of *Opera Quarterly* (no.34/Spring – Summer 2018) dedicated to the project. Other publications include *The Ring: An Illustrated History of Wagner's 'Ring' at the Royal Opera House* (Royal Opera House/Oberon Books, 2006) and *How to Enjoy Opera* (Oberon Books, 2016). For twenty years he worked at the Royal Opera House, Covent Garden, where he was Head of Publishing and Interpretation.

Pierre-Olivier Toulza is Assistant Professor of Film Studies at Université de Paris. He is a specialist in classical Hollywood cinema and seriality in cinema and television. He is the author of *Le Cercle rouge de Jean-Pierre Melville* (Atlande, 2010) as well as numerous journal articles and book chapters related to Hollywood genres (mainly the melodrama and the musical) and the relations between the performing body and attractions. He recently co-edited *Politiques du musical hollywoodien* (Presses universitaires de Paris Nanterre, 2020), *Star Turns in Hollywood Musicals* (Les Presses du Réel, 2017) in its English and French versions, and *L'Expérience du cinéma* (Hermann, 2015). Between 2015 and 20017, he led with Marguerite Chabrol the international research project 'Musical MC²: the Hollywood Film Musical in its Mediatic and Cultural Context'. He is currently working on a book for Presses universitaires de Tours's 'Serial' series entitled *Backstage: scènes et coulisses des series*.

INTRODUCTION

It was around the end of the 19th century that Paris gained the soubriquet 'Ville Lumière', the 'City of Light' (Rearick, 2011, p. 12), courtesy of the 56,000 gas lamps that had been installed in the 1860s. An important role in disseminating this and other conceptions of the French capital, in enhancing and cementing a Paris of the imagination has been ascribed to international guidebooks that came out in the same era,[1] because they 'were instrumental in framing individual experiences with a collective memory' (Rearick, 2011, p. 7).

One could argue that the Anglo-American entertainment industry fulfils similar functions to a Baedeker – in its own way, it is simply another authoritative travel guide for tourists: with its portrayals of places that might be worth a visit it offers road maps, instructions for the field and how-to manuals to ensure the audience will enjoy experiences that are both unique and communal. Its depiction of the French capital is a case in point: 20th century film and theatre quickly discovered Paris as one of their favourite topics, in the course shaping pre-conceptions and expectations while at the same time providing the prism through which individual exploits in the city have been viewed and interpreted.

For more than 130 years Paris has been promoted, glorified and exploited by mass culture. In this popularisation of the French capital as a perfect tourist destination for all kinds of adventures the stage and film musical, after all both born in strictly commercial environments, often played an important role. It is astounding how many famous Broadway/West End shows and Hollywood films have been set in the French capital, and this volume aims to investigate why the city has been of such importance to the musical and how it has developed as a trope, in the process offering an exploration of both varieties of musical entertainment.

From the early 20th century onwards, musical theatre responded to the fascinating reputation of the French capital and incorporated the iconicity of Paris as a state of mind into such global successes as Franz Lehár's operetta *The Merry Widow*

(1905) which was the first major work to make use of Paris as a glittering backdrop to an enchanting love story. Since then, the 'City of Light' has been a recurrent reference point in Anglo-American entertainment, from shows and movies set in Paris (*like Roberta, Funny Face* and *The Phantom of the Opera*) to those imported from there (i.e. *Irma La Douce* and *Les Misérables*). Over the decades, these and other musicals were instrumental in exploring, exploiting as well as celebrating the French capital as a symbol, and that mythology of Paris continues to this day.

This book covers widely known works (like *The Merry Widow, An American in Paris, Gigi, Les Miz* and *Phantom*) from a singular perspective, but also includes fresh approaches to musicals with cult status (such as *Dear World, Sunday in the Park with George* and *Moulin Rouge!*). In addition, it offers the first detailed discussion of important shows/movies that have rarely been investigated in depth (like *Bless the Bride, Can-Can, Irma La Douce, Marguerite*). It is divided into six sections with three chapters each, which are organised in vaguely chronological order.

Part I: 'Capital Paris'

The opening section of the volume highlights three key topics: the city itself as cultural symbol, *The Merry Widow* as the first important work to reflect its symbolic value and Cole Porter as the composer-lyricist who wrote most consistently about the metropolis.

In Chapter 1 Venita Datta explores the historic role of Paris as the capital of modernity, tracing not only the evolution of the city during this key period, but also examining the position it occupied in the cultural imaginary, as both emblem of French identity and of modernity. During the years spanning the Second Empire to World War I (1852–1914), Paris became not only a leading cultural and intellectual centre – the birthplace of the avant-garde and the capital of pleasure – it also emerged as the most modern city in the world, especially during what the French call the *belle époque*, roughly from 1880 to 1914. It boasted arguably the world's biggest department store as well as its largest press. The recently transformed city was also home to wide tree-lined boulevards, housing shops, cafés and theatres, which attested to a vibrant boulevard culture. Around this time, Paris also gained notoriety as an environment for pleasure and hedonism, or for some, a place of debauchery and depravity, especially in Montmartre, even though this was not to last: 'The way of life symbolized by the pleasure seekers of the *belle époque* would survive in some form after 1914, although much of it would disappear in the trenches of World War I.'

Chapter 2 charts the victorious journey of *The Merry Widow* around the world. If there is any one show that could be said to have established the global reputation of the French capital as a state of mind which goes to the head like champagne it must be *The Merry Widow* by Franz Lehár. The operetta presented the city as a whirl of revelry in glamorous nightspots, further enhancing its reputation for elegance, romance and high spirits; its depiction of the French capital jumpstarted a fascination with Paris that holds the musical under its spell to this very day.

FIGURE 0.1   A sophisticated love affair conducted in the 'City of Romance': Joseph Coyne as Prince Danilo and Lily Elsie as Sonia in the first London production of *The Merry Widow*, which opened in 1907.

Source: Postcard provided by the editor.

The essay compares the different adaptations, proceeding from Vienna's *Die Lustige Witwe* and focusing on the London version, but also surveying its French matrix, Henri Meilhac's comedy *L'Attaché d'Amabassade*. It then highlights the operetta's international reception, especially in the English-speaking world, where it was the very first production to make extensive use of merchandising, most famously with the '*Merry Widow* Hat'. Finally, Stefan Frey shows how the song 'Off to Maxim's' turned the restaurant into a household name even to those who had never travelled to Paris: 'In *The Merry Widow* Maxim's was . . . the essence of all that made Paris attractive – elegance, beautiful women and high spirits.'

Chapter 3 considers the intersection of Cole Porter's (1891–1964) personal and domestic life with his musical output. From the little-known revue *Mayfair and Montmartre* (1922) to the Broadway hit *Can-Can* (1953), Paris has frequently featured in the work of the beloved composer and lyricist. His stage musicals *You Never Know* (1938), *Can-Can* and *Silk Stockings* (1955) are all predominantly set in Paris, and the city is passingly represented in two scenes in *Nymph Errant* (1933). Hollywood has made regular use of Porter's talent, either in original film musicals or in screen adaptations of his Broadway hits. In addition to this, his songs have also lived on in the soundtracks of films, particularly those set in Paris. While he certainly referred to it in numerous ways, Porter was not continuously resident in the city from his rise to fame until his death.

Therefore, this chapter begins by considering the role Paris played in our perception of the first half of Porter's career, especially in the context of his relationship with his wife Linda and their social circle. It then considers how Porter and his collaborators used Paris within their work and how this interacts with our perceptions of the city. As Hannah Robbins concludes at the end of her text, although the songwriter employed the French metropolis as both milieu and background time and time again, his work lacks specificity: in his hit songs, Porter 'relies on clichéd imagery . . . to conjure up Paris without providing fresh details in his own voice', while in his stage and film productions, 'Paris is more substantially embodied by the work of the set and costume designers than through Porter's lyrics'.

Part II: 'Broadway Paris'

The discussion of how the three major entertainment centres in the Anglophone world (Broadway, Hollywood and the West End) have depicted Paris in a large number of musicals begins in the second section with a close look at the New York theatre industry.

Broadway has always been fascinated by the French capital as the following observations may illustrate. While researching his PhD thesis on self-reflexive songs in American musicals from the first half of the 20th century, Michael G. Garber, author of Chapter 5, noticed how many of these productions referenced Paris in one way or another. Of the 34 shows Garber examined which opened between 1897 and 1928, ca. 44 per cent (15 out of 34) have a Paris setting or allude to it in their lyrics or dialogue.[2]

TABLE 0.1 List of Broadway productions between 1897 and 1929 that reference Paris. Compiled by Michael G. Garber for his PhD thesis *Reflexive Songs in the American Musical, 1898–1947*.

Title	Year	Set in or near Paris	Reference in Lyrics	Dialogue reference
The Fortune Teller	1898		X	
Wirl-I-Gig	1899	X	X	
In Dahomey	1903		X	
Whoop-Dee-Doo	1903	X		
Fantana	1905		X	
Social Whirl	1906			X
Fascinating Flora	1907	X	X	
The American Idea	1908	X	X	
The Firefly	1912		X	
Dancing Around	1914		X	
Oh, Lady! Lady!	1918		X	
Innocent Eyes♪	1924	X	X	
The Vagabond King	1925	X	X	
Criss-Cross	1926	X	X	
The Desert Song	1926			X

Source: (Garber, 2006).

♪ the musical revue had an actual Parisian star, Mistinguett.

While these figures are admittedly impressionistic and do not aim to count as clear statistical evidence, they still indicate the appeal the French metropolis has had throughout the decades for the US musical, and that allure remains undimmed, if such recent screen-to-stage transfers as *An American in Paris* (2015), *Amélie* (2017) and *Moulin Rouge!* (2019) are any indication.

Chapter 4 explores how the Paris fashion industry both inspired Broadway glamour and offered a mirror for American national and cultural identity in three 20th-century Broadway musicals: Victor Herbert and Henry Blossom's operetta *Mlle Modiste* (1905), Jerome Kern and Otto Harbach's musical comedy *Roberta* (1933) as well as Richard Rodgers and Samuel Taylor's musical play *No Strings* (1962). In addition to exploiting the reputation of Paris as one of the world's leading fashion capitals they cunningly combined the fun of lively entertainment with the allure of beautiful dresses. These shows use images of Parisian couture to examine questions of gender and sexuality, as well as contradictory ideas about democracy and aristocracy; pragmatism and aesthetic style; Puritanism and sensual expression; and 'American' and 'European' worldviews.

Set in a Rue de la Paix millinery, *Mlle. Modiste* defines Parisian sophistication as a luxurious accessory to the more essential asset of American democracy, epitomised by the shop girl heroine of the title. Unfolding in the dress shop of a courtesan-turned-couturier, *Roberta* models sophistication via a more fluid concept of American gender roles, as a virile college fullback transforms into a chic 'dressmaker'. Centred in Paris' modelling world, and including locations on the French Riviera, *No Strings* aligns ideals of sophistication not only with the city's sartorial elegance but, by contrast with American bigotry, with Paris's history of expatriate freedom for African Americans. In Maya Cantu's words, the three works collectively

> suggest that American culture is never that far removed from Plymouth Rock. At the same time, the stylish vision of the *Parisienne* inspires much of the elegance, sensuality and defiant joie de vivre that . . . has always dressed and caressed the Broadway musical.

Chapter 5 seeks to rehabilitate the reputations of three Broadway musicals that were not commercial successes and are usually only acknowledged in order to identify the reasons for their failure. All three were created by acclaimed Broadway artists of the 'Golden Age'. *Miss Liberty* (1949) was led by the creative team of Irving Berlin, Robert Sherwood, Moss Hart and Jerome Robbins. *Ben Franklin in Paris* (1964), the musical retelling of the Founding Father's journey to France in 1876 to gain French recognition of the American Revolution, was staged by Michael Kidd, featured Jerry Herman interpolations and starred Robert Preston. *Dear World* (1969) was adapted by Robert E. Lee, Jerome Lawrence and Jerry Herman from the famous Jean Giraudoux play *The Madwoman of Chaillot* for Angela Lansbury, who got rave reviews for her star turn.

FIGURE 0.2   Angela Lansbury in *Dear World* (1969). The actress won her second Tony Award for her role as Countess Aurelia.

Source: Photo provided by the editor.

In all cases, the shows acted as important pivots or stepping stones in the artists' development. For *Miss Liberty*, this history reveals the considerable extent of its success, including that of its songs. As Michael G. Garber highlights, the

> differences between these three shows assuredly demonstrate the shift of topics and tonalities in the Broadway musical over a twenty-year span – from the

light-hearted charm of *Miss Liberty*; through the earnest assumptions, infused with comedy and romance, of *Ben Franklin in Paris*; to the allegorical social critique, overlaid with both whimsy and bombast, in *Dear World*.

In addition, 'they also demonstrate a shift in the rhetoric surrounding Paris which can be described schematically as a move from hedonism towards heroism'.

Chapter 6 addresses a musical about Paris that, somewhat surprisingly, originated there. In the wake of World War II, the importing of musicals written in a language other than English to the West End or Broadway was practically never heard of. In this context, *Irma La Douce* (1958) is a rarity: not only is it an original French musical, the musical comedy about a *fille de la rue* (streetwalker) and her *mec* (pimp) with music by Marguerite Monnot and libretto by Alexandre Breffort also became a hit in both London and New York. The essay charts the expansion and progression of the piece: from an intimate venue in the French capital to a London West-End playhouse, and eventually a large Broadway theatre. This is done by examining the context of French Musical Theatre, the development of post-war British musical theatre and the expectations of what was required for the Broadway stage in the 1960s.

The essay charts how English adaptors retained the piece's French atmosphere and charm whilst allowing it to mature to suit the tastes of both British and American audiences; and how creative practitioners brought their own influence to bear on the piece via their work in the world of opera, absurdist theatre, dance and popular music. Stewart Nicholls has interviewed key players for this essay, including the show's original Tony Award-winning star, Elizabeth Seal, thus yielding a first-hand view of its development. Can the musical be revived successfully today? Seal has some doubts: 'I think times have changed. At that time, Paris was this fairy tale place. *Irma la Douce* is a fairy story. It needs an innocence and naivety. It's a delicate piece.'

Part III: 'Hollywood Paris'

'Paris is always a good idea.'

This quote is regularly attributed to Audrey Hepburn, although doubts have been expressed as to whether she really made the statement (Keeper, 2014). Yet whoever first uttered it, the American film industry seems to agree: over 800 Hollywood films 'have been shot in Paris or feature reconstructions of the city', making it 'by far the foreign city [to appear] most often' in US movies (De Baecque, 2012, p. 11).

It is easy to compile a list of American films made by celebrated directors in which the French capital plays an important role for each decade of the last 100 years: *A Woman of Paris* (Charlie Chaplin, 1923), *The Hunchback of Notre Dame* (William Dieterle, 1939), *Casablanca* (Michael Curtiz, 1942), *Love in the After-noon* (Billy Wilder, 1958), *Charade* (Stanley Donen, 1963), *The Three Musketeers*

(Richard Lester, 1973), *Frantic* (Roman Polanski, 1988), *Prêt-à-Porter* (Robert Altman, 1994), *Before Sunset* (Richard Linklater, 2004) and *Midnight in Paris* (Woody Allen, 2011).

Yet while it is possible to name major Hollywood films set in other capitals in Continental Europe like Rome (*Roman Holiday*, William Wyler, 1953), Vienna (*The Third Man*, Carol Reed, 1949) or Berlin (*A Foreign Affair*, Wilder, 1948), how many US film musicals are set there? Less than a handful come to mind: Rome – *A Funny Thing Happened on the Way to the Forum* (Lester, 1966) and *Nine* (Rob Marshall, 2009), Vienna – *The King Steps out* (Josef von Sternberg, 1936) and *The Emperor Waltz* (Wilder, 1948), Berlin – *Cabaret* (Bob Fosse, 1972).[3] Only the last of these has left any mark in the annals of screen entertainment. This is in stark contrast to the rich history of Hollywood musicals linked to Paris, so Section III shines a spotlight on several of these.

Chapter 7 takes as its starting point director Ernst Lubitsch's famous description of 'Paris Paramount' as 'the most Parisian' when compared to MGM's and the real capital of France. Marguerite Chabrol analyses the early 1930s Hollywood operettas featuring Maurice Chevalier and Jeanette MacDonald, partially located in Paris and involving French culture and customs. Her close reading shows that Paris is not so much the spectacular setting it would become in the 1950s, as a series of conventions and codes built in a cross-cultural dialogue between Europe and the United States. This in turn allows her to explore the ideological boundaries in Pre-Code musical comedies.

The musicals, directed by Lubitsch and Rouben Mamoulian, entwine several pre-existing aspects of Paris, thus building their own myth: the sentimental and romantic Paris from the popular international 'Paris songs'; the place for sexual freedom inherited from theatrical traditions (the entertaining 'Gay Paree' or the setting of French farces); and a city socially divided between working class and aristocracy. That composite myth of Paris is common to Paramount and MGM, but does not exclude the nuances expressed in Lubitsch's view. Chabrol identifies as some of those nuances the

> use of the stars and the conception of Paris as an attraction. . . . What is obvious is that Paramount was more interested in French themes. . . . If Paris-Paramount is not necessarily 'more Parisian', Paris-MGM is, on the other hand, obviously 'more American'.

For self-evident reasons, the trend towards shooting in 'real' environments outside the studio lot which had started after the end of World War II took longer to affect the movie musical, a form of entertainment that relies heavily on artifice and more than other genres needs to be able to control filming conditions for its elaborate song-and-dance numbers. Yet in the late 1950s, partly as a response to the threat posed by television, Hollywood sent its filmmakers abroad to utilise Paris (which had become one of the most popular of holiday destinations for Americans) as a spectacular backdrop to potential box-office hits with a high budget, thus offering audiences an experience they could not find at home.

Chapter 8 takes a close look at how four movie musicals shot on location from 1957 to 1958 – *Gigi, Silk Stockings, Les Girls* and *Funny Face* employ the French capital to give their productions a special flair and allure, by presenting Paris as a set piece, a prettified site of parks, clubs and night-time street corners and courtyards. As Julia Foulkes underlines, in this quartet of major studio releases, the city still defined the essential joys of life as embodied in romance between a man and a woman. Having Americans travel, work and prosper in filmic Paris aligned the United States with the cosmopolitanism, beauty and sophistication that the place signified. These films emerged in the 1950s to assert Americans' claim over Paris and its tradition as a capital of culture; it was a takeover defined by nostalgia, desire and longing. More Americans experienced the city in person during that decade, but the images – and the imagining – in these films made their own point. They 'reinforced the idea that what is found in Paris is enduring, much as both French and American people in the newly fractious and explosive mid-20th century wanted to believe'.

FIGURE 0.3   When in Paris, do as the Parisians do: Maggie Prescott (Kay Thompson) and Dick Avery (Fred Astaire), pretending to be 'French Intellectuals', perform 'Clap Yo Hands' in *Funny Face* (1957).

Source: Photo provided by the editor.

In Chapter 9 Daniel Batchelder contrasts two cartoon movie musicals and investigates their reception history. In its long history, the Walt Disney Company has released several famous cartoons set in the French capital (for instance, *The Hunchback of Notre Dame*, 1996); however, the very first of the studio's animated movies to take place in Paris was *Aristocats* (1970). That release reached cinemas eight years after another cartoon musical depicted Paris through the eyes of cats, *Gay Purr-ee* (UPA, 1962). Yet while the former is now regarded as a family classic, the latter was a major box-office disappointment and has remained a curiosity item.

On the surface, these original film musicals possess numerous similarities. Both deploy all-star voice casts, and both feature romantic adventure narratives about anthropomorphic cats in Paris during the *belle époque*. Yet beyond these correspondences the two films betray radically different approaches to the unique expressive potential of the animated musical. The chapter considers the visual, musical and dramatic profiles of *Gay Purr-ee* and *The Artistocats*, arguing that, while the latter largely adheres to the Walt Disney Studio's traditional verisimilitude, UPA's film embraces a far more fractured system of aesthetics. The essay also examines the roles of the films' headline stars, Maurice Chevalier and Judy Garland, thus extending the study of animated film musical aesthetics to performers. For Batchelder, the muted reception for 1962 film is a consequence of Disney's 'stranglehold on audience expectations'; that the film reads 'as an exception to the rule' is due to the fact that for most of the 20th century the animation giant was the main reference point for the majority of cinemagoers not only when it comes to 'long-form narrative animated musicals, but [to] the representational strategies of animation itself'.

Part IV: 'West End Paris'

For a long while London seemed far less interested in the glittering metropolis just across the English Channel than New York; but then, within a year of each other, two shows opened that were closely associated with Paris and turned into the most successful musicals ever to play the West End: *Les Misérables* (1985), the Anglicised version of the 1980 French concept album,[4] and *The Phantom of the Opera* (1986), both of which were still running in their 35th and 34th year, respectively, when COVID-19 forced all of London's theatres to close in March 2020.

Yet apart from these two major examples, the number of British musicals with a Parisian setting or other links to the city is comparatively small: a few successes with respectable runs (*Bless the Bride*, 1947, 886 performances; *Wedding in Paris*, 1954, 411 perf.; *Aspects of Love*, 1989, 1,325 perf.) are matched by a few notorious flops, centred on famous French figures such as *Colette* (1980, 47 perf.), *Napoleon* (2000, 127 perf.) and *Lautrec* (2000, 84 perf.). The last two of these actually involved foreign talent and thus could be said to be international collaborations – the musical on the French emperor originated in Canada, while the one about the famous painter had music by Charles Aznavour. *Irma La Douce* (1956; British première in 1958; 1,512 perf.) and *Marguerite* (2008, 135 perf.) also combined French and British talents: songwriters from France and adaptors/directors from the United Kingdom. Another French import, *Notre Dame de Paris* (1998) – a huge hit in most of Continental Europe and Asia – was savaged by the critics when it reached London in 1990 and only lasted for 158 performances, while *J'Accuse. The Passion of Émile Zola*, about the Dreyfus Affair, with music by Petula Clark and lyrics/libretto by Dee Shipman, never moved beyond a 2010 concept recording.

The fourth section of the book examines a cross-section of these shows, looking in chronological order at both commercial success and failures. *Bless the Bride* (1947) by Vivian Ellis and A. P. Herbert, set against the backdrop of the Franco-Prussian war, depicts the dramatic love affair between an English rose and a handsome French actor and benefitted enormously from the casting of Parisian Georges Guétary as the male lead. The period piece, a genuine British operetta, may be set in 1870–1871, but historical displacement disguises many of the factors that relate to the recent experiences of its first audiences during World War II. Chapter 10 examines how that subtext is conveyed through the contrasts of stereotypical English and French 'types' alongside the more rounded characterisations of the leading romantic couple. The deconstruction of a political subtext of Anglo-French cooperation and respect is supported by similar approaches in two adjacent works (1946 and 1949) by the same creative team. As a crucial speech in the final scene of the musical makes clear, Paris is unusually made prominent here not as a setting for the main narrative but for what it could symbolise to a British audience in the wake of war. According to John Snelson, the end of *Bless the Bride* was fully understood by its original audience

> as a statement of 1940s post-war political and national conviction. It acknowledges the shared wartime history of France and England, using the neutrality of England in the Franco-Prussian war as a warning, with the correction of both World Wars implicitly acknowledging the importance of such an alliance.

Chapter 11 explores how the identity of Paris, which draws on a persistent awareness of historical and cultural memory rich in symbolism and linked in particular with the French Revolution is dramatised in musicals based on three novels set wholly or partly in Paris: *Les Misérables* (1985), based on Victor Hugo's 1862 Romantic masterpiece, *The Phantom of the Opera* (1986), a loose retelling of Gaston Leroux' 1910 gothic thriller, and *Aspects of Love* (1989), a faithful adaptation of David Garnett's 1955 novella of the same title.

In Hugo's epic tale the French capital is much more than a mere setting as large sections of the book are given over to detailed descriptions of the city's language, history and socio-political climate, to the degree that the metropolis could be said to constitute one of the novel's main protagonists. Leroux on the other hand set most of the action in *Phantom* in the vast premises of the famous building on the Boulevard de Garnier that gave his mystery its title. In contrast, Garnett spreads his love roundelay across several cities, regions and countries (including Montpellier, the Pyrénées and Venice), yet repeatedly returns to Paris for significant plot developments.

John Snelson examines the three literary sources to show how fact and fiction in the portrayals of Paris have been fused through the mediation of each author's biography. Comparisons with the London stage adaptations as 1980s musicals show further refinements to the characterisation of Paris, including through the temporal interplay of framing devices. Finally, these otherwise contrasting literary and dramatic works are linked through the refractions between past and present that Paris connotes, especially in relation to revolutionary ideals of freedom. As the author underlines:

> Life is the source of art here through identifiably Parisian geography, architecture, politics, society and culture. There may not be an equal necessity for a literal Paris across these shows, but they do share a sense of appropriateness to a way of thinking around history and memory that ties them together.

Chapter 12 will consider the reception of *Marguerite*, the 2008 musical retelling of Alexandre Dumas' novel *La Dame aux Camélias* (1848), which reset the story in occupied Paris during World War II. In spite of a beautiful score by Michel Legrand and a marvellous cast (Ruthie Henshall, Alexander Hanson and Julian Ovenden) the show, elegantly staged by Jonathan Kent, received mixed reviews and could not find an audience. Clare Chandler explores the British responses to an 'unsympathetic' female protagonist – a response that showed elements of xenophobia. Her text also investigates the musical's revisions, revivals as well as its reception outside of the United Kingdom. As the author emphasises at the end of her text, from a contemporary perspective, the musical's 'original staging with its political framing' and references to the cruel punishment of women who were accused of 'horizontal collaboration', 'feels all the more resonant in the current political climate, so maybe there is a way to revive and revitalise the show once more'. After all, musical theatre 'has come a long way since *Marguerite*'s 2008 première; perhaps now there is space in the canon for a flawed female protagonist at the heart of a complicated situation'.

Part V: 'Naughty Paris'

The next section focuses on how the reputation of the capital as a symbol of hedonism and libertinism is employed as a starting point or backdrop for shows and movies that challenge prudery, battle censorship and undermine gender stereotypes. Chapter 13 focuses on two of the various incarnations of *Victor/Victoria*. Most famous in its 1982 Hollywood version starring Julie Andrews, James Garner and Robert Preston, the story of the cross-dressing comedy has actually been around a lot longer: Blake Edwards' film musical is loosely based on the German movie *Viktor und Viktoria* (1933, directed by Reinhold Schünzel), which was followed by French (*Georges et Georgette*, 1934) and English (*First a Girl*, 1935) versions, before it was remade in West Germany under its original title in 1957. Florian J. Seubert explores how gay shame can be traced as a cinematic discourse in both the 1933 and 1982 films by illustrating how this psychological concept becomes manifest as filmic language.

Applying queer studies to a Weimar comedy and a Hollywood musical reveals their shared strategies in linking what can be called heteronormative value judgements to the presentation of non-mainstream sexual identities. Their visual language is intricately linked with tropes of Paris as the city of free love and is mapped out in the architectural and audiovisual renditions of the urban space. In a series of close readings, the chapter looks at how the various non-verbal elements of filmmaking, such as the composition of frames or editing, can create and reveal internalisations of gay shame in characters and viewers alike. Yet by exposing the visual codes of shaming at play, Seubert also shows the creative potential for rediscovering the topical subject matter of *Victor/Victoria*. It is his hope that '[i]ncreased awareness of those codes may help directors and cinematographers to develop a visual discourse for the depiction of free love in Paris and elsewhere, without shame'.

Chapter 14 explores how certain post-war stage and film musicals traded on the fluidity between 'timeless' Paris and much more localised recreations of its symbolic freedoms. With one of these, *Can-Can*, a curious double-image arises in the gap between its 1953 Broadway première during the height of the McCarthy era and the 1960 film, catering to an audience on the brink of the sexual revolution.

The stage version addresses such serious issues as censorship and the hypocrisy of prosecuting inhumane and unjust laws. The film adaptation twists the show's characters and songs to quite different ends, with a result accurately described as 'Las Vegas, 1960, not Montmartre, 1896'. How and why this happened provides the main content of the chapter, with special attention to the redeployment of songs and the realities of Parisian life that were strategically absent from one version or the other. Raymond Knapp and Mitchell Morris show that the screen adaptation has its own distinctive and serious aims despite its apparent betrayal of the stage show: to urge Americans to break free of their Puritan inhibitions. It thus reimagines Paris as a proto-Las Vegas, representing the eternal feminine of the *demi-monde* as the ideal playground for the kind of man who reads *Playboy*, and the quintessential town for such a man to be about. Contrasting the Broadway and Hollywood versions, the authors conclude that the French capital as the 'greatest of all Old-World models of luxurious commodities' was 'the perfect courtesan of hedonic dreams, endlessly available and accommodating. Its timeless charms, as *Can-Can* treats them, testify to the luminous spectacle of passions and their purchase.'

Chapter 15 discusses the major incarnations of the Lerner and Loewe musical *Gigi*: the 1958 movie, the 1973 stage transfer and the 2015 Broadway revival, which was substantially revised by Heidi Thomas. Adapted from Colette's 1944 novella, Vincente Minnelli's film has been praised as 'the last great musical of the fifties' (Sennett, 1981, p. 253); 15 years later it was transferred less successfully to the stage. Yet, although the film won nine Oscars (including 'Best Picture of the Year'), over the years it has acquired a reputation for being 'problematic': for instance, the movie's opening song 'Thank Heaven for Little Girls' has often been

FIGURE 0.4   A Paris-set musical starring a real Parisian Music Hall star: French actress Lilo making her US debut in Cole Porter's *Can-Can* (1953). She is pictured here in the 'Garden of Eden' number; on the far left is her co-star Eric Rhodes.

Source: Photo provided by the editor.

mistaken as a barely veiled paean to paedophilia, while the basic set-up of the story which sees a courtesan-in-training falling for an older and wealthy womaniser nowadays is regarded by many as unsavoury. Consequently the 2015 Broadway revival attempted to address these issues with a new libretto that altered several key plot elements in order to make the material more palatable for general audiences.

As Olaf Jubin underlines, all three versions are imbued with a strong sense of artifice and artificiality, although the form of these stratagems varies: whereas Minnelli, using a carefully calibrated colour scheme, depicted a stilted society averse to bodily spontaneity, the stage musical attempted in vain to replace the sensuous ambience of the screen original – the film was famously shot on location in Paris – with new songs which only underlined that the property seemed contrived outside its 'natural' habitat. The 2015 rewrite on the other hand overlaid the story with a 'modern sensibility' that went against the core of its source material and thus created its very own type of disingenuousness. Summing up the reasons why the theatrical versions have faltered where the movie succeeded, the author argues:

> It is Gigi's spark and sparkle that set her apart, and so far, imbuing the character with the same qualities on stage has failed, because they cannot be faked when the Paris of 1900 is not present in either atmosphere or spirit.

Part VI: 'Artistic Paris'

As Patrice Higonnet explains, between 1785 and 1940 'Paris was the undisputed capital of Western painting and, to a lesser degree, sculpture' (Higonnet, 2002, p. 347). The sixth section will examine how the city, often described as the spiritual home of artists everywhere, has been portrayed in musicals that feature painters and writers as protagonists.

Chapter 16 interrogates the popular trope of the struggling visual artist who tries to carve out a living while soaking up the inspiration that Paris can offer in two film and stage incarnations. The topic was given sophisticated treatment in the MGM movie, *An American in Paris* (1951) which is particularly famous for its 17-minute ballet set to George Gershwin's 'rhapsodic ballet' which gave the movie its title. Previous screen-to-stage adaptations of famous MGM classics, most notably *Singin' in the Rain*, were content to re-produce the respective movie without any major changes. When director-choreographer Christopher Wheeldon and librettist Craig Lucas adapted *An American in Paris*, however, they completely re-conceived the material. Together with scenographer Bob Crowley their 2014 version builds on yet nevertheless transforms basic story elements, utilising an imaginative new scenographic conceit that combines striking costumes, stylised digital projections and graphic set pieces that appear to be in the process of creation by an artist in the presence of the audience.

The chapter will compare the approaches to choreography, narrative and design of the movie and its stage adaptation to explore how differently they deploy their artistic means in dealing with the inter-involved tropes of music, painting, dance and love in the French capital. At the end of his comparative analysis Robert Gordon asserts the extraordinary qualities of both versions which celebrate similar cultural icons, forms and masterpieces through very different expressive means: 'Minnelli's film and Wheeldon's stage musical is each in its own way an art work that pays homage to Paris, Gershwin, ballet and French art of the *fin de siècle* and mid-twentieth century.'

FIGURE 0.5 The painter surrounded by the subjects he sketches on their day off on La Grande Jatte, an isle in northern Paris. Scene from the 2006 London revival of *Sunday in the Park with George*, starring Daniel Evans (seated) as George and Jenna Russell (second from the right) as Dot.

Source: Photo courtesy of Donald Cooper/Photostage.

The Pulitzer Prize-winning *Sunday in the Park with George* (1984) by Stephen Sondheim and James Lapine forms the focus of Chapter 17. Robert Lawson-Peebles begins his essay with 'The Last Time I Saw Paris', the 1940 song by Jerome Kern and Oscar Hammerstein II written in response to the German occupation of Paris, and utilises two paintings of Georges Seurat, *Sunday Afternoon on the Island of La Grande Jatte* and (to a lesser extent), *The Bathers* to examine the conflict between the demands of artistic production and the needs of human beings.

The next section of the chapter examines the contrast between Seurat's choice of a suburban Parisian park for his painting and the everyday concerns of the bourgeoisie during the *belle époque* through two minor figures from Act I, the American tourists. The author then illustrates Seurat's relation to Impressionist paintings of the Seine, the development of the art market and the consequent dispersal of his paintings to the United States and the United Kingdom. The final section explores the depiction in Act II of the monetisation of art (and the ironies involved in Seurat's *La Grande Jatte* being housed at the Art Institute of Chicago) with reference to novelist Saul Bellow, before concluding with a return to that Parisian park, now destroyed by suburban sprawl, but still a residuum of creative and personal integrity. For Lawson-Peebles, the final moments of *Sunday in the Park with George* represent 'a triumphant reaffirmation of the continued presence of Paris as a source of artistic imagination'.

In Chapter 18, Pierre-Olivier Toulza expounds how the French inspiration behind *Moulin Rouge!* (2001) fits in with a renewed interest in Parisian imagery and culture. Baz Luhrmann's film aimed at reinventing the musical for the 21st century, while referencing the cycle of 'Frenchness films' of the 1950s. The 'commercial Bohemianism' of *fin de siècle* Paris is echoed in the film's blurring of the line between art and business as well as that between entertainment, theatre and prostitution. Furthermore, the immersive vision associated in *Moulin Rouge!* with the iconic locations of the French capital – which in 1890 were already tourist attractions – is also reminiscent of spectacular strategies of 1950s musicals. Accumulation and profusion are part of Luhrmann's visual style and correspond to the type of attractions available in the cabaret culture at the turn of the century as well as to their reinterpretation in party scenes in those earlier films. The motif of the can-can as well as the visual effects (especially lights and colours) aiming at 'audience participation' are similar to the ones used in both the work of *fin de siècle* painters and the Hollywood musicals set in France. At the end of his analysis, Toulza attests that no filmmaker is 'better placed to so intimately understand all the paradoxes of Parisian culture in the *belle époque* as depicted in the musical genre' than Luhrmann.

À très bientôt à Paris!

Although this book aims to be wide-ranging, it does not claim to be exhaustive – any Paris fan and lover of musicals will realise that a number of famous works associated with the city are missing, most obviously the various musical adaptations of Victor Hugo's classic novel *Notre Dame de Paris/The Hunchback of Notre Dame* (1831), such as the 1996 animated musical by Disney and its stage incarnations, the 1998 French *spectacle musical* and Lionel Bart's unfinished *Quasimodo*, which got a belated stage production in 2013 at London's tiny King's Head Theatre. Some of these have been explored elsewhere,[5] but there remains a lot more material that awaits close analysis and/or re-discovery, including, but not limited to

- early stage hits such as *The Vagabond King* (1915).
- the less famous 1950s Hollywood musicals set in the French capital, including *Rich, Young and Pretty* (MGM, 1951), *April in Paris* (1952, Warner Brothers) or *So This Is Paris* (1954, Universal).
- the many musical versions of Alexandre Dumas' *The Three Musketeers* (1844).
- revues, for instance *Jacques Brel is Alive and Well and Living in Paris* (1968).
- theatrical 'flops', ranging from *Tovarich* (1963) and *Mata Hari* (1967) to *Thou Shall Not*, the 2001 musical version of Emile Zola's 1867 novel *Thérèse Racquin* with a score by Harry Connick Jr.

With this in mind, the eighteen chapters of this volume clearly constitute only a first foray into rich subject matter, but then, who doesn't want to return to Paris again and again once they have experienced what it has to offer?

Notes

1 They were partly necessitated by the Paris World Exhibitions of 1867, 1878, 1889 and 1900, the last of which attracted 50 million visitors from all around the world (Higonnet, 2002, p. 114).
2 Many thanks to Michael Garber for not only alerting me to his findings, but for making them available to me.
3 The irony is that *A Funny Thing . . .* and *The King Steps Out* were made entirely on studio lots in Los Angeles, while *Cabaret* was filmed in Munich and the exteriors of *The Emperor Waltz* were shot in Alberta, Canada. On the other hand, *Nine* only partially takes place in 1960s Rome, in scenes that were added to the screen version; the film's source material, the 1982 concept musical, is basically set in the protagonist's mind.
4 For more details on how the 1985 RSC production differed from the original French version, see Gordon et al., 2016, pp. 171–174.
5 For more on the Disney musical *The Hunchback of Notre Dame* on stage and screen, see Jubin, 2017, pp. 101–116.

References

De Baecque, A. (2012) 'Paris by Hollywood: Introduction,' in A. De Baecque (ed.) *Paris by Hollywood*. Paris: Flammarion, pp. 11–15.

Garber, M. G. (2006) *Reflexive Songs in the American Musical, 1898–1947*. Unpublished PhD, City University of New York, New York.

Gordon, R., Jubin, O. and Taylor, M. (2016) *British Musical Theatre since 1950*. London: Bloomsbury.

Higonnet, P. (2002) *Paris. Capital of the World* (Arthur Goldhammer, trans.). Cambridge and London: Belknap Press.

Jubin, O. (2017) 'Too Far "Out There"? *The Hunchback of Notre Dame* (1996),' in G. Rodosthenous (ed.) *The Disney Musical on Stage and Screen: Critical Approaches from Snow White to Frozen*. London: Methuen, pp. 101–116.

Keeper, B. (2014) 'Audrey Hepburn Never Said "Paris Is Always a Good Idea!",' http://thecollectedtraveler.blogspot.com/2014/07/paris-is-always-good-idea.html, accessed 15 May 2020.

Rearick, C. (2011) *Paris Dreams, Paris Memories. The City and Its Mystique*. Stanford, CA: Stanford University Press.

Sennett, T. (1981) *Hollywood Musicals*. New York: Harry N. Abrams.

PART I
Capital Paris

1

PARIS AS A SYMBOL (1852–1914)

Venita Datta

Paris, according to German literary critic and sociologist Walter Benjamin, was 'the capital of the nineteenth century' (Benjamin, 1999, pp. 3–26).[1] During the years spanning the Second Empire to World War I (1852–1914), Paris became not only a leading cultural and intellectual centre – the birthplace of the avant-garde and the capital of pleasure – it also emerged as the most modern city in the world, indeed, the 'capital of the world' (Higonnet, 2002, p. 232). While Americans tend to associate modernity with the United States, during the years of the late 19th and early 20th centuries, especially during what the French call the *belle époque*, roughly from 1880 to 1914, Paris was the capital of modernity. It boasted arguably the world's largest department store – the Bon Marché – as well as its largest press. The recently transformed city was also home to wide tree-lined boulevards, housing shops, cafés and theatres, which attested to a vibrant boulevard culture. Constructed in honour of the centennial of the French Revolution in 1889, the Eiffel Tower was the tallest manmade structure in the world and the perfect symbol of the newly renovated city. The Tower was the highlight of the 1889 Universal Exposition, which attracted visitors from all over the world. In the late 19th century, Paris became the major stop on Americans' world tours, as Mark Twain's *The Innocents Abroad*, published in 1867, illustrates. Around this time, Paris also gained notoriety as a place of pleasure and hedonism, or for some, a place of debauchery and depravity, especially in Montmartre. This reputation only served to increase the numbers of foreign visitors to the city.

In the 1950s, the Paris of the *belle époque* was immortalised in such major American motion pictures as *An American in Paris* (1951), *Funny Face* (1957) and *Gigi* (1958), to name just three.[2] These films, while often viewed as a nostalgic nod to Paris of the past, were actually a way for Hollywood filmmakers to celebrate the modernity of Paris and its status as home of the avant-garde, all the while laying claim to this legacy in the 20th century (Schwartz, 2007, p. 21). The story of Paris's role as the capital of

FIGURE 1.1   The Eiffel Tower upon completion in 1889. Today the most famous sight of Paris, the structure caused a lot of controversy when it was built.

Source: Photo provided by the editor.

modernity is the subject of this chapter. To that end, it will trace not only the evolution of Paris during this key period, it will also examine the role it occupied in the cultural imaginary, both as an emblem of French identity and of modernity.[3]

Paris in the mid-19th century

In the mid-19th century, Paris was a second-rate city, surprising visitors from London with its 'backwardness'. It was dirty and insalubrious, with waste thrown into the Seine, which was also the source of drinking water. Although the construction of sewers was begun under Napoleon I, little work was completed until the Second Empire (1852–1870) and even later in the century. Meanwhile, cholera epidemics wiped out tens of thousands of residents. Indeed, a major epidemic in 1832 killed more than 18,000 Parisians, mostly in poor areas (Horne, 2004, p. 218). Paris remained a medieval city until the second half of the 19th century, with narrow streets and warrens of old houses, immortalised in such novels as Eugène Sue's *Les Mystères de Paris*, published from 1842 to 1843, and Victor Hugo's 1862 novel, *Les Misérables*. Most of the poor lived in dingy, overcrowded hovels. Paris at this time was a series of little villages; travel both from east to west and from north to south was nearly impossible. Plunged in darkness at night, the city was often dangerous.

Worth noting is the mix of social classes in Paris in the earlier 19th century, often in the same buildings. The poorest residents occupied the higher floors, while the wealthy occupied the noble lower ones. Furthermore, many shopkeepers lived above their shops, meaning a variety of different types of buildings on the same street; modest wood and plaster homes could thus be found on the same block as more elegant ones in stone (Taunton, 2009, p. 21).

The restructuring of Paris was one of the largest urban renewal programmes in the world. This momentous economic and social change, however, could not take place without the growth of industrial production, which brought great wealth to the middle and upper classes. The development of a modern banking system was also necessary to raise the capital required, not only for public works in Paris; it also allowed for the establishment of private enterprises, among them department stores, many of which were founded at this time. By the middle of the 19th century, the Bourse – France's Wall Street – was the biggest money market on the continent. The extension of the railway too allowed for the facility of movement of people and goods. This economic growth brought greater numbers of workers to the city and led to overcrowding, contributing to the explosion of Paris's population from 786,000 to over a million between 1831 and 1851 (Horne, 2004, p. 232).

Haussmannisation

Napoleon's nephew Louis-Napoleon came to power in 1848, when he was elected president of the Second Republic. In 1851, he affected a coup d'état and established himself as emperor the following year, dubbing himself Napoleon III (Napoleon's son had died in 1832). Having travelled extensively and lived in London, Napoleon III wanted to create a Paris that would rival London on the world stage. He and Georges-Eugène Haussmann, a civil servant whom he named Prefect of the Seine, transformed Paris, truly making it the capital of the 19th century. Napoleon III ruthlessly appropriated buildings and land and partnered with private firms to build elegant houses and shops, a process brilliantly described in Emile Zola's 1872 novel, *La Curée*, in which the author used the language of the hunt to describe speculation in Paris during the Second Empire.

The goals of Napoleon III and Haussmann were economic, sociological, aesthetic and political. First and foremost, they sought to rid the city of congestion by facilitating the circulation of both people and goods. To that end, they built an east–west axis from the place de la Nation on the east side, to the place de l'Étoile, on the west, also building the avenues around the Étoile. They constructed a north–south axis with the boulevard Sebastopol cutting through the Île de la Cité to become the boulevard Saint-Michel on the Left Bank. The most radical change was on the Île de la Cité – site of Notre-Dame and also of some of the worst slums in Paris. In fact, hundreds of small shacks stood in front of Notre-Dame, blocking the view of the cathedral. Haussmann cleared out the hovels, giving us the panoramic view we have today, and established the Île de la Cité as an administrative centre housing law courts and police headquarters.

Haussmannisation also involved building the boulevards Arago, de Magenta, de Port-Royal, Voltaire (originally the boulevard du Prince-Eugène), de la Madeleine and Haussmann, which, ironically, was only completed in the early 20th century. The city also witnessed the multiplication of green spaces – represented by the construction of the Parc Monceau and the Parc Montsouris, the Bois de Boulogne to the west and the Bois de Vincennes to the east. A sewer system was built, although it was not finished until the early 20th century, at which time the metro was also constructed. Transforming Paris into the 'City of Light', 32,000 gas lamps replaced 15,000 oil lanterns, and by 1877, electric lights supplanted the gas streetlamps (Horne, 2004, p. 236).[4] Finally, Napoleon and Haussmann also authorised the construction of the uniform buildings on the new wide tree-lined boulevards. One of the crowning achievements of the plan was the construction of the Opéra Garnier, which became part of the neighbourhood associated with the new Paris and a destination for entertainment and shopping. While some *grands boulevards* predated Haussmann, the new ones henceforth came to be associated with modern Paris. As one contemporary noted: 'This place de l'Opéra, with its big ways that open onto everything, with these vast luxury stores, these gigantic cafés, the Grand Hôtel and the Opéra. This is modern Paris' (Gustave Fraipont, quoted in Schwartz, 1998, p. 23). Indeed, the process which became known as Haussmannisation pushed the city centre to the west of the city.

Furthermore, Haussmannisation doubled the area of Paris, which absorbed 500,000 inhabitants at this time. In 1860, Paris had just 12 arrondissements, when it expanded to 20, through the annexation of Auteuil, Passy, Grenelle and other areas, including Montmartre. Finally, Napoleon III and Haussmann also had new railroad stations built, such as the Gare de Lyon and the Gare du Nord, thereby facilitating visits to the capital by foreign and provincial visitors. Railway stations were a favourite subject of some of the Impressionist painters depicting modern life, among them Édouard Manet and Claude Monet. These changes led to the tremendous growth of the city. By 1870, the population stood at two million, and by 1914, three million (Jones, 2004, p. 299). Finally, political motivations, linked to aesthetic and economic ones, also motivated Napoleon III and Haussmann. Their goal to embellish Paris meant moving poor people out into the outer arrondissements. Paris had historically been the centre of the revolution – in 1789, 1830 and 1848 – when, ironically, Napoleon III himself came to power. Building

FIGURE 1.2   The epitome of 'modern Paris' in the 19th century: the place de l'Opéra with the Opéra Garnier, which was built between 1861 and 1875.

Source: Photo provided by the editor.

the *grands boulevards* made it both easier to bring in troops and artillery to fight rebels and harder to erect barricades, as opposed to the small, winding streets of the city before Haussmann (Jones, p. 318).[5] The consequences of Haussmannisation were thus of great import: 20,000 houses were destroyed, among them some of historical importance dating from the Middle Ages. Moreover, some 350,000 residents were displaced by Haussmannisation (Jones, 2004, p. 318). Perhaps the most important consequence of this gentrification was that it pushed the poor increasingly towards the outskirts of the city, especially towards the 18th, 19th and 20th arrondissements, a process catalogued by Emile Zola in *L'Assommoir* (1877), in which one of the major characters, washerwoman Gervaise, wanders the new streets of her old neighbourhood, feeling alienated from a world where she no longer belongs. As Gervaise's experience illustrates, workers could no longer afford to live in the centre of the city; while their wages went up 30 per cent during this time, rents and living expenses went up by 45 per cent (Horne, 2004, p. 244). Napoleon and Haussmann thus displaced the problem of class conflict. Indeed, these workers, feeling cheated and excluded by and from the new beautiful city, participated in the 1871 civil war known as the Commune, which took place in the wake of the French defeat in the Franco-Prussian War in 1870 and which had led to the abdication of Napoleon III.

Franco-Prussian war and Commune

When Mark Twain visited Paris in 1867, he was much impressed by the modernity of Haussmannised Paris and even attended the 1867 Universal Exhibition held there to celebrate the achievements of Napoleon III and his Empire. Three years later, this glittering world would come tumbling down when Napoleon III was maneuvered by Prussian Chancellor Bismarck into declaring a war that would result in the fall of the Second Empire on 4 September 1870 after a decisive loss at the battle of Sedan on the eastern border. The same day, the Third Republic was declared at City Hall. Soon thereafter, in September 1870, the Prussians besieged Paris until the end of January 1871.

Paris at this time was unrecognisable. No longer the city of light, it was plunged into darkness after rationing forced the government to limit gaslight. A journalist writing for the fashionable *Le Gaulois* wondered: 'This lugubrious city without illuminated windows, open cafés . . . and gaiety – is it still Paris?' (cited by Clayson, 2002, p. 53). Gas lighting, which had extended the interior to the exterior and had literally fuelled boulevard nightlife, gave way to a Paris in which the boulevards with all their entertainments and cafés reverted back to the street, used by pedestrians of all classes to get from one place to another rather than as a destination in and of themselves (Clayson, 2002, p. 58).

Various theatres around the city, including the Odeon theatre, became hospitals, and the Garnier Opera house, still under construction, became an arms depot. Many of the places of pleasure henceforth had utilitarian uses. The Bois de Boulogne was no longer a park but instead a place for grazing animals. By December 1870, food was so scarce that Parisians were forced to eat the animals, including those in the zoo, chief among them Castor and Pollux, the famous elephants housed there, although they were not destined for the poor but sold to the highest bidders (Spang, 1992, p. 757). Some of the more chic restaurants even featured menus that listed stuffed head of donkey, elephant consommé and roasted camel. Nathan Sheppard, one of the rare Americans who remained in Paris during the siege, lamented his boredom and claustrophobia (Sheppard, 1871, p. 185). The siege led to temporal and spatial anxiety, as the residents of Paris experienced a suffocation due to a lack of food and light and the simple feeling of being suspended in time and space (Clayson, 2002, pp. 55–56). It came to an end in the last days of January 1871 after the Germans began using Krupp canons to force Paris to surrender. The French were obliged to accept defeat, giving up the two provinces of Alsace and Lorraine, and to pay a hefty indemnity

The new French government, whose leaders were mostly republicans in name only, alienated many Parisians not only by capitulating to the Germans when many of them had wanted to continue fighting but also by moving the capital to Versailles, associated with the monarchy. When the Versailles government sought to disarm the poorer sections of the city, notably Montmartre, which had raised money for cannons by public subscription, a skirmish broke out, with combatants killed on both sides. Paris was once again besieged and became the site of a bloody civil war known as the Commune, in which thousands were killed.

The events of the Commune led to the destruction of key monuments after the Communards began a scorched earth policy, setting the Tuileries Palace, a symbol of royal power, on fire. The Communards also burned parts of the Palais Royal and the medieval city hall and toppled the Napoleonic statue atop the Vendome Column. The last week of the insurrection, from May 21–May 28, 1871, known as the Bloody Week, witnessed the execution of Communards by the Versailles troops in the Père Lachaise cemetery. Nevertheless, Paris was resilient. By the end of 1871, Cook's Tours was organising visits to Paris to see the ruins, and when Henry James visited the city in 1875, it had returned to its former glory (Brooks, 2007).

The Paris of the *belle époque*

The Paris of the *belle époque* remains enshrined in memory even today, and it was certainly celebrated in the musical comedies of the 1950s. Vincente Minnelli's *An American in Paris*, set in the French capital shortly after World War II, features a long ballet sequence in which a Toulouse-Lautrec painting comes to life. The term *belle époque* is a nostalgic one, born not in the wake of World War I, but rather in 1940, on the eve of World War II, and cemented during the German occupation of Paris (Kalifa, 2017, p. 21).[6] Moreover, the period was not 'beautiful' or golden for everyone – certainly not for the servants who made the leisured lifestyle of the bourgeoisie possible, nor for workers in the mines who toiled for long hours and little pay. However, for those who could afford it, the Paris of the *belle époque* was a city of pleasures and entertainments, and, moreover, the capital of the European avant-garde.

A number of key developments, however, first had to take place. The 1880s witnessed a number of important laws that contributed to the unification of the country. In 1881, the republicans, who finally gained control of both the Chamber of Deputies and the Senate (in 1879), passed a law establishing freedom of the press. In the following years, they enacted legislation mandating free, secular and compulsory primary school education. Finally, they undertook projects to build roads and construct railways, which facilitated the process of moving goods, including newspapers, thereby creating a national economy. Such improvements in technology, particularly in the production of newspapers and images, led to the emergence of a mass press and national opinion. Indeed, historian Benedict Anderson has dubbed the national conversation of citizens via the newspapers an 'imagined community' (Anderson, 1991). This national opinion, moreover, was increasingly formed in the new democratic space of the café, open to all who could pay the price of a drink, and no longer in the private aristocratic salon. In addition, the department store, which had emerged during the Second Empire, like the republican schools, also contributed to homogenising French society and forging national identity around certain kinds of consumption. While the schools created unity through patriotism and the speaking of French, department stores taught members of more modest classes how to dress and furnish their homes like members of the upper bourgeoisie (Miller, 1981, p. 183). The *belle époque* period thus marked the emergence not only of mass democracy but also of mass culture, both of which had a levelling effect on French society.

The pillars of this mass culture were the penny press and the boulevard theatre, buttressed by the café and the department store. All these institutions were not only housed on the boulevards, together, they created the new boulevard culture, which privileged the visual and turned all of Paris into what one historian has called a city of 'spectacular realities' (Schwartz, 1998, p. 2). Everyday events from visits to the morgue and Madame Tussaud's wax museum to watching a dentist pulling a patient's teeth in the street were turned into public entertainment. As French author Alfred Delvau noted with some hyperbole: 'The boulevards are not only the heart and the head of Paris, but also the soul of the entire world' (quoted in Schwartz, 1998, p. 21). When contemporaries spoke of the *grands boulevards* during the late 19th century, they meant the area west of the place du Chateau d'Eau, renamed place de la République in 1879, up until the Madeleine (Schwartz, 1998, p. 19).

The *grands boulevards* contributed to the myth of Paris as the capital of modernity. While some Parisian connoisseurs after World War I dismissed the *grands boulevards* of the *belle époque* as decadent because they attracted tourists, foreigners, women and workers, in the wake of World War II, the memory of the importance of the *grands boulevards* to Parisian life was restored by commentators (Rearick, 2006, pp. 88–90) whose observations no doubt influenced American filmmakers of musical comedies in the years that followed.

Consumption, visual and otherwise, took place on the *grand boulevards* (Hahn 2006, pp. 73–77); indeed, they housed not only shops and department stores, but also a constant barrage of advertising, from the posters plastered on the advertising columns known as the *colonnes* Morris to the *hommes sandwichs*, or the human billboards, and horse-drawn vehicles – later, automobiles – with advertisements for the department stores whose glittering shop windows also offered spectacles for sale. Moreover, the department stores hosted musical concerts and other entertainments, reflecting the activity on the *grands boulevards* outside. Such was the importance of the department stores to Parisian life that Emile Zola dubbed them the 'tabernacles' or cathedrals of the new culture of commerce (Zola, 1883/1999, p. 53).

The *belle époque* was the golden age of the press – the four major newspapers sold roughly four million copies in 1912 (Charle, 2004, p. 160). It is little wonder then that the major newspapers were housed on the *grands boulevards*, and they contributed in no small measure to the dissemination of the myth of Paris as a capital of entertainment and pleasure, with their articles discussing the latest events taking place in the city. Located next to cafés, some newspaper offices even housed their own cafés where members of the public could read newspapers. The café itself became a prime spot for people watching, and some contemporaries likened this experience to the entertainment of the theatre (Barrows, 1991, p. 17).

The *belle époque* was not only a golden age of the press but also a vibrant age for the boulevard theatre; these two institutions, both located on the *grands boulevards*, worked in symbiosis. The newspapers advertised the latest plays and highlighted the smallest details of famous actors' and actresses' lives, marking the beginning of the age of celebrity culture. Actress Sarah Bernhardt, who regularly played to sell-out audiences, starred as national heroes like Joan of Arc, whom she portrayed in two different productions, as well as Napoleon's doomed son, who died of tuberculosis in exile at the age of 21. Perhaps the greatest theatrical success of the *belle époque* was Edmond Rostand's *Cyrano de Bergerac* with the great actor Benoît-Constant Coquelin playing the lead role. The play commemorated its 1,000th performance in 1913 and made its dramatist a national hero – and the first celebrity author (Datta, 2011, p. 25; p. 105).

The theatre was a place for crafting heroes and forging national identity. The French public, weary of political quarrels, disheartened by the loss of the Franco-Prussian War and fearful of technological, cultural and social changes, including the rise of the socialist and women's movements, increasingly sought refuge in the fictions of the theatre and the press. The theatre often presented historical heroes like Napoleon and Joan of Arc, in common with the press, which promoted real-life heroes in the sensational news stories it published above the fold and fictional ones in the serialised stories published below it (Datta, 2011, pp. 28–29). As one historian has written, Paris during the *belle époque* was 'a stage, a vast theatre for herself and all the world' (Shattuck, 1968, pp. 5–6). He was referring not only to the important role the theatre played in French national life but also to the theatricality of *belle époque* life. In fact, many of the artists of this time, among them Henri de Toulouse-Lautrec, Edgar Degas and Jean Béraud, depicted scenes of the theatre in their work, illustrating both literally and figuratively the importance of the theatre in *belle époque* Paris.

This theatricality extended to politics. In the 1890s, Paris was the site of a number of bombings by self-styled anarchists, one in the Chamber of Deputies and another at the café of a busy railroad station. In 1894, President Sadi Carnot was assassinated by an anarchist. The 1880s and 1890s witnessed political and economic unrest, including numerous miners' strikes. The period was also marked by one of the greatest of French conflicts, an event that remains imprinted in French memory even today – the Dreyfus Affair. In 1894 a Jewish army captain was accused of selling secrets to the Germans and sentenced to life imprisonment on Devil's Island in French Guyana. Subsequently, his family and friends found out that he had been falsely accused and that a military cover-up had taken place. This military case became an affair of national opinion, centred less on the guilt or innocence of one man, but rather on a debate about the nature of French identity itself. The Affair divided friends and families and it pitted (for the most part) the conservative forces of the Church and the army against more progressive, republican ones, although neither group was a monolithic bloc (Datta, 1999, p. 5).

The Affair was in large part propelled by the press; indeed, it was the first mass media event in France. It also launched anti-Semitism as a mass movement whose ideas were disseminated by a virulently anti-Semitic press (Weber, 1987, pp. xxv–xxvii). The years of the Affair witnessed a good deal of street violence. While most musical comedies do not depict the political and social tensions of the time, these events marked the memory of Parisian contemporaries.

The World's Fairs of 1889 and 1900

The *belle époque* witnessed the flourishing of the entertainment industry, not only cabarets, circuses and music halls, but also the World's Fairs. Paris hosted five different Universal Expositions at an interval of 11 years from 1855 to 1900, earning it the title of 'Queen City of Expositions' (Geppert, 2013, p. 62). The 1889 and the 1900 World's Fairs, in particular, were huge successes, the first, attracting 32 million visitors and the second, over 50 million, both from France and around the world (Prochasson, 1999, p. 93). The French government sought to represent the sights of Paris as an extension of the marvels of the exhibition and the city itself as the centre of Western civilisation, indeed, a new Athens (Prochasson, 1999, p. 94). Dubbed 'the festival of the Republic' by Jean Frollo, the pseudonym of a group of journalists writing for *Le Petit Parisien* ('Les Trois étapes', 15 April 1900, in Frollo 1900/1994, p. 145), the 1889 Fair commemorated the centennial of the French Revolution. The major feature of the exhibition was the Eiffel Tower. Viewed by its creator and republican politicians as an ode to progress and technology, the Eiffel Tower became the tallest manmade structure in the world, until well into the 20th century (Levin, 1989, pp. 1055–1057). While Eiffel found the Tower both beautiful and useful, a number of conservative artists and writers published a public petition in *Le Temps* denouncing it as a 'profanation' of Paris, claiming, moreover, that 'even commercial America' would not want it ('La Protestation des artistes', *Le Temps*, 14 February 1887, in Lemoine, 1989, pp. 98–99). Among the signatories was writer Guy de Maupassant, who claimed he had to leave Paris because the sight of it annoyed him so much (Maupassant,1890, p. 1). Nevertheless, over time, the Eiffel Tower became an iconic symbol, both of the French capital and of France itself. Little wonder then that a key scene in Stanley Donen's *Funny Face* (1957) culminates with the three main characters all making their way to the Tower, where they meet up to celebrate both this great monument and Paris itself (see cover photograph).

For the 1900 World's Fair, as in the case of the 1889 exhibition, republican leaders envisaged new construction in Paris, in particular, such iconic buildings as the Grand Palais and Petit Palais, along with the baroque Pont Alexandre III, built to commemorate the Franco-Russian friendship treaty signed in 1896. The 1900 *Exposition Universelle* was described by the journalists of *Le Petit Parisien* as the 'apotheosis of peace', progress and civilisation (*Le Petit Parisien*, 15 April 1900, in Frollo, 1900/1994, p. 146). Nevertheless, the tensions that would lead to the hostilities of World War I were already present, notably, in the desire of the host nation to assert its superiority, in particular, against such traditional enemies as the Germans and the English.

One way of manifesting its power was to claim half of the exhibition space for French products (Prochasson, 1999, pp. 97–99), especially in the display of its colonies. In 1889, the colonial displays had been interspersed throughout the fairgrounds – although a number of the colonial exhibits were prominently located on the Esplanade of the Invalides. The French gave greater prominence to the colonies in 1900, devoting to them an entire section of the fairgrounds, in the Trocadero gardens. Not only were colonial subjects reduced to exhibits in 'human zoos' in these exhibitions, so too did the colonies become a source of visual consumption, as the public visited recreations of African villages, an Algerian *casbah* and a model of the Cambodian Angkor Wat temple (Young, 2008, pp. 349–354). The Rue du Caire exhibit in 1889 – with its souks, houses, cafés and female performers who titillated visitors with 'la danse du ventre' – was especially successful in packaging the colonies for the general public (Rearick, 1985, p. 139).

Beyond the official pavilions, meant to be (mostly) educative, were commercial entertainments on the fairgrounds, among them panoramas like the reproduction of the Bastille in 1889 and, in 1900, le Vieux Paris, a recreation of the old streets and sights of Paris from medieval times to the 18th century. Cafés and restaurants,

FIGURE 1.3   A showcase for the self-proclaimed 'centre of Western civilisation': the 1889 World Fair in Paris featured a '*Grande Galérie des Industries diverses*'.

Source: Photo provided by the editor.

including on the Eiffel Tower, also abounded, and the 1900 fair even featured the giant Ferris Wheel. Popular entertainments were also to be found off the fairgrounds. In 1889, Buffalo Bill's Wild West show, while located in Neuilly and thus not on the fairgrounds proper, attracted huge crowds who saw this entertainment as an extension of the fair, a notion encouraged by its American organisers. (Datta, 2018). Visitors could thus be forgiven for collapsing the notion of the entertainments on the fairgrounds and those on the streets of Paris.

Montmartre

One of the attractions designed to lure visitors to Paris during the 1889 Fair was the Moulin Rouge, which debuted the scandalous can-can. The Moulin Rouge became associated in tourists' minds not only with Montmartre but with Paris itself. Both a place of pleasure and crime (Chevalier,1980), Montmartre also had revolutionary associations – the events of the Commune had begun here. Montmartre was a working-class district in which bohemian writers and artists rubbed shoulders with anarchists, criminals and prostitutes. While Montmartre had been annexed to Paris in 1860, it was far enough away to seem rural – windmills and vineyards still dotted the landscape in the late 19th century. It was also one of the parts of Paris to escape Haussmannisation. Rents were cheaper, and it became a haven for artists like Toulouse-Lautrec and, later, Pablo Picasso, who had their studios there.

In 1880 a law was passed prohibiting the closing of any café for political reasons, leading to the growth of numerous cabarets, dance halls and drinking establishments, especially in Montmartre. One of the most well-known cabarets in Montmartre was Le Chat Noir, made famous, in part, by its advertising poster by Théophile Steinlen, which was plastered all over Paris. Founded in 1881 by painter Rodolphe Salis, Le Chat Noir succeeded in attracting writer Émile Goudeau, the organiser of gatherings of avant-garde writers and artists known as Hydropathes on the Left Bank (Goudeau, 1888/2000, pp. 254–257). In the wake of the launching of Le Chat Noir, these left-bank bohemians migrated to Montmartre (Hewitt, 2017, p. 37), where the cabaret's first home was on the boulevard Rochechouart. Goudeau became the official poet-in-residence of the cabaret as well as the editor of the journal *Le Chat Noir*, which publicised the cabaret's activities. He also wrote a novel chronicling the tribulations of Montmartre bohemians in *La Vache enragée* in 1885, penning his memoirs *Dix Ans de Bohème* three years later. In recognition of Goudeau's key role in publicising Montmartre life, a square in Montmartre was named in his honour in 1911.

A consummate showman, Salis greeted his clients either with insults or with exaggerated politeness – he had a man in a Swiss Guard costume greet his guests like royalty. On one occasion, he announced his own death and held a wake for himself at his cabaret (Rearick, 1985, p. 59; p. 65). Salis invited young bohemian artists, among them Adolphe Willette, Steinlen and Caran d'Ache, to hang their paintings in his establishment and singers such as Aristide Bruant, to perform, but he often exploited them. Bruant eventually defected from Le Chat Noir and founded his own cabaret Le Mirliton. The Toulouse-Lautrec poster series of Bruant, featuring his iconic hat, red scarf and cape, made him a celebrity.

Both Salis and Bruant, who sang songs extolling the virtues of the poor and downtrodden, saw themselves as outsiders, opponents of the establishment and the bourgeoisie. But the irony of these bohemians was that, in seeking to escape the commercial culture of the bourgeoisie, they availed themselves of advertising and publicity techniques for self-promotion, thereby attracting a broad public eager for a 'taste of Bohemia' (Seigel, 1987, p. 216). Upper-class men came to Montmartre to find their pleasures. Among the visitors to Le Chat Noir were the Prince of Wales, the philosopher Ernest Renan and General Georges Boulanger (Seigel, 1987, p. 221). On the occasion of the 1900 World's Fair, Victor Meusy and Edmond Deplas published a *Guide de l'étranger à Montmartre*, presumably destined for French-speaking tourists. In its preface, Émile Goudeau regretfully admitted that Montmartre was henceforth no longer separated from commercial Parisian life but had willingly embraced 'the golden calf' (1900, p. 7). The publicity elicited by such guidebooks brought in tourists seeking the thrill of the 'dangers' of Montmartre, allowing Bruant and Salis to grow rich from their counterculture exploits, with Bruant buying a country estate to which he retired, living the good life until his death at age 73.

Not all, however, accepted the commercialisation of bohemian culture. In 1896 and again the following year, some Montmartre denizens, led by artist Adolphe Willette, organised the 'Fête de la Vache enragée'[7] meant not only to parody the traditional Fête du Boeuf Gras, associated with Mardi Gras festivities, but also as a protest against the increased commercialisation of Montmartre by such residents as Salis and Bruant. (Datta, 1993, p. 196). While the poverty and suffering of bohemians in Montmartre were badges of honour for some artists, they were also a sign that behind the gaiety, Montmartre had a dark side.

But it is other celebrations like the costumed *Bal des Quat'z'Arts*, hosted by the students at the École des Beaux-Arts and which gave birth to the cabaret of that name, along with the *Bal du Courrier Français*, organised by the eponymous newspaper,[8] that marked historical memory, in part due to the arrest of one of the participants of the *Bal des Quat'z'Arts* for public nudity in 1893 and the subsequent riots in the Latin Quarter protesting the arrest. In fact, one of the last scenes of *An American in Paris* depicts its main characters – albeit fully dressed – cavorting at a Beaux Arts Ball.

Montmartre also became celebrated for the iconic Sacré-Coeur basilica, constructed by Catholics as a symbol of national atonement for the loss of the Franco-Prussian War and the national divisions of the Commune (Jonas, 2001, p. 99).[9] In locating the church here, they built upon the religious associations of Montmartre, which was reputed to be the site of the martyrdom of France's patron saint Saint-Denis. Construction of the Sacré-Coeur, which began in 1875, was not completed until 1914; the church was not consecrated until after World War I in 1919. The irony of its location was not lost on the habitués of Montmartre cabarets who mocked the religious pilgrims who henceforth flocked to the site, rubbing shoulders with disabused Montmartre bohemians. But both groups shared in the commercialisation and popularisation of Montmartre culture, the first, through its entertainment industry, the second, through the marketing of religious pilgrimages and related souvenirs.[10]

By the mid to late 1890s, some Montmartre entertainers moved to sites in central Paris, near the *grands boulevards*, the Folies Bergère and the Olympia music hall chief among them (Rearick, 1985, p. 74). Although these entertainers claimed that their departure signalled the end of Montmartre as a pleasure capital, Montmartre's reputation continued on well into the inter-war period (Hewitt, 2017, p. 9).

Conclusion

The Paris of the late 19th and early 20th centuries was a place to see and be seen. The recently urbanised capital had been transformed into a vast stage, which offered nightly entertainments not only in the theatres, cabarets and dance halls but also in the everyday spectacles of modern life, from the shop windows on the tree-lined boulevards to the cafés of major hotels where spectators could watch passers-by. The way of life symbolised by the pleasure seekers of the *belle époque* would survive in some form after 1914, although much of it would disappear in the trenches of World War I. Yet the memory of the Paris of pleasures and entertainments would live on well into the 1950s in American musical comedies, which packaged for their audiences a mythical and timeless city.

Notes

1 Benjamin wrote two essays with that title – the first in 1935, the second in 1939 – published in Eiland and McLaughlin, trans. 1999, pp. 3–26.
2 For more on these three films, see Chapters 8 (*Funny Face* and *Gigi*), 15 (*Gigi*) and 16 (*An American in Paris*).
3 Patrice Higonnet observes that the Paris of the French national imagination was not the same as in the imagination of other countries (2002, p. 232). But I would note that the images did sometimes converge, as they did during the late 19th and 20th centuries.
4 On lighting Paris at this time, see Clayson, 2019.
5 Although, as Jones, notes, 'no smoking gun exists in the shape of an order by Napoleon III or Haussmann to build boulevards for military and repressive purposes . . . there exists little doubt that the wish to undermine Parisian popular militancy' was on their minds, (2004, p. 318).
6 Historians disagree on the exact periodisation of the *belle époque* – while they agree with 1914 as the end point, some opt to start with 1880 or 1889, while others begin with 1900: Kalifa, 2017, pp. 17–18.
7 'Manger de la vache enragée' was a slang term for going hungry.
8 *Le Courrier Français* sponsored the balls of a group of Montmartre bohemians called 'Les Incohérents' before founding its own ball in 1888.
9 Associated with the Sacred Heart cult, it was thus meant as a powerful symbol of the French counterrevolutionary tradition (Jonas, 2001, p. 99).
10 Visits to Sacré Coeur also coincided with a visit to the sights of Paris; one of the most popular years for such pilgrimages coincided with the 1889 World's Fair (Jonas, 2001, pp. 108–109).

References

Anderson, Benedict (1991) *Imagined Communities: Reflections on the Origin and Spread of Nationalism*. New York: Verso.

Barrows, Susanna. (1991) 'Nineteenth-Century Cafes: Arenas of Everyday Life,' in Barbara Stern Shapiro (ed.) *Pleasures of Paris: Daumier to Picasso*. Boston: Museum of Fine Arts, pp. 17–26.

Benjamin, Walter. (1935; 1939/1999) 'Paris: The Capital of the Nineteenth Century,' in Howard Eiland and Kevin McLaughlin (trans.) *The Arcade Project*. Cambridge, MA: Harvard University Press, pp. 3–26.

Brooks, Peter. (2007) *Henry James Goes to Paris*. Princeton, NJ: Princeton University Press.

Charle, Christophe. (2004) *Le Siècle de la Presse (1830–1939)*. Paris: Seuil.

Chevalier, Louis. (1980) *Montmartre du Plaisir et du crime*. Paris: R. Laffont.

Clayson, Hollis. (2019) *Illuminating Paris: Essays on Art and Lighting in the Belle Époque*. Chicago: University of Chicago Press.

———. (2002) *Art and Everyday Life under the Siege (1870–1871)*. Chicago: University of Chicago Press.

Datta, Venita. (2018) 'Buffalo Bill Goes to France: French-American Encounters at the Wild West Show, 1889–1905,' *French Historical Studies*, 41(3), pp. 525–555.

———. (2011) *Heroes and Legends of Fin-de-Siècle France: Gender, Politics, and National Identity*. New York: Cambridge University Press.

———. (1999) *Birth of a National Icon: The Literary Avant-Garde and the Origins of the Intellectual in France*. Albany: SUNY Press.

———. (1993) 'A Bohemian Festival: La Fête de la Vache Enragée,' *Journal of Contemporary History*, 28, April, pp. 195–213.

Frollo, Jean. (1900/1994) 'Les Trois Étapes,' *Le Petit Parisien*, 15 April 1900 in Christophe Prochasson and Olivier Wieviorka (eds.) *La France du XXème Siècle*. Paris: Seuil.

Geppert, Alexander C. T. (2013) *Fleeting Cities: Imperial Expositions in Fin-de-Siècle Europe*. London: Palgrave-Macmillan.

Goudeau, Émile. (1900) 'Préface,' in Victor Meusy and Edmond Deplas (eds) *Guide de l'étranger à Montmartre*. Paris: J. Strass.

———. (1888/2000) *Dix Ans de Bohème*. Paris: Champ Vallon.

Hahn, Haejeong Hazel. (2006) 'Du Flâneur au Consommateur: Spectacle et Consommation sur les Grands Boulevards, 1840–1914,' *Romantisme*, 134(4), pp. 67–78.

Hewitt, Nicholas. (2017) *Montmartre: A Cultural History*. Liverpool: Liverpool University Press.

Higonnet, Patrice (2002) *Paris: Capital of the World*. Arthur Goldhammer (trans.). Cambridge, MA: Belknap Press of Harvard University Press.

Horne, Alistair. (2004) *Seven Ages of Paris*. New York: Vintage Books.

Jonas, Raymond. (2001) 'Sacred Tourism and Secular Pilgrimage: Montmartre and the Basilica of Sacré-Coeur,' in Gabriel P. Weisberg (ed.) *Montmartre and the Making of Mass Culture*. New Brunswick: Rutgers University Press, pp. 94–119.

Jones, Colin. (2004) *Paris: The Biography of a City*. New York: Penguin Press.

Kalifa, Dominique. (2017) *La Véritable Histoire de la 'Belle Epoque'*. Paris: Fayard.

Lemoine, Bertrand. (1989) *La Tour de M. Eiffel*. Paris: Gallimard.

Levin, Miriam R. (1989) 'The Eiffel Tower Revisited,' *The French Review*, 62(6), pp. 1052–1064.

Maupassant, Guy de. (1890) *La Vie errante*. Paris: P. Ollendorff.

Miller, Michael B. (1981) *The Bon Marché: Bourgeois Culture and the Department Store, 1869–1920*. Princeton, NJ: Princeton University Press.

Prochasson, Christophe. (1999) *Paris 1900: Essai d'histoire culturelle*. Paris: Calmann-Lévy.

Rearick, Charles. (2006) 'La Mémoire des Grands Boulevards du XIXème Siècle,' *Romantisme*, 134(4), 79–90.

———. (1985) *Pleasures of the Belle Époque: Entertainments in Turn-of-the-Century France*. New Haven: Yale University Press.

Schwartz, Vanessa R. (2007) *It's so French: Hollywood, Paris and the Making of Cosmopolitan Film Culture*. Chicago: University of Chicago Press.

———. (1998) *Spectacular Realities: Early Mass Culture in Fin-de-Siècle Paris*. Berkeley: University of California Press.

Seigel, Jerrold. (1987) *Bohemian Paris: Culture, Politics and the Boundaries of Bourgeois Life, 1830–1930*. New York: Penguin Books.

Shattuck, Roger. (1968) *The Banquet Years: The Origins of the Avant-Garde in France, 1885-World War I*. New York: Vintage Books.

Sheppard, Nathan. (1871) *Shut Up in Paris*. London: R. Bentley.

Spang, Rebecca L. (1992) '"And They Ate the Zoo": Relating Gastronomic Exoticism in the Siege of Paris,' *MLN*, 107(4), pp. 752–773.

Taunton, Matthew. (2009) *Fictions of the City: Class, Culture and Mass Housing in London and Paris*. London: Palgrave-Macmillan.

Weber, Eugen. (1987) 'Foreword,' in Norman Kleeblat (ed.) *The Dreyfus Affair: Art, Truth, and Justice*. Berkeley: University of California Press, pp. xxv–xxvii.

Young, Patrick. (2008) 'From the Eiffel Tower to the Javanese Dancer: Envisioning Cultural Globalization at the 1889 Paris Exhibition,' *The History Teacher*, 4(3), pp. 339–362.

Zola, Emile. (1883/1999) *Au Bonheur des Dames*. Paris: Garnier-Flammarion.

2

'YES, I'M A GAY PARISIAN!'

Establishing the trope of 'Gay Paree': *The Merry Widow*

Stefan Frey

> *'For I am quite Parisian*
> *A most distinguished man*
> *And try to look as English as I can.*
> *Yes, I'm a gay Parisian,*
> *And far above the common mob*
> *Je suis très snob!'*
> (Lehár, 1907, pp. 191–192)

This song with the title 'Quite Parisian' was composed by Franz Lehár for the 1907 production of his operetta *The Merry Widow* at Daly's Theatre in London. It was sung in the third act by the comedian W.H. Berry, who played Nisch, the messenger of the Marsovian embassy, accidentally his fatherland: 'I was born by cruel fate,/In a little Balkan state.' But he likes to dance with 'the girls in France . . ./ They are all so chic and the *dernier cri*,/kicking up lingerie!/Quite *épatant*; eh, what?/ *C'est joliment cocotte!*' (Lehár, 1907, p. 192).

In Lehár's original score of this act there is neither a song for 'Njegus', as the role of Nisch is called in German, nor the polka 'Butterflies', danced by Fifi and the chorus. There is only one song about those typical Parisian guises: 'Les belles grisettes' or – in the English version by Adrian Ross – 'The Girls at Maxim's'. Their song begins with the pretty verse: 'We are little Paris ladies,/Ev'ry one a Maxim's maid is'. Like Nisch's 'Quite Parisian', this song is also about Paris, celebrating the reputation of the French capital as a place for pleasure, entertainment and rapture, caused by champagne and girls and ending with the dance most widely associated with Paris: the can-can: 'Here is music, here is dancing,/playing, swaying, all night through!/We are Maxim's girls entrancing,/and we're here to welcome you.' (Lehár, 1907, p. 175).

FRANZ LEHAR   5125·14

FIGURE 2.1   Franz Lehár (1870–1948), the Austro-Hungarian composer of *The Merry Widow*.

Source: Photo provided by the editor.

London's *Merry Widow* 1907

The third act of the London version of *The Merry Widow* from 1907 is clearly a variation on this trope of 'Gay Paree', and it is this aspect which differentiates it from the original version. It is rather a touristic perspective of girls welcoming their customers with a French Can-can, a special form of the original can-can, which emerged as a combination of the individual style of the Parisian ballrooms and the typical chorus line of British music halls. The French Can-can did not arrive in

Paris until the end of the 19th century, first and foremost to fulfil the expectations of English and American tourists. And that is exactly, what the English version of *The Merry Widow* does, because for the London audience Paris is an exotic place to travel to where one forgets one's own moral standards. For the Viennese audience Paris was just another Vienna. So the whole third act of the German original is not located in 'Maxim's restaurant, Paris' like in the English version, but in a fake Maxim's, replicated by the widow herself in her house. The reason for this was acknowledged by librettist Victor Léon: '[T]he Viennese wouldn't have accepted that elegant society ladies visit a venue where men associate with cocottes' (Léon, 1931, p. 7).

But this was not adapter Basil Hood's only alteration. He replaced nearly all of the names, except that of Danilo, who became a prince instead of a count. The widow was now called Sonia instead of Hanna, Njegus turned into Nisch, the second couple was changed from Rossillon and Valencienne to Jolidon and Natalie, her husband from Zeta to Popoff and the country, whose ambassador he is, from Pontevedro to Marsovia. There was new dialogue, especially for the comical characters Nisch and Popoff; the latter was given a routine about his favourite hen named Hetty and her very special eggs. Hood, a former Captain of the army and experienced author of many musical comedies such as Arthur Sullivan's last work *The Rose of Persia* (1899), explained in the magazine *Play Pictorial*, why this was necessary:

> For more than one reason a translation would not suit or satisfy the taste of our English audiences; not – as is often suggested to me – because native improprieties would prove too startling for our British Mrs. Grundy, but because our audiences desire different matters of construction and treatment. . . . The third act [of most Viennese librettos] is to our taste so trivial in subject and treatment that it is necessary to construct and write an entirely new act, or to cut it away altogether.
>
> *(Hood, 1911, pp. 50–51)*

In the case of *The Merry Widow* the differences aren't as drastic as in Hood's later adaptations of other Viennese operettas. Ever since *Die Fledermaus/The Bat* (1874), third acts of the genre were infamous for their musical sparseness. But in this case, not only was the third act not eliminated, it was even enlarged, with the two other acts maintaining the dramaturgical structure of the original *Lustige Witwe*.

Director George Edwardes, the legendary 'Guv'nor' of Daly's Theatre, had signed a contract with Lehár's publisher Adolf Sliwinski as early as 27 February 1906, just two months after the world premiere, which guaranteed him the exclusive rights for all English-speaking countries (Abel, 1959, p. 88). It turned out to be the business deal of a lifetime. It cannot be verified whether Edwardes himself attended the performance in Vienna; however, it is most likely, because that was the usual procedure in the business. As musicologist Derek B. Scott reveals in his recently published book *German Operetta on Broadway and in the West End*, Edwardes originally wanted to hire the Viennese 'widow'

FIGURE 2.2   Joseph Coyne (Prince Danilo) and Lily Elsie (Sonia), sporting the famous *Merry Widow* hat, in the first British production of *Die lustige Witwe* in 1907.

Source: Photo courtesy of Alamy Stock Photo.

Mizzi Günther, although she was not really the type of leading lady he usually cast: the musical comedies he had produced before normally starred a young girl. He found one in 21-year-old Lily Elsie, a very attractive actress with a small light voice, who had never played a leading role before. But Edwardes was convinced that she would be a hit in the role of Sonia. He commissioned London's most famous designer Lady Duff Gordon to give her Parisian chic.

Even more risky was the casting of 40-year-old American comedian Joseph Coyne as Danilo. Not only had he never been a 'romantic lead' before he also couldn't sing at all – and had no desire to do so. But George Edwardes succeeded in persuading him that he alone would be the perfect Prince Danilo. The bigger problem was to convince the composer Franz Lehár, when he arrived for the London rehearsals. Coyne only spoke his dialogues. Lehár asked why he wouldn't sing, and Edwardes excused him with a cold. When the rehearsals with the orchestra began, Coyne couldn't avoid singing any longer – and recited his lines:

> When this happened Lehár was horrified. He stopped the rehearsal; he put down his baton. 'What was this?' he demanded. No chance for pleas of a cold or other evasions now! Edwardes assured Lehár that Mr. Coyne was a very funny man. 'But I have not written funny music,' retorted Lehár.
>
> *(MacQueen-Pope and Murray, 1953, p. 98)*

Nonetheless, Coyne remained as the lead. It is impossible to gauge from the London reviews how he performed the songs, whether he recited them rhythmically – 'anticipating Rex Harrison's technique in *My Fair Lady*' as Derek Scott assumes

(Scott, 2014, p. 65) – or whether he delivered them more in a melodramatic par-lando like his Viennese counterpart Louis Treumann.

Marsovia in Paris

Although the love story between Sonia and Prince Danilo – or Hanna Glawari and Count Danilo in the original version – takes place in Paris, both protagonists were actually 'born by cruel fate in a little Balkan state'. But the other couple, Natalie and Jolidon (or Valencienne and Camille) are citizens of the French capital and have a 'typical' Parisian affaire. Jolidon is a beau and Natalie is married to the ambassador of the fictitious Marsovia. The latter comes up with a scheme to prevent the merry widow from transferring all her money out of her home country to France. Thus, she is welcomed by a crowd of 'quite Parisian' gentlemen offering her compli-ments. In her entrance song Sonia admits her ignorance of those Parisian customs:

> I haven't been in Paris long,
> And when I meet a man,
> I'm always saying something wrong,
> I'm so Marsovian
> For when a man would wed a girl
> In my own native land.
> He doesn't call her star and pearl
> And want to kiss her hand.
> Says he, 'Let us get married now,
> We are both growing big,
> My father has a cow,
> Your mother has a pig.'
> (Lehár, 1907, pp. 19–21)

How Sonia becomes 'a gay Parisian' constitutes one part of her love story. The other part shows how Prince Danilo rekindles their previous romance. In the end they meet at Maxim's, the most Parisian place imaginable in this operetta. Danilo's entrance song is just about this restaurant. It is his adopted, but real home, where he feels com-fortable, while his native Marsovia is merely exhausting. At the start of the number, Danilo exclaims: 'My Fatherland, it is for thee, I ought to work from one to three.' It concludes with the line: 'Till I forget completely my dear old Fatherland', which implies that Danilo is the right man to divert Sonia's thoughts from her home country.

This is the topic of their central scene in the second act, a duet, which begins as a dialogue accompanied by music and ends in a dance. Their conversation is about what a modern woman should know about places like Maxim's, 'where men associ-ate with cocottes'. Hanna begs Danilo to introduce her into 'the mysteries of the demimonde' so that she might be able to show off to her future husband: 'I want to pretend that I had experienced all that. That puts the final touch to the modern woman.' At this moment, the orchestra starts playing the Maxim's song. When a

Kolo strikes up, Sonia refuses to dance this native Marsoviarian dance: 'It is not fashionable for such a woman to dance the patriotic "Heimathopser".' Then for the first time in the operetta, the famous 'Merry Widow Waltz' is heard which makes Sonia wish 'to forget in three-quarter time three quarters of her virtue'. In the copy of the libretto for the Viennese censorship office the scene ends with a 'Niggertanz':

DANILO: 'Look at me! O yes, my little baby . . . If a negro gives you a kiss, you
    have the proof of his love in black on white.'
HANNA: 'That is something really new!'
DANILO: 'That goes directly to your head. What? Hallo!'
HANNA: 'Hallo!'
    Their dance becomes wilder and wilder!

(Zensur-Textbuch, 1905, unpaginated)

This scene was the highlight of the Viennese production, because Mizzi Günther and Louis Treumann were famous for their dance routines. Most impressive was how they handled the waltz, which for the first hundred performances did not yet have any lyrics. This show piece was not only danced to perfection and played with an erotic charge but also a milestone in operetta history, as critic Ludwig Hirschfeld

FIGURE 2.3   A regular highlight of every stage production and film version of Lehár's operetta is the 'Merry Widow Waltz', here performed by Lana Turner (in black) and Fernando Lamas (white uniform) in the 1952 MGM screen adaption, directed by Curtis Bernhardt.

Source: Photo provided by the editor.

underlines: 'When Mr. Treumann held Mrs. Günther by the neck for the first time and the two of them spun around freely, it constituted a true exploit for operetta' (Hirschfeld, 1923, p. 12). It was this new kind of dancing which made the sensitive little waltz melody one of the genre's greatest hits. After the opening night it was 'this dance scene with the waltz, rather than a waltz fragment, which escorted the audience home' ('Sch', 1905).

The French matrix: *L'Attaché d'ambassade*

Librettist Leo Stein responded to a newspaper survey with the title 'How an Operetta Is Born' with the following verses: 'First you should assiduously read some books, then "suddenly" an idea forms in your mind, next you should get an advance from the theatre management, and everything else will fall into place' (Stein, 1905, p. 5). Stein, a lawyer and clerk at the railway company Südbahn, was born as Leo Rosenstein 1861 in Lemberg and, since *Wiener Blut/Vienna Blood* in 1899, had become the favourite writing partner of Vienna's most famous operetta librettist Victor Léon. Léon had discovered Franz Lehár for operetta in 1902 with their *Rastelbinder*, but it was Stein who suggested transforming *L'Attaché d'ambassade* by the Offenbach librettist Henri Meilhac into an operetta. The comedy premièred in 1861 in Paris; one year later it was performed for the first time in Vienna at the Carltheater before being shown at the Burgtheater, where it remained in repertory, from 18 April 1863 until 5 June 1905, as *Der Gesandtschafts-Attaché*.[1] Two days later, *Die Lustige Witwe* was announced as one of the new operetta productions of the Theater an der Wien in all Viennese newspapers. Instead of listing Meilhac's popular play as its source material, it was declared for copyright reasons that *Die Lustige Witwe* was 'partly based on a foreign idea' ('teilweise nach einer fremden Grundidee').

This 'foreign idea' in fact copied the plot of Meilhac's comedy. Just like *The Merry Widow*, the earlier work takes place in an embassy in Paris, although not that of a 'Balkan state' but that of a typical German petty state named Birkenfeld. The ambassador Baron Scarpa is tasked with preventing Madelaine Palmer, the Paris-born, young and rich widow of a Birkenfeld banker from marrying a Parisian. He delegates this task to his attaché Count Prax, a notorious ladies' man, even though he does not have the Parisian charm of his French rivals. Prax is described as a typical German rake ('débauché'), which is why he tells the widow straight away during their first meeting that he will never fall in love with her. Yet soon he does, and when his ruthless rival Frondeville tries to seize Madelaine's fortune via defamation, he challenges him to a duel. At the end Prax confesses to Madelaine that her Parisian charm has changed him into a real human being, which here means into a real Parisian. For Meilhac, being Parisian is neither exotic nor erotic, it is just a matter of manners, and consequently there is no Maxim's.

The Merry Widow tells the same story with a different premise and from another perspective: at the centre of the play is no longer the Parisian lifestyle and the development of Prax, but Sonia's emancipation and her unusual love affairs (Denscher,

2017, p. 304). What intrigues the audience is how a woman changes from a Balkan country girl into a Parisian lady. The new focus is not only shown in the title of the operetta, but also in Sonia's characterisation as self-determined person, who takes her life into her own hands and does not wait for the men to act like Madeleine does in the *Attaché*. The two widows only have in common that they have inherited 20 million francs.

In the 44 years between the two plays, many things had changed, especially the relationship between women and men. Thus, the operetta introduces another plot element: Hanna Glawari and Danilo have previous history. They had met as young people, but Danilo's noble family didn't allow them to marry. As a result of the interference, Hanna married the old banker Glawari and Danilo went to Paris to not only forget his 'fatherland' but also the love of his life. But when they meet again, they realise that they are both still in love.

Like Prax, Danilo tells the widow right from the start that he will never declare his love for her, but his reasons are different. He doesn't want to appear to be a fortune hunter, who loves her only for her money as his French rivals do. Hence, Danilo has a psychological problem with his mission to prevent the widow from marrying a Parisian. The task itself remains the same as that of Prax, but he is conflicted because of his own personal attachment to the widow. She is aware of his emotional state and so tries to provoke him into revealing his true feelings. The way he struggles against them delights her, because she still loves him without showing it. It is the widow who controls this battle of the sexes and who wins it in the end – a landmark in operetta history.

The other major change introduced by librettists Victor Léon and Leo Stein was that both protagonists come from the same country, the fictional Balkan state Pontevedro. In the original copy of the libretto submitted to the censorship office, Pontevedro was identified as the real Montenegro, which had been independent since 1878 and for the contemporary Viennese audience a 'synonym for a under-developed country' (Csáky, 1996, p. 90). On the one hand, the satire of the neigh-bour to the south catered to local resentments against those small Balkan countries that always provoked conflicts with the Austrian-Hungarian Empire. On the other hand, the 'Montenegro' of the operetta was a parody of the Empire itself, which seemed to be underdeveloped in comparison to its German neighbour to the north. The censorship office, however, had reservations; although they regarded it as 'harmless mockery' they still were concerned that it 'could be objected to by the diplomatic mission of Montenegro' (Anon, 1905a).

Vienna's *Lustige Witwe* 1905: modernity, psychoanalysis and operetta

> Our melody. In the *Merry Widow*, it can be heard. Everything that resonates and creates a buzz today, the things we read, write, think, chat about and the modern clothes our feelings are clothed in, it all is given sound in this operetta, resonates in it.
>
> *(Salten, 1906, p. 2)*

Felix Salten, the author of *Bambi*, was thrilled about the parallels between *The Merry Widow* and modern Viennese literature:

> It is not at all necessary that Lehár really reads everything we write or is concerned with what we think. . . . Lehár . . . sets the pace for our steps. . . . Lehár's music is hot with an open, scalding sensuality; is full of sexual lust . . . you could sing modern verses to her.
>
> *(Salten, 1906, p. 2)*

That sexual lust was exactly what 'Gay Paree' was famous for. But in Lehár's operetta this element was not only related to Paris but also to the Balkan. A Viennese critic claimed that the 'sensually beautiful "Vilja"', a 'Pontevedrinian' folk song, 'would certainly have been forbidden if it had been written in words the way it was put into music' ('bgr', 1908, p. 2). If 'sultry eroticism' is 'characteristic for the twentieth century', wrote another critic, Lehár 'gave the twentieth century its operetta with the *Merry Widow*' (Scherber, 1920, p. 90). For Felix Salten, Lehár's music was 'immersed in the exotic, was varieté-like, décolleté and hot sensuality. It was sensuality as we present it today: a breaking free of desire to the point of frenzy. The unveiling of the instinctive' (Salten, 1906, p. 2).

As Lehár's English biographer Walter MacQueen-Pope wrote, this unveiling begins with the first encounter of the protagonists:

> There was a thrill for everyone in that meeting . . . Danilo covered his embarrassment – and the widow took the initiative. . . . It was now evident that something new in musical plays . . . had arrived. In this one the woman was to be the pursuer.
>
> *(Macqueen-Pope and Murray, 1953, pp. 107–108)*

Hanna and Danilo, both unable to show their feelings, represented the emotional state of their generation. Here was a modern woman, financially independent and socially unattached, with swarms of men around her, and there a reckless, nervous, proud man, exhausted by the women at Maxim's and uncertain how to behave towards this emancipated woman. What was almost unthinkable in the 19th century – namely that a woman pursues the man she desires and even courts him – is exemplified in Lehár's operetta. The spark ignited at the première. The constellation of the courting woman and the man, who although 'brought into the most kissable situations by three acts . . . steadfastly refuses any tenderness', struck a nerve with the audience. 'She talks to him so nicely with her eyes, in the wild tenderness of Slavic dances, that he finally kisses her, with the whole house applauding' (Anon, 1905b, p. 14), and so she finally succeeds.

As a prototype of a woman of the 20th century, Hanna Glawari is not only economically but also sexually self-determined and thus embodies everything her female audience could only dream of. That she comes from an underdeveloped Balkan state is astonishing while Valencienne, her more conventional counterpart

FIGURE 2.4 Glamorous, economically independent and sexually self-determined: Jeanette MacDonald, as the eponymous character in MGM's 1934 film adaptation of *The Merry Widow*, directed by Ernst Lubitsch. MacDonald's costumes were designed by Adrian.

Source: Production still provided by the editor.

and the second major female role in the *Merry Widow*, comes from Paris, the capital of modernism. Yet she lives in an arranged marriage, like most women of the time, including for example Sigmund Freud's female patients. For these 'unfortunate women who struggle between desire and imposed conscience', as his first biographer Fritz Wittels explained in 1908, there were only two ways out of their situation: 'Infidelity or hysteria, the individual solution to the women's question.' The latter had been negotiated on the opera stage, but the operetta had always relied on infidelity. Offenbach's heroines had demonstrated how to do this with virtuosity, and Valencienne, the French wife of the Pontevedrinan envoy, is their late descendant. Outwardly a 'decent woman', she isn't averse to a date in the pavilion, since according to psychoanalyst Wittels she 'apparently wants nothing more from the man than to exert sexual freedom and sexual power' (Wittels, 1908, pp. 10–11).

It is more than a coincidence that *The Merry Widow* appears in the same year as Freud's *Three Essays on Sexual Theory*. For Karl Kraus, one of the harshest critics of both *The Merry Widow* and psychoanalysis, the point was finally reached where 'the colossal lack of humor that strains the modern operetta began to be interpreted as an excess of psychology' (Kraus, 1909, pp. 4–6). What that meant in Sigmund Freud's Vienna is obvious. The intersection of Viennese operetta and psychoanalysis is not only significant for the 'simultaneity of the inequality' prevalent at that time but is also thematically concentrated in one common focus: taboo sexuality. 'The impact of operettas' – similar to how dreams work – knows 'no logic anyway, but only lies in the unconscious game of associations' (Adorno, 1984a, p. 518). In reference to the Parisian take on the myth as presented by Jacques Offenbach, philosopher Theodor W. Adorno concluded that 'the real Orpheus migrated to the operetta and took possession of our underworld' (Adorno, 1984a, p. 517).

International reception: New York

> The fame of *Die lustige Witwe* must have preceded the coming of the opera, for the appearance of the composer was greeted with thunders of applause before ever a note had been heard. The applause seemed to increase in volume as the evening went on; we have hardly ever attended so uproarious a first night.
>
> *(Anon, 1907d, p. 4)*

With these sober lines, *The Times* began its review of the London première which took place on 8 June 1907. Only four months later *The Merry Widow* reached the United States, where she also had been anticipated with excitement. *The New York Dramatic Mirror* greeted her enthusiastically: 'The operetta is twice welcome, on account of its own excellence, and because it may start a new era in musical entertainment' (Quoted in Bordman, 1981, p. 75).

Producer Henry W. Savage had leased New York's largest theatre at that time, the New Amsterdam Theater on 42nd Street, which had 1,700 seats. The Broadway opening on 21 October 1907 was a big event, and the New Amsterdam Theater, only four years old, with its Art Nouveau architecture was the perfect setting for the operetta, attracting

> the most brilliant audiences which have attended a New York first night in recent years. . . . The applause was almost terrifying in its intensity at times

and there were as many shouts of "Bravo!" as at a performance of *Pagliacci* when Caruso sings.

(Anon, 1907c, p. 9)

The biggest surprise for the audience, however, was, as the *New York Telegram* stated, that the operetta, although it dealt with 'the specialty of the Parisian dramatists – the unfaithfulness of wives', did not make this its main topic:

> Had the book been written by a Frenchman instead of by Germans it would have been a great deal more brilliant. . . . But . . . praise to those German authors and the American adapter, there are no gags. . . . If there is anything foreign to the average Broadway production it is this self-same *Merry Widow*.
>
> *(Anon, 1907b)*

Unlike most American musical comedies, the piece had 'a real plot and captivating music'. What thrilled Broadway audiences was not 'Gay Paree', but, as the *The Sun* attested, 'that golden champagne of Viennese life which is so much softer and less biting than the wine of Paris' (Anon, 1907a).

How this *played* out especially in the dance scenes was something new for American audiences. Frederic McKay, the critic of the *Evening Mail*, wrote:

> It seems strange, now that its discovery has been made, that it remains for the authors of *The Merry Widow* to realize the value of a waltz of lovers as a dramatic expedient. If the polka and the two-step have been shoving the waltz to one side of late, I have no doubt in the world, that the wonderfully contagious waltzes of *The Merry Widow* will revive the glories of that strictly Viennese dance.
>
> *(McKay, 1907)*

Indeed, after its heyday as a collective pleasure in the 19th century, the dance experienced a worldwide renaissance courtesy of Lehár's operetta and seeped into everyday life, especially in the United States. The waltz and the couple who danced it awakened unexpected desires via identification. In this sense, Sonia and Danilo became the mythical couple of their era, the idol of the paying customers. Whether New York, London or Copenhagen, everywhere they became ideal figures whose behaviour started fashion trends. The operetta became the model for reality. Dance competitions were held to determine the best Danilo-Sonia couple. As the Viennese critic Ludwig Hirschfeld recalled, there were 'at that time a lot of otherwise normal people who . . . spoke, thought and felt in quotes and melodies culled from it' (Hirschfeld, 1923, p. 12).

Making fashion: The *Merry Widow* hat

The most striking example for this imitation of Lehár's operetta in everyday life certainly was the Merry Widow hat, big as a cartwheel, created by London's Sonia Lily

Elsie and inherited by Ethel Jackson in New York. MacQueen-Pope enthused: 'A hat? no, a HAT – the sight of which sent every woman into ecstasy and the quick resolve to have one just like that at the earliest possible moment' (MacQueen-Pope and Murray, 1953, p. 114). It hadn't appeared in the Viennese production and was designed by Lady Duff Gordon under her fashion name 'Lucile', London's most important couturière. She added the glamour that made Elsie a fashion icon of her era. All of her costumes in the London *Merry Widow* caused a sensation. The highlight, however, was undoubtedly the gown in the third act, when Sonia enters Maxim's for her erotic waltz showdown with Danilo, to show him how Parisian she has become in the meantime: a tight-fitting white chiffon dress with a spectacular headpiece – described by the Canadian theatre historian Marlis Schweitzer as 'an immense black crinoline hat, banded round the crown with silver and two huge pink silk roses nestling under the brim. . . . Not only youthful, feminine, and innocent but also, paradoxically, mature, sophisticated, and sexually aware' (Schweitzer, 2009, p. 197).

This connection between the waltz and the hat evidences the direct link between operetta and textile industry, as Adorno was keen to point out: 'The waltz from *The Merry Widow* may have exemplified the new style, and the jubilation with which the bourgeoisie greeted Lehár's operetta can be compared to the success of the first department stores' (Adorno, 1984b, p. 772). Thus for an operetta performer, the elegant presentation of her costume, the skilful handling of the props, in short, the ability to enliven commodities was more important than vocal perfection – not the cane, but how it was twirled, not Lucile's hat, but the symbolic meaning Lily Elsie gave it as the merry widow created the fashion. Hat and operetta became a symbol of a new attitude towards life which was honoured in its secular temples: the department store and the theatre. Both facilities shared the same urban space and offered women in particular the opportunity to use it effectively. The theatres offered the perfect role model, which the department stores were invited to imitate. Even though the hat as a fashion accessory was associated with Paris, London and New York provided the ideal stage for this interplay.

How popular the *Merry Widow* hat was in New York, emerged when the management of the New Amsterdam Theatre decided to instrumentalise this resolve to be fashionable when celebrating the 275th performance of the operetta by distributing hats from Paris 'as souvenirs to all the women occupying orchestra or balcony seats'. But they underrated both the intensity of the women's 'resolve' and the female power to execute it. Deciding 'that the fifty cent seats deserved souvenirs and [assuming] that there would be some men in the audience', they had only 1,200 hats for 1,600 female audience members. When this became evident, before the curtain even 'began to come down, everybody . . . made a rush to the improvised bargain counter', where the hats were to be distributed. What then happened went down in Broadway history as 'Hot Skirmish over *Merry Widow* Hats'. *The New York Times* reported that a

> throng of women . . . declared mob rule and began the attack. . . . One
> woman tackled a woman next to her with a vim that would have done credit

to the world's champion female wrestler. . . . The older women did themselves credit . . . and the ardor with which they threw themselves into the mêlée made their daughters look like the veriest mollycoddles.

(Anon, 1908, p. 11)

There could be no proof more striking that operetta had become a primary ingredient of everyday culture of modern urbanity. In addition to the hat, there have been *Merry Widow* shoes, corsages and creams as well as Merry Widow cakes, chocolates and liqueurs, as products for a very contemporary lifestyle. Under the permanent rule of capitalism such commodities became symbols of being up-to-date for a socially mobile middle class, which was still nascent but existed in nearly every part of the Western world as a new circumstance of both consumers and theatre audiences. Their global similarities were stronger than their local differences.

'Off to Maxim's': the right place for 'Gay Paree'

It was quite astonishing that the last stop on the *Merry Widow's* triumphant journey around the Western world was Paris, where it opened as late as 28 April 1909 at the Apollo Theater. But *La Veuve Joyeuse* quickly prevailed over the initial scepticism of the press. This was not only due to the aforementioned copyright dispute with the heirs of the Offenbach librettist Henri Meilhac but also to the fact that France, the motherland of the genre, had previously been rather hostile to foreign works especially when they dealt with Paris as did *The Merry Widow*. The French translators Gaston Arman de Caillavet and Robert de Flers were therefore allowed to use the original freely and were mainly guided by the English version. In their version, the title heroine did not come from the Balkans but only grew up there and was actually an American, and consequently she was cast with the Englishwoman Constance Drever. Her name changed to Missia Palmieri, based on the Baroness Palmer from the *Attaché*, and Danilo was a count, indebted because of his passion for gambling. That made it even more difficult for him to admit his love to the rich widow. He was played by the baritone Henry Defreyn, whose Maxim song 'C'est tout un demi-monde/Où jamais on n'dit non' was a great success as a recording.

This song was the most effective one in Lehár's operetta to advertise Paris as the city where people revelled in glamorous nightspots, turning Maxim's into a household name even for those who had never travelled to the French capital. Of course, the real restaurant, which was known for always having stunningly attractive girls sitting by the window, was the model for the one in Lehár's operetta and benefited from it, but in *The Merry Widow* Maxim's was more than that: it was the essence of all that made Paris attractive – elegance, beautiful women and high spirits:

> I go off to Maxim's,
> Where fun and frolic beams,
> With all the girls I chatter,
> I laugh and kiss and flatter!

Lolo, Dodo. Joujou. Cloclo,
Margot, Froufrou.
For surnames do not matter,
I take the first to hand
and then the corks go pop.
We dance and never stop.
The ladies smile so sweetly,
I catch and kiss them neatly:
Lolo, Dodo. Joujou. Cloclo,
Margot, Froufrou –
Till I forget completely
My dear old Fatherland.
(Lehár, 1907, pp. 32–34)

The screen adaptations of *The Merry Widow*, all released by Metro-Goldwyn-Mayer which bought the rights in 1923, used Maxim's as their basic setting, with the exception of Erich von Stroheim's outstanding silent movie from 1925. In Ernst Lubitsch's version, which was released nine years later, it is at Maxim's where Sonia and Danilo meet for the first time in Paris. This Sonia, played by Jeanette MacDonald, disguises herself as a Parisian cocotte in sexy dresses. The casting of her partner further emphasised the Parisian background: Maurice Chevalier, in one of his last Hollywood performances before returning to his native country, as the French sunny boy – a character for which he had become famous. The actor announced:

I am tired of playing forever only the stupid boy who is madly in love, the Playboy of Paris, London and Hollywood. . . . But I will still equip the Danilo in Lehár's masterpiece with everything I have at my disposal.
(Quoted in Salzer, 1933, p. 7)

A Danilo with a French accent was the most fitting incarnation of 'Gay Paree' in the history of *The Merry Widow* and the personification of the man Nisch dreamed to be in his song from the 1907 London version: 'For I am quite Parisian' (Lehár, 1907, p. 193).

Note

1 It was performed 111 times altogether.

References

Abel, P. (1959) 'Copyright in *The Merry Widow*,' *American Journal of Comparative Law*, 8(1), Winter, p. 88, https://doi.org/10.2307/837167, accessed 6 January 2020.
Adorno, T. W. (1984a) 'Arabesken zur Operette (1932),' in T. W. Adorno (ed.) *Gesammelte Schriften 19 – Musikalische Schriften VI*. Frankfurt a. M.: Suerkamp, pp. 517–518.
———. (1984b) 'Zur gesellschaftlichen Lage der Musik,' in T. W. Adorno (ed.) *Gesammelte Schriften 18, Musikalische Schriften VI*. Frankfurt a. M.: Suerkamp, p. 772.

Anon. (1908a) 'Hot Skirmish Over *Merry Widow* Hats,' *The New York Times*, 14 June, p. 11.

———. (1907a) 'Hail to *The Merry Widow*. She Is Captivating, Graceful and Chic,' *The Sun* (New York), 22 October.

———. (1907b) 'Pranks of *The Merry Widow*. Franz Lehar's Operetta at the New Amsterdam,' *New York Telegram*, 22 October. Pressespiegel, Weinberger-Archiv, Vienna, unpaginated.

———. (1907c) '*The Merry Widow* Proves Captivating,' *The New York Times*, 22 October, p. 9.

———. (1907d) 'Daly's Theatre: The Merry Widow,' *The Times* (London), 10 June, p. 4.

———. (1905a) *Niederösterreichisches Landesarchiv*. St. Pölten (1905) NÖ Reg, Präs: Theater ZA 1905/3098 K 45.

———. (1905b) 'Theater an der Wien,' *Neue Freie Presse*, 31 December, p. 14.

'bgr'. (1908) 'Theater an der Wien,' *Die Zeit*, 22 January, p. 2.

Bordman, G. (1981) *American Operetta. From H.M.S. Pinafore to Sweeney Todd*. Oxford: Oxford University Press.

Csáky, M. (1996) *Ideologie der Operette und Wiener Moderne: ein kulturhistorischer Essay zur österreichischen Identität*. Wien, Köln and Weimar: Böhlau.

Denscher, B. (2017) *Der Operettenlibrettist Victor Léon, Eine Werkbiographie*. Bielefeld: Transcript.

Hirschfeld, L. (1923) 'Wiedersehen mit einer Witwe. Ein Rückblick im Operettenformat,' *Neue Freie Presse*, 23 September, p. 12.

Hood, B. (1911) '*The Count of Luxembourg*. A Letter to "My Dear Mr. Findon",' *Play Pictorial* 18/108, February, pp. 50–51.

Kraus, K. (1909) 'Grimassen über Kultur und Bühne,' in K. Kraus (ed.) *Die Fackel*, 275–271, 9 January, pp. 4–6.

Lehár, F. (1907) 'The Merry Widow,' New Musical Play, Adapted from the German of Victor Leon and Leo Stein by Basil Hood, Lyrics by Adrian Ross, Vocal Score Arranged for the Piano by H. M. Higgs. Chappell, London.

Léon, V. (1931) '"Das is ka Musik . . .". Die wahre Wahrheit über die *Die Lustige Witwe*,' *Neues Wiener Journal*, 6 January, p. 7.

MacQueen-Pope, W. and Murray, D. L. (1953) *Fortune's Favourite. The Life and Times of Franz Lehár*. London: Hutchinson & Co.

McKay, F. E. (1907) '*Merry Widow* Wins an Instant Success,' *The Evening Mail* (New York), 22 October. Pressespiegel, Weinberger-Archiv, Vienna, unpaginated.

Salten, F. (1906) 'Die neue Operette,' *Die Zeit*, 8 December, p. 1–3.

Salzer, E. M. (1933) 'Maurice Chevalier verfilmt die *Lustige Witwe*. Gespräch mit dem berühmten Tonfilmstar,' *Neues Wiener Journal*, 29 November, p. 7.

'Sch'. (1905) 'Theater an der Wien,' *Illustriertes Wiener Extrablatt*, 31 December. Pressespiegel, Weinberger-Archiv, Vienna, unpaginated.

Scherber, F. (1920) 'Franz Lehár Feuilleton,' *Österreichische Rundschau*, LXIII, April/June, p. 90.

Schweitzer, M. (2009) '"Darn That Merry Widow Hat". The On- and Offstage Life of a Theatrical Commodity, Circa 1907–1908,' *Theatre Survey*, 50, pp. 189–221.

Scott, D. B. (2014) 'German Operetta in the West End and on Broadway,' in L. Platt, T. Becker and D. Linton (eds.) *Popular Musical Theatre in London and Berlin*. Cambridge: Cambridge University Press, pp. 62–80.

Stein, L. (1905) 'Wie eine Operette entsteht. Eine Rundfrage,' *Neues Wiener Journal*, 11 June. p. 5.

Wittels, F. (1908) 'Die Feministen,' in K. Kraus (ed.) *Die Fackel*, 248, 24 March, pp. 10–11.

Zensur-Textbuch. (1905) *Die lustige Witwe*. Niederösterreichisches Landesarchiv St. Pölten, NÄ Reg. Präs. Theater TB K 338/27.

3

'COME AND PLAY WIZ ME IN GAY PAREE'

Approaching Cole Porter's Paris

Hannah Robbins

From the little-known revue *Mayfair and Montmartre* (1922) to the hit stage musical *Can-Can* (1953), Paris has frequently featured in the work of beloved composer and lyricist Cole Porter. His stage musicals *You Never Know* (1938), *Can-Can* and *Silk Stockings* (1955) are all predominantly set in Paris, and the city is represented in passing in two scenes in *Nymph Errant* (1933), which include the songs 'Georgia Sand' and 'Si Vous Aimez le Poitrines'. Paris is also directly referenced in six titles from Porter's stage works: 'Bad Girl in Paree' (*Paris*, 1928), 'Do You Want to See Paris?' and 'You Don't Know Paree' (*Fifty Million Frenchmen*, 1929), 'I Love Paris' and 'Who Said Gay Paree?' (*Can-Can*), and 'Paris Loves Lovers' (*Silk Stockings*).

Porter's work has been frequently presented on screen whether as original films (e.g. his song contributions to little known film musical *The Battle of Paris*, 1929) or as screen adaptations of his stage hits like MGM's 1957 version of *Silk Stockings*. Porter's songs have also lived on in the soundtracks of films, particularly those set in Paris. Examples include the 1990s romantic comedies *Forget Paris* (1995) and *French Kiss* (1995), which both partially take place in Paris, and several feature spots in Woody Allen's *Midnight in Paris* (2011). While a small part of Porter's ongoing legacy, these specific uses reinforce a subtextual relationship between Paris as iconic city and Cole Porter's body of work.

Porter began his first European tour, including a stop in Paris, with his grandfather in the summer of 1909 before starting his studies at Yale. Forty-eight years later (in April 1957), he returned for the last time. He was married there. He had a famously luxurious home there. He met and entertained the rich and famous there. Porter's repeated references to the city may stem from the joy and nostalgia of the period in which he and wife Linda particularly frequented its society events.

In the decade he studied composition at the Scholar Cantorum, wrote music for his ballet *Within the Quota* (1923) and contributed to a number of now-forgotten revues (1919–1929), Paris acted as a hub for diverse creative enterprises. American

FIGURE 3.1 Cole Porter rehearsing with Hildegard Knef and Don Ameche, the two stars of *Silk Stockings*. The 1955 Broadway show was the last of the composer's musicals to be set in Paris.

Source: Photo courtesy of Photofest New York.

composer Aaron Copland also travelled to France to study under legendary teacher Nadia Boulanger. Igor Stravinsky premiered his one act ballet *Pulcinella* (1920) at the Paris Opera. The piece, commissioned by ballet impresario Sergei Diaghilev, featured set designs by Pablo Picasso. In 1921, Coco Chanel became the first major fashion designer to produce a fragrance, cementing her commercial empire with the iconic Chanel No. 5. Modernist architect Le Corbusier opened his Parisian office and began to construct new buildings in the city. Artists, including René Magritte, Salvador Dali, Joan Miro and Max Ernst, thrived, founding new art movements including Cubism and Surrealism. In the mid-1920s, Maurice Ravel collaborated on his second opera *L'Enfant et les Sortilèges* (1926) with a libretto by Colette, while Josephine Baker arrived in Paris to perform in a show *La Revue Nègre* at the Théâtre des Champs-Élysées (1927). The success of Baker's first performances facilitated her return to the city a year later as the star of the Folies Bergère where she first created the infamous 'Dance Sauvage'. This coincided with Chanel's next great invention, 'the little Black dress'.

Significantly, Porter was not alone in monumentalising his time in Paris during 'les Années Folles'. Fellow composer George Gershwin visited the city in 1928 and composed his jazz concerto *An American in Paris*. Ernest Hemingway's posthumously published *A Moveable Feast* (1964) documents his residency in the city for six years while working as a foreign correspondent for the *Toronto Star*. In this memoir, Hemingway recorded his various encounters with members of the 'lost generation' including authors F. Scott and Zelda Fitzgerald, Ezra Pound, James Joyce and American writer and *salonnière* Gertrude Stein. Picasso would create numerous cityscapes of the vista including Notre-Dame Cathedral.

However, Porter's allusions to Paris are made more complicated by his parallel experiences to many of these creators. His ballet, an isolated creative project in his career, led him to work with the Ballet Suédois alongside influential French composer Darius Milhaud (a member of the legendary group Les Six), but the negative American reception of the work halted his progress in this area. Meanwhile he produced lots of 'one-off' contributions to projects happening elsewhere. While no creator is tied to a location, it is vital to recognise that Porter's productivity during his longest residency in Paris was focused on projects that did not take place there. Indeed, this is shown in programming about Porter's life in the city, NBC's 1973 television special *Cole Porter in Paris* – featuring performances by Louis Jourdan (who had appeared in 20th Century-Fox's adaptation of *Can-Can*, 1960), Charles Aznavour, Perry Como and Diahann Carroll – focused as much on *Kiss Me, Kate* (1948) and 'non-Parisian' hit songs as on the score of *Can-Can*.[1]

With their regular suite at the Ritz, a town house near Les Invalides and parties with the Princesse de Polignac, the romantic appeal of Cole and Linda Porter's life in Paris, including their connections with the European elite, frame cultural readings of Porter's works. Indeed, the enduring popularity of many of his songs and some of his musicals have clouded our representation of the shape of his professional career. Although Porter wrote popular music during his time at Yale University (1909–1912), including the music and lyrics for football song 'Bull Dog' (1911) and numerous college shows, much of his work before *Paris* (1928) met with limited success. Similarly, our image of Porter and his social set is frequently constructed with reference to Porter's privilege of birth rather than as a result of his marriage to the wealthy divorcée Linda Lee Thomas (née Linda Belle Lee), ten years his senior. As details of Porter's numerous extra-marital relationships have become more public, including Porter's passionate (if one-sided) correspondence with his lover Boris Kochno, Linda's influence has assumed less significance in our understanding of Porter's life.

Porter's position in the 'gay international set that gathered at Paris, the Riviera and Venice' (Anon, 1964, p. 1) and his numerous trips to purportedly 'exotic' places including Egypt and the Lebanon are also relevant to our perception of his Parisian lifestyle and the textual details of his lyrics. Indeed, Porter's extensive travel has

FIGURE 3.2 Diahann Carroll (left), Perry Como (centre), Louis Jourdan (above) and Connie Stevens (right) celebrating *Cole Porter in Paris*. The Shakespeare portrait in the background provides a clue that this 1973 TV special included many of the composer's hits not related to the French capital, like those of *Kiss Me, Kate*.

Source: Photo provided by the editor.

formed an important thread in the witty barbs and socialite archetypes familiar in works including *Anything Goes* (1934) and *High Society* (1956). Nevertheless, there is a special mystique around Porter's relationship with Paris that goes beyond his physical time in the city. (Paris was often a familiar interim destination on his travel itinerary rather than the focus of Porter's entire European existence.) By analysing the relationships between the perception of his identity and its reality, this chapter considers the intersection of Porter's personal and domestic life with his musical output.

While he certainly referred to Paris in numerous ways, Porter was not consistently resident in the city from his rise to fame until his death. Therefore, this chapter begins by considering the role Paris plays in our perception of the first half of Porter's career, especially in the context of his relationship with Linda and their social sets. It then considers how Porter and his collaborators used Paris within their works and how these musicals represent the city through the lens of their construction.

Cole and Linda in Paris

In *Travels with Cole Porter*, Jean Howard prefaces her account of her international trips in Porter's company with an introduction to his marriage to Linda (1991, p. 10). She explains how they met at a society wedding in January 1918 but does not allude to the fact that Porter initially took against Linda before forming a serious attachment to her. By March 1918, he wrote to friend Monty Woolley of his infatuation with Linda:

> With the exception of my occasional soirees with the half-world, I'm in a complete rut. I lunch and dine with Linda Thomas every day, and between times, call her up on the telephone. She happens to be the most perfect woman in the world and I am falling so in love with her that I'm attractively triste. It may be merely the Spring, but it looks dangerously like the real thing and I'm quite terrified, for there's nothing like it to kill concentration.
> *(Eisen and McHugh, 2019, p. 30)*

The warmth of Porter's affection for Linda is clear and continued to be present in his correspondence about her throughout their marriage.

The balance of passion for Linda against his affairs with men is communicated in the framing of Porter's life in the 2004 biopic *De-Lovely*. In the film, 'Linda' (Ashley Judd) appears for the first time, during a lavish Parisian soiree, in an ornate room bedecked in French flags. 'Cole' (Kevin Kline) and 'Gerald Murphy' (Kevin McNally) perform 'Well Did You Evah!' for the company. The biographic narrative then transports us to the Champ de Mars under the shadow of the Eiffel Tower, presenting their enigmatic relationship with some of the heteronormativity found in Warner Brothers' earlier account of the composer's life *Night and Day* (1946), as Porter serenades Linda with a semi-diegetic performance of 'Easy to Love'. Yet this modern rendering also has the couple pass Diaghilev's 'premier danseur' (a reimagining of Kochno) during their walk [12:07 min.], retaining a queer context and acknowledging the complexity of their private lives.

Even in this representation of their relationship where Linda is generally portrayed as glamourous and worldly if slightly humiliated by Porter's affairs, Porter commands the social environment they meet in and is the centre of each of their scenes. Yet Jean Howard frames Porter's milieu by Linda's connections, explaining:

> Linda brought Cole into the rich, glittering world that would hold an irresistible fascination for him most of his life. It fit him like a glove. If not for

Linda, I don't know if he would have known that world – certainly not on the same level of sophistication.

(1991, p. 10)

Similarly, playwright Moss Hart described falling in love with Linda as a rite-of-passage for young men arriving in Paris following his own trip to Paris in 1933. The Porters bought a house in Paris in 1930 which they maintained until 1939, and Hart (quoted in Kimball, 1971, p. 129) outlined his impression of their domestic situation:

They were rich, they were gifted, and they moved about with infinite ease and lightheartedness in two worlds – the worlds of fashion and glitter and the pantaloons world of the theatre. Their house in Paris was exquisite, one of the most beautiful houses I have ever seen, and Linda Porter, a legendary beauty herself, lent something of her own radiance and splendour to their life together so that everything and everyone in their house seemed to sparkle and shine with her own special grace.

Their ability to navigate their environment (an understated description of pronounced social agency) and the impact of their home seems to reinforce the impression of a decadent, champagne-quaffing society which is depicted in English, Conservative politician and diplomat Duff Cooper's diary extracts (see below). As illustrated by Hart's picture of the Porters' married life, their home became a second focus of interest for public and private audiences. In May 1932, *American Vogue* produced a one-page feature on 'The Cole Porters' Music Room', illustrated with photographs. The copy begins:

Born – as beautiful rooms often are – of a necessity, the music room in Mr. and Mrs. Cole Porter's Paris house centres on the piano, screened in straw marquetry, and the composer's worktable. Silver lacquer panels give the effect of mirrors reflecting the beech trees in the garden. White leather covers the sofas and chairs; the only rugs are zebra skins. The musical library, bound in white parchment, is set in niches on each side of a fireplace.

(Anon, 1932, p. 54)

As such, Porter's identity is connected to the power and charisma of Linda and their combined wealth but not specifically to the place they are in. Paris is the backdrop to sections of this period of their lives but is not foregrounded in any way.

In a professional context, there are examples illustrating that, until Porter achieved acclaim in the mid-1930s, he received press coverage through his social environment or was presented as 'husband to Linda'. For example, when the *Washington Post* (Anon, 1923, p. 71) reported on his ballet *Within the Quota*, which

FIGURE 3.3   Cole Porter and his wife Linda Lee Thomas, whose social standing gave
the composer access to the most sophisticated circles of the international
jet set.

Source: Photo courtesy of Alamy Stock Photo.

premiered in December 1923, the article uses Linda's fame as a context for Porter's
identity:

> The ballet itself is by two Americans – former classmates at Yale and now
> prominent in Parisian art circles, the music having been composed by Cole
> Porter, well-known to Washington society as the husband of the famous
> Linda Lee, one of the most rated beauties of the south, and the settings hav-
> ing been designed by Gerald Murphy.

Later, in 1928, the *New York Times* reported a Paris dinner, celebrating George Gershwin 'whose ingenious modern compositions have delighted Parisians, giving them a taste for more American music' (Birkhead, 1928, p. 34). Porter, 'who added to the jazz feast by playing his own compositions', is introduced as part of a list of over 25 guests, rather than the centre of attention as is suggested in films including *Night and Day* and *De-Lovely*. Significantly, Porter and his creativity are distanced from the spotlight of this coverage. He was a contributor to the ambiance of fête society but, unlike the celebrated newcomer Gershwin or well-recognised classical composers including Stravinsky, Maurice Ravel and Darius Milhaud's *Les Six* compatriot Francis Poulenc, in those days Porter was not notable for or perhaps not interested in contributing to 'the sound of the city'.

Cole Porter's international jet set

While the extravagance of the Porters' lives and the role this has played in forming Porter's cultural identity is not in question, it is clear that Paris was, in part, significant for Porter because it was where Linda and her friends happened to be. Later in their marriage, the Porters would pass through the city, but it was no longer their European base in the way that Venice became the backdrop for their summer gatherings in the 1920s. Yet Duff Cooper's diary, the *Vogue* editorials and similar examples remain part of his legacy, and it is striking that Jean Howard recalled seeing the same community of people in Paris 31 years later, continuing as though no time had passed: 'Lunched with Cole at the Berkeley. He looks very well indeed. Paris has done him a world of good. Saw the Duchess of Windsor, Lady Diana Cooper, and Mainbocher, all lunching together' (Howard, 1991, p. 50). This lack of change is important to recognising how Porter's circle were not forced to negotiate the same post-war realities that faced numerous Americans and the European expatriate community they had been part of in the 1920s. However, the superior sophistication of his social life was not limited to Paris nor was it unique to his experiences there, or indeed in New York, in California or in any other place he chose to reside.

The Porters were part of an exclusive community of wealthy Americans who frequented the French capital as part of a circuit of international travel. An *Associated Press* obituary published in the *New York Times* (Anon, 1964, p. 1) explains that 'the glossy opulence of the scores Porter wrote was a valid reflection of his own manner of living'. Stories about Porter in company with well-recognised individuals from society celebrity Wallis Simpson (later the Duchess of Windsor), playwright Noël Coward and the philanthropist Winnaretta Singer (also known as the Princesse de Polignac) have enhanced the image of Porter at the heart of cosmopolitan French culture in the 1920s, 1930s and 1940s. This context is perhaps characterised by a fun note in the diary of Duff Cooper on January 24, 1924, which reads:

> I thought I was dining with Cole Porter at the Ritz as he had sent me a telegram saying 'Can you dine with us Ritz Thursday night nine o'clock'. I, of

course, assumed that he meant the Ritz in London but apparently he meant the Ritz in Paris.

(2006, p. 189)

Cooper and his wife, Lady Diana, became acquainted with Cole and Linda Porter by the summer of 1923 when they holidayed in Venice. Cooper's inference that Porter meant to dine in London and Porter's assumption that Cooper would come to Paris indicates the freedom of travel their social class enjoyed as well as offering an insight into the contemporary attitude to being resident at the exclusive Ritz hotel chain in whichever country one happened to be in.

The public appeal of Porter's social circle is characterised by a mischievous prank he played on a number of American society columnists while based in Paris during 1930. Porter invented a 'bogus social-climbing couple' called Mr. and Mrs. S. Beach Fitch whom he and his friends then invited to and shunned at their events for a period of several months (Kimball, 1971, p. 107). He and his friends wrote letters to papers and columns including *The New York Herald* pretending to be Mr. Fitch and responding to 'Fitch's' letters, which were regularly published as legitimate. According to Robert Kimball (1971, pp. 108–109), the game was halted when the writers Walter Winchell and Cholly Knickerbocker (a pseudonym identity used by columnists in the *New York American*) exposed what was happening. A clipping documented in *Cole* (taken from Cholly Knickerbocker's column) explains that 'Cole and the rest of the razzle-dazzle American set in Paree were astounded to read in their favourite Paris journal, a notice in the obituary column announcing the sudden death in Rome of Mr. and Mrs S. B. Fitch!' (Kimball, 1971, p. 109). The appeal of this story, where a community of wealthy friends take advantage of gossip columnists, illustrates a connection between a hedonistic, elite environment and Porter's life in the French capital.

In contrast with the frivolous partying that inspired strikingly bleak novels by F. Scott and Zelda Fitzgerald (*Tender is the Night*, 1934, and *Save Me The Waltz*, 1932, respectively) Porter has also been connected to a socially liberal expatriate community that supported displaced African American performers who found more favourable working environments in Paris than at home. Porter was one of several wealthy Americans to support Ada 'Bricktop' Smith's emerging career in Paris, hiring her to entertain at his parties and to teach guests the Charleston after seeing her perform in 1926. He had Smith, rising star Josephine Baker and popular cabaret singer Leslie 'Hutch' Hutchinson perform at numerous social events merging their respective cultural capital with his own before patronising Smith's nightclub, Bricktop, through which she was a renowned Parisian hostess until 1939 (Levenstein, 2010, p. 51).

In the context of this behaviour and his involvement in progressive writing for Black actors in his most commercially successful musical *Kiss Me, Kate* (1948), it is equally important to acknowledge that Porter was an active participant in some of the racist behaviour associated with his peers (including their acquaintance Wallis Simpson), especially in the years preceding World War II. Unused verses of songs in his draft lyrics at the Library of Congress show how he embedded racist slurs about Chinese and Japanese characters into comedy songs even if the content was cut before Broadway. These 'jokes' remain in the song 'Come to the Supermarket (In Old Peking)' from the television musical *Aladdin* (1958), a comic number which was given enduring life when it was recorded by Barbra Streisand on her debut album in 1963. Recently, it also has been heard on the soundtrack for Amazon's hit series *The Marvelous Mrs Maisel* (2017–). Still, Porter's forward-looking collaborations with Black artists including Ada 'Bricktop' Smith and Josephine Baker characterise his time in Europe more vividly than the politics of his residencies in New York and California.

'Si vous aimez les poitrines, come to Gay Paree'

The mystique of Porter's Parisian sophistication, the public fascination with Linda's society life and Porter's rendering of the city as an emblem of romance and sex in his work did not come together to form a coherent whole. This is exemplified by a *New York Times* review of the original Broadway production of *Can-Can* on 8 May 1953. *Times* critic Brooks Atkinson (1953, p. 28) writes: 'Mr. Porter and Mr. Burrows are fascinated by the wickedness of Montmartre in the Nineties. But it is Mr. [Michael] Kidd, the choreographer, who makes real theatre out of the revelry in the dance halls.' Atkinson felt that *Can-Can* was not one of Porter's most original works, with some 'recognizable clichés in both the music and the lyrics'. Perhaps Atkinson identified that, although it was veiled by the layers of puns, pop-culture references and appealing melodies, Porter repeatedly avoided characterising Paris beyond superficial references to landmarks including prominent hotels and shopping streets.

Porter's familiarity with trends in American tourist travel to the French capital repeatedly informed his representation of Paris in works largely written for a New York audience, initially made up of his peers. Phenomena like 'Paris By Night' tours, which took American travellers to see the Folies Bergère and the sex workers in Montmartre and offered socially-approved peep shows of artists working in cafés with their muses, correspond directly with the repeated references to the spectatorship of naughtiness within his work (Levenstein, 2010, p. 4), even if this frivolous and frequently irreverent representation of Parisian identity was not unique to Porter's musicals.

For example, in *Fifty Million Frenchmen* (1929), the hero, a young American called Peter Forbes, works as a tour guide in Paris, having wagered with his friends that he can live without money while securing the hand of Looloo, the girl of his dreams. In Act One, Scene Six, Peter takes a group of American tourists to view the hugely lavish Café de la Paix, once a famous haunt of Oscar Wilde and, at another period, Emile Zola. In an early script draft, this scene (then Scene Three of the musical) begins with two Frenchmen breaking their lunch date to avoid the Americans. One exclaims:

> They come over here and they think because they spend a few million francs they own Paris . . . And how they speak the French! *Espèce d'andouille*! Terrible! It is like when you scrape you [*sic*] knife on a plate.
>
> *(Fields and Porter, 1929b, pp. 1–3–1)*

As they leave, one of the Frenchmen takes a fancy to Julia (a young woman in the American party), pinches her cheek twice and asks in French if she'd like to take a tour with him. Julia slaps him in the face and he has her arrested by a Gendarme. This and the following three pages of vignettes, with a postcard seller offering the Americans rude postcards and a drunk who accosts their table, were removed from the script before the original Broadway version. Herbert Fields also rewrote Peter's opening tour patter to include a joke about Napoleon coining a 'Not Tonight Josephine' catchphrase, while painting a bawdy history of the establishment (Fields and Porter, 1929a, pp. 1–6–42). When the woman he is addressing asks Peter if the café is respectable, he responds: 'Madam, [the café] is a notorious hangout for all sort of thugs and gangsters' (Fields and Porter, 1929b, pp. 1–3–3). In the earlier draft, Fields had then added ' . . . and French politicians' in blue biro to the end of the line. This tweaks the meaning of 'notorious', signposting the quippy, satirical representation of 'Frenchness' found in the abridged scene, prefacing the performance of 'Do You Want to See Paris?' (a reworked version of 'Omnibus' from *La Révue des Ambassadeurs*, 1928), with lyrics including 'We're on the Champs Elysées now, a street of great renown/You see that fellow there, he's the only Frenchman left in town'.[2] As indicated in this example, we can see a creative rapport between Porter and Fields in their representation of this stereotypical if irreverent cosmopolitan behaviour.

In the lyrics for 'Omnibus' in *La Révue des Ambassadeurs*, Porter returns to 'the only Frenchman left in town' as the tour arrives at the theatre to see a show. However, in *Fifty Million Frenchmen*, his revised lyric mirrors the pattern of change outlined above. The lyrics in 'Omnibus', where the lone Frenchman has found a renowned beauty he wants to attend the show with, are removed from 'Do You Want to See Paris' and replaced with 'We are now in the theater called the Moulin Rouge,/An old Parisian Pet/Where the men the girls remember meet the girls that men forget' (Fields and Porter, 1929a, pp. 1–6–47). This shows how Porter's representation of soubrettes, dancing girls and nightclub singers is used as a way to characterise 'Paris'. Across three decades of musicals, Porter collaborated on numerous creative projects that foreground women in traditionally sexist roles. While beloved examples like Reno Sweeney in *Anything Goes* (1934) and Lois Lane in *Kiss Me, Kate* (1948) are associated with all-American stereotypes like the evangelist and the 1930s gold-digger (after Anita Loos), Porter here capitalised on the subtextual identification of the *Parisienne* with the sexually libertine to construct another stereotype of feminine identity, this is based on the city's louche connotations as a milieu with few taboos.

In the 'Bad Girl in Paree' from *Paris* (1928), the lyrics of the refrain describe the allure of the girl with 'the kind of eyes that advertise' (Kimball, 1984, p. 106):

> She gave me one long look
> And I understood
> That was about all it took
> To forget to be good.

Porter's words offer a seedy representation of lust and sex work as well as alluding to a disapproving sense of social propriety. Meanwhile, in the second act of *Nymph Errant* (1933), his lyrics make more overt reference to sex and promiscuity. The musical's heroine Evangeline has a school friend, Madeline, and she has become a star of the Folies de Paris. In this late scene, Madeline performs the bawdy 'Si vous aimez les poitrines' (which can be translated as 'If You Like Tits'). In the lyric, Porter follows his traditional list format eliminating locations including Bali, Spain and Eastbourne in favour of the women of 'Paree'. In the short song, Porter naughtily suggests that, where one might favour exotic beauty or local charm, Parisian women understand sex.

In *Can-Can* (1953), Porter's 'Maidens Typical of France' works as a satirical vehicle for the female chorus (the can-can dancers) to decry 'the wicked clutches of romance' while advocating their training in the domestic arts. As the song builds to its close, the women, performing in can-can outfits to the customers of the dance hall, proclaim: 'And if, when we dance, we show our derrières/It is to show that, even when we dance,/We are maidens' (Kimball, 1984, p. 422). Porter simultaneously draws attention to the 'traditional' mode of performing the can-can and the potentially questionable virginity of the dancers in the chorus.

There is no sense that Porter is censorious about sex work or sexual activity throughout his work. In fact, many of his songs including those noted above challenge audiences to confront their squeamishness about sex and the realities of commodified sex. When *Can-Can* was proposed for the West End, the Lord Chamberlain's office required Porter to change the lyric from 'Maidens Typical of France' quoted above with the Reader's Report (Anon, 1954, p. 1) noting that: 'Even without the supply of powerful telescopes, I feel this verse should be altered.' The line 'And if, when we dance, we show our derrières' was changed to 'And if, when we dance, we show *we have no cares*' (Williamson Music Ltd., 1953, p. 1). Despite the potential prudishness of this change, the Lord Chamberlain's office generally defended *Can-Can* against several complaints of indecency from London audience members. After nearly a year's run in the West End, the Office requested some minor changes to the staging through a series of meetings with the company manager and director, suggesting that this might extend the run and the popularity of the forthcoming British tour. In an internal memorandum (dated August 8, 1955), one of the reviewers outlined the Lord Chamberlain's requests:

> The actions of the male partners to be considerably modified and especially their heads to be raised so that they did not do large parts of the dance with that part of their bodies in proximity to the girls' drawers.
> No bumping of male faces into ladies' drawer-clad posteriors. [The male dancers had been on their knees in front of the can-can line, *HR*]
> No 'flapping' of ladies' skirts in the manner described to the Brigadier.
> The ladies when having been ostensibly deprived of their drawers by the men, not to pull their skirts up between their legs loin cloths fashion.
>
> *(Anon, 1955)*

While the concerns about the dancing focus on the depiction of sexualised move-ment, it is important to acknowledge that other Porter musicals away from the dancehalls of Montmartre, such as the less well-remembered *Out of this World* (1950), provoked similar interventions during out of town try-outs in Boston, because the risqué component of Porter's songs frequently was part of his wider lyric tropes. That the artist's musicals were regularly bowdlerised is illustrated by the notable censorship of lyrics in the MGM film adaptation of *Kiss Me, Kate* (1953), which also cut many more lines from Shakespeare's *Taming of the Shrew* than had already been omitted by book authors Sam and Bella Spewack.

Embodiment and othering

While Porter and his collaborators used Paris as a vehicle or even a code for prom-iscuity and sexual liberty, they also have the French capital (and – in extension – 'Frenchness') represent or embody emotions or other traits associated with Paris' symbolic status as a city for lovers. For example, the whimsy of his hit song 'I Love Paris' (*Can-Can*, 1953) does not address any geographic or unique detail of the city apart from associating it with being in love. In what initially appears to be a ballad about one of his international homes, Porter evokes the romantic construc-tion of Paris as communicated by impressionist artists and members of the Art Nouveau movement but does not really characterise the metropolis in the lyrics of this or his many other songs set in or about the city. Instead, one of the powers of 'I Love Paris' is the effective way audiences and listeners respond to the mode of the music, conjuring specific images to represent Porter's 'timeless town' (Kim-ball, 1984, p. 429) and projecting their own romantic visions. Later on, in the same musical, the less-well remembered song 'Who Said Gay Paree' dampens the romance of 'I Love Paris', souring its imagery with: 'Who failed to add/Paris could be sad?' (ibid, p. 434). Out-of-context, as 'I Love Paris' so frequently is used, the city merely represents the home of love lost and found. Considering that the lyrics of the title song from *Can-Can* do not include Paris in their tour of the world and that 'Paris Loves Lovers' (*Silk Stockings*, 1955) describes a city of lights that facili-tates romance but never looks beyond it, Porter's Paris feels both vivid and elusive.

By contrast, there are several stereotypical or deliberately clichéd representations of Parisian society in the details of Porter's 'French' musicals; there is also an under-lying 'othering' and even xenophobia within the 'humour' of some of his songs and in the books of many of his shows. In the opening scene of *Paris*, Cora, a loud and overbearing matriarch, travels to the French capital in order to rescue her son, Andrew, from his attachment to a French actress. She arrives suffering terribly from travel sickness. When offered medical assistance, she responds aggressively: 'I'll have no frog-eating Frenchmen filling me full of foreign physics' before lamenting the state of the compartments on French railway cars because they accommodate 'little rooms . . . for their French goings-on' (Brown and Porter, 1928, p. 7). Although Cora is portrayed as unsympathetic, librettist Brown nonetheless caters to prejudice for the sake of laughs, a feature all too common in scripts from shows of this period.

FIGURE 3.4 Cole Porter congratulates Lilo, star of his 1953 musical *Can-Can*, to the successful opening of the show which introduced one of the composer's most famous hits, 'I Love Paris'.

Source: Photo provided by the editor.

Additional examples, including (the frequently renamed) characters Ching and Ling in *Anything Goes* or many of the uncomfortable representations of culturally-undefined 'Asians' in *Aladdin*, reveal the most insidious potential of this kind of characterisation. Meanwhile, the (Nazi) German and British ambassadors in *Leave It to Me!* (1938) constitute other kinds of cultural stereotypes. While acknowledging the use of recognisable character traits as an integral tool of writing comedy in any form, it is important to comprehend that Porter and his co-authors frequently exploited extreme characterisation for the American (and, sometimes, British) gaze.

Porter also relied on highly recognisable popular cultural and geographic images to construct a sense of place in many of his works without committing to produce any dramaturgically meaningful imagery. This is evidenced by the splicing of mock-Shakespeareana in *Kiss Me, Kate* (1948) with a list of names of famous Italian landmarks in 'Where Is the Life That Late I Led?'. While Petruchio's lyric 'You give a new meaning to the leaning tow'r of Pisa' (Kimball, 1984, p. 393) combines Porter's well-documented passion for double-entendres with a 'legitimate' local reference, this innuendo reminds the audience of the play's Italian setting without further engaging with the sense of place. Any hypothetical 'authenticity' that might be conjured up by nods to Milan or the Duomo are counterbalanced by a joke about Italian American migration ('I'm lucky I missed her gangster sister from Chicago').

Similarly, temporal and spatial disruption form part of Porter's lyricist identity, whether that's quoting 'La Marseillaise' in Lois's declaration of sexual emancipation, 'Always True to You (In My Fashion)', also from *Kiss Me, Kate*, or in the show-shopping 'I'm Taking the Steps to Russia' from *Leave It To Me!* In the playfully titled second example, the wife of a bathtub manufacturer who has just been appointed the American ambassador to Russia performs a boisterous number about 'making Communithm/Thwing' (Kimball, 1984, p. 239). Here Porter naughtily promotes American dance modes over the indigenous 'gloomy op'ras' and 'corn-fed folk songs' of Soviet Moscow they are traveling to. Meanwhile, in *Silk Stockings*, Porter represents Paris as home to the hedonistic pleasures of capitalism in opposition to the grey, puritanical communism of Stalinist Moscow. Consequently, his lyrics frequently move beyond their dramaturgical contexts, speaking to the biases of his American audience and the comic 'traditions' of US showbusiness, rather that creating an authentic sense of place.

'You don't know Paree'

From his first successful Broadway musical, *Paris* (1928), to his last, *Silk Stockings* (1955), Cole Porter has repeatedly exploited the tropes of the city's affluent transnational community, café society and chorus girls, especially (but not exclusively) when composing songs performed 'in Paris'. For example, the stereotypes and caricatures outlined in this chapter are set in sharp contrast by the composer's songs with powerful imagery including 'I Love Paris',[3] the flirty insistence of hit list song 'Let's Do It, Let's Fall in Love' or the playful mischief of 'Let's Misbehave', both from *Paris*. Yet in each of these examples, it is clear that Porter understood the creative potential of invoking Paris, whether for playful, saucy or romantic reasons.

Porter's work has also been recognised for overt and underlying sexual coding in his lyrics with authors including John M. Clum (2001), Joseph Morella and George Mazzei (1995) arguing that this masks homosexual analogies throughout his work. ('Gay Paree' is itself an innuendo for those in the know.) Indeed, this phenomenon appears to be part of a wider theme in Porter's work, using Paris as a palatable (civilised, even) abstract location that becomes a means of discussing promiscuity and generalised romance. This theme is characterised, on the one hand, by seemingly contradictory references to purchasing sex and protecting female virginity to be found in Porter's more humorous songs about Paris, and on the other hand, by a lack of specificity in such beloved ballads as 'I Love Paris' or the romantic duet 'Paris Loves Lovers' from *Silk Stockings*. In these hit songs, Porter relies on clichéd imagery of couples walking in the mist under Art Nouveau streetlamps to conjure up Paris without providing fresh details in his own voice.

When it comes to Porter's stage and film productions, Paris is more substantially embodied by the work of the set and costume designers than through Porter's lyrics. Instead his 'Paris' is situated within the broader representation of sexual freedom and unashamed libido in his catalogue of work. This Paris marries the voyeuristic puritanism of American tourism with the *lassez-faire* of Continental European liberalism that made space for African American artists abroad but not at home. His representation of the city is as the home of romance, possibly inspired by the experience of his early infatuations with Linda and with lover Boris Kochno. In his depictions of Paris, Porter cleverly codes romantic and sexual liberation while not fully moving beyond the gendered and exotic tropes that permeated the patriarchal society of his time.

Notes

1 The special began with an arrangement of songs from films of Porter's shows (including 'From This Moment On' and 'Be a Clown'), was followed by a medley of music from *Kiss Me, Kate*, a medley from *Can-Can* and then a series of standalone hits, including 'Anything Goes' and 'Begin the Beguine'.
2 According to Robert Kimball (1984, pp. 92–93), the lyric in 'Omnibus' goes 'We now are going up the Champs Elysées, if you please./You see those poles sticking out the ground, those are trees.'
3 'Every time I look down on this timeless town/Whether blue or grey be her skies./Whether loud be her cheers or soft be her tears,/More and more do I realise:/I love Paris.' (Kimball, 1984, p. 429)

References

Anon. (1964) 'Cole Porter is Dead; Songwriter Was 72,' *The New York Times*, 16 October, p. 1.
———. (1955) 'Internal Memorandum,' 8 August. Lord Chamberlain's Play Correspondence, 1954/6795. British Library, London.
———. (1954) '*Can-Can* Reader's Report,' 31 August. Lord Chamberlain's Play Correspondence, 1954/6795. British Library, London.
———. (1932) 'The Cole Porters' Music Room,' [American] *Vogue*, 15 May, p. 54.
———. (1923) 'American Jazz Plays Part in Swedish Show,' *The Washington Post*, 9 December, p. 71.
Atkinson, B. (1953) 'First Night at the Theater: Cole Porter's "Can-Can" Includes a Book by Abe Burrows and Ballets by Michael Kidd,' *The New York Times*, 9 May, p. 28.
Birkhead, May. (1928) 'Paris Life Is Quiet during Half-Season: Parisians Follow Code in Taking Flight, While Visitors Catch Up on Tours,' *The New York Times*, 15 April, p. 34.
Brown, Martin and Porter, Cole. (1928) *Paris* [Script deposited for copyright]. New York Public Library Billy Rose Theatre Division Play Scripts RM50885.
Clum, John M. (2001) *Something for the Boys: Musical Theater and Gay Culture*. New York: Palgrave for St. Martin's Press.
Cooper, Duff. (2006) *The Duff Cooper Diaries: 1915–1951* (John Julius Norwich, ed.). London: Phoenix Books.
De-Lovely: The Cole Porter Story. (2004) Directed by Irvin Winkler [DVD]. Santa Monica, CA: MGM Home Entertainment.

Eisen, C. and McHugh, D. (2019) *The Letters of Cole Porter*. New Haven and London: Yale University Press.

Fields, Herbert and Porter, Cole. (1929a) *Fifty Million Frenchmen* [Script deposited for copyright]. New York Public Library Billy Rose Theatre Division Play Scrips RM 4681.

———. (1929b) *Fifty Million Frenchmen* [Unpublished Script]. New York Public Library Billy Rose Theatre Division Play Scrips RM 450.

Howard, Jean. (1991) *Travels with Cole Porter*. New York: Abrams.

Kimball, Robert (ed.). (1984) *The Complete Lyrics of Cole Porter*. New York: Vintage Books.

———. (1971) *Cole*. New York: Holt, Rinehart & Winston.

Levenstein, Harvey. (2010) *We'll Always Have Paris: American Tourists in France since 1930*. Chicago: University of Chicago Press.

Morella, Joseph and Mazzei, George. (1995) *Genius and Lust: The Creativity and Sexuality of Cole Porter and Noel Coward*. London: Robeson Books.

Williamson Music Ltd. (1953) 'Letter to the Assistant Comptroller', 27 August. Lord Chamberlain's Play Correspondence, 1954/6795. British Library, London, 1p.

PART II
Broadway Paris

4

DRESSED BY PARIS

Mlle. Modiste, Roberta and *No Strings*

Maya Cantu

'I've got *quelque chose*' Paris fashion and the Broadway musical

In *Paris*, Cole Porter's, 1928 musical comedy *billet doux* to his adopted city, a scandalous Parisian actress named Vivienne Rolland discovers the most persuasive way to sway her prospective mother-in-law's heart: through her closet. Determined to overcome the staunch disapproval of Mrs. Cora Sabbot, a New England Puritan, Vivienne (played originally by Irene Bordoni) compels Cora towards couture. At first, Cora protests: 'The Sabbots never wear anything but navy black and blue!' (Brown et al., 1928, pp. 1–8). Yet, before long, Cora has been transformed by the alluring Vivienne, who has that '*quelque chose*/That brings me beaux' (as Bordoni would have sung in an unused song for *Paris* [Porter, 1928]). Ditching her 'Whistler's Mother'-like apparel, the Massachusetts matriarch undergoes a dramatic makeover, trading a scarlet-accented chiffon and lace frock for an 'exceedingly daring and smart' gold evening gown ('Act Three description'). Emboldened by her new wardrobe, Cora sips cocktails at the Ritz, flirts with beaux and relishes her newfound glamour, exclaiming: 'Oh, to hell with the Sabbots!' (Brown et al., 1928, pp. 1–8).

While the spectacle-oriented theatrical genre bears little surface resemblance to the prim Mrs. Sabbot, the Broadway musical has similarly expressed a longing to be 'dressed by Paris'. In a long parade of shows extending from late-19th century operetta and revue, to the Paris-set musicals of Cole Porter and to mid-century shows and films like *Funny Face* (1957) and *Coco* (1969), the Broadway musical has sought to drape its manifold mythologising of American democracy with the irresistible 'quelque chose' of Paris fashion, embodied in the elegant feminine icon of the *Parisienne*. In the Broadway musical, settings of Paris fashion have served both as mirrors and measurements for the American character: allowing creators of Broadway musicals to both project elaborate materialist fairy tales and to chart the ideological distance from Cora Sabbot's Plymouth Rock to the 20th century's aspirations towards cosmopolitan modernity. Many Broadway musicals closely link settings of Parisian fashion with discourses of sophistication: an ethos most dominant in the interwar era, but influential throughout the 20th century. 'If there was ever an Age of Sophistication, it was surely the 1920s and 1930s', as Faye Hammill observes in describing the era's various conceptions of sophistication as urbanity, sleek modernity in fashion, 'world-weary' irony and sexual open-mindedness (2010, pp. 113–120) as well as its basis in 'transatlantic cultural exchange' (2010, p. 163).

In the three 20th-century Broadway musicals discussed in this essay, the operetta *Mlle. Modiste* (1905), the musical comedy *Roberta* (1933) and the musical play *No Strings* (1962), settings of Paris fashion have inspired elaborate glamour and spectacle. At the same time, these musicals reflect sharply upon American national and cultural identity, using images of Parisian couture to explore contradictory ideas about democracy and aristocracy; pragmatism and aesthetic style; Puritanism and sensual expression; and 'European' and 'American' worldviews. Populated with the models, shop-girls and modistes that Agnès Rocamora describes as aspects of the *Parisienne* (2009, p. 25), all three musicals use Paris fashion to examine questions of gender and sexuality and constructs of femininity and masculinity.

Mlle. Modiste, Roberta and *No Strings* all employ Parisian fashion settings to variously explore the meanings of sophistication and its translation to American cultural mores. Set in a millinery on the Rue de la Paix, *Mlle. Modiste* (music by Victor Herbert; book and lyrics by Henry Blossom) defines Parisian sophistication as a luxurious accessory to the more essential asset of American democracy, epitomised in the enterprising shop-girl heroine of the title. Unfolding in the boulevard dress shop of a courtesan-turned-couturier, *Roberta* (music by Jerome Kern; book and lyrics by Otto Harbach) models sophistication via a more expansive and fluid concept of American gender roles as a virile college fullback transforms into a chic *modiste* and 'dressmaker'. Centred in Paris' modelling industry and spanning locations in Monte Carlo and the French Riviera, *No Strings* (music and lyrics by Richard Rodgers; book by Samuel Taylor) aligns ideals of sophistication with not only the city's sartorial elegance but with France's traditions of racial tolerance – as contrasted with American bigotry – and its history of expatriate freedom. Written as a starring vehicle for Diahann Carroll, the Civil Rights-era musical recounted the interracial romance between two expatriates: an African American model from Harlem and a white novelist from Maine. Framing Paris, and its fashion industry, as a site of liberation and self-determination for African American women, *No Strings* substantially expanded the vision of fashion as democratising agent evoked in *Mlle. Modiste*, while pointing to racial dynamics left unexplored in the 1905 musical fairy tale.

'She ought to be an American': grisettes, the 'square deal' and Mlle. Modiste

Opening at the Knickerbocker Theatre on December 25, 1905, Herbert and Blossom's *Mlle. Modiste* drew upon an atmosphere of Parisian elegance as set in a millinery on the Rue de la Paix. On this fashionable boulevard in 1858, couturier Charles Frederick Worth had opened his historic high-fashion salon, catering to aristocrats of France's Second Empire and *belle époque* eras. In its plot of an industrious and clever shop girl who dreams both of becoming an opera star and marrying the Viscount Etienne de Bouvray, *Mlle. Modiste* also drew upon the close proximity of the Rue de la Paix to the Paris Opera House: another cultural magnet for the city's elite. A comic operetta, *Mlle. Modiste* drew rave reviews for the star performance of Fritzi Scheff, its production 'trimmed with rare taste and skill' (Hubbard, 1906), and its skilful integration of music and narrative.

At the same time that *Mlle. Modiste* evoked elite Parisian luxury, Herbert and Blossom stitched their adaptation of Charles Perrault's *Cinderella* with American themes and values. 'From beginning to end, *Mlle. Modiste* scintillates with brightest wit. Its humor is thoroughly American, but somehow suits well the Parisian setting', observed *Town and Country* (Anon, 1905b). In their retelling, Herbert and Blossom placed the *Parisienne* figure of the *grisette* into conversation with the more familiar American archetype of the shop girl who worked as a labourer in the fashion industry and first appeared in British Cinderella musicals like *The Girl Behind the Counter* (1906), many produced at George Edwardes' Gaiety Theatre. Like the shop girl, the *grisette* pervaded French cultural discourse as a 'worker in the Parisian fashion trade', though she drew upon a distinctively Gallic context. Jules Janin's definition of the *grisette* as a versatile working 'girl who is good at everything' (quoted in Rocamora, 2009, p. 94) aptly characterises the artful Fifi, whom Madame Cecile (the exploitative, wicked stepmother-like owner of the millinery) concedes is 'pretty and chic and a clever saleswoman' (Blossom and Herbert, 1905, pp. 1–11). While drawing upon the glamorous Parisian proximity of the *grisette* to 'fashion's latest pose' (Blossom and Herbert, 1905, pp. 1–1), *Mlle. Modiste* also foregrounded her identity as a worker and a symbol of American democratic values.

Though set in the world of Paris consumer fashion, *Mlle. Modiste* epitomised the values of President Theodore Roosevelt's 'Square Deal'. Roosevelt promoted this Progressive-era domestic policy throughout his two-term presidency from 1901 to 1909. In 1902, Roosevelt promised 'a square deal for every man, big or small, rich or poor' (Lewis, 1906, p. 74). In 1906 (the year following *Mlle. Modiste*'s opening), Roosevelt published his book, *A Square Deal*, outlining his vision of equal opportunities for all Americans: an egalitarianism contradicted by his imperialist policies in Latin America and the Caribbean. Roosevelt's promise of a 'Square Deal for the Negro' (Roosevelt, 1906) also fared weakly against the realities of Jim Crow violence and voter suppression raging in the South and the persistence of racial segregation throughout the country. At the same time, Roosevelt instituted numerous social and economic reforms and made efforts to reign in corporate power while expanding consumer protections (the 'Square Deal'). These measures appealed powerfully to American myths of a meritocratic distribution of wealth and opportunity.

The president's visit on 9 October 1905 to *Mlle. Modiste* during its out-of-town try-out at the Columbia Theatre in Washington, DC, underscores the musical's political contexts. *The New York Times* observed:

The audience rose and cheered repeatedly when the President came in. He was in jovial humor and laughed heartily, led the applause, started all the encores, headed the demand for curtain calls, and was the first to ask Mr. Herbert for a speech.

The *Times* also reported Roosevelt laughing at an allusion to his Long Island summer home:

> In one song by Bertha Holley (as Mrs. Bent), entitled 'Our Culture Club in Keokuk', occurred the lines: 'We've argued politics and such/We don't think Kaiser Bill so much/We even send advice to Oyster Bay'. The President enjoyed this so much that the audience compelled several repetitions of the verse just to see him laugh.
>
> *('President Has Good Laugh', 1905a)*

Mlle. Modiste succeeded with Roosevelt-era American audiences by blending the sophistication of Paris fashion with Square Deal values, both represented in the heroine of the title. As Fifi, Viennese-born leading lady Fritzi Scheff drew praise from *The Syracuse Herald*: 'Hers is the elusive and piquant charm that is generally attributed to the Parisienne. . . . Fritzi Scheff has this innate knowledge of how to dress and what to wear' ('Fritzi Scheff's Career', 1908). *The New York Tribune* also noted the modish millinery fashions displayed in the show and in numbers like 'Hats Make the Woman' ('Notes on the Stage', 1906).

At the same time that *Mlle. Modiste* marketed Paris fashion, the musical balanced its consumerist spectacle with attentiveness to themes of feminised labour. Rocamora writes of Paris's image as a world 'fashion city', opposing

> two versions of Paris fashion and of Paris more generally – one spectacular, polished to attract consumers, the other unencumbered by the imperative to impress the consuming gaze, a Paris of sweatshops, workshops and unglamorized trade – (conjuring) up Erving Goffman's notions of front and back regions.
>
> *(2009, p. 49)*

Mlle. Modiste's opening number, 'Furs and Feathers', featured a chorus of shop girls singing about 'Hard work! Very little pay' and the 'distress' of working 'ten hours every day'. As if realising their status as characters in an operetta, the shop workers suddenly switch to Goffman's 'front region' of a performative surface. They chirp, 'Yet we're as happy as can be!' (Blossom and Herbert, 1905, pp. 1–1) and sing about their anticipation of the evening's romance.

Mlle. Modiste framed its heroine as an industrious *grisette* consonant with American values and Roosevelt's own 'conservative progressivism' (Riccards, 1995, p. 57). Fifi represents the enterprise and ambition of the Protestant work ethic and opposes the snobbery associated with the aristocratic Rue de la Paix. The musical mixed the Cinderella narrative with the Horatio Alger rags-to-riches story, as Blossom and Herbert provide Fifi with a fairy godfather in the form of American

FIGURE 4.1   A Parisian shopgirl with American values: Fritzi Scheff as the eponymous character in *Mlle Modiste* (1905).

Source: Postcard provided by the editor.

millionaire Hiram Bent, who passes onto Fifi a gospel of pluck-and-luck. He endows her with a loan to go out and pursue her dreams, both of becoming an opera singer and marrying Etienne. Impressed by Fifi's fairness with customers, Hiram praises the shopgirl's honesty and industry in what he considers the highest terms. When asked if she's American, he responds, 'She ought to be. I found her in a shop' (Blossom and Herbert, 1905, pp. 2–15).

The musical's denouement illustrated its *Mlle. Modiste* achieving her own 'Square Deal'. She triumphs over the condescension of the Count de Bouvray, who had forbidden the 'pert little minx' (Blossom and Herbert, 1905, pp. 2–1–7) and saleswoman from marrying his nephew. At the end of the musical, as Fifi demonstrates her new opera fame as Madame Bellini, the Count makes his apologies to Fifi at a charity bazaar. There, he carries out the conditions, explained by Fifi earlier in the musical, for her willingness to wed Etienne: that 'you come to me with your hat in your hand and beg me to do so!' (Blossom and Herbert, 1905, pp. 2–1–13). Evoking its heroine's millinery both as a symbol of high fashion and egalitarianism, *Mlle. Modiste* thus tipped its hat to Continental glamour while most vigorously saluting Rooseveltian values and myths.

'Paris has done something for him': fashioning the male 'Parisienne' in Roberta

Like *Mlle. Modiste, Roberta* extols American democratic ideals. One of the hits of the 1933–1934 Broadway season, the New Deal-era musical – described as an 'operetta, revue, and fashion show all rolled into one' (Barron, 1933) – opened at the New Amsterdam Theatre on November 18, 1933, and featured music by Jerome Kern, lyrics and book by Otto Harbach as well as show-stopping gowns by the costume designer Kiviette. Yet, by contrast to the Roosevelt-era patriotism of the former musical, *Roberta* asserted that American character might be beneficially broadened and refined by exposure to French style and sophistication. It also suggested that an appreciation of Paris fashion could lead to a more expressive concept of American masculinity.

Herbert and Blossom's musical had recounted the story of a *modiste*-turned-opera diva. By contrast, *Roberta* followed John Kent (played by Ray Middleton), who transforms from football fullback to male *modiste* after inheriting the 'Roberta's' dress shop of his Aunt Minnie Roberts (Fay Templeton), who reconnects with him in Paris shortly before her death. Spurned by his snobbish college girlfriend, Sophie Teale (Helen Gray), John finds new love with Stephanie (Tamara), the expatriate shop assistant who has secretly been working as Roberta's head designer – and concealing her identity as the daughter of a Russian grand duchess. Like *Mlle. Modiste, Roberta* drew upon the Broadway musical's classic Cinderella narrative. At the same time, *Roberta* presented a witty gender reversal of the trope of the Parisienne: the feminine icon long coded as synonymous with Paris style, who 'sets trends and embodies Parisian distinction' (Rocamora, 2009, p. 90).

Based on Alice Duer Miller's best-selling 1932 novella, the musical adaptation adhered relatively faithfully to the Miller story: an elegant and 'delightfully capricious' soufflé (dust jacket of *Gowns by Roberta*, Miller, 1933). At the same time, the musical expanded Miller's Paris setting – opening the musical's action at a New England fraternity house at Haverhill College – and added screwball roles for star comics Lyda Roberti and Bob Hope (respectively cast as fashion-plate Polish chanteuse Madame Scharwenka and wisecracking collegiate bandleader Huckleberry 'Huck' Haines, a character 'who did not exist in Miller's novel' [Block, 2019, p. 19]). The dust jacket of *Gowns by Roberta* described the light-hearted gender satire and sophisticated ethos of Miller's plot:

> When a man is handsome, six foot two, captain of his college football team, and goes to Paris to forget the girl who jilted him, anything can happen. But to find himself, as John Kent did, in all his masculine virility, co-proprietor of the swankiest dressmaking shop in the Rue Pavane, staggers the

imagination. . . . In truly active American fashion, the metamorphosis took place while John learned the ways of the cosmopolitan world.

(1933)

Though considered by critics to be less narratively and musically ambitious than Kern's previous musicals *Show Boat* (1927), *The Cat and the Fiddle* (1931) and *Music in the Air* (1932), *Roberta* flourished at the box office on the strength of melodic song hits like 'Smoke Gets in Your Eyes' (performed by Tamara, on guitar) and a spectacular production geared by producer Max Gordon to 'knock (audiences') eyes out' (Gordon, 1963, p. 174).

Produced just after the darkest days of the Great Depression, as the New Deal launched a long process of economic recovery, *Roberta* captured the zeitgeist through its elaborate escapism. The musical offered American audiences the recreated spectacle of Paris *haute couture* at the height of its interwar style and influence. When Minnie/Roberta scoffs at the temperamental Scharwenka, 'Let her go back to Worth or (Jeanne) Lanvin' (Harbach and Kern, 1933, p. 32), Broadway audiences would have placed these designers among a Parisian fashion landscape that included Coco Chanel, Elsa Schiaparelli and Paul Poiret. Among the most prolific and influential designers of interwar musical comedy and revue, the American designer Kiviette, born to

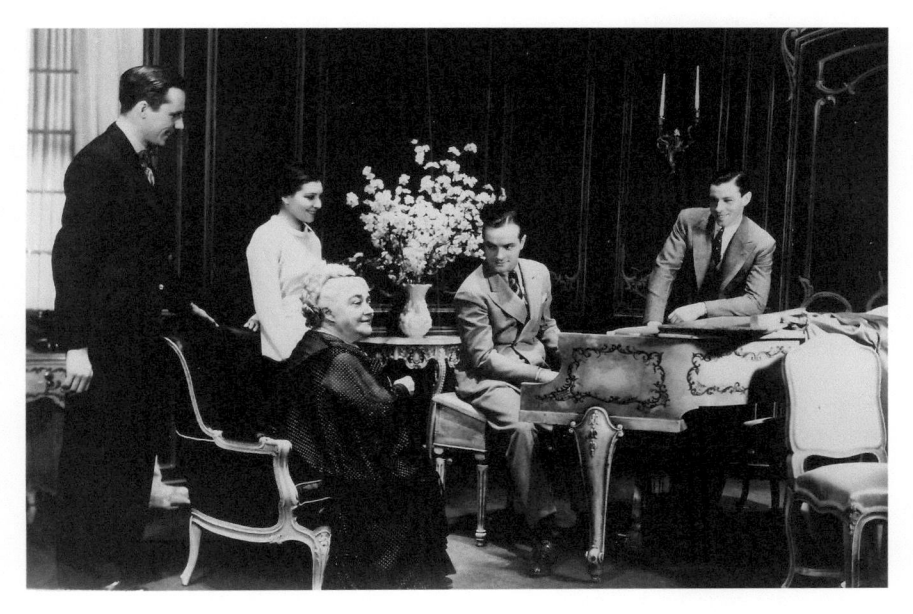

FIGURE 4.2   The original Broadway cast of *Roberta*, a musical set in the alluring world of Paris fashion. From left to right: Ray Middleton (John Kent), Tamara (Princess Stephanie), Fay Templeton (Aunt Minnie, aka Madame Roberta), Bob Hope (Huckleberry Haines) and George Murphy (Billy Boyden).

Source: Photo by George Rinhart, provided by the editor.

a Russian-Jewish Staten Island family as Yetta Schimansky (López-Gydosh, 2018, p. 207), earned raves for her stunning evocations of French couture that, incorporating American synthetic fabrics, influenced the next Paris fashion season.[1] *The Baltimore Sun* asserted, 'Kiviette should have equal billing with the author' (Barron, 1933).

Roberta's setting drew not only on the exceptional 'chic and allure' of Paris fashion but on a number of cultural discourses that dominated American popular culture between the two world wars. Transatlantic narratives of cultural exchange, created by writers like Sinclair Lewis, drew upon the waves of expatriate experiences in 'Lost Generation' Paris. This late 1920s/early 1930s cycle of works typically featured American protagonists seeking after sophistication as they contemplated more leisured lifestyles and culturally expansive values than the materialism and efficiency of American 'Babbitry'.[2] In fact, Max Gordon's quartet of Broadway hits during the 1933–1934 season also included a stage adaptation of Sinclair Lewis' 1929 novel *Dodsworth*, in which the European travels of the Midwestern industrialist title character broaden his perspectives while dooming his marriage. *Roberta*'s protagonist, John Kent, resembles a younger version of Sam Dodsworth, whom Lewis describes as a former college football star. While Sam's status-conscious wife, Fran, views him as 'provincial as a prairie dog' (Lewis, 2014, location 2419), *Roberta*'s Sophie Teale similarly compares John to a 'big, affectionate blundering Newfoundland dog' (Harbach and Kern, 1933, p. 24).

Described as an author with a 'carefree intimacy with the sophisticated upper set' (dust jacket of *Gowns by Roberta*, Miller, 1933), Alice Duer Miller's work, and its Broadway musical adaptation, contributed to pervasive interwar discourses of sophistication. Born into a 'blue-blood' American family (Hammond, 1933) descended from a Revolutionary War general, Miller chafed against the Puritan roots with which she characterises John Kent, the son of a Yankee farmer, in *Gowns by Roberta*. A noted feminist and suffragette, Miller created a prolific body of novels, light verse and screenplays and also gained publicity as a member of Manhattan's bastion of performative sophistication, the Algonquin Round Table.

In addition, both *Gowns by Roberta* and the musical *Roberta* drew from the influential discourse of the *Parisienne*. In the 1952 Hollywood musical remake of *Roberta, Lovely to Look At*, Tony Naylor (played by Howard Keel) inscribes the image of Paris as embodied in luxurious femininity: 'Paris is a beautiful woman' (*Lovely to Look At*, 1952). Rocamora elaborates on the multi-faceted aspects of the Parisienne as she has appeared as an 'icon of modernity' (2009, p. 105) in popular culture: as not only the shop girl *grisette* portrayed in *Mlle. Modiste*, but in roles including the fashionable courtesan and the 'universal woman', who might 'equally well be a foreigner' as Paris-born (2009, p. 98). As Rocamora observes, these various personae have drawn from the image of the 'quintessential *Parisienne*' as 'sophisticated, perfectly groomed, elegantly dressed, urban and independent', as well as possessing an 'emancipated sexuality' (2009, p. 105).

Roberta, like its source, the Miller novel, flips the traditional gender of the Parisienne in the metamorphosis of John Kent. The musical portrays John's transformation under the elegant wing of his courtesan-turned-couturier Parisienne aunt, born as the American Minnie Roberts. 'Minnie in her day was hot stuff!' (Harbach and Kern, 1933, p. 9), Huck Haines breathlessly describes John's aunt, who had been the kept mistress of a French marquis before striking out on her own as Madame Roberta to become 'the greatest dressmaker in Paris' (Harbach and Kern, 1933, p. 9). Vowing to help her favoured nephew, John, thwart Sophie Teale's perception of her ex-fiancé as 'unsophisticated' (Harbach and Kern, 1933, p. 11), Minnie resolves to give him a full makeover. When John confesses that Sophie has broken off their engagement, Minnie pledges that she, with the help of her immaculately tailored English aristocrat friend, Lord Henry Delves, can help John shed his provincialism. By the time Roberta's opens under John's new management, in partnership with Stephanie, Minnie's nephew has been transformed into not only a 'King of Couturiers' (Harbach and Kern, 1933, p. 65), but a masculine reflection of the Parisienne. Sophie expresses her astonishment at John's metamorphosis: 'Paris has done something to him. His clothes, his manner, his hair . . .', while Huck effuses, 'Did you ever see such a change in a man?' (Harbach and Kern, 1933, p. 60).

By contrast, the Old World Russian expatriate Stephanie undergoes a reverse arc in *Roberta*. She acquires the vernacular, New World sophistication of 'the American Language' and increasing fluency with American popular culture. From Huck, she learns to perform risqué numbers like 'Let's Begin' and to pepper her speech with American slang. Through the character of Stephanie – who changes from a 'drab little modiste' (Harbach and Kern, 1933, p. 88) into her mother's imperial ball gown at the end of the show – *Roberta* reflected the cosmopolitanism of the French fashion industry. In interwar Paris, numerous exiles from the Russian Revolution had re-established their names in French couture, among them the Grand Duchess Maria Pavlovna.

John and Stephanie's romance evoked a fusion of American democracy and European aristocracy (by way of a romanticised Tsarist Russia). Similarly, *Roberta's* score and choreography fused the elegance of Parisian style with the spontaneity of American jazz. As Sarah Berry observes of *Roberta's* 1934 Hollywood film adaptation,

> This struggle, however, is also about the nature of fashion, as articulated in a contest between American practicality and European aesthetics; this contrast is ultimately mediated by the popular stylishness of American music and dance, represented by Fred Astaire (as Huck) and Ginger Rogers (as Scharwenka).
>
> *(2000, p. 66)*

In the stage musical *Roberta*, Minnie and Stephanie perform songs aligned with the vocabulary of European operetta (e.g. 'Yesterdays'), while American jazz is represented by both the Polish bombshell, Scharwenka and the California Collegiate jazz band headed by Huck. The latter invents the idea of a musical fashion show scored to the band's tunes.

Framing Paris fashion as an aspirational model of sophistication, *Roberta* also espoused increased flexibility in American concepts of gender through its story of a 'stalwart young All-American fullback' (Gabriel, 1933) turned couturier. Like Miller's book, the Kern-Harbach musical dramatises cultural anxieties directed upon the 'virility' of John Kent. In the source novel, Miller critiques American puritanism and rigid ideals of masculinity. John receives a disapproving letter from his mother: 'A man dressmaker! All your friends here agree with me, and I assure you the jokes I hear – and read, for even the papers have taken it up – are far from pleasant' (Miller, 1933, p. 119). As in the Miller book, John faces initial dismay as his new 'feminine' career is satirised in the American press and a profile entitled 'Football Player Goes Modiste' appears in *The New Yorker* (Harbach and Kern, 1933, p. 65). Similarly, when Huck teases John about the likely headlines ('All-star fullback goes in for dressmaking. Swish!'), the latter responds with a homophobic epithet, 'Speak for yourself, Nellie!' (Harbach and Kern, 1933, p. 44). Yet, throughout the course of *Roberta*, John becomes increasingly comfortable with more gender-fluid Parisian notions of masculine sophistication. As Huck tells Sophie, 'Say, he likes being a dressmaker. And why shouldn't he? It seems to be dazzling you once again' (Harbach and Kern, 1933, p. 88).

Roberta premiered at a time in which the Paris fashion industry was dominated by numerous female and male European designers but by few American men. In later decades, American fashion designers, such as Norman Norell and Donald Brooks, acquired influence, and by 1952, when *Roberta's* second Hollywood musical version premiered (as the heavily adapted *Lovely to Look At*), the shocking novelty of a male American fashion designer appeared outmoded: the character of John Kent was reconceived as Tony Naylor (Howard Keel), a playboy Broadway producer rather than a college football fullback.

No Strings, with costume designs by Brooks, appeared against an American cultural context that created more room for men's sartorial expressivity. During the Civil Rights era, America's fashion industries also made increasing space for African American women, a development which was reflected in media discourses of Paris. In the 1962 musical, Paris continued to be represented as the 'capital of style and sophistication' ('Top Negro Model', 1960), as described by the pioneering African American expatriate model Helen Williams: a likely inspiration for the character of Barbara Woodruff in *No Strings*.

'For once, I was just an American': Civil Rights-era fashion and the universal woman in *No Strings*

Roberta illustrated the cosmopolitan style of the *Parisienne* as a beneficial influence on American masculinity. By contrast, *No Strings* celebrated the city as a beacon of 'Parisian racial sophistication' (Cook, 1962), offering a fashion industry more inclusive and tolerant than its mid-century American counterpart. According to

Agnès Rocamora, the icon of the *Parisienne* encompassed an ideal of a 'Universal Woman', one 'impervious to borders':

> 'She is even sometimes born a *Parisienne* on the other side of the ocean.' In 1932, writer Léon-Paul Fargue wrote that '*La Parisienne* can be the colour of milky coffee, like Josephine Baker, or Jewish like Sarah Bernhardt. Here is a first point: *la Parisienne* is well able to come from Moscow, from the Sugar Islands, or from Castelsarrasin.
>
> *(2009, p. 1998)*

No Strings flouted American racial taboos by portraying its Harlem-born heroine Barbara Woodruff as the embodiment of the 'spirited, emancipated and fashionable Parisienne' (Rocamora, 2009, p. 118). Romance with David Jordan (played by Richard Kiley), a white expatriate novelist from Maine, threatens the freedom and independence that Barbara considers as symbolised by her clothes: a hard-won closet of 'beautiful Paris dresses' by Dior, 'Balmain and Balenciaga and Givenchy' (1962, p. 81) that she has acquired as the 'highest-paid model in Paris' (Rodgers and Taylor, 1962, p. 60). When David asks Barbara, in a final scene heavy with racial subtext, for the model to return to small-town New England with him, Barbara responds: 'I don't think I have the clothes for a rugged, coast-of-Maine woman' (1962, p. 117).

No Strings drew upon Paris's decades-long traditions of expatriate freedom experienced by dozens of African American women like Josephine Baker. At the same time, the musical equally engaged with the gains made by Black women during the Civil Rights era, as designers, models, actresses and glamour icons. As the fabric-abundant New Look turned Paris designers like Christian Dior and Hubert de Givenchy into American household names in the 1950s, the Harlem-based designer Zelda Wynn Valdes (also fabled as the original creator of the Playboy Bunny costume [Diehl, 2018, p. 223]), attained unprecedented crossover success during a time in which 'racial segregation was enforced and a fashion system created by and for Black Americans existed alongside the mainstream fashion industry'. As Nancy Diehl notes, Valdes' 'roster of clients was filled with internationally known celebrities including Josephine Baker, Ella Fitzgerald, Mae West, Jessye Norman, . . . Diahann Carroll, Dorothy Dandridge [and] Eartha Kitt' (2018, p. 223).

While Valdes commanded publicity as a designer during the 1950s and early 1960s, African American women, such as Dorothea Towles and Helen Williams, also crossed the colour line as fashion models. Paris, rather than New York, welcomed these women on its runways. In June of 1962, towards the start of *No Strings'* Broadway run, *Life Magazine* reported:

> For [African American] models, the breakthrough is a dream come true, a dream which is coincidentally being celebrated nightly in the big Broadway

musical hit *No Strings*, which tells about a Harlem girl who becomes a famous mannequin and takes Paris by storm.

(Anon, 1962, p. 87)

Life captioned a glamorous photo of the exuberant, Texas-born Towles: 'Prototype for *No Strings* may have been Dorothea Towles, who was Dior's first Negro model in 1949. Here, she wears a Balmain gown' ('Negro models', 1962). Known for her statuesque beauty, Helen Williams, who modelled for Dior and Jean Dessès, may also have influenced Rodgers and Taylor in the writing of *No Strings. Ebony Magazine* profiled the model in 1960:

> It's a long way from Riverton, NJ, to the salons of the great Paris couturiers, but Helen Williams, America's most successful Negro model, made that journey this year, scored a glittering success, and realized a life-long dream.
>
> *('Top negro model', p. 61)*

While drawing upon the convergence of Civil Rights-era progress and New Look fashion, *No Strings* was also conceived by Rodgers as a star vehicle for Diahann Carroll after seeing her on 'The Jack Paar Show'. Throughout the 1950s, Carroll performed on Broadway (e.g. 1954's *House of Flowers*) and in Hollywood where she appeared in film adaptations of *Carmen Jones* and *Porgy and Bess* as well as 1961's *Paris Blues*, a film that will be explored in depth later in this chapter. Yet, Carroll encountered persistent racial obstacles in her career, and by 1961, she was frustrated by the persistent stereotyping of African American women in Broadway and Hollywood casting as what she called the 'the nauseatingly "good" girl who naively trusts everyone' or 'the high-living, easy-come-easy-go sportin' lass' (Cooper, 1962). Carroll recounted to *The Chicago Defender* on being approached by Rodgers for a possible collaboration: 'I told him I wanted to do a contemporary piece, preferably a comedy . . . The idea [of *No Strings*] thrilled me and I said of course I was interested' (Cooper, 1962).

For her work as Barbara in *No Strings* Carroll earned rave reviews as well as a Tony Award for Best Actress in a Musical: 'She is beguiling and lithe and graceful and endowed with that star quality that is encountered all too seldom these days', observed *Newsday* (Oppenheimer, 1962). Carroll also dazzled reviewers and fashion columnists in her array of costumes designed by Donald Brooks. Known for the elegant simplicity and lean lines of his dresses, the American fashion designer created gowns for Jacqueline Kennedy, linking *No Strings* to the liberal idealism of JFK's 'Camelot' presidency and its support of the Civil Rights movement.

The interracial romance at the centre of its narrative featured among numerous elements of Broadway risk-taking in *No Strings*, the first musical embarked upon by Rodgers after the death of Oscar Hammerstein II. Written in collaboration with book-writer Samuel Taylor, a playwright known for the 'smart set' air of his settings (e.g. *Sabrina Fair*, the source of the 1954 film *Sabrina*), Rodgers considered *No Strings* among his most adventurous musicals, telling *The New York Herald Tribune*: 'Playing it safe and doing the old-fashioned thing is really playing it dangerous . . . It is much safer to be new and fresh' (Ross, 1962).

Opening to generally admiring, though not rapturous, reviews, the out-of-town try-out of *No Strings* included performances in Detroit, Toronto, Cleveland and New Haven before the show premiered on Broadway on 15 March 1962 at the 54th Street Theatre. The show had a moderately successful run of 580 performances, its lack of smash-hit status likely influenced by the musical's unhappy ending and uncomforting view on America's racial progress as well as by numerous critics finding the libretto 'on the dull side' (Robert Colman, quoted in '*No Strings, Rodgers Musical . . .*', 1962). Yet, for *No Strings*, Rodgers not only composed a versatile, jazzy score without a string section but experimented with the onstage use of the orchestra: 'In *No Strings*, the orchestra has been taken out of the pit and put on the stage. Several of the musicians have been incorporated into the action and the others are invisible behind a screen' (Ross, 1962).

A structurally sophisticated book by Taylor accompanied Rodgers' musical innovations. The romance between Barbara and David unfolds within a bittersweet framing device of the lovers performing 'The Sweetest Sounds' in twin soliloquies recalling the earlier duet in *South Pacific*. Both sing, on separate parts of the stage, 'The sweetest sounds I'll ever hear/Are still inside my head' (1962, p. 3). In both prologue and epilogue, Barbara and David pass each other by, 'not seeing, unaware' (1962, p. 4), first, because they have yet to meet, later, because the fleeting 'no strings' love affair has been so once-in-a-lifetime intense that its memory must be reframed as unborn possibility. David responds to Barbara's question of 'How can I live without you?' with the proposition: 'Only one way. To say to ourselves that this never happened. . . . You are something that hasn't happened to me, yet' (1962, p. 119).

If words that are 'waiting to be said' comprised a powerful subtext in *No Strings*,[3] Rodgers' reluctance to openly allude to Barbara's race in the Broadway musical sparked intense controversy. Rodgers had drawn upon Carroll's own personal history in the creation of Barbara Woodruff, who tells David that she hails from New York City's 'uptown. Way uptown' (1962, p. 29). *The Pittsburgh Post Gazette* profiled the star's similarities to Barbara Woodruff: 'Our backgrounds are similar. (Like me), she is from Harlem. She has a father who was a bus driver. My father was a subway conductor' (Glover, 1962). Yet Rodgers and Taylor encapsulated their reticent approach to the question of Barbara's race in an opening 'Authors' Note':

> The part of Barbara Woodruff is designed to be played by an American colored girl in her early twenties. It is proposed that she also be beautiful, have style, and wear clothes well; be intelligent, witty, warmly human and wise. The play itself never refers to her color.
>
> *(Rodgers and Taylor, 1962, p. 1)*

The composer elaborated to *The New York Times*:

> We are not dealing with race relations. One of the reasons the setting is France is because such a situation is completely acceptable there. In our show, the point never comes up. The role could be played by a white girl

without a line being changed. We chose Miss Carroll because we've wished for a long time to see in her in something on the stage.

(Funke, 1961)

Walter Kerr, in the *LA Times*, was among the critics who charged that, for all its risk-taking and 'experiments (extending) to virtually every aspect of stagecraft' (1962), Rodgers played it too safe on issues of race: 'It seems unlikely that these two attractive people would not, even causally, mention the matter of race for month upon intimate month. . . . A narrative that means to be courageous instead seems ambiguous' (1962). At the same time, Rodgers and Taylor's hesitance to frankly discuss facts of race in *No Strings* might have emphasised them further and underscored the reluctance of many white Americans to engage in honest and rigorous discussion, despite the progress of the Civil Rights movement.

Yet, while Rodgers' and Taylor's libretto frames 'the interracial aspect of the relationship (as) a muted but significant part of the plot' (Glover, 1962), its cultural subtexts resonate clearly in evoking Paris as a site of liberation for African American women. For the rootless novelist David, a 'Europe bum' (Rodgers and Taylor, 1962, p. 39) who struggles with writer's block, Paris is only the centre of a pinwheel of European pleasure-spots, as he 'knocks around' (1962, p. 11) from Paris to the French Riviera and Monte Carlo. Mollie Plummer, the sardonic, Helen Gurley Brown-like editor of French *Vogue*, advises Barbara to send David home to Maine: 'Back to America, to work. It's the only thing that can save him' (1962, p. 96).

For Barbara, the Paris fashion industry not only signifies work but identity, freedom and a sense of belonging that she has not been able to find in the United States. As a top Paris model, Barbara pursues a life of sexual and economic independence that aligns with the values of Gurley Brown's *Sex and the Single Girl*, published in 1962 (the same year as *No Strings*) and which Stacy Wolf describes as a key influence on 1960s Broadway musicals such as *Sweet Charity* (Wolf, 2011, pp. 58–67). Although she accepts jewels and furs from her infatuated, middle-aged French suitor, Louis de Pourtal, Barbara declares that her modelling work allows her 'to organize her life' romantically, just as it fulfils her professionally: that no one 'annoys' her or 'enjoys' her 'unless we're equal partners in the fun' (Rodgers and Taylor, 1962, p. 31). Barbara expresses no regret about her choice to leave America for France, where she desires – and 'will settle for' – nothing less than 'the world' (1962, pp. 29–30). 'I didn't leave much' (1962, p. 27), Barbara explains to David, elaborating that she tore up her return ticket to America 'the very first hour' after winning a round-trip to the city as first prize in a dressmaking contest: 'As soon as I breathed the air of Paris, I knew I was home' (1962, p. 61). Barbara expresses her sense of Parisian freedom and self-definition in terms that recall the blunter statements from the models from whom *No Strings* drew inspiration. Dorothea Towles told *Women's Wear Daily*: 'For once, (in Paris) I was not considered Black, African American or Negro. I was just an American' (Rourke, 2006).

While leaving much explicitly unsaid on issues of race, Rodgers and Taylor's libretto for *No Strings* clearly evokes Paris's history of African American expatriate

FIGURE 4.3   The African American fashion model and the white writer from Maine: Diahann Carroll as Barbara and Richard Kiley as David in Richard Rodgers' *No Strings* (1962).

Source: Photo by Friedman-Abeles, provided by the editor.

migration, which swelled during the periods following World War I and World War II. Attempting to persuade Barbara not to leave him for the self-destructive David, Louis tells her that only she belongs in Paris: 'And then there are some Americans who have come to Europe to be born', as Barbara replies, 'You're so right; that's me' (1962, p. 40). In the 1920s, dozens of African American artists and performers, including Ada 'Bricktop' Smith, Adelaide Hall and Sidney Bechet, sought artistic rebirth in the City of Light. The pattern recurred in the 1950s, as not only models like Dorothea Towles, but writers and musicians like James Baldwin, Miles Davis and the jazz percussionist Kenny Clarke fled segregated 1950s America, many settling in the expatriate (and Existentialist) colony of Saint-Germain-des-Prés.

Rodgers and Taylor also likely drew upon the previous year's film *Paris Blues*, also featuring Carroll and set in the world of the city's jazz clubs. Although the film elided the interracial romance of the film's 1957 source novel by Harold Flender, the film explored themes of African American expatriatism. In *Paris Blues*, Carroll played Connie Lampson, an independent young woman searching for romance and adventure in Paris. Vacationing with her friend Lillian (Joanne Woodward), Connie falls in love with expat jazz saxophonist Eddie Cook, played by Sidney Poitier. Committed to the Civil Rights struggle back in the United States, Connie attempts to persuade Eddie to return to New York with her. In a film that explores tensions between collective activism and individual self-determination as contrasting methods of racial resistance, Poitier's Eddie explains his reluctance to return to America. Eddie's dialogue anticipates Barbara in *No Strings*, as he describes his sense of a new home and safety in Paris, where he has resided for five years:

CONNIE: You've never wanted to go back?
EDDIE: You stick around Paris for a while and stretch a bit. Sit down for lunch somewhere without getting clubbed for it, and you'll wake up one day, look across the ocean and you'll say, 'Who needs it?'

(Paris Blues, 1961)

In the final scene of *No Strings*, in which David asks Barbara to return with him to America, the musical's racial themes assert themselves less ambiguously. According to *The Globe and Mail*, script changes made between the Detroit and Toronto try-out runs clarified the American racial prejudice and social ostracism that cuts the strings on the couple's romance:

> But on opening night (in Detroit), this idea of (Barbara and David) finally parting because of the difference in skin color was not at all clearly conveyed. However, with the introduction of new dialogue and eloquent pauses during the lovers' final conversation and duet (of the title song), the fact is made abundantly plain . . . that she, a Negro, would not be socially acceptable in the small community of his birth – even as his wife.
>
> *(Thomson, 1962)*

Over the course of the scene, David realises the extent of Barbara's likely unhappiness in his provincial New England hometown. In Bear Isle, Maine (a state painted less idyllically here than in 1945's *Carousel*), Barbara would have to give up the 'beautiful Paris dresses' that have liberated her in the fashion industry. To Barbara's protests of 'How do I live without you?', David reminds her that she has embraced France as her home: 'You're going to stay here, where you belong.' He laments: 'What a damned foolish thing it is . . . That your warm, lovely world should be so bad for me, and the world I'm going back to so impossible for you' (Rodgers and Taylor, 1962, p. 118). Continuing to explore the themes of interracial romance prominent in his work with Hammerstein (e.g. *South Pacific*), Rodgers drew upon the Paris setting of *No Strings* to glamourise the professional advancements of African American women in fashion – but also to point to the daunting inequitable distances remaining in the United States. If hesitant to join its voice to the full volume of the Civil Rights movement, *No Strings* used resonant contexts and subtexts to celebrate Barbara Woodruff's Parisienne sophistication and her unabashed hunger for the world.

Conclusion: Paris fashion, the Broadway musical and the world

In setting the world of Paris fashion on the Broadway musical stage between 1905 and 1962, *Mlle. Modiste, Roberta* and *No Strings* varied in their themes and contexts. Yet the musicals all evoked the emancipated spirit of the Parisienne who puts her claims upon her presence in 'the world': whether epitomised by Fifi in *Mlle. Modiste* wanting to go out in it; by the ex-courtesan Minnie Roberts/Madame Roberta savouring her slice of it; or Barbara Woodruff declaring she'll settle for nothing less than it in *No Strings*. All three musicals also used Paris fashion as a mirror against which to define and reimagine American values. Fifi's epitomising of Theodore Roosevelt's 'Square Deal' in Blossom and Herbert's *Mlle. Modiste* transforms in Kern and Harbach's *Roberta* into the gender fluidity and economic rebounding of early-1930s 'New Deal' America, while the notion that a 'Square Deal' has been achieved equally by all Americans is critiqued and questioned in the more liberated Paris fashion world of Rodgers and Taylor's *No Strings*.

Finally, all three Broadway musicals model American ideals of sophistication, reflecting how its definitions and interpretations have changed silhouette throughout the decades. *Mlle. Modiste, Roberta* and *No Strings* measure Parisian values of sexuality and cosmopolitanism against America's enduring Puritan ideals. These musicals contrast the diaphanous silk of Cole Porter's '*quelque chose*' against the rockbound Protestant Work Ethic that brings David Nolan in *No Strings* back to rugged Bear Isle, Maine. Collectively, *Mlle. Modiste, Roberta* and *No Strings* suggest that American culture is never that far removed from Plymouth Rock. At the same time, the stylish vision of the Parisienne inspires much of the elegance, sensuality and defiant joie de vivre that – despite the censure of the nation's Sabbots – has always dressed and caressed the Broadway musical.

Notes

1 For Lyda Roberti's Scharwenka in *Roberta*'s bar scene, Kiviette designed a 'black sheer, lustrous striped gown with full skirt and jacket . . . made out of a woven cellulose acetate material called Sylph-Sheen by the Sylvania Industrial Corporation'. Dubbed the 'Gown of Tomorrow', the dress 'appeared in French collections the following season, albeit in different styles' (López-Gydosh, 2018, p. 211).
2 Sinclair Lewis's 1922 satirical novel, centered on the Midwestern businessman George F. Babbitt, led to the coining of the words 'Babbitt' and 'Babbitry' to refer to a 'person and especially a business or professional man who conforms unthinkingly to prevailing middle-class standards' (Merriam–Webster Online).
3 Barbara and David's duet 'Nobody Told Me' also reflects the show's themes of the tacit, the subliminal and the unsaid.

References

Anon. (1962) 'Negro Models: A Band of Beautiful Pioneers,' *Life Magazine*, 29 June, p. 87.
———. (1960) 'Top Negro Model Makes Debut in Paris,' *Ebony Magazine*, September, p. 61.

————. (1908) 'Fritzi Scheff's Career,' *The Syracuse Herald*, 22 March, p. 15.

————. (1906) 'Notes on the Stage,' *The New York Tribune*, 22 August, p. 7.

————. (1905a) 'President Has Good Laugh,' *The New York Times*, 10 October, p. 5.

————. (1905b) 'The Theatre: Henry de Vries' Remarkable Impersonations,' *Town and Country*, 27 January, p. 21.

Barron, M.(1933) 'Jerome Kern Scores Again with *Roberta*,' *The Baltimore Sun*, 26 November 19333, p. TM4.

Berry, S. (2000) *Screen Style: Fashion and Femininity in 1930s Hollywood*. Minneapolis, MN: University of Minnesota Press.

Block, G. (2019) 'Refashioning *Roberta*: From Novel to Stage to Screen,' in Dominic McHugh (ed.) *The Oxford Handbook of Musical Theatre Screen Adaptations*. New York: Oxford University Press.

Blossom, H. and Herbert, V. (1905) 'Mlle. Modiste,' Original Broadway Libretto Typescript, Scherer Library, Goodspeed Opera House, East Haddam, Connecticut.

Brown, M., Porter, C. and Goetz, E. R. (1928) 'Paris,' Original Broadway Libretto Typescript, Cole Porter Collection, Irving S. Gilmore Music Library, Yale University, Cole Porter Collection, Box 10, Folder 78.

Cook, L. (1962) '*No Strings* Is Sure Moneymaker,' *The Detroit Free Press*, 16 January, p. 15.

Cooper, M. (1962) 'Diahann Carroll is Broadway's Cinderella Girl,' *The Chicago Defender*, 19 November, p. 24.

Deihl, N. (2018) 'Zelda Wynn Valdes: Uptown Modiste,' in N. Diehl (ed.) *The Hidden History of American Fashion: Rediscovering 20th-century Women Designers*. London: Bloomsbury Academic.

Funke, L. (1961) 'News of the Rialto: Rose's Future,' *The New York Times*, 26 November, p. X1.

Gabriel, G. (1933) 'With Song and Laughter,' *Town and Country*, 15 December, p. 28.

Glover, W. (1962) 'Negro Girl Star Living Her Dream,' *The Pittsburgh Post-Gazette*, 19 April, p. 31.

Gordon, M. (1963) *Max Gordon Presents*. New York: Bernard Geis.

Hammill, F. (2010) *Sophistication: A Literary and Cultural History*. Liverpool: Liverpool University Press, pp. 1–22.

Hammond, P. (1933) 'The Theaters: White Tie', *The New York Herald Tribune*, 20 November, p. 12.

Harbach, O. and Kern, J. (1933) 'Roberta,' Original Broadway Libretto Typescript, collection of Tams-Witmark Music Library, author's personal copy.

Hubbard, W. L. (1906) 'News of the Theaters: *Mlle. Modiste*,' *The Chicago Tribune*, 25 December, p. 8.

Kerr, W. (1962) 'Mr. Rodgers Entangled in *No Strings*,' *The LA Times*, 29 April, p. A14.

Lewis, A. H. (1906) *A Compilation of the Messages and Speeches of Theodore Roosevelt, 1901–1905*. Volume 1. Washington. DC: Bureau of National Literature and Art.

Lewis, S. (2014) *Dodsworth*. Bucharest: Romania: BP Publishing. Kindle Books (Original work published 1929).

López-Gydosh, D. (2018) 'Kiviette: Star Performer,' in N. Deihl (ed.) *The Hidden History of American Fashion: Rediscovering 20th-century Women Designers*. London: Bloomsbury Academic, pp. 207–221.

Lovely to Look At. (1952) Directed by Mervyn LeRoy. DVD 2010, Los Angeles: MGM.

Miller, A. D. (1933) *Gowns by Roberta*. New York: Grosset and Dunlap.

'*No Strings*,' Rodgers Musical, Draws 1 Rave and 3 So-Sos'. (1962) *The New York Times*, 16, March, p. 2C.

Oppenheimer, G. (1962) 'On stage: Rodgers and Rodgers,' *Newsday*, 21 March, p. C3.

Paris Blues. (1961) Directed by Martin Ritt. DVD 2014. New York: Kino Lorber.

Porter, C. (1928) 'Quelque Chose. (Unused)' from *Paris*, Cole Porter Collection, Irving S. Gilmore Music Library, Yale University, Cole Porter Collection, Box 9, Folder 75.

Riccards, M. P. (1995) *The Ferocious Engine of Democracy: A History of the American Presidency*. Volume 2. Lanham, MD: Madison Books.

Rocamora, A (2009) *Fashioning the City: Paris, Fashion, and the Media*. London: I.B. Tauris.

Rodgers, R. and Taylor, S. (1962) *No Strings*. New York: Random House.

Roosevelt, T. (1906) 'The Square Deal,' Theodore Roosevelt Center at Dickinson State University website, www.theodorerooseveltcenter.org, accessed 3 July 2019.

Ross, D. (1962) 'A Look at Richard Rodgers Taking a Chance on Himself,' *The New York Tribune*, 11 March, p. C1.

Rourke, M. (2006) 'Dorothea Towles Church: Model Was Trailblazer on Paris, US Runaways,' *The Boston Globe*, 27 July, http://archive.boston.com, accessed 1 July 2019.

Thomson, H. (1962) '*No Strings* Benefits by Facelift,' *The Globe and Mail*, 14 February, p. 8.

Wolf, S. (2011) *Changed for Good: A Feminist History of the Broadway Musical*. New York: Oxford University Press.

5

LIBERATED BY PARIS

A reconsideration of three Broadway 'flops' – *Miss Liberty, Ben Franklin in Paris* and *Dear World*

Michael G. Garber

The place: the Broadway stage. The time: the mid-20th century, the 'Golden Age of the American Musical'. The shows: *Miss Liberty* (1949), *Ben Franklin in Paris* (1964) and *Dear World* (1969). The link: the setting of Paris. The people: many of the genre's most significant figures, celebrated for their other works – songwriters, Irving Berlin (*Annie Get Your Gun*, 1946) and Jerry Herman (*Hello, Dolly!*, 1964); a director, Moss Hart (*My Fair Lady*, 1956), and director-choreographers, Jerome Robbins (*West Side Story*, 1957), Michael Kidd (*Guys and Dolls*, 1950) and Joe Layton (*The Sound of Music*, 1959); stars, Robert Preston (*The Music Man*, 1957) and Angela Lansbury (*Mame*, 1966). The irony: despite their illustrious personnel, all three productions were critical and commercial failures.

These works survive primarily through their original Broadway cast recordings plus published scripts (in two instances), photographs and written or (still, in 2020) remembered experiences of playgoers.[1] The shows demonstrate Broadway craftspeople engaging with the ambience of Paris in narrative musicals that did not make money. The rhetoric surrounding these shows, in histories, biographies and critical works, is dominated by the extent of and reasons for their failure. The shows are defined by what they did not achieve rather than by what they did achieve. Yet, in the careers of their creators, they often provided important stepping stones.

Further, the semantic and semiotic significance of these works proved prescient in terms of the historical employment of Paris as setting in English-language musical theatre. Peter Langer (1984) clarifies the conventional ways that cities are described – for example, as jungles of heartless struggle, bazaars of pleasure and plenty or containers for homely neighbourhoods. Particularly the last two of these patterns of representation have been applied to Paris, which is usually imagined as a place of both sensuality and bonhomie. This trio of flops, however, helped to amplify the connotations of Paris, which becomes a powerful locus for meditations on freedom.

Miss Liberty (1949)

The action for *Miss Liberty* is set in 1886, as pieces of the Statue of Liberty lie stored in crates in New York City awaiting a pedestal. The hero, news photographer Horace (Eddie Albert), is enthusiastic and naïve but not savvy. He is poised between dichotomies: two newspapers – one for the elite financial class, the other for the common worker; two venues – the small town of his origins versus the big city where he almost despairs of making his career; and, most germanely for the purposes of this anthology, two contrasting women. One is his chummy American colleague, Maisie (Mary McCarthy). The other is an impoverished Parisian street gamine, Monique (Alyn McLerie), whom by accident Horace mistakes for and passes off as the model for the Statue of Liberty – thus creating the farcical plot complications.

The love triangle might conceivably place its Broadway audience in a dilemma: should the hero mate with a representative of their own American culture (whom he likes but does not love) or a representative of French culture (whom he loves)? The impasse is resolved when Monique becomes associated with that quintessential American type, the immigrant – one of the 'huddled masses yearning to breathe free' – by means of Emma Lazarus' famous poem about the Statue of Liberty, which becomes the lyric for Monique's (and the show's) final song, 'Give Me Your Tired, Your Poor'. (Sadly, the likeable Maisie ends up without a mate – a lack of resolution apparent even on a cursory perusal of the script. Gerald Bordman later suggested this was the main damper on audiences' enthusiasm; 569.)

The production is notorious in the career of its songwriter Irving Berlin for being his first theatrical failure in a then 35-year Broadway career. The critic's response was – and, as a result, the play's latter-day reputation remains – exaggeratedly negative because of the overly high expectations placed on its distinguished creative team. Besides Berlin, with his recent successes of *Annie Get Your Gun* (1946) on stage and *Easter Parade* (1948) on screen, these included playwright Robert Sherwood (fresh from his third Pulitzer Prize); director Moss Hart (basking in the glory of his Oscar-nominated screenplay for the 1947 Best Picture-winner, the 'social conscience' film *Gentleman's Agreement*); and choreographer Jerome Robbins (associate artistic director of the newly created New York City Ballet). The last-mentioned was the only one of the four who received unanimous rave reviews for the show.

Historians of *Miss Liberty* have perpetuated a myth that 'only its advance sale, coupled with a lack of competition, allowed it to run into April' (Bordman, 2001, p. 569; see also Bergreen, 1990, p. 496; Mordden 1999, p. 199). Trade journals reveal otherwise (Anon, 1949a). When the show opened on Broadway on 15 July 1949, the advance sale was impressive ($435,000). Yet, this was predominantly for tickets through October; only 20 per cent of that advance sale was for November and December performances. Even after the middling-to-bad reviews, mail orders kept pouring in (Green, 1949). Further, according to the weekly column in *Variety* reporting Broadway grosses, the theatre frequently sold its limit of thirty standing-room tickets well into October. After that, the show continued to break even or make a profit for all but two weeks, from November through mid-February. The slowing of ticket sales coincided both with the fading popularity of its songs and the increased competition: the serious *Lost in the Stars*; the revues *Touch and Go* and *Alive and Kicking*; and a bevy of musical comedies, including *Arms and the Girl*, *Texas L'il Darlin'* and particularly the hit *Gentlemen Prefer Blondes* (which opened on 8 December), another light-hearted period piece in which the characters travel from New York to Paris. When it closed on 8 April 1950, *Miss Liberty*, after over 300 performances, had paid back about 84 per cent of its investment, and the subsequent brief post-Broadway tour broke even (Anon, 1950a). A shortened version, broadcast on television in early January 1951, was praised as 'highly enjoyable' with much of the 'freshness', 'charm, gayety [*sic*] and nostalgia' of the stage original (Rose, 1951, p. 29).

Meanwhile, in a probably synergistic relationship, the score was generating hits. Trade journals disprove Laurence Bergreen's emphatic statement that 'none of the songs in *Miss Liberty* became a smash hit, to be sung and cherished in homes across the country – not one' (496). In fact, 'Just One Way to Say I Love You' and 'Let's Take an Old-Fashioned Walk' were among the top Billboard charting hits of the year and on the prestigious *Your Hit Parade* radio programme (Anon, 1950b; Elrod, 1994, pp. 637–638). 'Homework' was also a solid hit on radio and disc, and 'Little Fish in a Big Pond' enjoyed one week of strong radio play (Anon, 1949b, 1949c, 1949e; Whitburn, 2002, p. 131). Moreover, the original Broadway cast recording charted higher and longer than that of *Annie Get Your Gun* and *Gentlemen Prefer Blondes*, and a studio-cast album also briefly charted (Whitburn, 2002, pp. 556–558). Overall, Berlin's score was second only to that for *South Pacific* on the year's honour rolls.

Since 1949, two numbers have enjoyed frequent airings. Berlin's second-act duet for the two heroines, 'You Can Have Him', became a nightclub and album favourite of powerhouses from Ella Fitzgerald to Liza Minnelli. Finally, Maisie's sporting solo, 'Falling out of Love Can Be Fun', found a home in the stage version of *White Christmas*, an early 21st century holiday favourite.

In the face of critics' repeated complaints of 'disappointing', the writers steadily claimed for *Miss Liberty* the status of an 'audience show' (Green, 1949; Anon, 1949d; Kimball and Emmet, 2001, p. 411). Published audience responses support this view, printed by the *New York Times* as a counter to the harsh judgment of their own critic, Brooks Atkinson. From Fishkill, New York, W.J. Hammond opined: '*Miss Liberty* is tops in theatrical entertainment. The music, the ballets, the costumes and scenery were all that one could ask for; and the fact that each principal gave his and her all made a memorable evening' (Hammond, 1949, p. X1).

Abraham Gelbfish went further, affirming that it was

> an altogether brilliant, charming and delightful production, and, indeed, so eloquent and fascinating that we regard it as a lofty contribution to the theatre, as well as a ringing tribute to the talents and imaginations of the Messrs. Berlin, Sherwood and Hart.
>
> *(Gelbfish, 1949, p. X1)*

Judging by his word choice ('lofty', 'ringing') this man-in-the-street was probably moved by the sober and patriotic finale, 'Give Me Your Tired, Your Poor'. To some, this heartfelt element appeared as too little, too late – too great a tonal shift from the light-hearted overall proceedings – but audience members such as Hammond and Gelbfish apparently held no such objections.

Theatre historian Miles Kreuger, then age 15, went to see it repeatedly, and in 2019 reported that the production remained 'still vivid in my mind's eye, among the most vivid of that era – very airy and light, brightly colored (except the lamp-lighting scene, which was moody and charming), as cuddly as a puppy' with a 'patriotic finale that worked wonderfully' (Kreuger). The equal of any other musical in two seasons of wonderful examples, *Miss Liberty* 'was old-fashioned and not a forward-looking musical theatre piece, but moment-by-moment it was simply marvelous'. Kreuger continues, 'With *South Pacific* I was impressed, but *Miss Liberty* gave me more pleasure'.

The evening's strongest sequence may have been the latter half of Act One, those scenes set in Paris. Berlin's daughter relates that, in retrospect, the songwriter-producer assessed how well 'the Paris parts of the show had worked, with the wonderful Motley costumes, straight out of Toulouse-Lautrec, the Robbins can-can, the pretty waltz "Paris Wakes up and Smiles", and the rowdy, cynical "Only for Americans"' (Barrett, 1994, p. 252). The musical follows Horace as he travels to Paris to find the sculptor of the Statue of Liberty, Bartholdi, and photograph his model. Bartholdi (in this fictionalised version) has just met the penniless Monique, eager for a job as a model. When he shows her the sketches for the statue and Lazarus' poem, she is enraptured by its final lines about the homeless and poses with Liberty's props, just as Horace enters the door. Not fully understanding what Horace is after, the sculptor and the young woman agree to him photographing her in the pose.

Being without funds, Horace and Monique then declare 'Let's Take an Old-Fashioned Walk' (a waltz, the score's biggest hit). They step onto a treadmill and the tiny Parisian buildings start to flow past them, pausing whenever the protagonists do then ambling on as they continue to walk. It rains, and the couples of Paris swirl on with umbrellas (Kreuger, 2019). The world strolls and dances to the cheerful, infectious waltz as the protagonists fall in love. For this episode, the set designer, Oliver Smith, and the costume design firm of Motley collaborated to evoke the paintings of Renoir (Leopold, 2005, p. 184). Kreuger remembers it as 'one of the loveliest moments I've ever seen'.

The next scene moves back to New York, with Maisie interfering in the clash between the conservative and liberal newspapers. This assertive career woman affirms, rather out of character (but by way of a hit song), that she wants to be a housewife and do 'Homework'. Back with Monique in Paris, the audience meets her grandmother, the 'Countess' (Ethel Griffies); the two are trying to sell wilted flowers near the bridge under which they shelter.[2] At dusk, the lamp lighters sing a waltz, the atmospheric 'Paris Wakes up and Smiles', and there ensues another dance interlude, this one rhapsodically envisioning 'a Seine fisherman – an *Apache* – a pimp – a tourist guide – an artist' (Sherwood, 1949, p. 41). Even the gendarme who has threatened to arrest the two women for vagrancy becomes part of the picturesque scene.

Horace appears with cash, and the Countess welcomes him with open arms. He suggests a night on the town, but she decries this, in a march-like fashion, as being 'Only for Americans'. In the lyric, Berlin deflates approximately 18 clichés about Parisian life as merely for the tourist trade, which Griffies 'packs with malice', her delivery making for a wildly 'insane specialty' (Atkinson, 1949a). For this number, the designers evoked Toulouse-Lautrec. It was the 'solidest showstopper' of the evening (Waters 1949). Robbins embodied the stereotypes in a 'bizarre harlequin-ade', 'a street masquerade' featuring the ensemble's singing and 'super-stepping' (Atkinson, 1949b). While the lyric dismisses the conventional associations of Paris common to previous musical comedies, the staging flaunts them. This can be seen as a typical example of the genre's ironic deprecation, allowing it to criticise the cake and yet serve it too (Garber, 2007).

Monique reappears, still pining for Horace, and he exuberantly promises to convey her and her grandmother to America in luxury. Only after this does he learn of his mistake but is now too deeply in to confess and back out of the plan for a publicity tour of this supposed model for the Statue of Liberty. The two duet on the score's second great hit and its third waltz for these Parisian scenes, 'Just One Way to Say I Love You'.[3] After this, the action returns to the United States for the play's duration. Yet Waters in *Variety* pointed out that the scenes in Paris 'are livelier, more spontaneous and generally more interesting than most of the American scenes' with the action going 'into high' with 'Let's Take'; after which the one-two impact of 'Paris Wakes up' and 'Only for Americans' 'keeps the ball rolling'.

Miss Liberty played various roles in the careers of its creative team. For Sherwood: unfortunately, it ushered in his final six years, years of alcoholism and unproductivity. For Robbins, who had actively sought the job, it resulted in the best reviews among the creatives, and it got him in with Berlin with whom he would soon reunite for another 'American in Europe' musical, the 1950 hit, *Call Me Madam* (Leopold, 2005, p. 182). For Berlin, it strengthened the theme running through his oeuvre of nationalist (military, political) themes, which would continue through to the eponymous hero of *Mr. President* (1962). For Hart, it served as a bridge between his directorial work on *Lady in the Dark* (1941) and *My Fair Lady* (1956). Through his uncredited writing contributions to *Miss Liberty*, Hart continued to hone his libretto-writing skills, previously evinced in *I'd Rather Be Right* (1937) and *Lady in the Dark* (1941) and soon to be further manifested in his screenplays for the movie musicals *Hans Christian Andersen* (1952) and *A Star Is Born* (1954).

Tentatively, *Miss Liberty* foreshadows later developments in Paris-set musicals. Firstly, Smith and Motley combined to create visual imitations of Renoir and Toulouse-Lautrec (Leopold, 2005, p. 184). This mise-en-scène can be seen as prefiguring that of the culminating ballet in the Oscar-winning *An American in Paris* (1951), which also evoked Toulouse-Lautrec alongside other iconographic Parisian artists.[4]

Secondly, the role of the Countess takes on greater significance within the era's context. The English-language production of Jean Giraudoux's *The Madwoman of Chaillot* (1943) was in the middle of a long run on Broadway as *Miss Liberty* opened. Sherwood's character shares some traits with Giraudoux's eponymous protagonist. Brooks Atkinson probably had the resemblance in mind when he dubbed the Sherwood creation as 'the madwoman of a Paris bridge' (1949a). In this musical, she prefigures the musicalisation, 20 years later, of Giraudoux's Madwoman in *Dear World*. Although the Countess in *Miss Liberty* is a far earthier personality than the more spiritual, romantic Giraudoux heroine, they are both elderly women, eccentric, of great vitality, authority and strength of character – and the most vivid figures in their worlds. Ethel Griffies probably deserves credit for helping to shape the Sherwood supporting character; the result is that even on the page the Countess is the most riveting of all the personae and steals the show.

Thirdly and most importantly: when Monique first reads aloud the Lazarus poem, while the melody that will eventually be married to those words sneaks in as underscoring, she is surrounded by the stereotypical artist's studio (from which the stereotypical group of beautiful models has just exited). This juxtaposition captures in a nutshell the early stages of the genre's transition from Paris as bohemian pleasure ground to Paris as site for rhetoric about liberty.[5] This trend would continue in *Ben Franklin in Paris*.

FIGURE 5.1   Monique (Allyn Ann McLerie) strikes the Miss Liberty pose in the studio of Bohemian artist Bartholdi while being photographed by Horace (Eddie Albert). Scene from the 1949 Broadway production of *Miss Liberty*.

Source: Photo by Will Rapport, provided by the New York Public Library for the Performing Arts.

Ben Franklin in Paris (1964)

There is a very clever conceit at the heart of *Ben Franklin in Paris*. It is hinted at in the reviews, and yet the critics missed its generic wit: Sydney Michaels, the lyricist-librettist of *Ben Franklin in Paris*, takes its eponymous historical hero and makes him the ultimate version of musical comedy's energetic go-getter. Musical comedy is well populated with such brash Americans injecting Yankee vitality into the Old World, from Kid Connor and Con Kidder conning and kidding their way through picturesque Amsterdam in *The Red Mill* (1906) and Stephen Hustleford hustling in Paris, thereby conveying *The American Idea* (1908), through to Sally Adams sallying forth in mythical Lichtenburg asserting *Call Me Madam* and can-do Steven Canfield in Paris serenading his beloved's *Silk Stockings* (notice the symbolic character names). As Raymond Knapp points out, American musicals often aim for 'the construction of a collective sense of "America"' (Knapp, 2005, p. 104). Thus, no matter where the action is set, stories told by Americans can almost always be interpreted as being at a deep level about America.

In collaboration with choreographer-director Michael Kidd, Michaels turned Benjamin Franklin's real-life years in Paris into a version of the American's clichéd jaunt to the Continent. As a result, the dramatic stakes are raised nearly as high as possible, at least for its intended homegrown audience – the success or failure of the American war of independence. As an additional result, an idolised Founding Father becomes imbued with musical theatre values – deliciously or jarringly so, depending on the viewpoint.

The fortuitous casting of Robert Preston meant that this fictionalised version of Franklin conjured up the star's recent roles: the conman Harold Hill in *The Music Man*; the slick television writer in *Nobody Loves an Albatross*; and, for some, another historical revolutionary, Pancho Villa, of *We Take the Town* – which, ironically, closed out of town (Taubman, 1964; Mordden, 1999). Preston's performance was the only element of the production to receive universal praise. The production ran almost 27 weeks but often with poor attendance, so it paid back only about 10 per cent of its investment (Miller, 2019).

Michaels collaborated on the score with composer Mark Sandrich Jr.[6] Jerry Herman also contributed two ballads, at first anonymously but eventually openly. Although the Broadway cast recording ambled along for two months in a low position on the *Billboard* album charts, the score produced no hit songs or standards. Herman fans may know 'To Be Alone with You', clearly the main contender for the take-home ballad from the show, which Herman himself recorded twice in later years, latterly with Michael Feinstein (Dietz, 2014, p. 270).

The action depicts Benjamin Franklin arriving in Paris to solicit funds from King Louis XVI for the American Revolution and to receive diplomatic acknowledgment of the new nation. He spars with the king's (fictional) right-hand advisor who is Franklin's former lover, the now wealthy widow Madame la Comtesse Diane de Vobrillac, played by Ulla Sallert. The Countess is his equal in experience, intelligence, competence and grasp of politics. They are powerfully attracted

FIGURE 5.2   Robert Preston as the eponymous character in the 1964 Broadway production of *Ben Franklin in Paris*.

Source: Photo provided by the editor.

to each other, but are pulled away from romance by their strong sense of duty
and responsibility to their countries, their pride and their emotional and financial
independence.

Rather late in the first act a secondary romance is introduced between Franklin's
16-year-old grandson, Temple Franklin (Franklin Kiser) and the youthful Janine
(Susan Watson, playing a non-historical character) who idolises Ben Franklin. She
is one of a small group, a few handfuls who hope to start a French Revolution but
by the end realise the time is not yet ripe. Ben Franklin at first functions unwit-
tingly as a blocking force against this romance yet ultimately encourages it. Here is
a parallel to other older protagonists who aid a youthful romance while also pursuing their own affairs in shows such as *Call Me Madam* and two shows that opened

in the same year as *Ben Franklin, Hello, Dolly!* and *Fiddler on the Roof*, with the latter two providing stiff competition for the Paris-set show.

Franklin achieves his goal of securing funding at the end of Act One, thanks firstly to Diane's advice that the king should co-fund the rebel colonies if Spain also contributes; after which Franklin wins over the Spanish ambassador by means of a drinking bout at the vineyards, in 'God Bless the Human Elbow'.[7]

But any further support is denied. In the penultimate scenes, Franklin determines to accept the invitation to England, where – despite their assurances – the British will surely kill him, and thus to martyr himself. Instead of a closing song, he speaks a final soliloquy about the value of freedom and the need to be willing to die for it. Diane grasps his fatal plan. In the final moments, Franklin is acknowledged officially as the Ambassador of the United States of America – an announcement that signals the true birth of the new nation and also saves Franklin's life. As the Countess curtseys to the newly appointed Ambassador Franklin, the audience realises that she is responsible and the curtain falls.

Because its action is set in the 1770s, *Ben Franklin in Paris* cannot draw on the set of clichés exploited by so many other works of popular culture – no can-cans, no visual allusions to Renoir or Toulouse-Lautrec, no concertinas. Nevertheless, the play manages to tip its hat to some conventions of representing Paris. Act One sneaks in a street café; later, the legendary wines of France become the focus of a pivotal scene. The genre's typically mature, sophisticated, quarrelling central lovers can evoke any Continental setting, but perhaps are identified most strongly with Paris via the iconic *The Merry Widow* (Altman, 1987, pp. 138, 144).[8] The adult nature of the relationship between Franklin and the Countess is explored when she offers to build him luxurious accommodations within her own house, which he refuses out of a fierce sense of his own independence. The notion of such an implied unconventional amatory liaison is decidedly Continental and perhaps most specifically Parisian. However, in this context, the casting of the female lead was not entirely successful: Sallert was a musical theatre star in her native Sweden, and – judging by the cast recording, photographs and an online-posted television clip – a powerful, subtle and sensuous presence on stage. Nevertheless, both the intended Parisian atmosphere and the comprehensibility of the script was somewhat diluted by her decidedly Swedish accent.

The 'Paris' song, such a staple of American musical comedy since the 1890s, rears its generic head in the first act. Temple worries he will never unwind – that he is old before his time – but learns to loosen up under the influence of Justine and her song, 'You're in Paris'. In Michaels' lyric Paris is a place of garrets, laughter and wine; it has music that will set one's heart dancing. Here the 'fashion is romance' with couples in street cafés at night or walking along the Seine at dawn. Meanwhile, Sandrich's melody is catchy, alternately flowing and tripping.

Yet the piece also reveals less helpful traits that manifest at various points throughout the score and weaken it. Many of Michaels' lyrics are precepts: 'Half the Battle'; 'Look for Small Pleasures'; much of Diane's torch ballad, 'How Laughable It Is'. Thus, Justine avoids any personal statement in 'You're in Paris'. Rather than focusing on their own emotions, these lovers instruct the listener with general truths.

Another trait is perhaps a sign of the Michaels' literary origins: the lyrics tend to impress more on the page than when performed.[9] An example of this in 'You're in Paris' is in the phrase 'dare to listen': Watson struggles to make audible the word 'dare' on a relatively high note – it sounds like 'care' or 'there'. Inevitably 'dawn by the river' is heard as 'down by the river' and 'of an evening' would sing more intelligibly as 'in the evening'. Each is a minor glitch; however, the accumulation of such instances in line after line and song after song might eventually irritate the listener and weaken the score's appeal.

In addition, Sandrich and Michaels – typically, for Broadway in the late '50s and '60s – often incorporate during their refrains a change in texture of phrasing, rhythm, tempo and texture.[10] The effect of this technique is twofold. On the plus side, it makes the song more sophisticated, adding drama, variety and invention. On the negative side, it discourages renditions in steady dance rhythm, such as by the dance bands, jazz improvisers and early rock'n'roll arrangers who had helped create the overlap of Broadway and pop. In 'You're in Paris' the first such insertion occurs at the mid-point, before the return of the main strain, when an eight-note figure interrupts the flow; the second, in the final section, shifts the tune from a ballad-like lyricism to a gentle soft-shoe feeling.

The chorus takes up 'You're in Paris' behind a scrim evoking the Pont Neuf, a Parisian icon legitimate to utilise because it dates to circa 1600. After this, there ensues one of the few opportunities director-choreographer Michael Kidd found in this show for an extended dance sequence. In the 'Ballet', 'the rabble army' of which Justine is a member 'reveal themselves to be about as clumsy and inept as one could imagine – Temple takes over and shows them how to fight from behind trees, etc. He rapidly turns them into a crack precision marvel' (Michaels, 1965, p. 60). The *Variety* reviewer harshly criticised Kidd's work in *Ben Franklin*, including this sequence, which he described as 'a weird *sans culottes* manual at-arms, which is at best glazed Kidd' (Gagh, 1964).

All this takes place in front of the stereotypical street café setting. In parallel to the scene in *Miss Liberty* in Bartholdi's studio, the creators of *Ben Franklin* take a time-honoured musical comedy mise-en-scène and fashion within it a tribute to the ideal of freedom from poverty and oppression. The scene ends with Janine inspired with an admiration for Temple's grandson so strong that she urges him to toss away his grandfather's writings in order to become his own man – which he does. Then the two wander off, hand in hand, as the chorus partially reprises 'You're in Paris'.

For Preston, *Ben Franklin in Paris* brought rave reviews and a Tony nomination, bridging his Broadway musical career between the hits *The Music Man* and *I Do! I Do!* (1966). In 1974, in *Mack and Mabel*, he would once again embody on Broadway the driven American go-getter, once again introducing Jerry Herman ballads to the Broadway stage. For Michaels, it weakened the career momentum created by his two hit plays, *Tchin-Tchin* (1962) and *Dylan* (1964), but did lead to some further

FIGURE 5.3   The military training number in *Ben Franklin in Paris*, choreographed by Michael Kidd. Scene from the 1964 Broadway production.

Source: Photo by Friedman-Abeles (Billy Rose Theatre Division, NYPL), courtesy of the New York Public Library for the Performing Arts.

minor contributions to the American musical – a never- completed project with Richard Rodgers in the shape of a musical about Nefertiti designed for Diahann Carroll (Anon, 1965); 1967 television adaptations of *Carousel* and *Kismet*; and the 1968 screenplay *The Night They Raided Minsky's*. For Sandrich, the failure of the show resulted in the abandonment of his composing career and the resumption of his work as an assistant director for television. For Kidd, it continued a streak of disappointments after *Destry Rides Again* (1959) that would not end until his dances for the 1969 Hollywood version of *Hello, Dolly!* and the directing-choreographing of Broadway's *The Rothschilds* (1970). The historical period setting of *Ben Franklin* was so different from that of his earlier Paris-set credit, *Can-Can*, that the two scarcely seem connected. The choreographer would engage one more time with musical comedy tropes of Paris, this time depicting yet a third era – the 1920s – in the 'Parisian Pierrot' number from the Gertrude Lawrence biopic *Star!* (1968).

In some respects, *Ben Franklin* as a whole prefigured the once-filmed and oft-revived *1776* of five years later. This foreshadowing was noted by Tom Dash when *1776* opened on Broadway (Dash, 1969, p. 15); and the point has been reiterated by Ethan Mordden in his praise of *Ben Franklin* as a musical play that deserved a happier fate: 'Considering that a major show of 1969 also gave us Ben Franklin and closed in a moving tableau on a bit of early-American history, we should remember that *Ben Franklin in Paris* did it first' (Mordden, 2001, p. 52). Lacking a major revival, this Michaels-Sandrich collaboration remains a show for (musical theatre) historians to remember. But through the script, the cast recording and photographic records, an image lingers of the mature Franklin and the youthful Temple, framed within the setting of Paris, wrestling with what independence means to both a lover and a nation.

Dear World (1969)

Some works resist a critical rhetoric focused on anything but their failure. Such is *Dear World*, which has achieved a particular kind of notoriety in the saga of musical theatre flops for its troubled history, which included a series of three directors (the final one, Joe Layton, also took over as choreographer), a delayed opening and an unprecedented number of preview performances (57), mixed-to-bad reviews and a lack of hit songs. Compounding these problems was the misplaced expectations of the public, eager for a repeat of the bright and cheery *Mame* (1966). This was an earlier collaboration by many of the same hands: songwriter Jerry Herman, arrangers Philip J. Lang and Don Pippin, librettists Jerome Lawrence and Robert E. Lee and star Angela Lansbury. *Mame* had been a smash hit but, in contrast, the commercial outcome for *Dear World* was dire. It closed 16 weeks after the long-delayed première with a loss of the entire investment. The original Broadway cast album, like that for *Ben Franklin*, drifted in the lower regions of the album charts in *Billboard* for two months. Yet, for various reasons – the renowned source material, the story's counter-cultural stance, the reputation of Jerry Herman, a score that yielded a trio of cabaret favourites and the strong central role for which Lansbury won a Tony Award – the piece has gone through two stages of revision to enjoy revivals regionally and in intimate settings in London and New York and may continue to be put on the boards.

The musical follows the outlines of the famous play on which it is based, *La folle de Chaillot*, written by Jean Giraudoux in the midst of the Nazi occupation of Paris and produced posthumously to great acclaim in 1945; its charm lies in its delicate touch, whimsy, satirical absurdity and symbolism. It was translated to the American stage as *The Madwoman of Chaillot* for a successful Broadway run in 1948 and a subsequent tour.[11] In both versions, a corporation realises there is oil beneath Paris, to be best tapped underneath a bohemian café, and plans to bulldoze the city to get to it. The plot is discovered by the café's habitués because the young man blackmailed by the corporation into bombing the environs does not have the heart to do it and attempts suicide. As he revives, the Countess Aurelia (the 'madwoman') helps him feel life is worth living. Meanwhile, the café's waitress falls in love with him, creating another 'young lovers' subplot similar to those in *Call Me Madam*, *Ben Franklin in Paris*, et alia. The romantic, whimsical, nostalgic Countess, up till now blind to the dire changes in the human condition, sets forth to save the city and the world from the soulless corporate villains. Through the help of the Sewerman, and after a surrogate trial of the villains facilitated by the café crowd and her two fellow madwomen (three in the Giraudoux original), the Countess reveals a mysterious endless stairwell. The corporate clique willingly descend it in search of oil – never to be heard from again. The Countess closes the door and the world is saved.

The most prevalent Paris stereotype utilised by *Dear World* was the frequent incorporation of the concertina in the arrangements. In contrast with the recordings of *Miss Liberty* and *Ben Franklin*. which do not feature accordions or concertinas, prominent use of this quintessential Parisian timbre is heard on 9 of the 14 tracks of the *Dear World* original cast album. The central café setting is another powerful Paris trope, here archetypally labelled the Café Français; and the bonhomie of the denizens of the Chaillot district evokes a related Paris tradition – the city as neighbourhood. Unlike *Madwoman* which had only two settings, one per act, the musical version opened up the action to include multiple locations. The adaptation starts off in a boat on the Seine and eventually descends to the city's sewers and wanders out to its streets (in the rain, naturally), flea markets and parks.

Here, Paris is not a place for illustrating the dynamic between Continental Europe and an American abroad; it is, rather, its own self-contained enclave. The situation in Paris becomes a synecdoche for the state of the world. As Mordden points out, the original play 'presciently bears the anti-corporation politics so

FIGURE 5.4   The Café Français in *Dear World* as designed by Oliver Smith; at the centre sits Countess Aurelia (Angela Lansbury), the 'madwoman'. Scene from the 1969 Broadway production.

Source: Photo by Friedman – Abeles (Billy Rose Theatre Division, NYPL), courtesy of the New York Public Library for the Performing Arts.

trendy in the 1960s', to which can be added the environmentalism and concern for the preservation of urban neighbourhoods characteristic of the later 20th century (Mordden, 2001, p. 259). This is probably one reason why Herman, Lawrence and Lee chose to create a musical version at that particular historical moment. Yet they failed in their appeal to the popular imagination, not quite hitting the right note to echo the zeitgeist of the late '60s. The reasons for this failure were many and are well outlined by Mordden (2001, pp. 259–263) and the original critics as summarised (and supplemented) by Mark Kirkeby (1992, pp. 9–13) and Dan Dietz (502–503). Nevertheless, with their attempt, the show's creators depict Paris as a locus of discourse concerning the encroachment of corporate culture on individual human freedom. In this way, it amplifies the trend seen in *Miss Liberty* and *Ben Franklin in Paris*. In emphasising politics – the struggle of the bohemian and lower classes against those in power – *Dear World* foreshadows a topic that would so memorably dominate the megahit *Les Misérables* (1980/1985). The story also explores the struggle to protect the environment, a subject pursued with even more absurdist satire in the long-running *Urinetown* (2001), which itself parodied *Les Misérables*.

In some structural aspects *Dear World* also echoes *The Phantom of the Opera* – the 1910 Parisian tale that has been filmed, broadcast and staged multiple times – and in particular foreshadows the famous Andrew Lloyd Webber 1986 musical theatre version. Descents into the cellars and underground water systems beneath the city; villains on a boat riding over the waters of Paris; central characters who are viewed as crazy and use secret passages to manipulate their opponents and enforce their judgment on others; a pair of relatively innocent young lovers; and a satiric view of society's shallowness and cruelty – all are factors shared by these two musicals. Despite their differences in milieu, themes and tone as well as the different age and gender of the shows' respective protagonists, the two musicals may be seen as a pair. This resemblance indicates the place *Dear World* holds in the development of Paris as a setting in the musical.

For Layton, this show allowed him to pick up again the Continental thread he had helped unspool with considerable success in *No Strings* (1962) and with less success in *Sail Away* (1961). *Dear World* also fit into the trajectory of his career as a trusted designer of showcases for star performers, from Mary Martin to Diana Ross and many more. For Lansbury, the role (and the Tony) confirmed her status as a singing actress with an indelible reputation for versatility. The Countess can be seen as a preparation for her more acclaimed and better documented role as Mrs. Lovett in *Sweeney Todd* (1979). Different as the characters are – indeed, in many ways they are opposites – they are both 'mad' women past their youth whom Lansbury played with a skilful, witty stylisation and a touch of grotesque exaggeration.

For Jerry Herman, *Dear World* signalled the end of his uninterrupted winning streak which lasted from off-Broadway's *Nightcap* (1957) through *Mame* (1966). The songwriter would have to wait 15 years for one last success with *La Cage aux Folles* (1983). Like *Hello, Dolly!*, *Mame* and *Dear World*, that was another musical with a strong central feminine figure (in this case a female impersonator), concerning eccentric or bohemian types who assert a viewpoint that is disruptive to society's status quo.

Certain numbers from *Dear World* are kept alive in cabaret, concerts and Herman anthologies. 'Kiss Her Now' and 'I've Never Said I Love You' feature recitative-like opening strains yielding to brooding passages and declamatory climaxes. 'One Person' is an optimistic march espousing the agency of the individual and the viral nature of social change. Coming at the end of the play, 'One Person' encapsulates the role the Countess has come to fulfil as society's saviour. It is, arguably, at odds with the protagonist's earlier proclamation 'I Don't Want to Know', which is probably the most famous song from the score.[12]

As Herman later wrote, singers find 'I Don't Want to Know' 'exciting to work with because it builds and builds in emotion like a Jacques Brel song' (Herman, 1996, p. 171). Indeed, although the composer remembers striving 'for a sound that was much more legitimate, more classical', Jacques Brel might have been an equal influence (Herman, 1996, p. 171). Brel, a Belgian singer-songwriter and star of the French pop music scene, developed a dramatic, astringent style that had brought his songs increasing fame in the United States after 1964. The 1968 off-Broadway revue of his works, *Jacques Brel Is Alive and Living in Paris*, was in the middle of a long run while Herman was writing *Dear World*. Therefore, Herman may have felt that inflecting the score with Brel's style would help evoke Paris.

In 'I Don't Want to Know', the Madwoman affirms that she would rather live in memories of a past world of beauty and happiness, if the current world will not offer those values. This conservative stance was, presumably, at odds with the desire by many, in the late-1960s, for social and aesthetic changes. Yet it also is an implicit declaration by Herman himself that, in a world in which rock musicals were flourishing, he would stick with the optimism, bittersweet romanticism and melodic lyricism of the Golden Age tradition.

Conclusion

Oliver Smith designed the sets for all three of the Paris-set musicals analysed in this chapter. More than just a curiosity, Smith's recurring involvement demonstrates the continuity of the mid-century Broadway tradition over a span of 20 years.[13] The trio of shows focused on in the present chapter also display other odd connections: two sets of Herman song contributions; two closely associated early exponents of American ballet (Kidd had been a dancer in Robbins' works); two sets of fictionalised historic personages; two youthful romances assisted by two older protagonists; and three countesses, of various ilks.

The three shows also share a trait even more germane to the evolution of the musical: they manifest political themes within the setting of Paris, each evincing concern for issues surrounding human liberty. They contributed to the changes in the Broadway musical genre overall, with productions at least from *Show Boat* (1927) onwards setting social commentary within locales that had previously been places only of exoticism or romantic idealisation. The three financial failures analysed in this chapter did not neglect the connotations of Paris as a locus for playfully flirtatious sexuality or delicate, bittersweet glamour. Nevertheless, they also demonstrate a shift in the rhetoric surrounding Paris which can be described schematically as a move from hedonism towards heroism. They thus served in some small way to pave the road for the acceptance on Broadway, decades later, of *Les Misérables*.

The differences between these three shows assuredly demonstrate the shift of topics and tonalities in the Broadway musical over a 20 year span – from the light-hearted charm of *Miss Liberty*; through the earnest foundations, overlaid with comedy and romance, of *Ben Franklin in Paris*; to the sobering social critique, overlaid with both whimsy and bombast, in *Dear World*. Overall, these three productions reveal major Golden Age creators contributing to the transformation of the signification of Paris on the American musical stage.

Notes

1 The Goodspeed Opera House revived *Miss Liberty* in 1983 and *Dear World* in 2000; and the latter is available in a revised version premiered there and then further altered for the Sundance Theater in Utah.
2 There is no hint in the *Miss Liberty* script or cast recording that the accents or speech patterns of Monique and the Countess are French. This choice may have somewhat weakened the show's evocation of Paris.
3 Berlin never used three-four meter more extensively in one show than in the Paris portions of *Miss Liberty*. The songwriter might have been drawing on the conventional association of the waltz with all things Continental, though usually it connotes not Paris but Vienna. Equally, he might be responding to the era's increasingly prominent Richard Rodgers waltzes.
4 Perhaps tellingly, the producer (Arthur Freed) and director (Vincente Minnelli) of *An American in Paris* discussed the concept of its ballet finale with Irving Berlin (Fordin, 1984, p. 320).
5 *The Vagabond King*, the 1925 operetta about French self-rule during the late Medieval period, can be interpreted as an even more distant and romanticised start of the association of Paris with the ideals of freedom. Perhaps two Cole Porter musicals set in Paris also contributed to this line of development: *Can-Can* (1953), with its light-hearted depiction of the conflict between artistic freedom and censorship; and *Silk Stockings* (1955), with its simplified debates between capitalist and communist viewpoints.
6 Sandrich's father, Mark Sandrich Sr., had been one of Hollywood's most successful directors, particularly notable for his seven films with Fred Astaire.
7 This is one of several opportunities for the male chorus. The choral arrangements are particularly strong in the male ensembles, perhaps one factor, along with its legit soprano heroine and Continental setting, that led Walter Kerr to analyse the show as an operetta (Dietz, 2014, p. 269).
8 In a bow to the conventions of romantic comedy, the show's hero is 20 or more years younger than the historic Benjamin Franklin during his years in Paris.
9 Sometimes Michaels overloads his songs with a bewildering series of metaphors. As well, the lyrics as heard on the cast recording differ in many details from those in his published script. Both of these may be symptoms of the author's continued difficulties in honing his lyric-writing skills.
10 An instance of this trend can be found in Alan Jay Lerner and Frederick Loewe's 'I Loved You Once in Silence', from *Camelot* (1960). Lerner spoke of deliberately emphasising harsher consonants in its final section, to force the singer at that point to shift to a slower tempo (*Songwriters*).
11 Martita Hunt won a Tony Award in 1949 for playing the Madwoman, just as Lansbury would do in 1969.

12 One shortcoming of *Dear World* is hinted at in the fact that all four of its enduring songs, along with the title tune, build to an emphatic climax bordering on stridency. This is perhaps a misjudgment on Herman's part in fashioning what he himself dubbed 'a very fragile show' (Kirkeby: 10). Notably, too, Herman creates a handful of melodies that feature the brief shift in phrasing, texture or rhythm noted above in relation to the score of *Ben Franklin*.
13 Smith also designed Paris scenes for Broadway in *Gentlemen Prefer Blondes* and the 1973 stage adaptation of *Gigi*.

References

Altman, R. (1987) *The American Film Musical*. Bloomington, IN: Indiana University Press.
Anon. (1965) 'Diahann Carroll Set in Musical by Rodgers-Michaels,' *Variety*, 240(7), 6 October, p. 69.
———. (1950a) '*Liberty* Closing in Chi after Two Mild Weeks,' *Variety*, 178(12), 31 May, p. 47.
———. (1950b) 'Peatman Annual Survey of Song Hits with the Largest Radio Audiences,' *Billboard*, 62(2), 15 July, p. 12.
———. (1949a) '*Miss Liberty* in Ticket Toils,' *Billboard*, 61(30), 23 July, pp. 6, 40.
———. (1949b) 'Songs with Greatest Radio Audiences,' *Billboard*, 61(35), 27 August, p. 25.
———. (1949c) 'Songs with Greatest Radio Audiences,' *Billboard*, 61(37), 10 September, p. 27.
———. (1949d) '*Liberty* Can Pay off Cost by Jan. at Current Pace,' *Variety*, 164(2), 21 September, p. 57.
———. (1949e) 'Songs with Greatest Radio Audiences,' *Billboard*, 61(41), 8 October, p. 24.
Atkinson, B. (1949a) 'At the Theater: *Miss Liberty*,' *The New York Times*, 16 July, p. 6.
———. (1949b) 'Mediocre Musical,' *The New York Times*, 24 July, p. X1.
Barrett, M. E. (1994) *Irving Berlin: A Daughter's Memoir*. New York: Simon and Schuster.
Bergreen, L. (1990) *As Thousands Cheer: The Life of Irving Berlin*. New York: Penguin Books.
Bordman, G. (2001) *American Musical Theatre: A Chronicle*. 3rd edition. Oxford: Oxford University Press.
Dash, T. (1969) 'Critic-at-Large: *1776* – the Birth of a Nation,' *Back Stage*, 10(13), 28 March, p. 15.
Dietz, D. (2014) *The Complete Book of 1960s Broadway Musicals*. Lanham, MD: Rowman and Littlefield.
Elrod, B. C. (ed.) (1994) *Your Hit Parade and American Top Ten Hits: A Week-by-Week Guide to the Nation's Favorite Music, 1935–1994*. 4th edition. Ann Arbor, MI: Popular Culture Ink.
Fordin, H. (1984) *The Movies' Greatest Musicals: Produced in Hollywood USA by the Freed Unit*. New York: Frederick Ungar.
Gagh. (1964) 'Show out of Town: *Ben Franklin*,' *Variety*, 236(1), 26 August, p. 56.
Garber, M. (2007) 'Songs about Entertainment: Self-Praise and Self-Mockery in the American Musical', *Studies in Musical Theatre*, 1(3), Fall, pp. 227–242.
Gelbfish, A. (1949) 'Assorted Views in the Drama Mailbag: Loves *Liberty*,' *The New York Times*, 24 July, p. X1.
Green, A. (1949) 'Songsmith Opines Critics Reviewed Sherwood, Berlin and Hart, Not Show,' *Variety*, 175(6), 20 July, p. 48.
Hammond, W. J. (1949) 'Found in the Drama Mailbag: Satisfied,' *The New York Times*, 31 July, p. X1.
Herman, J. (1996) *Show Tune: A Memoir*. New York: Donald I. Fine.

Kimball, R. and Emmet, L. (2001) *The Complete Lyrics of Irving Berlin*. New York: Alfred A. Knopf.

Kirkeby, M. (1992) 'Dear World,' Liner Notes for *Dear World*. CD. New York: Sony Music Entertainment, pp. 7–13.

Knapp, R. (2005) *The American Musical and the Formation of National Identity*. Princeton, NJ: Princeton University Press.

Kreuger, M. (2019) Conversation with the author, 31 October.

Langer, P. (1984) 'Sociology – Four Images of Organized Diversity: Bazaar, Jungle, Organism, and Machine,' in Lloyd Rodwin and Robert M. Hollister (eds.) *Cities of the Mind*. New York: Putnam Press, pp. 97–117.

Leopold, D. (2005) *Irving Berlin's Show Business: Broadway, Hollywood, America*. New York: Harry N. Abrams.

Michaels, S. (1965) *Ben Franklin in Paris*. New York: Random House.

Miller, D. (2019) Private email to the author, 16 October.

Mordden, E. (1999) *Beautiful Mornin': The Broadway Musical in the 1940s*. New York: Oxford University Press.

———. (2001) *Open a New Window: The Broadway Musical in the 1960s*. New York: Palgrave, St. Martin's Press.

Rose. (1951) 'Miss Liberty (Musical Comedy Time),' *Variety*, 181(5), 10 January, p. 29.

Sherwood, R. E. (1949) *Miss Liberty*. New York: Samuel French.

Taubman, H. (1964) 'The Theater: *Ben Franklin in Paris*,' *The New York Times*, 28 October, p. 52.

Waters. (1949) 'Plays Out of Town: *Miss Liberty*,' *Variety*, 175(1), 15 June, p. 52.

Whitburn, J. (2002) *Billboard Pop Hits Singles and Albums: 1940–1954*. Menomonee Falls, WI: Record Research.

6

SEDUCED BY PARIS

Irma la Douce and its journey to Broadway

Stewart Nicholls

In the 19th century, opéra bouffe was the dominant home-grown fare for Parisian audiences following composer Jacques Offenbach (1819–1880) creating such enduring pieces as *Orphée aux Enfers/Orpheus in the Underworld* (1858*)*, *La Belle Hélène* (1864) and *La Vie Parisienne* (1866). Excepting the operettas of Robert Planquette who attained success with works including *Les Cloches de Corneville/The Bells of Corneville/The Chimes of Normandy* (1878) and *Rip Van Winkle* (1882), there was little commercial French musical theatre entertainment for most of the 20th century.

The 1980s and after brought forth very few Gallic musical theatre voices, although the country arguably produced one of the most successful musical theatre song-writing teams of modern times, Claude-Michel Schönberg and Alain Boublil (*Les Misérables*, 1980/1985; *Miss Saigon*, 1989). On *Marguerite*, which premiered in 2008 in London, they collaborated with three-time Oscar-winner Michel Legrand (1932–2019), a late career bloomer in theatre, who also composed *Le Passe Muraille/Amour* (1997). Riccardo Cocciante's *Notre-Dame de Paris* (1998) and Gérard Presgurvic's *Roméo et Juliette: de la Haine à l'Amour/Romeo and Juliet* (2010) were home-grown pieces and found international exposure. Modern day French musical theatre appears to thrive in the medium of large-scale arena events, but these find negligible support in Anglophone cultures.

Before *Irma* – musical theatre in France

What was produced in French musical theatre throughout most of the 20th century? Offenbach's works were regularly revived (and to some extent still are), giving much pleasure to Parisian audiences, but there was hardly any new writing during this period that warrants comment. Major musicals from the American golden age found very little success in France, although Parisians had particular affection for Vincent Youman's *No! No! Nanette* (1924), Rudolf Friml's *Rose-Marie* (1924) and

Irving Berlin's *Annie Get Your Gun/Annie du Far-West* (1950). These were commercially recorded – either with their original casts or as comprehensive studio
recordings – in their French translation.

Few imported musical comedies were embraced by Parisian audiences, and
there was negligible indigenous writing of note through the middle part of the
20th century. If the denizens of Paris showed little interest in musical theatre, what
musical entertainment did they frequent? Four classical orchestras and the *Ballets Russes* led in classical music and dance whilst the *Orchestre de Paris* embraced
modernist music. Jazz music, a popular Parisian entertainment, flourished in the
1930s with numerous jazz clubs emerging; the most famous being the *Hot Club de
Paris*. These intimate clubs flourished throughout the 1950s and the large *Olympia
Music Hall* was consistently inhabited by American jazz icons. Music Hall, which is
essentially 'jazz revue' in France, was a very popular entertainment at such famous
venues as the *Folies Bergère*, *Les Ambassadeurs* and the *Moulin Rouge* with the singer
and entertainer Josephine Baker being the pre-eminent female performer in this
entertainment genre, later succeeded by Zizi Jeanmaire.

One entertainment genre; *chanson réaliste*, (almost wholly particular to France),
thrived in the Parisian cabaret club circuit in the Pigalle area of the city. *Chanson
réaliste* (in English: 'realist song') is an intensely emotional and passionately heart-
rending delivery of a song, often depicting stories of underworld figures and poorer
classes. Usually presented by female performers, the leading exponent of the genre
was Édith Piaf. Piaf had a string of popular songs to her name and often wrote
her own lyrics, collaborating with numerous composers: 'La Vie en Rose' may
be her most famous song (and one of her signature pieces); it was composed by
Louiguy. 'Mon Legionnaire', a 1936 song with lyrics by Raymond Asso and music
by Marguerite Monnot (1903–1961) was an international success for both Piaf
and Monnot. The two had met earlier that same year through an introduction by
rival singer Annette Lajon after Piaf allegedly appropriated the song 'L'Étranger'
(winner of the Grand Prix du Disque by L'Académie du Disque Français in 1935).
The meeting between Monnot and Piaf led to a fervent friendship and a successful
song-writing partnership; they formed that rarest of entertainment commodities: a
female song-writing team.

Monnot, a child prodigy pianist, was classically educated by one of most notable
teachers of composition of the 20th century, Nadia Boulanger, and found popular
music to be her true *métier*. Although Piaf recorded songs by Monnot; including
'La Goualante du Pauvre Jean' ('The Poor People of Paris'), which would become an
international hit, it was their collaboration that produced many successful pieces
such as the 1949 ballad, 'Hymne à l'amour', which not only triumphantly showed
off Piaf's vocals but brought the writing duo global fame.[1]

The partnership of composer and lyricist/performer led to an unusual occur-
rence: an original work of French musical theatre: *La P'tite Lili* (1951). This piece,
featuring a libretto by admired French playwright Marcel Achard had a moderately
successful production at Théâtre de l'ABC, where it played for seven months. This
was Piaf's only performance in a musical (she also collaborated on the lyrics with

FIGURE 6.1   Marguerite Monnot, the French composer of *Irma La Douce*, in the early 1940s.

Source: Photo by Keystone-France, courtesy of Getty Images.

Achard), and most probably found an audience on her name alone as the piece has never been revived. An original cast album, probably only waxed due to Piaf's ascendance as France's premiere chanteuse, reveals a charming score although there is little of the musical exuberance found in Monnot's compositions for *Irma la Douce*.[2] For a piece billed as a 'comédie musicale', the synopsis reads as rather dramatic:

> Lili, a little seamstress who sings the whole day long, has an admirer, a night por-
> ter named Mario. Dismissed from the sewing workshop because she sings during
> her work, she finds herself mixed up in the murder of a pimp. She falls under the
> spell of Spencer, a crook who seduces then leaves her. She tries to kill herself,
> but the pharmacist has, fortunately, replaced the arsenic with a harmless liqueur.
>
> *(Laurent, 2015)*

The recording preserves a score relatively serious in tone in accordance with the plot; although a joyous number sung by co-star Eddie Constantine, 'Petite Si Jolie' ('So Pretty'), already hints at Monnot's later development as a theatrical composer.

Irma in Paris

Although *La P'tite Lili* was a rarity – a home-grown piece of Parisian musical theatre – it served as an important springboard for Monnot's primary musical theatre work: the international hit *Irma la Douce* (1956). The plot of *Irma* originally appeared in the satirical French newspaper *La Canard Enchaîné* (*The Chained Duck*) as a short story feature written by Alexandre Breffort (1901–1971). Breffort, a maverick, who spent his formative years moving from job to job (including printer, typewriter salesman and cartoonist) eventually found success as editor of *La Canard Enchaîné*, followed by a productive career as an author of books, films and plays. His most famous work, *Mon Taxi et Moi/My Taxi and Me*, a book written in 1951, humorously recounts his early life as a taxi driver. The encouraging response to the newspaper publication of his short story of *Irma* inspired Breffort to adapt it into short play/sketch which, in itself, was pleasing enough for a musical theatre adaptation to be considered.

Irma la Douce (*Irma, the Sweet*) is a Parisian tart with a heart of gold. She walks the narrow backstreets of the Pigalle area of Paris; an area inhabited by prostitutes and pimps. The police are happy to 'turn a blind eye' to the dealings occurring around them. Nestor-le-Fripé, a penniless law student, falls in love with Irma and once he is her boyfriend, decides that in order to ensure that he is Irma's only partner, he has to become her only client. Thus he disguises himself as an elderly man, Monsieur Oscar, complete with a false beard. Not only does Nestor have to take on additional work in order to pay Irma for her services to Oscar, he also becomes incredibly exhausted at the exertions he has to undertake in his double life of both Nestor and Oscar. Nestor decides the only course to take is to effectively 'kill' Oscar, which he does, but he gets convicted of the crime and imprisoned on Devil's Island. He escapes, rows back to Paris, is greeted by Irma who thinks he is Oscar (he hasn't been able to shave – so his beard is now real), therefore proving that Nestor couldn't have killed Oscar as he is alive. Nestor is reprieved and Oscar 'says' he will leave Paris, thus bringing forth a happy ending, crowned by the birth of Irma's twin babies.

The location, plot, atmosphere of the piece and the character of Irma all have strong connections to *La P'tite Lili*. It is easy to comprehend why Monnot would be attracted to the source material. Breffort, writing book and lyrics in a collaboration with the composer, adapted his story himself, working alongside René Dupuy, artistic director of the tiny Théâtre Gramont, where the piece premiered on 12 November 1956. The title role was undertaken by popular band singer Colette Renard:

> As soon as I saw her, I called her Irma. . . . Her voice is the sort that rises from the suburbs and holds you spellbound without effort, because it rings true. Indeed, everything is true about Colette Renard . . . right down to her Montmartre nose, retroussé enough for a certificate of origin.
>
> (Breffort, 1956)

Nestor was played by Michel Roux, recreating and building on the role he had previous undertaken in Breffort's initial short play/sketch. The trio of principal roles was completed by director Rene Dupuy assuming the role of Bob Le Hotu; essentially a narrator. The intimate production was complemented by ten male performers undertaking various supporting roles, accompanied by a three-piece orchestra. The production was minuscule, intimate, raw; it had a close relation to a certain 1928 ballad opera by Bertolt Brecht and Kurt Weill:

> the show itself is not unconventional: its attitude is. It treats underworld folk from the viewpoint of the underworld. These are to an extent the people of *The Threepenny Opera* [originally produced in Berlin as *Die Dreigroschenoper*, SN] – only here they're supposed to be loveable.
>
> *(Mordden, 2001, p. 11)*

An intimate production, *Irma la Douce* instantly found an audience – an astounding achievement:

> in a city where, despite their great appeal everywhere else, musicals had constantly been shunned by audiences. What attracted the sophisticated and worldly Parisians could have easily been the shady glamour of the seedy back streets, with its small-time crooks and good-time *cocottes*, living out their lives in sleazy bars to the accompaniment of a nostalgic accordion waltz; that was something the French could relate to, not, some American import, like *Oklahoma!*, which meant absolutely nothing to them.
>
> *(Deutsch, 1991, p. 16)*

The show was so popular that it transferred to a slightly larger venue, the Théâtre de l'Athénée, where it continued to run for four years; unprecedented for a French musical comedy. Renaud shot to stardom and went on to become one of France's most popular recording artistes. During the original run she recorded four songs from the show accompanied by her future husband, Raymond Legrand, and his orchestra. These recordings, although charming, feel quite underpowered, especially 'Ah! Dis-Donc', when compared to those of other productions. The musical arrangements differ from those used in the theatre production; the orchestra consisting of a small brass and woodwind section, accordion, harp and a rhythm section is fuller than the trio of piano, bass and guitar listed in the programme of the original staging (Anon, 1956, unpaginated). Considering the success of the production, it is surprising that not more of the score was recorded by the original cast or popular French singers of the period.

The English *Irma*

BBC bandleader Henry Hall had a stake in the French music publishers of *Irma*. After attending a performance early in the initial Paris run, he immediately spotted that the show was a potential commercial hit outside of France. He quickly negotiated ownership of the English-speaking rights to the show and the music. Hall then enticed the two most powerful post-war British theatre producers, Donald Albery and Hugh Beaumont (known as Binkie), to mount a London production under the auspices of their production companies, Donmar Productions and H. M. Tennent.

Beaumont took the singular producing step of casting a performer for the title role for the London production before a translation of the script was anywhere near completion. This was even more unusual considering that the actress he cast, Elizabeth Seal, had never played the lead in a musical. Seal found overnight success in the 1955 London production of the American musical *The Pajama Game* at the London Coliseum playing the secondary role of Gladys. Her home-grown triple-threat performance was a refreshing tonic in this British version of a post-war Broadway show, as often the key performers were American artistes imported to play major roles. Film appearances and a non-musical leading part in the 1957 London production of Tennessee Williams play *Camino Real* (1957) directed by Peter Hall put Seal's career in the ascendant. Stepping into the shoes of performer Belita (aka Maria Belita Jepson-Turner), who had proved ineffectual as Lola in the 1957 British première of *Damn Yankees*, Seal was greeted in her dressing room at the Coliseum by Beaumont with a question: 'What role would you like to do next?' (Seal, 2020). Seal was keen to play the lead in the forthcoming staging of Broadway musical *Bells Are Ringing*, due to follow *Damn Yankees* into the Coliseum. Beaumont had other ideas:

> Binkie said to me one day: 'How would you like to go to Paris for the weekend?! I want you to go and have a look at this show.' And I went to see this little show; I hadn't seen anything like it before . . . I was in this tiny little theatre, and there are four musicians[3] in the right-hand box, and a tacky curtain, and this trombone kept coming out – it was great fun! I loved all the music; I thought it was wonderful. I couldn't understand the dialogue, but people were laughing a lot. Colette Renard was terrific, but she was a singer – she didn't do any dancing. I came back to London, Binkie called me and asked: 'What did you think?' I said, 'I loved it,' and he said: 'Well, I think you'll be wonderful as Irma!' I said: 'Oh Yes – but there's no dancing in it, you'll have to put some dancing in it!'
>
> *(Seal, 2020)*

As Beaumont's biographer notes: Seal was perfect casting: She was exquisitely pretty with elfin looks, bursting with talent and personality and wholly delightful (Huggett, 1989, p. 446). The producer put Seal on a seven-month financial retainer. Except for a few film and television appearances, she had had very few performance opportunities until *Irma la Douce* was ready. Beaumont said to Seal: ' "First we need to get a director, and we have to have it translated." I was on board before anyone else – I was very lucky' (Seal, 2020).

FIGURE 6.2 The multi-talented Elizabeth Seal as *Irma la Douce* in the 1958 London production.

Source: Photo by Michael Ward, provided by the actress.

Albery and Beaumont enlisted Peter Brook to realise the physical production on the London stage. Brook, the pre-eminent British theatre director of his generation, was not known for staging musical theatre; his only previous experience of the genre consisted of helming the disastrous 1954 American musical *House of Flowers* by Harold Arlen (music) and Truman Capote (book and lyrics), where he was replaced in all but name prior to the show reaching Broadway. Presumably Brook's background in opera, his pioneering work on French theatre practitioner Antonin Artaud and his successful realisations of the works by Bertolt Brecht were strong factors in motivating his engagement on *Irma*.

Irma in English

A strong English translation was imperative for the intrinsically Parisian piece to become a property which would be fully comprehended and embraced by British audiences. It also had to be skilfully adapted in order for it to be suitable for the Lord Chamberlain to grant a performance license. It was Brook who discovered the adaptors – almost by accident: David Heneker, Monty Norman and Julian More.

Heneker, a colonel in the British army, had a second career as a songwriter and, since the 1930s, had created many stand-alone songs for British singers for both films and London stage revues. He wanted to write full-length musicals and had teamed up with More to work on an original piece entitled *The Apple and Eve*. More, a Cambridge graduate, had had immense success immediately following graduation with the book and lyrics to the musical *Grab Me A Gondola* (1956), a fast-paced, modern musical comedy which achieved a long run in London's Lyric Theatre on Shaftesbury Avenue. Norman, a band singer and recording artist, was bought in by Heneker and More to cut some demonstration recordings of songs from *The Apple and Eve*. This resulted in him joining them to form a writing trio. *The Apple and Eve* was soon aborted, following the success of *My Fair Lady* as unfortunately there was no room for two musicals set in Covent Garden. The trio were then approached by writer Wolf Mankowitz who, like Breffort, was adapting a novella he had written for a newspaper to the musical stage, *Expresso Bongo*. He needed songwriters, and the Heneker-Norman-More trio fitted the subject matter perfectly as they understood the seedy side of Soho and the cut-throat music business that the show inhabits. *Expresso Bongo* was the first commercial musical of the 'kitchen sink' school of theatre, and it needed a strong director. The writers approached Brook, and although the piece was not for him, he was impressed with the writing and could see clear connections in style and theme to *Irma la Douce*. The trio were immediately commissioned to undertake the British translation. As More commented in 1999: 'This was a complete act of faith on his part as we were then an untried team' (More, 1999, unpaginated). The threesome would soon have two of the most highly regarded and critically acclaimed post-war musicals running in London, with both *Irma la Douce* and *Expresso Bongo* opening in 1958.

Heneker, Norman and More grappled with how to translate the multitudinous amount of argot used in Breffort's text:

> After several versions had been thrown in the wastepaper basket, we eventually hit on the right way to present *Irma* to English audiences; to avoid use of Bronx or Cockney slang equivalents so beloved by subtitlers and so killing to the Gallic atmosphere; to use instead a few French 'argot' terms in their original . . . and to adapt the lyrics freely, taking Breffort's thought line but creating our own shapes, and in some cases writing completely new lyrics to Monnot's music.
>
> *(More, 1999, unpaginated)*

They hit on the right formula to adapt the show, but they still needed to inform the audience about what the French slang terms actually meant. The theatregoers would understand the argot terms if helped by strong direction and excellent acting, but they had to comprehend them from the outset or there was a risk of losing the spectators' attention. The translators' solution was to write an introductory musical scene which gave the audience the knowledge to comprehend the language and style of the piece. The original French production opened with a spoken introduction by the character of Bob; there was no opening number. The trio of adaptors retained the convention of having Bob narrate, yet interwove his monologue with melodies from the title song, thus creating a musical sequence that set the scene clearly for the rest of the performance.

From the first line of dialogue, Heneker, Norman and More needed to settle the 1950s London audience and the Lord Chamberlain in one fell swoop and allow them to fully comprehend the piece straight from the start. Bob introduces the show as follows: 'Don't worry – it's quite suitable for the children. This is a story about passion, bloodshed, desire and death. Everything in fact that makes life worth living' (*Irma la Douce*, 1960, pp. 1–1–1.) The writers then immediately have Bob explain the argot in two ways, both verbally and visually: 'We call this part of Paris the "Mileu", where the only crime is to get caught . . . (he turns upstage, looking at the Gendarme) . . . and avoiding the Flics is our favourite pastime' (*Irma la Douce*, 1960, pp. 1–1–1).

After giving the theatregoers a brief lesson in French slang – which subconsciously tells them that it must be important information as it is explained at the very beginning of the show – the adaptors then permit the audience some mood and colour:

> This is the Paris that blossoms at night
> Hiding in whispers away from the light
> This is the Paris that turns in its sleep
> Up on the hill where the sad gutters weep
> (*Irma la Douce*, 1960, pp. 1–1–1)

They then gently introduce the eponymous character by describing her in slang, allowing the spectators to visualise her just as she subtly vocalises her profession, before giving the audience one final lesson in argot:

BOB: Now once upon a time there was a Poule. You don't know what a Poule is? You'll soon find out . . .

IRMA: . . . You've got the time, Cheri?
> Pretend my love is free
> And why not come with me
> Dancing the *Valse Mileu*

BOB: This is the way the Poule would earn money for her boss – or as we say in the Milieu, Grisbi for her Mec.

This is the system: Mec sends out Poule . . . Poule gets Grisbi . . . Grisbi goes
to Mec . . .

(IRMA and CLIENT waltz on . . . They twist and turn,
and HE gives her money . . .)

(*Irma la Douce*, 1960, pp. 1–1–2)

As a perfect opening number, this helps the theatregoers both visually and aurally
with grasping what the show is about. They are allowed to discover who the heroine is, what the slang actually means and why it has been retained in its original
language. The original Paris production did not require the 'Valse Milieu'; the
Parisian audience already had all that information from the real life on the streets
outside the Théâtre Gramont.

Most likely, Monnot did not compose a new piece of music for the 'Valse
Milieu' because she wasn't asked for one. The adaptors already had the perfect
piece of music; the melody of the title song. It fits the mood perfectly and thus
from the outset as a theme permeates the show, so that when it builds to be sung
in full in Act Two, it feels like the 11 o'clock number it deserves (or is required)
to be. Aside from composing one new piece of music for the British production,
a solo song for Irma entitled 'Bravo!', Monnot had little involvement with the
piece outside of France, while Breffort had even less, since he didn't speak English.
Seal recalls:

> I had to sing for Marguerite Monnot and David [Heneker] played the piano
> for me. The attitude was: 'Oh, this little English girl – there's no way she's
> going to be able to be Irma.' I had to sing 'The Language of Love', . . . and
> afterwards Marguerite Monnot kissed me and said: 'Merveilleux! Fantastique!'
> (Marvellous! Fantastic!). I had approval from the team, which was wonderful.
>
> *(Seal, 2020)*

Mirroring the Paris production, the rest of the cast was all-male; an unusual, yet
inspired artistic strategy, giving the piece its distinct vocal and visual individuality.
Keith Michell, a handsome and charismatic Australian actor, who was building a
successful career in the United Kingdom on the classical stage, on film and television, was cast as Nestor.[4] With his charm, physique and strong singing voice, he
had the required range to make the juxtaposition of the characters of Nestor and
Oscar believable. Michell's casting elevated the quality of the acting; he also had a
strong bond with Seal, which can be witnessed in a clip of the duo recreating the
duet *The Language of Love* in a rare television appearance from 1971, *Presenting Keith
Michell* (Mitchell and Seal, 1971).

To complete the dynamic trio of leading players, a further antipodean actor, Clive
Revill, was cast as Bob. Revill, like Michell a successful stage actor, brought creativity and flair to the role. A company of 12 inventive male performers completed
the cast, including many actors who would go on to achieve notable careers, such
as Ronald (Ronnie) Barker, Julian Orchard, Gary Raymond and Frank Olegario.

Brook's long-time collaborator Rolf Gérard, a notable opera and ballet designer, created the settings and costumes as well as drawing the delicately simple artwork adorning posters, programmes and published sheet music. The rest of the creative team was completed by Beaumont's highly regarded regular lighting designer Joe Davis; choreographer John Heywood, who had previously found success staging the dances for *The Boy Friend* (1954) in both London and New York; renowned composer and conductor Cyril Ornadel (as musical advisor) and Bert Waller who created the appealing vocal arrangements. His use of Christmas bells in the song 'Christmas Child', is particularly charming. Waller initially conducted the orchestra, although he was quickly succeeded by highly regarded conductor and composer Alexander Faris and film and theatre conductor Marcus Dodds during the London run.

The sound of *Irma*

The orchestrations for the London production were created by André Popp, whose career encompassed many spheres of the French popular music scene; arranging music for Jacques Brel's earliest albums, the top French female pop singers and many 'space age' experimental orchestral recordings. He was also a prolific composer and is probably best known for his popular pieces, 'Les Lavandières du Portugal/*The Portuguese Washerwomen*' and the hits songs 'L'amour est Bleu/*Love Is Blue*' and 'Tom Pillibi', the latter of which won the 1960 Eurovision Song Contest. Popp's contribution to *Irma la Douce* was paramount to the success of the show as he brought a genuine French orchestral texture to the score, at the same time imbuing the songs with theatricality; his use of percussion in the song 'That's a Crime' is a key example. His arrangement of the title song is obviously influenced by Piaf and demonstrates a clear trajectory to his work with Brel. A delightful piece of orchestration worthy of comment is Popp's use of flute in Irma's reprise of 'Our Language of Love' in Act Two. Using a small nine-piece instrumentation, Popp instantly creates a rich Parisian underworld atmosphere, enhanced by the use of tack-piano, xylophone and accordion. The audience can immediately inhabit the atmosphere of the back streets of Pigalle. Coincidentally, he also conducted and orchestrated a French studio cast recording of *Irma la Douce*, released in 1958, starring international French star Zizi Jeanmaire (*Irma la Douce*, 1958a). Although conjecture on this author's part, it is possible that the orchestration was initially created for that studio recording and then adapted for the London production under the supervision of Ornadel, Waller, Faris and Dodds; all theatre men, as a opposed to studio arranger Popp.

Irma en route to London

The British production of *Irma la Douce* had its out-of-London try-out in Bournemouth and Brighton during the summer of 1958; audiences responded favourably. Seal recounts:

> We didn't know if it was going to work. Binkie said: 'Bournemouth is far enough away, nobody's going to go there!' I don't think Peter [Brook] was

quite sure I'd be OK! After I'd done 'Dis-Donc', and the place erupted, I knew I absolutely had Peter on board as he could see the public liked me!

(Seal, 2020)

Although the piece was playing well, Seal recalls the book was substantially reworked en route to London; quite a lot of dialogue was changed: 'I don't think the "powers-that-be" realised that I could be quite funny. I did it instinctively – I wasn't trying to be clever' (Seal, 2020). The choreography required some additional work as audiences wanted to see more of Seal's dancing:

> Binkie said: 'We've got a find a place in Act Two where she can dance.' It was decided to put something in during the raft sequence . . . 'Freedom of the Seas' . . . but we didn't have any dance music, so I said: 'We've got the drums, haven't we? When we get to that point, play the drums, double it, and I will dance.' That's what I did. I made it up as I went along!
>
> *(Seal, 2020)*

This was perfected and entitled 'Fever Dance'.[5] One casualty of the try-out was Monnot's new song, 'Bravo!' Seal recalls:

> It was made for me to sing in Act Two when Irma had had her baby, or was waiting for her baby. Somehow it didn't have the weight we needed at that point and was replaced with a reprise of 'Language of Love'.
>
> *(Seal, 2020)[6]*

More's *Grab Me A Gondola* closed at the Lyric Theatre on 12 July, closely followed five days later by the opening of *Irma la Douce*, which was the last time Seal saw Monnot. The show was well received by the press, as were Seal and Michell, and audiences embraced the saucy topic, absurdist qualities and intimate nature of the production. The show ran for three years at the Lyric, totalling 1,512 performances. Throughout the run, Seal was succeeded by Shani Wallis and Mary Preston, while Michell was replaced with John Neville, Denis Quilley, Gerard Healy and Gary Raymond.

The original London cast recording is utterly charming (*Irma la Douce*, 1958b); the characters come alive, and it has abundant atmosphere – no doubt a result of the occasional use of dialogue throughout, which allowed the understated theatrical flair to be preserved.

The American Irma

Due to its London success, American producers began showing great interest in bringing the piece to New York. Very few London musicals had transferred to Broadway since the 1930s, therefore in order to ensure box-office appeal, financial security and a long run, those producers inevitably demanded an established star to open a potential Broadway production. As Seal remembers:

> It was ghastly! People were coming in to look at my performance. All the major stars: Juliette Gréco, Brigitte Bardot, Leslie Caron . . . you name

them . . . coming in to see if they'd like to do it. This went on for weeks and weeks and weeks. It upset me greatly. I had Donald Albury coming to my dressing room − literally at the half hour − saying: 'We're not taking you to Broadway. Those houses are so big − you wouldn't be able to fill them.' They had to hold the show one night, because I was so distraught.

(Seal, 2020)

Much as Beaumont had sought out Seal in her dressing room during the run of *Damn Yankees*, American producer David Merrick did the same at the Lyric Theatre: 'He walked into my dressing room. He was a big, big, successful Broadway producer . . . and he said: "Miss Seal, you *are* my Irma." He put the show back a season on Broadway, and waited for me.' (Seal, 2020). It was a gamble, but Merrick was a risk taker and *Irma la Douce* was a safe bet: a relatively small physical production that would take little time or cash outlay to remount; particularly as he took the leading players, director, set, costume and lighting designers with him. What he was determined to do, was give the show an additional sheen expected by American audiences; by engaging an American choreographer, enlivening the orchestrations and encouraging the adaptors to revisit the lyrics to some of the musical numbers to ensure that New York audiences could fully comprehend the piece. In particular, one song was considerably altered lyrically; even its title 'Tres Tres Snob' (taken from the original French title 'C'est Polyte-Le-Mou'), was amended to 'Sons of France' for Broadway. This fast-paced number, sung by the Mecs, immediately follows the gentle 'Valse Mileu' and introduces additional argot and plot as well as many of the characters. It was wise to revisit it for Broadway, as the masterly revision enhances the clarity of the song, without oversimplifying it for an American audience.

Onna White, a former Broadway dancer, who had attained immediate success choreographing her first Broadway musical, *The Music Man* (1957), was engaged to create the new dances for *Irma la Douce*. White, a lone-female choreographer on Broadway was an inspired choice by Merrick as the show was a musical featuring a lone-female protagonist. At the behest of Merrick, White came over to London to see the British production. Seal then travelled to America in advance of the Broadway rehearsals where she worked closely with White who interpolated Seal's special dance abilities into the numbers:

Onna was very clever. Before she choreographed anything, she said to me: 'I want to find out what you do that's great.' She worked out that I was very good at turns and turning split jumps . . . I could do kicks. She used them all!

(Seal, 2020)[7]

Although Andre Popp's orchestrations were used for Broadway, the musical side of the show underwent considerable revision. Veteran musical director Stanley Lebowsky was contracted to conduct the orchestra and enhance Waller's vocal arrangements. The added lustre Lebowsky brought to the show is preserved on the

Broadway cast album; in particular, the title number is greatly enhanced by his use of the male voices in the latter sections of the song.

A role almost unheard of in London musical theatre of the period was that of the dance music arranger whose task it was to work closely with the choreographer to ensure that the music and dances fit seamlessly together:

> [D]ance music is derived from the songs written for the score . . . the chore-ographer and dance arranger often sketch these numbers thematically; work them in sections, with the dancers; and then once the ideas formulate, assemble the pieces.
>
> *(Suskin, 2009, p. 194)*

The London production of *Irma la Douce* had no such position credited, but for Broadway, the job was undertaken by a young John Kander, at the start of his career. One of the main elements of the show he worked on was the 'Arctic Ballet' (when the Mecs are crossing the Ocean on a raft, having escaped from Devil Island) which replaced the 'Fever Dance':

> The Ballet in Act Two, was a brand-new part of the show. I remember it step-by-step. Onna and I worked very closely creating the ballet. She would say: 'John, can you play me some Penguin music?' She was such fun to work with. It was a very special time.
>
> *(Kander, 2020)*

As the main dance numbers underwent considerable revision, they required new orchestrations, thus Robert Ginzler, one of Broadway's finest and most highly regarded orchestrators,[8] was engaged to adapt Popp's arrangements where necessary. (Kander and Ginzler had already undertaken the same roles the previous year for the musical *Gypsy*.) Ginzler's excellent work, matched by strong musicianship (documented on the Broadway cast recording) expounds Popp's work and allows the score of *Irma la Douce* to achieve additional sparkle and sheen; this is particularly remarkable considering that the orchestra still only consisted of nine pieces. A pit band of such a small size was rare during the period, because Broadway theatres with a large seating capacity were under agreement with the American musician's union to pay for a set number of instrumentalists (usually around 25 pieces). These were called 'union houses', and producers of musicals were contractually obliged to pay these wages – irrespective of how many players were actually required for the show. As producers thus had to shell out for a set number of musicians anyway, it was standard to orchestrate for all of them; alternatively, the musicians would simply collect their payment but not actually play.

Don Pippin, Lebowsky's assistant on *Irma la Douce* recalls:

> *Irma* played at The Plymouth Theater – a non-union house. Merrick didn't have to pay for a large orchestra. For *Irma*, we had some of the finest

> Broadway musicians in the pit. It was wonderful to have an orchestra exactly the right size for the show.
>
> *(Pippin, 2020)*

The Plymouth Theater was considered a 'dramatic house': 'These range between 700 and 1,100 seats . . . For most of the period from about 1940 into the 1980s, union minimums were roughly . . . for a dramatic house twelve players' (Suskin, 2009, p. 235).

Revill and Michell reprised their roles, with Quilley taking over from the latter after six months. As with the London production, the supporting cast of male performers for the Broadway production included actors that would soon become a who's-who of American Theatre, TV and Film talent: Stuart Damon, Fred Gwynne, George S. Irving and Elliott Gould. Also in the cast was a young singer/dancer named Zack Matalon who would soon become Seal's husband.

Under Brook's direction and with the key trio of players in place, the American *Irma la Douce* retained the charm, effective storytelling and strong acting of its London incarnation. Kander recalls: 'At the start of the very first day of rehearsals, Peter [Brook] asked me to play 'Dis-Donc' to the cast. I played it very fast, and he said: "*That* is our show!"' (Kander, 2020). With White's choreography, Kander's dance music, Lebowsky's revised vocal arrangements and Ginzler's enhanced orchestrations, the show became a slick production able to compete with the big American musicals running concurrently on Broadway. The joyous and infectious Broadway cast recording is a wonderful testament to the production: from the vibrant 'Overture' to Seal's cry of joy 'the fireworks in the sky' during the title song, which makes for an utterly jubilant moment. It is a thrilling recording.

Following a short try-out in Washington, D.C., at the National Theater, *Irma la Douce* opened in New York where it was greeted enthusiastically. Merrick, famous for his advertising stunts, thoroughly utilised the Parisian setting to promote the Broadway production: he 'had sandwich men parade around midtown wearing French berets and, around their middle, portable pissoirs like those you see on the streets of Paris, with posters for *Irma la Douce*' (Kissel, 1993, p. 223). Merrick's publicity was enhanced by numerous nominations for the 1961 Tony Awards, with Seal winning 'Best Performance by a Leading Actress in a Musical' – an impressive achievement considering her much better-known competition: Julie Andrews for *Camelot*, Carol Channing for *Show Girl* and Nancy Walker for *Do Re Mi* – 'I was young, I took it in my stride . . . I didn't realise it was such a big deal!' (Seal, 2020). Overnight, Seal became the toast of Broadway. Kander recalls Seal's impact very clearly: 'The whole city adored Elizabeth. She was a bundle of loveable energy' (Kander, 2020).

On Broadway, Seal *was* the show. It is likely that the production would have had a much longer run had Seal not become pregnant. Rather than continue the show without Seal, Merrick closed the production – still doing well at the box office – after 524 performances. Given the show was a significant success on Broadway and that it was small enough to break even quite quickly, Merrick sent the show on a

FIGURE 6.3   The Broadway company of *Irma la Douce* perform 'Dis-Donc, Dis-Donc';
pictured from left to right: George Del Monte, Rudi Tronto (leaning
down), Fred Gwynne, Stuart Damon (head only), Elizabeth Seal, Zack
Matalon (legs only on stool), George S. Irving, Aric Lavie (half face),
Osborne Smith, Clive Revill (behind bar centre), Byron Mitchell (kneel-
ing), unknown and Eddie Gasper (leaning on table).

Source: Photo provided by the editor.

national tour starring Taina Elg and Denis Quilley. The producer cunningly had
Elg play the role in the last performance on Broadway (denying Seal that opportunity) so that he could bill the tour as 'Direct from Broadway'.

Life after *Irma*

Monnot did not witness the success of her music on Broadway first hand. She
continued to compose with various lyricists, and for a while her association with
Piaf continued to prove artistically and financially rewarding; particularly when
Piaf introduced 'Milord', a 1959 song with lyrics by Georges Moustaki. However,

once Piaf met composer Charles Dumont and found vast success with his 1956 song 'Non, je ne regrette rien' ('I Have No Regrets'), which she recorded in 1960, she gradually began to discard Monnot. This affected the composer considerably, and having neglected to undergo surgery for appendicitis, she died in 1961, aged just 58.

Brook developed an excellent working relationship with Merrick, which later led to the another incredibly well received Broadway transfer: in 1965, the producer imported Brook's hit production of Peter Weiss' play with music *The Persecution and Assassination of Jean-Paul Marat as Performed by the Inmates of the Asylum of Charenton under the Direction of the Marquis de Sade*. Musicals, however eluded Brook; a further collaboration with Norman and More, *The Perils of Scobie Prilt* (1963), produced by Albery and Beaumont and designed by Gerard, barely managed a week's run in Oxford. Heneker on the other hand found enormous success in the same year with *Half A Sixpence*, which then transferred to New York two years later with White choreographing and Lebowsky conducting.

Seal was asked to play *Irma* in Australia in 1961, but having performed the show for three years and having recently become the wife of Zack Matalon, decided against it. She took a break from performing, brought up three children, divorced Matalon, married photographer Michael Ward and then went back to performing, appearing (among other productions) in the 1976 London revival of *Salad Days*, the original London staging of *Chicago* (1979), the 1983 Broadway revival of the play *The Corn is Green* and the 2012/3 London revival of Ivor Novello's *Gay's The Word*.

International *Irma*

Irma la Douce proceeded to find an international audience. Various key productions included performances in Australia (1961), Germany (1961/2), the Netherlands (1961) and South Africa (1961). As with many musicals of this period, the film rights were sold for a considerable sum. Yet the 1962 screen adaptation, directed by Billy Wilder and starring Shirley MacLaine and Jack Lemmon differs greatly from the stage show most significantly in that the songs were cut with Monnot's score being relegated to background music.[9] Although the film bears little resemblance to the musical, its box-office success allowed the title of the musical version to stay in the public mind; something which aided further productions of the stage show.

The work continued to be performed globally throughout the 1960s and 70s, with many stagings receiving cast recordings. Notable presentations include a Parisian revival in 1967 starring Colette Renard and René Dupry reprising their original roles (*Irma la Douce*, 1967) and a short-lived 1979 London revival starring Helen Gelzer and Charles Dance. An acclaimed actor-musician production was directed by John Doyle at the Watermill Theatre Newbury with revisions by Norman and More, while a 2015 revised Parisian adaptation at the Théâtre de la Porte Saint-Martin starred married couple Marie-Julie Baup and Lorànt Deutsch. Intriguingly, both of these stagings used a female actress in the role of Bob-Le-Hotu.

However, a concert staging by Doyle for the New York City Center *Encores!* series in 2014 was poorly received, with *The New York Times* labelling the piece a 'rusty relic' (Isherwood, 2014). One major stumbling block for modern audiences seems to be that Irma is so gullible not to realise that Nestor and Oscar are one and the same person. Yet because this constitutes one of the key plot points, the question is whether theatregoers today might still allow themselves to accept the artifice of this farcical element. Sixty years ago, the comic timing and artful delivery of the leads clearly charmed the audience and thus helped them to go along with the far-fetched story-telling conceit. Perhaps the musical is not really suited for our more jaded era with its less rose-coloured view of streetwalkers. Seal contemplates: 'I think times have changed. At that time, Paris was this fairy tale place. *Irma la Douce* is a fairy story. It needs an innocence and naivety. It's a delicate piece' (Seal, 2020).

Breffort died in 1971 having lived in luxury in Valais, Switzerland, from the enormous royalties brought in by a short story that became the foundation of an international hit, both as a stage musical and a film: *Irma la Douce*. He was purported to declare: 'I am the only man who lives honourably from a prostitute' (quoted in Merlin, 1966, p. 316).

Acknowledgement

The author wishes to thank Richard Stirling for his help with translating the French texts.

Discography

Irma la Douce. (1967) Live Recording of the French Revival Cast with Colette Renard and René Dupry. CD: Vega 465–826–832.
———. (1961) South African Cast Recording. Album: RCA 30122.
———. (1960) Original Broadway Cast Recording. CD: Sony Broadway 48018.
———. (1958a) French Studio Cast Recording with Zizi Jeanmaire. Album: Philips B76093R. (Selections are available on CD: Sepia 1120).
———. (1958b) London Cast Recording. CD: Sepia 1120.
———. (1956) French Cast Recording with Colette Renard. Album: Disques Vogue EPS 7 300. (Selections available on CD: Sepia 1120).
La P'tite Lili. (1951) CD: Milan Music 399 651–652.

Notes

1 In 1960 the song found enormous popularity in Japan as 'Ai no sanka' in a version by singer Fubuki Koshiji.
2 There are some additional songs in the score by other writers, including Charles Aznavour, although the majority are by Monnot/Piaf/Achard.
3 The programme of the production at Théâtre Gramont actually lists only three instruments: piano, bass and guitar. (Anon, 1956, unpaginated.)
4 Michell is billed as 'By courtesy of The Rank Organisation' in the programme of the British production (Anon, 1958, unpaginated).
5 Seal originally wanted Kenneth MacMillan to choreograph; she believes Beaumont was worried that the two egos of MacMillan and Brook would not gel (Seal, 2020).

6 The song 'Bravo!' was included in the 1961 South African production and can be heard on the rare cast recording (RCA 30122). The song was also published in the United Kingdom in the More-Heneker-Norman translation by Trafalgar Music Ltd. Study of it backs up Seal's comment; it feels inappropriate for the position in Act Two, Seal describes.
7 Some of Seal's skills can be observed on an unnamed 1961 American TV variety show where she performs the song 'Hey, Look Me Over', choreographed by Peter Gennaro (Elizabeth Seal, 1961).
8 Ginzler's career encompassed orchestrations for many celebrated musicals including *Bye, Bye, Birdie* (1960) and *How to Succeed In Business Without Really Trying* (1961).
9 A similar fate befell the 1961 film adaptation of the Merrick-produced 1954 Broadway musical *Fanny*: all of the songs by Harold Rome were either cut or used as underscoring.

References

Anon. (1958) *Irma la Douce*. Programme. London: Saville Theatre.
———. (1956) *Irma la Douce*. Programme. Paris: Théâtre Gramont.
Breffort, A. (1956) 'Sleeve Notes,' *Irma la Douce* (1956). French Cast Recording. Album: Disques Vogue EPS 7 300.
Deutsch, D. (1991) 'Sleeve Notes,' *Irma la Douce* (1960). Original Broadway Cast Recording. CD: Sony Broadway 48018.
Huggett, R. (1989) *Binkie Beaumont. Eminence Grise of the West End Theatre 1933–1973*. London: Hodder & Stoughton.
Irma la Douce. (1960) 'Music by Marguerite Monnot,' Original Book and lyrics by Alexandre Breffort. English Book and Lyrics by Julian More, David Heneker and Monty Norman. Unpublished manuscript. New York.
Isherwood, C. (2014) 'Tis Pity She's a . . . Busy Young Professional,' *The New York Times*, 8 May 2014, www.nytimes.com/2014/05/09/theater/irma-la-douce-back-on-the-streets.html, accessed 15 February 2020.
Kander, J. (2020) Telephone Interview with the composer, 1 March.
Kissel, H. (1993) *David Merrick: The Abominable Showman*. New York: Applause Books.
Laurent, F. (2015) 'Sleeve Notes,' *La P'tite Lili*. *La P'tite Lili* (1951). CD: Milan Music 399 651–652.
Merlin, L. (1966) *C'était formidable! Mémoires*. Tome II. Paris: éditions René Julliard.
Mitchell, K. and Seal, E. (1971) 'Our Language of Love,' www.youtube.com/watch?v=wvpCEnebk8A, accessed 15 February 2020.
Mordden, E. (2001) *Open A New Window. The Broadway Musical in the 1960s*. New York: St. Martin's Press.
More, J. (1999) 'Programme Notes,' *Irma la Douce*. Programme. 1999 revival, Bagnor: The Watermill Theatre. Unpaginated.
Pippin, D. (2020) Telephone interview with the Assistant Musical Director, Wednesday 19th February.
Seal, E. (2020) Interview with the Actress. London, 29 January.
———. (1961) 'Elizabeth Seal – Hey, Look Me Over – 1961,' www.youtube.com/watch?v=10okXhLU3Co, accessed 15 February 2020.
Suskin, S. (2009) *The Sound of Broadway Music. A Book of Orchestrators and Orchestrations*. New York: Oxford University Press.

PART III
Hollywood Paris

7

THE CAPITAL OF PRE-CODE OPERETTAS

Paris at Paramount and MGM

Marguerite Chabrol

Ernst Lubitsch's definition of 'Paris Paramount' is one of the most cited jokes in Hollywood history. 'There is Paramount Paris, and Metro Paris, and of course the real Paris. But Paramount's is the most Parisian of all' (Corlis and Clarens, 1978, p. 31; Eyman, 1993, p. 197). Another version of that quotation is 'I've been to Paris, France, and I've been to Paris Paramount. Paris Paramount is better' (Bingen and Wanamaker, 2017, p. 7). Both foreground the supposedly genuine 'Parisianness' of Paramount films. Among other real or fantasy European capitals, Paris was indeed a major diegetic place in the studios' early sound films, particularly the operettas featuring Maurice Chevalier and Jeanette MacDonald: *The Love Parade* (Lubitsch, 1929), *One Hour with You* (Lubitsch assisted by George Cukor, 1932) and *Love Me Tonight* (Rouben Mamoulian, 1932). The cycle ended at MGM with *The Merry Widow* (Lubitsch, 1934). Though outstandingly successful at first, these operettas did not survive the commercial failure of *The Merry Widow*. As Tino Balio explains (1993, p. 214), not only was it a casualty of the Hays Office but 'the producers of the picture were [also] out of touch with the audience'. Whilst Paris would reappear as a fantasy setting in later Hollywood musicals, the mid-1930s audiences preferred Busby Berkeley's backstage films (Warner Bros.), rooted in the New York of the Great Depression, or Astaire and Rogers' more American romantic comedies (at RKO).

Lubitsch's words could suggest that the French settings were more realistic and accurately designed at Paramount. Art director Boris Leven considered Paramount to value that field, and according to him, German decorator Hans Dreier, invited by Lubitsch, set up a freer atmosphere than Cedric Gibbons, his counterpart at MGM, ever did, and thus stimulated the creativity of his team (Corlis and Clarens, 1978, p. 49). But a close look at the settings of the early 1930s Paris musicals reveals that the city does not necessarily provide a picturesque *décor*, contrary to non-musical films like *Design for Living* (Lubitsch, 1933). The operettas foreground it neither as the 'City of Light', full of attractions from the late 19th and early 20th centuries, nor as the capital of vibrant entertainment and cabarets depicted in Robert Siodmak's 1936 *La Vie Parisienne* (Phillips, 2004). The Paris of 1930s film operettas is also not the pictorial city of 1950s Hollywood musicals, that of the *belle époque* and Toulouse-Lautrec (Schwartz, 2007, pp. 19–53). Far from being mainly the paradigm of European art, Paris is rather an imaginary space constructed by sound and a set of conventions implying a pact with the audience. The Lubitsch and Mamoulian musicals entwine several pre-existing aspects of Paris, thus building their own myth: the sentimental and romantic Paris from the popular 'Paris songs'; the place for sexual freedom inherited from theatrical traditions (the entertaining 'Gay Paree' or the setting of French farces); and a city socially divided between working class and aristocracy, between the underworld of *Apaches* – Parisian ruffians or gangsters – and highbrow social rituals. That composite myth of Paris is common to both studios, but does not exclude the very nuances expressed in Lubitsch's view.

International Paris and cosmopolitan films

Before the early film musicals, Paris was already prevalent in American popular culture through songs. The epitome of bohemian cosmopolitanism (to American eyes), Paris was both the capital of entertainment and a place inspiring nostalgia, as many artists had experienced a stay there. Paris was celebrated by international stars, especially in a Franco-American mirror effect: Josephine Baker was as popular in Paris as Maurice Chevalier was to become in the United States. The 'Paris song' was a genre in itself, and the lyrics of many American songs from the 1910s and 1920s celebrated Paris in the way 19th century French stage operettas did (Blaszkiewicz, 2018, p. 71). Mistinguett garnered international acclaim with 'Ça c'est Paris' in 1926, as did Baker with 'J'ai deux amours (mon pays et Paris)' ('I have two loves, my country and Paris') in 1930. On Broadway stages, Paris had been endowed with a particular erotic appeal since the early 20th century. Cole Porter's *Paris* (1928) turned Irene Bordoni into the ultimate fashionable French woman (though the title song is not by Porter). She embodied the 'naughty' French attitude: Bodoni's hits from *Paris*, '(Let's Do It) Let's Fall in Love' and 'Let's Misbehave', have obvious Parisian overtones, although the city is not mentioned in the titles. Hays' Studio Relations Committee (SRC, the predecessor of the Production Code Administration) actually observed that the dialogue in *The Love Parade* recalled the contents of Bordoni's songs (Anon, 1929, 'Heron'). 'Should I misbehave?', asks Chevalier in the song 'Oh That Mitzi!' (*One Hour with You*): everyone knows indeed that Paris is definitely the place to 'misbehave'.

Paris is sometimes represented more as a brand than as a place. The first version of the stage musical *Gay Paree* (1925) did not even take place there, but the name is a signal for frivolity, pleasure, comedy. Its 1926 incarnation includes a few songs about France whose titles summarise the archetypes later to be found in the Chevalier movies: songs praising the city ('There Never Was a Town Like Paris') and love songs ('Je T'aime [Means I Love You]'). On Broadway, the presence of Paris in a show title (like *A Night in Paris*, 1926, and other lavish Shubert revues) advertised exotic numbers (not necessarily French, but also African, German, Venetian . . .). Gay Paree typified the cosmopolitan capital in the late 1920s.

Some numbers in the film operettas rely on the standard tropes of the Paris songs of the time, except for *One Hour with You*, because the story takes place entirely in Paris. 'Paris, Stay the Same', by a Chevalier leaving the city in *The Love Parade*, initially has the sentimental tone of many Paris songs, immediately replaced by erotic innuendo, when all the women he is leaving behind appear to share his nostalgia. In *The Merry Widow*, the recurring 'Melody of Laughter', whose lyrics praise 'a melody of Paris in the Spring', is the typical Gay Paris song: MacDonald first sings it when she decides to drop her mourning by anticipating her stay in France. She, typically, performs it in lingerie, which is also a way to associate the French capital with refined and erotic underwear.

As exotic as it may feel to American audiences, the Paris of Hollywood operettas is also meant to be seen by foreign audiences, including French ones. What Vanessa Schwartz showed about the 1950s musicals – the fact that Paris is a privileged setting when film production has an international scope (Schwartz, 2007) – holds true for the 1930s. Film operettas are made transnational by the directors and participants' diverse nationalities. But Paramount might also have been especially sensitive to French topics at a time when American producers needed to reconquer European markets. Indeed, their domination was challenged by sound (and dialogue in native languages) as well as by the growing protectionism of European countries (Vincendeau, 1988, p. 28). Paramount was one of the Hollywood majors most strongly established in Paris, with its foreign office located there and with its sound stages in Joinville where films were shot in French for the local public.

The prestige film operettas were made in Hollywood, but most were shot in multiple versions. Some early talkies were commonly shot several times in different languages instead of being dubbed (Barnier, 2004). These operettas rank among the most famous of all multiple language films, because they feature major stars like Chevalier and MacDonald who could recreate their parts in French. The original *Love Parade* was reedited by Paramount to become *Parade d'amour*, with the English dialogue but with its songs translated into French (Barnier, 2004, p. 36). *One Hour with You* and *The Merry Widow* were made in full French versions in order to sell the recordings of the songs in two languages (Barnier, 2004, p. 37). *Love Me Tonight* is the exception, but the SRC Files confirm that the film was clearly meant for a French audience too: the Hays Office was deeply preoccupied with the image of French characters, especially the 'Royalists' who might be hurt by their depiction.[1] (Indeed a scene where MacDonald whips her domestic servant was cut.)

Sophisticated pleasures: Pre-Code Hollywood

Lubitsch's operettas, like his contemporary comedies, are considered typical of the so-called 'Pre-Code' era, the period between the writing of the Production Code in 1930 and its full application by the Administration (PCA) founded in 1934

(Balio, 1993; Doherty, 1999). This was not a time of complete freedom. Films were already under surveillance, but they mostly underwent cuts from local censorship boards rather than self-censorship, often because the production process did not follow the SRC's suggestions. The PCA was created halfway through the production of *The Merry Widow* and the film has suffered slightly more than the previous films, but still resisted many rewritings as we will see.

Chicago or New York – whether they are explicitly named or not – are the Pre-Code capitals of gangster films. Paris is that of comedies and musicals. The Motion Picture Producers and Distributors of America (MPPDA) archives show that the operettas were aimed at a mature audience. Within the industry and the world of critics, they were, at first, more 'sophisticated' – the word is often used, in connection with Lubitsch, or French culture – than utterly transgressive, though they appeared simply immoral in the eyes of some local censors. Paramount was indeed the most 'sophisticated' studio in the Pre-Code era: alongside Lubitsch its lead personalities were Mae West, Marlene Dietrich and Josef von Sternberg. *The Love Parade*, for example, met remarkably good reviews, but raised local protests in Palo Alto, CA (AMPAS), from admirers of Chevalier's first American film, *Innocents of Paris* (1929), who disapproved of what they saw as the star's immoral turn. The censorship boards' reactions to the prologue of the film in Paris were not consistent: in Pennsylvania or Alberta, it was partially cut and the film had to start with the ambassador's arrival (AMPAS). The stereotypical French comic adultery was impossible according to conservative conventions. But in other places, the Parisian sequence remained and the censors rather focused on another scene showing MacDonald in bed and in her bath. This suggests that for some, the French stereotypes allowed some license and made the introduction more comic than morally subversive.

The Paris operettas all operated on what was at the time a thin line between frivolity and vulgarity. *The Love Parade* 'is light, sophisticated, frivolous [*sic*], but never vulgar' (Anon, 1929, 'Fischer'). In *Love Me Tonight*, only one song was problematic ('A Woman Needs Something Like That'), but

> [t]here is such a real place in pictures for the delightful and clever Chevalier pictures that it is more than ever important not to jeopardize that field by going too far beyond the line between the risqué into the suggestive.
>
> *(Anon, 1932, 'Joy')*

In 1934, the new PCA envisioned *The Merry Widow* in a similar manner and first perceived its lightness. But after negative public reactions, PCA Head Joseph Breen expressed afterthoughts: '[T]he picture as it now stands is not the light, gay, frivolous, operetta which it is intended that it should be but rather the typical French farce that is definitely bawdy and offensively – in spots – suggestive' (Anon, 1934). Lubitsch in particular benefited from strong artistic recognition, which reinforced the 'sophisticated' reading of the operettas within the Hays Office. The creation of the PCA did not change that notion. But the public reception did, the Legion of Decency in particular being responsible for redefining vulgarity and immorality within the industry. Initially, Breen shared the views of his predecessors on sophisticated comedies and musicals (as less dangerous than criminal stories), which explains his first reaction about *The Merry Widow*. But although he changed his mind, the film production actually resisted many of his suggestions.

Paris as a code

The Chevalier–MacDonald operettas worked well in the Pre-Code context precisely because they suggested (including in heavy-handed ways) more than they showed. The Hays Office initially did not censor the content (sex) as long as it was expressed symbolically. Paris played a part in that process. In the films, the city is less a picturesque setting than a set of codes, conventions and winks to the audience, which fits in with Lubitsch's style, understood by the Hays Office as the elegant treatment of disgraceful matters. Rick Altman pointed out that these films were the most explicit among what he calls 'fairy tale musicals', for they treat 'sex as sex' (1987, p. 141). The French culture, capital and language all provided immediate symbolism for that purpose: phrases like 'Ooo, la, la' (also the title of a song in *The Love Parade*), the words 'French' or 'Paris' are in themselves passwords. The codes work as well in publicity. The press book for *One Hour with You* does not promote the attractive features of the French capital, but summarises everything in the word 'it'. Maurice Chevalier has 'got that thing called "It!"' – like Clara Bow had previously. The opening argument in French at the beginning of *Love Parade* obviously means that the dispute is about sex even if the language is not understandable to everyone. Every 'Madame' or 'Monsieur' in *One Hour with You* is fraught with innuendo. The SRC sometimes singled out those words. In *The Love Parade*, it requested in vain to cut the line: 'I lost my independence, but I had a terrific French accent [referring to an affair with a French woman]' (Anon, 1929, 'Sell'). When Paramount asked for the re-issue seal in 1936, Breen was more careful with the mentions of France or Paris and asked for a removal in the lyrics of 'Anything to Please the Queen': 'A good night watchman I will be; I learned that duty in Paris.'

Many reviewers or scholars have underlined that Paris is equal to pleasure and desire in Hollywood films (De Baecque, 2012). As Nancy Schwartz cleverly put it in her discussion of *The Merry Widow:* 'Paris represents joy, music, sensuality – an id to Marshovia's superego' (Schwartz, 1975, p. 15). To be more specific, 'Paris' means 'sex' as different both from love (sentiment) and social order (marriage as an institution). In *The Love Parade*, Chevalier is punished for his adulterous affair by having to leave Paris. In *The Merry Widow*, ironically, the king punishes him for the same crime by sending him *to* Paris – obviously a reward! Before Reno became the ultimate divorce location, Paris was the place for it. At the end of *The Love Parade*, during the opera scene, Chevalier declares his intention to go back to Paris to get a divorce. The expression 'a Paris divorce' was as commonplace as 'a Paris affair' and both meant the separation of married couples. The press book of *The Merry Widow* offers a novelisation including a dialogue between Danilo and the King which is a little spicier than that in the film:

KING: Ever been in Paris?
DANILO: I spend all my holidays there, Your Majesty.
KING: So you know Paris.
DANILO: You want some addresses, Your Majesty?
KING: No, no, I'm a married man. Are you married?
DANILO: No, Your Majesty.
KING: You don't know what you're missing.

Paris is definitely incompatible with marriage. It is more implicit in the film, but nonetheless true, even for the main couple who has to get married back in Marshovia. When the story has multiple locations, Paris is only a place for evasion, not for resolution or denouement. Moreover, Paris is the only possible city which is suggestive of prostitution and sexual arrangements in parks (the opening of *One Hour with You*) or in private salons (*The Merry Widow*). After the Code became enforced, that convention remained and is alluded to in *Camille* (George Cukor, MGM, 1936) and *Angel* (Lubitsch, Paramount, 1937). One of the cuts made to the *Widow* was a shot of a sign 'French Massage in All Languages – Madame Louise'. Breen also perfectly understood that '[t]he Café Maxim's, of course, is nothing more than a high-class whore house' (1934, AMPAS). He demanded that the film never implied prostitution and was fearful about the use of 'the dining room upstairs'. But most of the required removals were not made, and that sequence kept its intended flavour.

Paris is sometimes described as one utopia among others in American film musicals (Altman, 1987, p. 158). But it is not simply any imaginary kingdom. Except for *One Hour with You*, it is part of a dialectical process typical of the duality that Altman pointed out in the musical genre, one that can be expressed as a number of oppositions: male/female, city/country, common/aristocratic, Chevalier/MacDonald (1987, pp. 45–58, 154). In *The Love Parade* and *The Merry Widow*, Paris is opposed to a more unrealistic 'mythical kingdom', the old Europe with its customs and royal courts. In *Love Me Tonight*, the other polarity is the French countryside where the aristocracy lives. This world of fox-hunting and masked balls in 18th century costumes also seems to belong to older times. Compared to these worlds, Paris feels modern and free of social conventions.

Between French farce and Viennese operetta

American operettas inherited features from the Viennese tradition, while the Viennese operetta in turn 'borrows from nineteenth-century French boulevard comedy' (Altman, 1987, p. 140). It notably inherited diplomatic themes and a parallel between international and sexual intrigues. Breen was right in labelling the *Widow* a 'typical French farce', for this theatrical genre was the basis for many international types of comedies. The expression 'French farce' is not always mentioned; it is even silenced in film promotion, for in puritan eyes it is immoral. But this genre also has a direct link with American comedies and, since the Sardou play *Divorçons* (1880), many others have been translated. French theatre has enjoyed a long-standing presence on American stages, with many adapters specialising in keeping the English versions 'quite close to the originals while cleaning them up for a more moralistic audience' (Brewster, 2001, p. 373). Lubitsch's films owe much to French farces; this is especially the case with *Bluebeard's Eighth Wife* (1937) and *That Uncertain Feeling* (1941) (Chabrol, 2016). All Chevalier-MacDonald operettas are more or less directly based on straight plays, sometimes via a musical version. *The Love Parade* is adapted from *The Prince Consort* by Leon Xanrof and Jules Chancel, a play that opened on Broadway in 1905. *Love Me Tonight* is based on a 1924 French play that was never staged on Broadway, *Le Tailleur au Château / The Tailor in the Castle*, by Léopold Marchand and Paul Armont. *One Hour with You* extends silent films that Lubitsch directed at Warner Bros. It is the musical remake of *The Marriage Circle* (1924), adapted from another French play; the adultery is also reminiscent of *This Is Paris* (1926). All these stories about married couples distinctly recall the pattern of the operetta *Die Fledermaus*, also an adaptation of a French farce, *Le Réveillon* (1872), by Meilhac and Halévy (see Brewster, 2001). *The Merry Widow*, one of the most famous operettas on American stages in the early 20th century, is adapted from *L'Attaché d'ambassade* (1861).

FIGURE 7.1 Mitzi (Genevieve Tobin) consults her best friend's husband (Maurice Chevalier) as a doctor, which starts the French farce's mechanics of *One Hour with You* (1932).

Source: Publicity still provided by the editor.

Those dramatic sources are perceptible in the film operettas and account for the fact that Paris constitutes more a key to the narrative structure than a spectacular place for visitors. The quantity of musical numbers is indeed relatively limited: there are fewer numbers in the Chevalier-MacDonald films (less than a quarter of the whole film's length) than in the contemporary Berkeley or Astaire-Rogers musicals (about a third). In the operettas, the numbers sometimes end early in the narrative and there is no final one (*One Hour with You, Love Me Tonight*), or there is a very short musical ending, after a long time without any number, during which the couple's separation and reconciliation is foregrounded (*Love Parade, Merry Widow*). These films thus rely very much on farcical dramaturgy. *The Love Parade* has a typical French farce ending, showing the couple in a bedroom and hiding the bed where everyone knows the real denouement is going to take place. Paris is also a frequent location in French farces and as the staging of *This Is Paris* (1926) clearly demonstrates (with its two opposite apartments), what is important is not so much the visual quality of the city than the fact that it is a place that allows free movement.

These features might be related to the ambition to reach the French audience. Analysing the reception of multiple version films in France, Ginette Vincendeau underlines: 'Clearly, the major element in box-office appeal was not production values, but the audience's familiarity with certain narrative patterns' (Vincendeau, 1988, p. 35). She then quotes a commentary from the 1930s[2] and concludes:

> What is brought out here is the crucial importance of intertextual familiarity with genres and narrative patterns in the source material – in this case the boulevard play and its archetypal plot revolving around illegitimacy and adultery – for audience appeal and identification.

It seems that some American audiences were receptive to that template too, especially in comedies, as it remained present on stages (and screens until the PCA redirected the narratives). In spite of its long theatrical tradition, this pattern was perceived as 'modern' as far as morals and lifestyles are concerned.

In the film operettas, the on-screen fidelity of the stars is the opposite of what is implied in the stories: Chevalier's character (and sometimes MacDonald's) have multiple sex partners and the very integrated musical numbers are the main place where this is expressed quite freely. Lubitsch's and Mamoulian's stagings often give a musical form to that narrative. The serial lover Chevalier has many list songs about his partners (whether girlfriends or possibly prostitutes), more than any other male lead of the time. Thus 'Paris, Stay the Same' (*Love Parade*), or 'Girls, Girls, Girls' (*Widow*) are strong opening statements, all the more so than they are made in Paris (for the second version of the song in *Widow*). Even his love song to MacDonald in *Love Parade* is a list song ("My Love Parade"), although she is supposed to be all girls at once. MacDonald visually gets her revenge in *Merry Widow*, when during 'Widows Are Rich' she waltzes with numerous men. In *The Merry*

Widow, the remarkable dance numbers take place in Paris, whether at Maxim's or the Marshovian Embassy. William Paul closely analysed the 'new sense of space in Paris' compared to the earlier scenes (1983, pp. 103–111). In the operettas, Paris is associated with mobility (often indicated by camera movements) and a broadening of possibilities and connections between characters. The number carrying the central theme, 'One Hour with You' could only happen there, even if the ballroom decoration is not typically French. This ensemble number shows all possible combinations of the couples – the very principle of the farce – and it visually summarises the narrative scheme. This number stands out in the film as it is the only one that starts as a diegetic song (played by the band). The situation then becomes more ambivalent when the main characters start singing and the ending is blurred, with the music continuing in the background as underscoring. These fluctuations in the nature of the number also underline the fluidity and volatility of the moment, in ways typical of what can happen in Paris in a Pre-Code film. Although the lyrics are clearly a romantic love declaration, the staging never takes them seriously and puts them into perspective.

Distance and humour, embodied in particular by Chevalier, are indeed another feature of the French style in those films. The reviews of the star's American films point out that these qualities are inherently attached to his persona. His frequent addresses to the camera, omnipresent in *One Hour with You*, are understood as mostly ironic and establish a complicity with the audience. They also recall his status as a music-hall performer (Altman, 1987, p. 146). One of the differences between the studios is that *The Merry Widow* tries to counterbalance the distancing, although humour remains very much present (the lyrics of 'Melody of Laughter' state that 'It's Paris and it's playtime'). Chevalier stops speaking or singing to the camera after the introductory 'Girls, Girls, Girls', which is a brief reminder of what is expected from him. In the press book, Lubitsch explains how he had to balance distance and seriousness to satisfy American audiences:

> We tried to blend the American and European viewpoints in the story. The lilting Viennese music is, in this country [the United States], associated with sheer romance, and viewed with more seriousness than in Vienna where it rather represents gayety [*sic*] and happiness more than romance and love.

The film is indeed more suffused by romanticism and is a hybrid between the French farce tradition and the American romantic notion of the waltz. It is the only Chevalier-MacDonald film where the couple actually dances and the waltz takes on a special meaning at the crossroads of highbrow art and popular lyricism (Schwartz, 1975). The film publicity clearly intends to 'Americanise' the movie compared to older operettas. Indeed, Paris-Paramount was utterly theatrical in its disregard for conventions, whereas Paris-MGM is divided between fun and romanticism. Less French is spoken in the MGM film, implying a little less sex and a little more sentimentality.

Paris as spectacle

In *Love Parade* and *The Merry Widow*, the Central European countries provide scope for lavish and monumental settings that find no match in the French capital. Showing too much of Paris would probably ruin the fantasy. Even if Mamoulian gives Paris a strong visual presence at the beginning of *Love Me Tonight*, most scenes rely on off-screen dynamics, triggered by the verbal codes I have described, as well as by the soundtrack (French tunes or Paris songs as underscoring) and Maurice Chevalier's image.

Surprisingly, the Paris operettas make no abundant use of the typical montage sequences that can be found in contemporary American films: the realistic ones (series of location shots of the streets of Paris, famous places, cafés, like at the beginning of the Chevalier vehicle *Playboy of Paris* or *Half Shot at Sunrise*, an RKO musical; both 1930), and the festive ones (shots of the Moulin Rouge, champagne bottles, Folies-Bergères girls . . .). In the American stage tradition, as well as in many Hollywood films from the 1920s and 1930s, Paris was in itself a spectacle providing dazzling attractions: the *café chantant* in *Zaza* (on stage and in the 1923 film), the jewellery from Place Vendôme, which can be seen in other Paramount films like *Desire*, the world of fashion (the ironic publicity song 'Colet and Company' in another Lubitsch film, *Trouble in Paradise*, accompanies a montage sequence about fashion). Many clichés are actually absent from the operettas, especially at Paramount. The beginning of *Love Parade* makes a statement on that issue: the opening credits show the French magazine *La Vie Parisienne* – a composite shot features a champagne bottle, a revue, the Eiffel Tower and the Moulin Rouge, but none of these takes on a specific meaning afterwards and they remain no more than subtext.

Instead of showing Paris as a series of postcards, the operettas evince the sense that the city enjoys an especially vibrant energy, its own rhythm and movement, and a magic way to connect characters. The numbers located there are often ensemble songs with several characters taking over the same melody ('Paris, Stay the Same' in *Love Parade*, 'Song of Paree' in *Love Me Tonight*, 'One Hour with You' in *One Hour with You*), or having a virtual dialogue in song ('I'm Going to Maxim's/A Melody of Laughter' in *The Merry Widow*). There is definitely an 'increase in vitality felt with the introduction to Paris' (Paul, 1983, p. 106). The innovative sense of rhythm in 'Song of Paree' has been often noted: it has been employed as a parallel to René Clair's aesthetics in *Under the Roofs of Paris* (1930), but it is also inspired by Mamoulian's own staging of *Porgy* (1927) on Broadway (Altman, 1987, p. 299; Jacobs, 2015). The director significantly associates the same aesthetics with on the one hand a Black neighbourhood in Charleston (South Carolina) and on the other with working-class Paris. As in Gershwin's musical piece *An American in Paris* (1928), the French capital is perceived as swarming with an exotic energy, which makes it an epitome of modernity.

MGM's Gay Paree

The Merry Widow is the only film in the cycle to resort to the more conventional spectacle of Paris in order to meet American taste. It is the only operetta of the four to significantly promote 'Gay Paree' in the advertisements (even if it is not the prime angle). It resembles the stage shows inspired by French farces: the American versions re-enact the stories with a little less bluntness and a few more picturesque details. A typical example, the show *Gay Paree* (1899) related how a married couple found new partners during their honeymoon and added a can-can and numbers in refined lingerie (Bordman, 2001, p. 189), all stereotypes which are also present in the 1934 *Merry Widow*.

Paradoxically, the only can-can scene in the operetta cycle was shot during the 'conservative retreat' (Paul, 1983, p. 89) of Lubitsch at MGM and while the PCA strengthened its control on films. The editing of that number is of note in Hollywood historiography, for in 1935, Paramount mentioned it to prove to the Breen Office that the can-can was not technically forbidden (Anon, 1934, 'Kelly and Breen'), contrary to fan dances for example. The exotic appeal of the can-can seems to have justified its on-screen survival, though in a very mild version. *The Merry Widow* has strong erotic overtones and the major difference to the Paramount operettas is not so much conservatism as the fact that this eroticism meets the stereotypical expectation of American audiences. According to Breen, 'the shot of Sonia partially undressed has a Minsky flavor' (Anon, 1934, 'Breen'), which addresses the thin line between chic French lingerie and vulgar American burlesque. Even if the PCA tried to remove the can-can (Anon, 1934), what was sacrificed was a heavy comment in the dialogue ('I've heard that's where a man can see ladies dance the can-can') and some close-ups of the legs and garters. Breen helped to edit the scene, after being invited to do so by Lubitsch (Anon, 1934, 'Thalberg'). The film publicity tried to make the short can-can seem naughtier than it actually was: '[T]he dance that startled the whole world with its "naughtiness" and for several years was the byword that summed up all the frothiness of gay Paris, has been brought to the talking screen in its original form and surroundings.' It made use of a voyeuristic argument: 'To have seen it is to have achieved the ultimate sophistication, even in these days of bolder "fan dances" and similar offerings.' Lubitsch's directing and Albertina Rasch's choreography make the scene both abstract in the close shots and picturesque in the large ones. The contrasted black and white costumes give the impression of a cartoon, which makes the image stand out. Though the number is concise, it is striking enough visually and musically to make the spectator believe he has seen a true can-can.

The press book nevertheless suggests that Paris was not the biggest attraction in the film. The embassy set was the actual asset: it is located in Paris, but with its stricter ballroom dancing it is culturally a Marshovian space. Moreover, the press book, obviously published before the final cut, mentions another 'Paris song' that is not in the movie. 'We'll Go to Café de Paris', by a male chorus, was probably a patter song interpreted by Sonia's suitors, interpolated in her 'Melody of Laughter' before she goes to Maxim's. The reason for this erasure is not clear and might be manifold: the film might have been too long and that very part was already packed with two songs. Or perhaps the 'Paris song' was perceived to be out of fashion by 1934.

FIGURE 7.2   The can-can dancers of *The Merry Widow* (1934) represented both as alluring and stylised visual material.

Source: Publicity still provided by the editor.

FIGURE 7.3   The formal ball at the Marshovian Embassy in the 1934 *Merry Widow* is one of the most lavish sequences in the film and counterbalances the one capturing the vibrant atmosphere of the Café Maxim's.

Source: Publicity still provided by the editor.

Social Paris at Paramount: Maurice Chevalier

In the Paramount operettas, Gay Paree is not the typical attraction. Paris is not a woman, it is neither the gamine (like in *Kiki*, a play adapted by Belasco that was filmed several times) nor the great actress (from Sarah Bernhardt to Irene Bordoni). Paris is Maurice Chevalier. Even before he was paired off with MacDonald, Chevalier 'began to personify Paris to the outside world' (Phillips, 2004, p. 83). This is represented in 'Song of Paree' (*Love Me Tonight*) where Chevalier appears in the middle of a choral number defining the city: Paris becomes Chevalier even as the drawing of his profile on a wall becomes the flesh and blood actor. Chevalier was already famous in France when he arrived in Hollywood. *Innocents of Paris*, his first film, can be regarded as a risk taken by the studio considering his heavy accent and lack of experience in the United States (Barnier, 2004, p. 63). But its huge success, reinforced by the star's status as a stage and radio singer, gave him a quick international following. He was a major catch for Paramount and the 'big thing' in the operettas (*One Hour with You*, 1932). Chevalier is also responsible for the box office success of the French versions of his films, stimulated in return by his newly acquired Hollywood notoriety (Barnier, 2004, p. 72).

The Chevalier vehicles may include alluring scenes of the French capital, but always in connection with the star. In the operettas – and also true at MGM – Paris is his territory and therefore a masculine city. Because the films were meant for release in France, the Paris embodied by Chevalier is actually closer to the image expected by French spectators (which does not mean that it is not another stereotype). In France, Chevalier's modest origins were well-known, turning him into the embodiment of a social success story. His commonplaceness is as asserted as his dandy character. This 'heterogeneous star image' was part of his appeal to the bourgeois audience (Vincendeau, 1996, p. 94, my translation). Though not quite as complex as in his French films, the Chevalier duality is also present at Paramount (although less so at MGM). Chevalier was both a dandy and an *Apache*, and several ads show him with a 'double' (for example he wears a cap and his shadow behind him wears his signature straw boater). A 'millionaire waiter' in *The Little Café* (according to Paramount's catchphrase), he 'was born in the humble section of Paris known as Ménilmontant', yet he is 'the aristocrat of the people! As a poor Paris tailor, he's rich!' and 'He kisses like a prince and loves like an *Apache*!' (*Love Me Tonight* press book).

Love Me Tonight stresses Chevalier's duality and trusts its publicity to enlarge the myth. The press book includes a full-page article signed by Chevalier about the Paris he loves (with the title 'So You're Going to See Paris! Chevalier Tells Night Delights of Joydom Capitol – Montmartre'), which was meant for publication in newspapers. This depiction of Paris mentions of course, wine, girls and explains that 'the demi-monde and the haute-monde [*sic*] enjoy themselves side by side'. This is not seen in the film, but it recalls his dandy image even though Chevalier is a modest tailor in the narrative. His character is associated with a revolutionary feeling: when he arrives at the indebted count's castle to get his payment, the musical underscoring employs the tune of a French revolutionary anthem 'Ah, ça ira' to imply that Chevalier is tempted to follow the unquoted lyrics' claim of

FIGURE 7.4 At the masked ball in *Love Me Tonight* (1932), Chevalier's working-class outfit is less a disguise than his 'real' look, creating a social contrast to the aristocrats in period costumes.

Source: Publicity still provided by the editor.

bringing the aristocrats to the gallows. Chevalier personifies two Parises and thus brings a tension into the Paramount operettas (beyond the general duality defined by Altman). The *Apache* sometimes shows through the military uniform when he makes brutal gestures, displaying a 'violent male domination' often associated with American clichés about French sexuality (Altman, 1987, p. 169). The *Apache* number in *Love Me Tonight* is aligned with the one from *Paramount on Parade* (1930), directed by Lubitsch. Chevalier played a tuxedo-ed *Apache*, whose fight with his wife became physical and led to an erotic undressing. He is less elegant in *Love Me Tonight*, but the *Apache* number is visually striking, the giant shadow on the wall suggesting real brutality behind the disguise (this is a masked ball) as well as serving as a reminder of the guillotine. The costume anyway looks particularly convincing on Chevalier and is anything but a mask.

In the Paramount operettas, Chevalier is the major star with the more complex persona. He has more musical numbers than MacDonald. *The Merry Widow* establishes a new balance between the leads: MacDonald's aura increased at the time; she was one of the studio's important assets and therefore she got most of the solo numbers. In the *Widow*, her classically trained voice perfectly suits the lead part; she is also the one with the richer image and more complex identity, as an aristocrat masquerading as a prostitute.

FIGURE 7.5   Maurice Chevalier's 'Apache Number' in *Love Me Tonight*, with the menacing shadow.

Source: Publicity still provided by the editor.

Conclusion

Like any *aperçu*, the Lubitsch joke that opened this essay is both revealing and exaggerated. The use of the stars and the conception of Paris as an attraction constitute the main differences between the studios, if we consider one film (*The Merry Widow*) as representative of the whole MGM style. What is obvious is that Paramount was more interested in French themes; so many films from the studio, whether musicals or not, were located in the capital. If Paris-Paramount is not necessarily 'more Parisian', Paris-MGM is, on the other hand, obviously 'more American'. This cycle of operettas nevertheless remains consistent overall.

The many nuances notable in the depiction of Paris are not all grounded in the studios' policies and aesthetics. With the beginnings of the PCA self-censorship the times had changed, while different directorial styles were an additional factor: *Love Me Tonight* could be considered as the most singular film of the cycle in its portrait of Chevalier as an *Apache*. The turn in Franco-American relationships and cultural exchanges were another important factor. On the one hand, the new commercial agreements between countries led to growing protectionism in Europe and a reorientation of national markets, while on the other, the symbolic importance of Paris in American culture transformed slightly from irresistibly fashionable to merely fancy. The press book for *The Merry Widow* formulates the issue by trying to resist the notion that the film could be outdated at the time of its release. In 1929, *The Love Parade* was obviously a novelty and was perceived as innovatory. In 1934, *The Merry Widow* had to strive to seem 'modern': 'Anticipate your public's probable reaction. . . . There is a chance they might think *The Merry Widow* is a re-issue or an old picture. It's new! Modern!'

The succeeding cycle of MacDonald operettas at MGM confirmed the need for a change. Chevalier went back to France and MGM found a fresh partner for the soprano – Nelson Eddy. The new formula established a confrontation between Old Europe and the New World, and the stories mainly took place on the American continent. *Naughty Marietta* (1935) symbolically showed the heroine flee from France very early in the narrative. When France or Paris was a location in that series, the vision was different: it was a Paris of the more remote 18th century and not the Gay Paree of the 19th (*Naughty Marietta*) or the high society Paris of Napoleon III's court and life at the Opera (*Maytime*, 1937). Paris was then less modern than 'historical'. For Hollywood, it temporarily became an emblem of the seriousness of Old Europe.

The author would like to express her thanks to Kerry-Jane Wallart.

Notes

1 The Hays Office notably wanted the 'light references to Bastille Day' suppressed because 'the Royalists in France may take exception to them' (Joy, 1932, AMPAS). So it tried to avoid any caricature of the French aristocracy in *The Love Parade* and especially to contain the notion that the characters are of royal lineage.
2 Vincendeau analysed reviews from *Variety* to explore the journalists' understanding of the cultural differences between the French and American receptions of the mystery film *The Unholy Night* (MGM, 1929). That movie failed in the United States but was successful in France.

References

Anon. (1929) *The Love Parade*. Motion Picture Association of America, Production Code Administration Records. Los Angeles: Academy of Motion Picture Arts and Sciences (AMPAS).
———. (1932) *Love Me Tonight*. Motion Picture Association of America, Production Code Administration Records. Los Angeles: Academy of Motion Picture Arts and Sciences (AMPAS).

————. (1934) *The Merry Widow*. Motion Picture Association of America, Production Code Administration Records. Los Angeles: Academy of Motion Picture Arts and Sciences (AMPAS).

Altman, R. (1987) *The American Film Musical*. Bloomingdale and Indianapolis: Indiana University Press.

Balio, T. (1993) *Grand Design. Hollywood as a Modern Business Enterprise, 1930–1939*. New York: Charles Scribner's Sons.

Barnier, M. (2004) *Des Films Français Made in Hollywood. Les Versions Multiples 1929–1935*. Paris: L'Harmattan.

Bingen, S. and Wanamaker, M. (2017) *Paramount. City of Dreams*. Guilford: Taylor Trade Publishing.

Blaszkiewicz, J. (2018) 'Writing the City: The Cosmopolitan Realism of Offenbach's *La Vie Parisienne*,' *Current Musicology*, 103, pp. 67–96.

Bordman, G. (2001) *American Musical Theatre. A Chronicle*. 3rd edition. New York: Oxford University Press.

Brewster, B. (2001) 'The Circle: Lubitsch and the Theatrical Farce Tradition,' *Film History: An International Journal*, 13(4), pp. 372–389.

Chabrol, M. (2016) 'Deux comédies françaises à la mode de Lubitsch: Paris-Broadway-Hollywood,' in P. Alexandre-Bergues and M. Laliberté (eds.) *Les Archives de la mise en scène. Spectacles populaires et culture médiatique 1870–1950*. Lille: Presses du Septentrion, pp. 245–259.

Corlis, M. and Clarens, C. (1978) 'Designed for Film,' *Film Comment*, 14(3), pp. 27–84.

De Baecque, A. (ed.) (2012) *Paris by Hollywood*. Paris: Flammarion.

Doherty, T. (1999) *Pre-Code Hollywood. Sex, Immorality and Insurrection in American Cinema 1930–1934*. New York: Columbia University Press.

Eyman, S. (1993) *Ernst Lubitsch: Laughter in Paradise*. New York: Simon & Schuster.

Jacobs, L. (2015) 'Lubitsch and Mamoulian,' in *Film Rhythm After Sound*. Oakland: University of California Press, pp. 109–165.

Love Me Tonight (1932). Press book. Press book collection. New York: New York Public Library for the Performing Arts.

The Merry Widow (1934). Press book. Press book collection. New York: New York Public Library for the Performing Arts.

One Hour with You (1932). Press book. Press book collection. New York: New York Public Library for the Performing Arts.

Paul, W. (1983) *Ernst Lubitsch's American Comedy*. New York: Columbia University Press.

Phillips, A. (2004) *City of Darkness, City of Light. Emigré Filmmakers in Paris 1929–1939*. Amsterdam: Amsterdam University Press.

Schwartz, N. (1975) 'Lubitsch's *Widow*. The Meaning of a Waltz,' *Film Comment*, 11(2), pp. 13–17.

Schwartz, V. (2007) *It's So French. Hollywood, Paris, and the Making of Cosmopolitan Film Culture*. Chicago: The University of Chicago Press.

Vincendeau, G. (1996) '"Avez-vous lu Freud?" Maurice Chevalier dans *Pièges* de Robert Siodmak,' *IRIS*, 21, pp. 89–98.

————. (1988) 'Hollywood Babel,' *Screen*, 29(2), pp. 24–39.

8

PARIS AS LOCATION

Funny Face, Les Girls, Silk Stockings and *Gigi*

Julia L. Foulkes

It's always springtime in Paris – in the movies. A(n) (older) man and a (younger) woman are destined to fall in love in Paris – in the movies. Song and dance are the preferred mode of communication for all in Paris – in the movies. And Americans find their true selves in Paris – in the movies.

Four movie musicals from 1957–1958 embody these Hollywood ideas of the French capital. *Funny Face, Les Girls, Silk Stockings* and *Gigi* present Paris as the location of love that is more like a bus tour of stops by the Eiffel Tower, the restaurant Maxim's, and the gardens of the Tuileries on the way to a declaration of love on a night-time cobblestone street. Paris is most often a set piece, a prettified site of parks, monuments, fountains, nightclubs, and night-time street corners and courtyards. The contemporary city of that moment does not appear – the changing demographics and physical landscape of the post-World War II city that struggled to recover from Nazi occupation, the ending of imperial power in Vietnam and Algeria, and the build-up of housing projects ringing the historical centre of the city. The imaginary filmic Paris exists as a place to escape to in a world heaving with the turmoil of two devastating wars in quick succession, unchanged by contemporary politics and steady – and historic – in its focus on personal pleasure. These movies strengthen the image of the French capital as still definitive of the essential joys of life, embodied in romance between a man and a woman.

These movies captured the endurance of Paris in new ways, however: by shooting on location there. Vanessa Schwartz estimates that over one-hundred American film productions requested permission to film in France between 1947–1963 (Schwartz, 2007, p. 22). While soundstages still were the primary set for these four films, even minimal shooting in Paris gave them a new kind of authenticity, inviting filmgoers to see the city from its actual streets in addition to its imagined hotels, cobblestoned cul-de-sacs, and working theatres. The vaunted realism also perhaps lent more weight to the inevitably fantastical genre of movie musicals. The actual sights of Paris grounded the singing and dancing superimposed on daily life.

The location shooting also paralleled and abetted Americans' travel to – and consumption of – Paris. No longer an exclusive destination, the French capital was within reach for more Americans after the war as air travel and economic prosperity made the city a destination for the middle class. If it was previously a mark of bohemia or the wealthy class, a Parisian sojourn became an aspiration accessible to more Americans than in any other previous period. In many ways, Americans' fascination with Paris buoyed the recovery of the city after World War II, particularly in these movies that celebrated its past as a birthplace of modern cultural and intellectual life (Endy, 2004; Schwartz, 2007; Wakeman, 2009).

Gigi

The movie *Gigi* debuted a year following *Les Girls*, *Silk Stockings* and *Funny Face*, all of which came out in 1957. But the era represented in the film is chronologically earlier than the other three movies; *Gigi* is set in the *belle époque* at the turn of the 20th century while the other three movies are contemporaneous to the time they were filmed. Even more, *Gigi*'s story and filmic realisation contain those stereotypes and symbols all four of the movies reinforce. It is also the only movie of the four that is actually about Parisians with not an American in sight – at least in the world of the movie.

Gigi began as a novella by Colette, published in 1944, became a French film in 1949, then a Broadway play with Audrey Hepburn in the title role in 1951, before becoming a movie musical produced by MGM in 1958. The story focuses on a young woman being groomed as a courtesan and winning the love – and a proposal of marriage – from a man who watched her grow from teenager to young woman. The film fills out the story with winning songs by Lerner and Loewe, lush costumes and set designs, and use of Parisian parks and palaces. It sets up Paris as a place of romance but, even more, as the apogee of high society. Gigi's transformation, then, from girl to potential courtesan to wife is a rise in class status – a success story in achieving what Paris represents, even if one tightly circumscribed by gender restrictions.

The movie begins with a scene in the Parisian park, Bois de Boulogne, with a quintessential Parisian as the narrator, Maurice Chevalier in the role of Honoré, the wizened society man who has forsaken marriage for perpetual romance. The song 'Thank Heaven for Little Girls' introduces Gigi, playing with other school girls, as well as the overriding thrust of the plot that women exist for the pleasure of men – with the now-uncomfortable as well as sexist overtones of older men eyeing younger girls as sexual objects or, as Honoré describes himself, 'a lover and collector of beautiful things'. Chevalier exudes a patronising gaze and beatific smile over the scene, as well as the whole movie, giving this thoroughly Hollywood film a whiff of Parisian authenticity. A famous singer by the 1920s, Chevalier became a stabilising force after the Nazi occupation, reminding Parisians of their enduring grandeur and joie-de-vivre. His role in *Gigi* is a bit of the same: he is a stand-in for the city itself, suggesting its long history and embrace of pleasure.

If Chevalier gave a Parisian air to the production, two other French-born actors as the romantic leads whipped the whiff into a waft. Leslie Caron and Louis Jourdan – both solid Hollywood stars by this point – looked the parts and played them with ease. Caron cast off the shy ingénue of her debut role in *An American in Paris* to be a gregarious tomboy, chaffing at the rules imposed on females and then bowing to them with clear-eyed frankness. In a pointed song, 'The Parisians', Caron questions the city's obsession with love. She walks by monuments of anguished love, even asking Gaston, played by Jourdan, 'Do you make love all the time?' She resents the fact that this is always the stated goal, whether in the vague hopes of her grandmother or directed lessons in manners, dress, and jewellery by her aunt. Her initial relations with Gaston exist outside of those rules, carefree and unbidden. But the rules take over and she bends to them by deciding to be his mistress even as he declares his love for her.

FIGURE 8.1   An added dose of authenticity? French actors Leslie Caron (Gigi) and Louis Jourdan (Gaston), the stars of *Gigi* (1958).

Source: Photo provided by the editor.

Interior spaces depicted in the film re-create a kind of gilded cage that represents the restrictions that bind Gigi's life in particular. Her more modest home, a flat reached by stairs, is still decorated in brocaded red. But a slumbering cat on a chair suggests the more informal atmosphere that attracts Gaston to the place – and the chamomile tea and playful game of cards that await him. Gigi's aunt's home, however, is the place for learning what is required by high society. A large marble building with an entrance directly from the street, door opened by a butler, draws Gigi into rules regarding how to pour coffee from a silver teapot, how to walk across a room or pick a cigar for an amour. But Gaston's apartment represents the end-goal of high society residences, filmed on location in the Museé Jacquemart-André. Scenes filmed at Maxim's restaurant make explicit what all the lessons are for: to see and be seen. This is the *belle époque* alive on film: colours, dress, luxury abounds – it is a decorated, built edifice of the spectacle of time-honoured society.

Exterior spaces present more personal and bare truths of emotions and relations. The public spaces of Paris are where the story begins, where Gaston declaims his social life as all a bore, where Gigi questions Parisians' devotion to love, and where Gaston changes his mind, first in realising that Gigi is no longer a child and, then, from desiring her as his wife instead of his courtesan. These scenes unmask the social contrivances and striving. In his night-time wandering of Parisian streets, Gaston questions himself – what he knows and what he wants. The streets allow him to see himself – and his future – anew. (And the director Minnelli avoids the visual clichés of the capital, such as Notre Dame and the Arc de Triomphe, another reinforcement of the idea that this is a Parisian's view of the city.)

But perhaps the most telling song of the movie is 'I Remember It Well', revealing the wrinkles of memory, the volley of competing remembrances. Even more, though, the song suggests that we create our memories as we wish the past to have been. Paris exists in the film in much the same way – created in a way that Americans might have wished the city to be. *Gigi* offers a visual feast of the *belle époque* when Paris laid claim to being the centre of the world – released at a time when New York City aimed to assume that status. It is a story of class striving – perhaps more typical of American social aspirations than French – and success in securing both love and status. The mythology of the American dream did not yet extend to an overt embrace of luxury and excess in the 1950s even as it moved ever more into an age of conspicuous consumption. The Paris of *Gigi*, then, was a not-very-subtle projection of American aspirations for wealth, luxury, and pleasure.

Les Girls

Conflicting memories and truths form the plot of *Les Girls*. The primary story of the adventures of an entertainment act in Paris is told three different times, from three different perspectives: two female dancers and the male lead and director of the troupe (Lennard, 2015). Gene Kelly as Barry Nichols leads the act, choreographing the lives as well as the dances of the three main female leads. The British Lady Sybil Wren, played by Kay Kendall, starts off the narrative as the writer of a memoir about her time as a dancer in Paris. She defends her account in a libel suit brought by Angèle, a French dancer in the act played by Taina Elg. Sybil begins her testimony in court in London by describing the city of Paris – it was springtime, of course, and all was exciting in the city of light and love.

Two primary places form the visual picture of Paris in *Les Girls*: the flat shared by the female dancers, in a building they call Liberty Hall, and the Musicale Hall Parisienne, the venue where they perform. The house is similar to the residences in all four films: it is at the end of a street in a circular stone courtyard lit by gas streetlamps with room for dancing. Flats are always reached by a winding stone staircase. This one at the top of the building allows vistas into the courtyard to spy on the activities of others as well as panoramic views of the city.

The flat itself is a cramped space, with steps into and out of bedrooms and the kitchen. It is a workers' apartment: small, basic, and dilapidated – in fact, a relatively typical residence in central Paris at the time when newer, more modern housing was being built in the ring outside the city centre. A cranky gas lever to the stove demonstrates the noble dilapidation – and also becomes a key plot point. Most musical numbers in the film are part of the act in the music hall, a small theatre without distinctive features, neither old nor modern but just a stage, backstage, and audience, a workaday presentation of theatrical life. There are a few scenes in

FIGURE 8.2 In *Les Girls* (1957), Paris offers its female protagonists the freedom to perform before settling down as a wife: Angèle (Taina Elg), Sybil (Kay Kendall) and Joy (Mitzi Gaynor) in the musical number 'Ladies in Waiting'.

Source: Photo provided by the editor.

public spots, such as a neighbouring flower market, a drifting boat on a leafy pond, and people lounging at a café – but primarily Paris at night dominates, with its theatres, dark stairways, and courtyards, after hours.

More palpable and notable than particular scenic locations in the city, then, are the opportunities the French capital affords. For these three *les girls*, it is a place of relative freedom. The job delays marriage, which is portrayed as a more constraining situation for at least two of them. Their act is a chance to be in the spotlight, to travel Europe on tour, to dally with romance while even drinking too much. For Sybil and Angèle, the song and dance job – and the companionship of women in the apartment and in the troupe – is a moment of single, working life before stepping into prescribed if privileged roles as wives of successful, adoring men. Their conflict at the start of the film, which sets up the lawsuit, vanishes at the end, when they embrace and renew female friendship as their husbands now bear the brunt of their ire.

It is the American man who resolves the conflicting stories by Sybil and Angèle. When Angèle asks Barry why he is in Paris, he replies that he is just a dancer in the US, but here he's 'something special'. Being an American in Paris was a familiar role for Kelly; so too was finding love in the film's city, this time with another American. It's a romantic pairing that reinforces these films as Americans touring European capitals and peoples, having liaisons, but with little intent to settle down there. When Barry announces his love for Joy, played by Mitzi Gaynor, she holds out for marriage – an echo of the conflict between Gigi and Gaston. Barry's version of the troupe's adventures takes the spotlight off Sybil and Angèle and their passing dalliances with him to focus on Joy. The closing shot of the film shows the director in London after the trial – having created a version of the truth that rescues the marriages of both Sybil and Angele – getting in to a taxi, where the aptly-named Joy awaits.

If *Gigi* shows the world of Paris encompassing both the apex of manners and courtliness as well as the frivolity of ice skating at the Palais de Glace and going out to Maxim's, *Les Girls* confirms the association of Paris with entertainment as well as class. Paris is where one could go from cabaret to palace in one night, and from a job as a dancer to wife of a wealthy man over a few months. Entertainment and art are linked in Paris, as part of an embrace of sensuality and enjoyment.

Silk Stockings

The character of Angèle in *Les Girls* situates at least one French person in a tale of the French capital, but *Silk Stockings* restores the more common trope in three of these films that the city is filled with those other than Parisians. (The Americanisation of France after World War II, particularly its film industry, is a topic that has long occupied scholars: see Grazia, 2005; Kuisel, 1993; Schwartz, 2007; Shandley, 2009.) In this movie, the capital city of France is a meeting point for the Cold War adversaries of the Soviet Union and the United States. Based on the movie *Ninotchka* (1939) with Greta Garbo, the musical first appeared on Broadway in 1955.

The plot involves the making of a film on location in Paris, a knowing contrivance as shooting moved outside of soundstages more often in the 1950s. The French capital was a compelling and attractive site, ready-made with grand backdrops and symbols. In *Silk Stockings*, these associations reinforce another, the geographic position of Paris between the United States and the Soviet Union. In the movie, the film producer Steve Canfield (played by Fred Astaire) wants to use the music of Peter Illyich Boroff, a Russian composer. Obtaining the rights to do so requires the consent of the Soviet Union, represented by three bumbling comrades who are in Paris to make sure Boroff returns to Moscow. When the Russians linger, the Soviet commissar sends his best envoy to corral the group, worried that they have been 'seduced' by Paris. Nina Yoschenko (Ninotchka, played by Cyd Charisse), who gave up all bourgeois pleasures at the age of 16, arrives in Paris and notes that the hotel looks like a palace. From that initial comment, Paris is presented as the epitome of consumption and capitalism, with women's lingerie as an indication of the end of civilisation (Wood, 1975, pp. 29–30).

Canfield and Yoschenko clash over their opposing views of Paris. She wants to see the workers and factories during the day; he wants to show her the Cartier store, a women's spa, and the sparkling lights and monuments at night. Even gender roles are viewed as capitalist in Yoschenko's ideology: under communism, all men and women do the same work, wearing similar basic brown clothing. What breaks through the barrier between them? Dance, of course. There is no purpose in dance except pleasure. Dance – and then love – renders utility meaningless. The inhibiting, depersonalised system of the Soviet Union cannot last under the assault of fresh flowers every day, champagne and, of course, silk stockings. Love also means an ardent return to conventionally sexist gender roles so that Nina sings to Steve, 'a man to a woman is her life'. Utility, practicality and ruthless attention to work lose to aimlessness, sensual pleasure, and love. Paris embodies beauty, even if the Champs-Élysées is three feet narrower than Nevesky Prospekt in St. Petersburg.

But the Russians are soon betrayed by the American film industry: they are horrified by the rendition of 'Ode to a Tractor' as a sexy siren song for the American star. They leave Paris immediately – and return to dress and surroundings of beige, brown, and grey. Scenes in the Soviet Union relay utility and government oppression in the form of hanging laundry on the patio and vistas of Red Square. When Nina and her comrades get together, they remember Paris with its enormous cigars, marble bathrooms, and the women of the Folies Bergère. Nina especially remembers the glittering lights of night-time. The composer Boroff then plays his latest composition that has been inspired by his time in Paris, his growing fascination with popular song, having succumbed to that which had earlier offended him. 'The Red Blues' brings out the workers in the building to sing and dance, except when everyone stops as a boss walks across the room. The spirited actions defy the background, returning to colour and energy in contrast to the drabness

FIGURE 8.3   Breaking down the barriers of the Cold War with dance: Fred Astaire as Steve Canfield and Cyd Charisse as Nina Yoschenko, aka Ninotchka.

Source: Photo provided by the editor.

around them. The Russians embrace self-expression, spontaneity and fun – for no logical reason at all.

In a familiar cycle, the comrades return to Paris to sell Russian films and Nina is sent to corral them again because of reports that they are being 'decadent' by entering a dance contest and winning. She returns to Paris and finds them in 'La Vielle Russia' nightclub where Canfield is the main attraction in a song and dance act titled 'The Ritz Roll and Rock'. The comrades are staying in Paris to run the nightclub and her love for him convinces Nina to stay with Canfield.

As in *Les Girls*, the physical spaces of the French capital are less important than what the city represents. Whether in nightclubs or cafes, silk stockings or films, Paris is primarily a spectacle to gaze upon. No Parisians have any major role in the film, no places render the unique appearance of the city beyond a flash of the Arc de Triomphe or a lyric that references the Champs-Élysées. It is a surface charm of glittering lights and romantic possibilities, a fantastical temporary movie set rather than a lived daily experience. Paris exists in the film much like the location of the movie being filmed there – as a meeting point that has brought these people together.

In other ways, Paris stands in for the United States in its heralding of individualism and capitalism, encapsulated in the portrayals of women. As with Paris, women are to be looked at and displayed – consumed. High heels, chic dresses, sexy linge-rie, and needing men to love define women in Paris. The other featured American in the movie, the film star Peggy Dayton, is more brash and ambitious than the Parisian model of womanhood that Nina emulates in her transformation. Paris allows Nina to step towards capitalism and individualism without a full capitulation to Americanism.

Paris is also a point of mediation between entertainment – represented by the United States, its popular song and fanciful movie-making – and art, the latter symbolised by Russian Boroff's serious classical 'Ode to a Tractor'. Astaire's final song and dance routine, 'The Ritz Roll and Rock', muddles the two, soft tap in a tux with just a splash of the harder rhythms of rock n' roll. If that came off as an immediately outdated mélange – Astaire announced his retirement from movie musicals upon the première of *Silk Stockings* – the place of Paris as a meeting ground for people, social, economic, and cultural forces made it a central metropole in the bifurcated Cold War world. In Paris, there is no need to pick mass entertain-ment or refined art or to denigrate one at the expense of the other. The city allows one to embrace all that is offered. Ultimately, the Paris of *Silk Stockings* represents the height of cosmopolitanism, trading on its long past and its surface pleasures. National borders fade, political ideologies get skewered by human interests, and enjoyment overwhelms all other endeavours.

Funny Face

Funny Face brings together what *Silk Stockings*, *Les Girls*, and *Gigi* focused on sepa-rately: crossing class borders, the place of spectacle and entertainment, and the construction of a cosmopolitan culture. Paris is more central to the plot of *Funny Face* as well, not just a decorative, almost incidental, location but one built into the plot of the story. Like the other films based on earlier stories, though, *Funny Face* repurposes an older production. The film uses the name of a 1927 Gershwin musical, eschewing the plot but keeping some of the tunes and also the star, Fred Astaire. (Astaire headlines the movie at the end of his career, an indication of the very different trajectories of men in entertainment, given that his co-stars in *Silk Stockings* and *Funny Face* were 23 and 30 years younger than him respectively.) In the first half of the 20th century, the recycling of Paris as a location of various sto-ries signalled its centrality in cultural imagination as well as its ability to stand in for common tropes, such as class ascendency and high culture.

Funny Face is a story about fashion, and the film features striking visual design. The photographer Richard Avedon served as the film's visual consultant – and also a kind of model for the male lead, Dick Avery, a photographer for a fashion maga-zine, played by Astaire. The first scene sets up the film's visual distinctiveness: a stripped rounded office of all white with doors in primary colours. The head of the magazine, Maggie Prescott, played by Kay Thompson, reconsiders the next issue of the magazine, deciding that it needs to 'go pink'. The white background then becomes aglow in bright pink. The attention to colour highlights the palette and spectacle of photography and filmmaking, with new technical advances throughout this era that sharpened images and saturated colours. Modern life was in rich and varied colour – sumptuous and vivifying – and often displayed in stark contrast to bland and dull settings. As in *Silk Stockings*, colour signalled the sensual spontaneity of Paris; brown was the unforgiving utility of the Soviet Union.

In a photo shoot concurrent to 'Think Pink!', Dick attempts to capture a 'woman who can think'. When the model herself is shown as incapable of projecting that idea, Maggie and Dick decide that a 'sinister' bookstore in Greenwich Village would be the ideal backdrop. They find Embryo Concepts Book Shop, also characterised by drab colours, and where Jo Stockton, played by Audrey Hepburn, works as an earnest bookseller. They ransack the place for the photography shoot; Dick stays behind to help clean up; Paris becomes the topic of conversation between Jo and Dick. He claims that she would love it there – parties, champagne, perfume, and a 'new love affair every hour on the hour'. She, however, wants to go to the French capital for none of that but for lectures, especially those of Professor Flostre, the important philosopher of 'Empathicalism', and this spoof is one of the few nods to contemporary French culture in these films. Paris as *haute couture* and elite socialising, Paris as intellectual vanguard – the battle lines between the lead characters have been set in the city itself.

When the magazine decides it needs a new 'it' girl, Dick recommends Jo because her face is 'funny'. He convinces Maggie when he strips a portrait picture of Jo's face down to its structure, an outline of nose, mouth, eyes, and eyebrows. Dick convinces Jo to accept the idea of being a model for the photo shoot after the always requisite – and always persuasive – dance. She sees it as a chance to go to Paris. The journey there showcases the standing of the city in that era in a song entitled 'Bonjour Paris'. The air travel itself begins the scene, with the lead characters looking out of plane windows interspersed with shots of Notre Dame, the Arc de Triomphe, and the Eiffel Tower. The thrill of the city begins with the excitement of air travel and the ability not only to go to new places but to see the sights anew, from above. The scene continues on the ground as each of the three primary characters goes off in three separate cabs to see the version of the city that draws them – Maggie goes shopping; Dick walks down the Champs-Élysées; Jo seeks out philosophers. And they all lie to do so, claiming the need to rest while instead they wander and discover their own version of the city. It's as if they cannot admit that pleasure supersedes work. Paris is presented as a city with many facets, enough to please everyone. A side-by-side triptych in the number visualises this, the three actors in different places of the city but singing the same song.

'Bonjour Paris' is a tourist vision of the city, one grand building and panorama after another, that ends with all three ending up at the iconic site that unites their different paths through the city: the Eiffel Tower. Its construction in the mid-19th century symbolised science and progress but its widespread imagery in the 20th century helped define urbanity, spectatorship, and tourism (Shandley, 2009; Stephens, 2015). The Eiffel Tower defines the French capital by means of one iconic structure but also relays the city to the world. A scalable open tower gives height to what could be seen; an airplane adds even more height and also speed, bringing parts of the world closer. Filmmaking then rendered that effect to an even broader audience. If postcards that featured a photograph of the Eiffel Tower distributed a vision of the future in the 19th century, these films of Paris brought the city in action to even more people around the world in the mid-20th century. As Jo, Dick and Maggie sing in 'Bonjour Paris': 'Is it real? Am I here?' – a summation of the questions that changes in technology, communication, and travel prompted in a newly knit-together world.

As 'Bonjour Paris' announces, Americans take over Paris in the rest of the film. There are occasional appearances by Parisians, but, as in *Les Girls* and *Silk Stockings*, the city's residents do not seem that necessary to stories of the city. Instead, Dick knows where to find Jo when she does not show up for a fitting. He goes directly to a smoky underground café in the Left Bank, filled with a person standing on his head, others strumming an instrument – a synoptic sense of bohemia. Sure enough, Jo is there, talking excitedly about Empathicalism to French men, who Dick reveals cannot understand any English. She insists on her belonging there nevertheless, with a jazzy, expressionistic dance.

Jo shows up the following day for her assignment, emerging as a model made for the moment and the place. Dick photographs her around Paris in narrative

FIGURE 8.4 Jo Stockton (Audrey Hepburn) confirms that she belongs among French philosophers by expressing her feelings in modern dance.

Source: Photo provided by the editor.

scenes inspired by what's around him, or perhaps, even more, by the countless love stories associated with Paris in the public imagination: hopeful in the Tuileries in a sudden rain, holding balloons; heartbroken in a train station; thinking of love in a flower shop; leaving the opera, unhappy because a lover did not show up; playful, fishing on the Seine; reverent, in night-time in front of a fountain holding a dove; elegance unbound, in the Louvre, with the winged angel behind her. The final scene, a wedding in the park, brings their love into the open.

Their interests diverge again, though, as Jo hears about an upcoming lecture by Emphaticalist Professor Flostre and escapes from the fashion world to meet him. She confirms her position in Paris by telling Flostre that she lives in Greenwich Village, 'our Left Bank'. Dick arrives to drag her to the press review and insists that the professor is not interested in her intellect but only her sexual attractiveness. Their anger disrupts the press review and Jo leaves again to seek out the professor at his home. Dick and Maggie follow, disguised as Parisian intellectuals, he in goatee, she with beret. While Jo resists them again, the philosopher Flostre reveals his sexual interest in her. The mishap reveals to Jo that Dick was right and that she should return to fight for his love. While she appears in the fashion show, Dick is on the way to the airport. Despite attempting to get a message to him, she watches a plane fly by the Eiffel Tower, believing that he has chosen to leave Paris without her. Dick, though, sees the injured professor at the airport and realises that Jo found out about his character. He finds her in the garden of the wedding shoot, and they reprise ''S Wonderful' in celebration of their love.

Funny Face reveals more of Paris than the other three films even as it centres Americans' experiences there. The film defines the city by its *haute couture* and intellectualism – albeit highly satirised – but also as a destination of American tourism, fascination, and self-discovery. Jo matures there, with the unmasking of her intellectual idol and her embrace of love. As in *Gigi*, it is a story of class ascension, moving from clerk in a bookshop in the United States to fashion model in Paris. Much of the character's reinvention, though, is accomplished by consuming: what is important can be bought – a dress or a trip to Paris. All of this is channelled through a keen attention to visuality, using colour to compel attention and the eye of the airplane or camera to focus on the future in a place so redolent of the past.

Aspiring to Paris

These films all present compelling visions of Paris, gleaming with possibility, sophistication, and romance. This was not a wholly accurate vision of the French capital at that time, which was struggling to recover from a devastating war and occupation. Municipal politics was as mired in conflict as national politics, all centred in the capital city and playing out in its streets. Even as the historic core of the city became more of a tourist playground and replica of what was once, the outer zone represented the future – the imposition of modernist, large-scale public housing projects, the marginalisation of immigrants, and rise of student and youth protests. The 'picture book of the past', as historian Rosemary Wakeman calls the centre of the city, became a nostalgic view of what Paris was no longer (Wakeman, 2009, p. 347).

And it was a view that both Parisians and Americans promoted. Film musicals were an ideal way to present this nostalgic picture. Fill the quaint night-time streets and beautified parks with song and dance, let romance and spectacle glide over contemporary conflicts and intractable politics, imagine it is always springtime as a moment of renewal and new possibilities! These tributes to Paris, though, occurred at a time when the United States and New York City were ascendant in the global order, as a dominant political force but also an increasingly dominant cultural and artistic one as well. The global power and reach of the US film industry itself was a leading example, an indication of economic strength.

But proving the idea that the United States could be the standard bearer of arts and culture was more difficult. Thinking through Paris – having Americans travel, work, and prosper in the city – aligned the United States with the cosmopolitanism, beauty, and sophistication that the place signified. These films emerged in the 1950s to assert Americans' claim over Paris and its tradition as a capital of culture; it was not a violent or dramatic takeover but one defined by nostalgia, desire, and longing. More Americans experienced the city in person during the 1950s, but, as in these films, what Americans brought home with them after the trip was not shown – and not necessary. Because far more fulfilled their dreams of Paris through these movies. The images – and the imagining – were the point. These films' endings in Paris only reinforced the idea that what is found in Paris is enduring, much as both French and American people in the newly fractious and explosive mid-20th century wanted to believe.

References

de Grazia, V. (2005) *Irresistible Empire: America's Advance Through 20th-Century Europe*. Cambridge: Harvard University Press.

Endy, C. (2004) *Cold War Holidays: American Tourism in France*. Chapel Hill: University of North Carolina Press.

Kuisel, R. (1993) *Seducing the French: The Dilemma of Americanization*. Berkeley: University of California Press.

Lennard, D. (2015) 'Libel, Scandal, and Bad Big Names: *It Should Happen to You, Les Girls, Camille,* and *Romeo and Juliet,*' in M. Pomerance and R. B. Palmer (eds.) *George Cukor: Hollywood Master*. Edinburgh: Edinburgh University Press.

Schwartz, V. (2007) *It's So French! Hollywood, Paris, and the Making of Cosmopolitan Film Culture*. Chicago: University of Chicago Press.

Shandley, R. (2009) *Runaway Romances: Hollywood's Postwar Tour of Europe*. Philadelphia: Temple University Press.

Stephens, S. (2015) 'Framing the Eiffel Tower: From Postcards to Postmodernism,' in N. Edwards, B. McCann and P. Poiana (eds.) *Framing French Culture*. Adelaide: University of Adelaide Press.

Wakeman, R. (2009) *Heroic City: Paris, 1945–58*. Chicago: University of Chicago Press.

Wood, R. (1975) 'Notes on *Silk Stockings,*' *Film Comment*, 11(3), pp. 28–31.

9

PARIS BY HAND

Gay Purr-ee and *The Aristocats*

Daniel Batchelder

The animated film musical contains enormous expressive potential. By its very nature, the medium of animation reconfigures and recalibrates reality into a theoretically limitless diegetic space. What would otherwise be immutable physical laws now become mere suggestions, and familiar modes of communication may be exaggerated, distorted or discarded entirely in favour of metaphor and abstraction. Add to this hyper-theatrical world the no less artificial conceit of characters expressing themselves through bursts of song and it begins to become clear why the idea of representation in animated musicals is such a complicated issue. Yet despite the animated musical's potential to distance itself from realistic depiction, the history of mainstream American animation has largely been one of relatively close adherence to recognisable forms. What's more, once one comes to grips with the animated musical's peerless powers of expression, it becomes possible to untangle the form's complexities and reveal the specifics of its relationship to reality.

This chapter tackles the task of uncovering the representational strategies of the animated musical by addressing two films: 1962's *Gay Purr-ee*, produced by the United Productions of America (UPA), and the Walt Disney Studio's *The Aristocats* (1970). Their punning titles betray that these films both adopt a primarily light-hearted, comic tone that has long typified the American animated feature's characteristic mode of address. Though both films offer dramatic variety by engaging with elements of adventure, peril and fear – again, all typical signifiers of the Hollywood animated feature's narrative priorities since the form's inception – both maintain cheery romantic comedy as a generic resting state. Both utilise the voices of well-known actors: Eva Gabor, Phil Harris and Maurice Chevalier in Disney's case, while the UPA production prominently features Judy Garland alongside Red Buttons, Hermione Gingold and relative newcomer Robert Goulet, then best-known to theatregoers as the co-star of Lerner and Loewe's *Camelot* (1960). Most obviously, both *Gay Purr-ee* and *The Aristocats* feature anthropomorphic cats as their main characters, and both films unfold primarily in and around the city of Paris. Finally, and most importantly for the present purposes, both films deploy musical numbers that offer a distinct departure from the linearity of spoken dialogue. Though *The Aristocats*' musical profile is slim in comparison to *Gay Purr-ee*'s – four songs compared to eight, plus reprises, respectively – the presence of these numbers qualify both films as animated musicals and therefore as appropriate foci for this study.

That neither *Gay Purr-ee* nor *The Aristocats* presents a precise semblance of Paris should come as no surprise. This loss of fidelity can be attributed in part to their shared animated medium, but perhaps even more to the fact that both are products of the Hollywood film industry, a system that has historically privileged production values over precise depiction, flashy spectacle over factual accuracy. Yet while both films maintain an essential distance from reality – a reality that includes the actual city of Paris populated by real people (and real cats) – it is not unreasonable to probe each film's individual relationship to reality. How, in other words, do these films' projections of Paris attempt to evoke the actual city?

Notwithstanding their surface-level similarities, comparing these two films will reveal a wide variety of approaches to representation in the animated musical. In the following pages, I map each film's aesthetic and expressive strategies on a general spectrum of fracture and cohesion. While *The Aristocats*' relationship to reality largely remains consistent throughout the film's running time, *Gay Purr-ee* embraces a far more fragmented and malleable system of representation. The ways in which each film deploys musical numbers further contributes to the respectively multivalent and cohesive natures of their diegeses. Finally, I extend this reading to these films' headline performers, Judy Garland and Maurice Chevalier, in order to present a phenomenological analysis of major stars in an animated film. Though this chapter cannot stand as a comprehensive guide, by focusing closely on the relationships between this expressive form and reality I intend to continue the project of opening up scholarly considerations of the unique creative potential of the animated musical.[1]

Historical background

By the time of *The Aristocats*' première in December 1970, the Walt Disney Animation Studios had been at the forefront of feature-length American animation for over three decades. After a few false starts, the studio, headed by brothers Walt and Roy Disney, found its first significant success with the 1928 cartoon short *Steamboat Willie*. Though its star character, Mickey Mouse, was similar in appearance and behaviour to the average 1920's cartoon character, what distinguished Mickey from his competitors was sound. Though *Steamboat Willie* was not the first ever sound cartoon, it was the first with a fully synchronised soundtrack complete with music and sound effects that accompanied the short film from beginning to end. Critics responded vociferously to the quality of the short's synchronisation, and Disney quickly established itself as a major force in the American animation industry (Barrier, 1999; Goldmark, 2007; Batchelder, 2018).

As rival studios began to incorporate fully synchronised sound into their cartoons, Disney sought to further distinguish itself. Though in part this differentiation came from developing technological advancements in the medium, the studio also moved away from the slapstick zaniness typical of animated films: Disney emphasised cohesive narratives, relatable characters with human-like personalities and an overarching attention to aesthetic beauty. Rather than setting their parallel series of *Mickey Mouse* and *Silly Symphony* shorts in wildly mutable cartoon spaces in which anything can (and does) happen, Disney increasingly pursued what scholar Paul Wells (1998, p. 25) refers to as a hyperrealist aesthetic: an approach to the animated medium in which 'the design, context, and action . . . approximates with, and corresponds to, the design, context, and action within the live-action film's representation of reality'. As the studio embarked upon ever more ambitious projects, its artists hewed progressively closer to a mode of mimesis grounded in reality. In *Snow White and the Seven Dwarfs* (1937), the world's first feature-length animated sound film, acts of magic and fantastical creatures are in many ways secondary to the film's emphasis on lifelike personalities, compelling drama and beauty – all of which are aided by Frank Churchill's lush, operetta-infused score (Thomas and Johnson, 1981; Care, 2002; Knapp, 2006; Batchelder, 2018).

Disney's hyperrealist project reached a zenith in 1942's *Bambi*, an isolationist quasi-musical whose impressionistic renderings of forest life at times borders on photographic verisimilitude. Upon the release of this film the United States' entry into World War II, coupled with a bitter animators' strike at the studio, left Disney facing bankruptcy and therefore ill-equipped to continue to produce laborious and expensive, realistic animated films. The studio survived the decade in part by producing a large number of propaganda films for the US government. *Cinderella* (1950) marked a return to form, a hyperrealistic fairy tale musical that privileges expression and drama over abstraction and flagrant artifice. While the studio continued to release acclaimed feature-length animated musicals, over time its founder began to pursue alternatives to animation, including live-action films, television programming and theme parks. Once a monolithic creative figurehead overseeing every step of the creative process, Walt Disney became increasingly less involved with the production of individual films (Barrier, 1999; Furniss, 1998).

Disney's sudden death in late 1966 set the studio reeling. Unsure of how to go on, the studio simply continued working as it had under his direction. *The Jungle Book* (1967) became the last film that Disney had personally overseen; its follow-up, *The Aristocats*, was therefore the studio's first animated feature made without its founder's participation (Watts, 1997; Barrier, 1999; Gabler, 2006). The 1970 movie reveals little sense of experimentation and is in many ways derivative of the Disney films that had preceded it. The broad strokes of the film's plot – a pampered house pet finds her way back home with the help of a charming stray – echo those of *Lady and the Tramp* (1955).[2] In addition to reusing a significant amount of *The Jungle Book*'s talent (including songwriters Terry Gilkyson and Richard and Robert Sherman, underscoring composer George Bruns and actors Phil Harris and

Sterling Holloway), *The Aristocats* likewise retains Disney's trademark hyperrealist aesthetic priorities.

The origins of *Gay Purr-ee* grow directly out of the history of the Disney studio. Among the hordes of talented animators fired during Disney's 1941 strike were Zack Schwartz, Stephen Bosustow and Dave Hilberman. During their tenure at Disney, this trio shared a common distaste for the studio's restrictive realist sensibilities. Now jobless, the three joined forces to create a new studio that would eventually bear the name United Productions of America (UPA). Under the creative leadership of urbane art school graduate Schwartz, UPA immediately rejected Disney's sentimental, cutesy aesthetics and instead embraced modernist abstraction. Due in part to budgetary restrictions, the studio turned to a technique known as limited animation, in which animators condense on-screen movements to a bare minimum, thereby reducing the number of individual drawings needed to complete a film. UPA's style replaced the constant, fluid motion associated with the Disney studio with minimalist design, stylised colours and dynamic sound editing (Barrier, 1999; Furniss, 2007; Abraham, 2012).

The new studio initially struggled to find a distributor – like Disney, it also produced propaganda cartoons during World War II – until landing a contract with Columbia Pictures in 1947. The 1950s represented a decade of creative and financial prosperity for UPA: the studio won Academy Awards for their shorts *Gerald McBoing Boing* (1950), *When Magoo Flew* (1954) and *Magoo's Puddle Jumper* (1956), the latter two of which featured the studio's near-sighted star character Mr. Magoo. The studio's bold visual style proved immensely influential, as the exaggerated angles and extreme colour palettes of limited animation began to appear in cartoons by Warner Bros., MGM and even Disney (Furniss, 2007; Abraham, 2012).[3] As Adam Abraham (2012, p. x) expresses in his monograph on the studio,

> UPA stood as a point of intersection among the arts. The lessons of modern masters such as Picasso, Matisse, and Mondrian combined with the stylings of *New Yorker* illustrators such as Saul Steinberg. We find the influence of ballet as well as syncopated jazz. Further, the UPA artists consciously avoided the talking animals, lowbrow humor, and cartoon violence typical of American animation. Dr. Seuss, James Thurber, and even Edgar Allan Poe provide the source material for some of UPA's striking creations.

To viewers and critics, UPA's expressive modernism represented a refreshing departure from the Disney studio's iron grip on mid-century animation aesthetics.

Yet it was ultimately Disney that caused UPA's downfall. In 1947, Walt Disney testified before the US House of Representatives Committee on Un-American Activities (HUAC). The strike at his studio had pushed Disney's politics sharply to the right, and in his testimony he named Hilberman as a potential communist sympathiser. UPA had, in fact, partially formed around leftist political aims: the studio's first major film, *Hell-Bent for Election* (1944), was a propaganda cartoon in support of Roosevelt's re-election. Yet Disney's testimony cast a long shadow over the studio, one that ultimately heralded its demise. By the time UPA released its first foray into feature-length animated films – a form that had been the near-exclusive domain of the Disney studio – with the 1959 Mr. Magoo vehicle *1001 Arabian Nights* the studio was in dire financial straits (Abraham, 2012).

Acclaimed animator Chuck Jones submitted the story for what would become UPA's second and final animated feature, *Gay Purr-ee*. Despite their fiscal predicament, the studio hired megastar Judy Garland to play the film's protagonist, Mewsette, a provincial cat who seeks fame and fortune in 1890s Paris as she is romantically pursued by skilled mouse hunter Jaune Tom (Goulet). At Garland's request, director Hank Saperstein engaged songwriters (and long-time Garland collaborators) Harold Arlen and E.Y. 'Yip' Harburg to compose the film's musical numbers. *Gay Purr-ee* thus became Arlen and Harburg's first time collaborating on a Hollywood score since 1944, due to Arlen's own struggles with the Hollywood anti-communist blacklist (Rimler, 2015, p. 183).

In spite of its major performing and creative talent, *Gay Purr-ee* was an abject critical and box-office failure. *Newsweek* (1962, p. 92) snarkily submitted that 'there seems to be an effort to reach a hitherto undiscovered audience – the fey 4-year-old of recherché taste'. By the mid-1960s, UPA had abandoned its pursuit of animation, and *Gay Purr-ee* had been largely lost to history: even Abraham's (2012, pp. 215–217) book-length study of the studio devotes only three pages to the feature.

Nevertheless, *Gay Purr-ee* and *The Aristocats* serve as useful case studies for the present purposes. In many ways *The Aristocats* represents an archetypal Disney feature, and thus serves as an emblem of the typical American approach to the animated musical. By contrast, *Gay Purr-ee* stands as an *alternative* to this approach, a non-Disney animated feature that was all too rare until the last decades of the 20th century. While we may read *Gay Purr-ee* as an example of UPA's modernist priorities, we may also interpret the film – and, indeed, nearly all of UPA's aesthetic profile – as specific reactions to the Disney style. To this end, despite their varying receptions and legacies, these two dissimilar films provide rich material for an examination of the animated musical's representational and expressive potential.

The hand of the artist

The differences in Disney and UPA's aesthetic priorities can be observed in a purely visual realm. Though an in-depth examination of these representational strategies lies beyond the scope of this article, it is noteworthy that Disney's version of Paris in *The Aristocats* maintains a relatively close connection to visual realism throughout. This is not to say that one could mistake this for a live-action film – the brightly coloured images that fill the screen read as unquestionably animated, to say nothing of the cast of talking animals. Yet it is fair to say that Disney's approach to caricaturing reality remains predominantly consistent and coherent throughout the film's running time. Although anthropomorphic animals constitute the majority of its dramatis personae, the film retains a stubbornly close and persistent relationship

FIGURE 9.1 Consistent visual verisimilitude in *The Aristocats*.

Source: Photo provided by the editor.

with reality. Once viewers accept that the diegesis of *The Aristocats* is one populated by talking (and singing) cats living in Paris at the turn of the 20th century, no individual character, object or piece of scenery appears to be out of place.

The relative verisimilitude of Disney's Paris becomes much more apparent in comparison to UPA's rendering of the city and its surrounding environs in *Gay Purr-ee*. This version of Paris betrays the latter studio's clear indebtedness to modernist design: hyper-saturated colour palettes include extreme yellows (including a yellow sky) in Provence, while Mewsette's arrival in a vividly green and pink-skied Paris immediately mark this diegetic space as blatantly artificial. Compared to Disney's consistent and detailed background paintings, UPA opts for a more conspicuously aestheticised approach in its settings, often featuring visible brush strokes that cut across scenery. A jaunty, almost expressionistic play with perspective informs this space, as the typically straight lines of doors, walls, horizons and so forth now take on improbably skewed angles. In short, UPA's approach to visual representation in this film thus maintains a further distance from reality than Disney's.

What's more, while *The Aristocats* exhibits a largely cohesive visual aesthetic throughout its running time, *Gay Purr-ee* dares to modulate its representational strategies. These shifts are most apparent during the film's several musical numbers which seem to provide implicit permission for UPA's artists to engage in flights of fancy,

FIGURE 9.2 Conspicuously artificial settings in *Gay Purr-ee*.

Source: Photo provided by the editor.

leaning even more heavily into abstraction. For instance, while Mewsette appears on screen several times during the song 'Take My Hand, Paree', each time she appears she seems to take on a different form. Here she appears as a mere suggestion of herself, with only sparse features; there she is no more than an outline against a kaleidoscopic background; there again a lyric reference to Modigliani motivates a caricature of the character in the style of that artist, with enormous eyes and a dramatically elongated neck. In this sequence, as in the vast majority of *Gay Purr-ee*'s other musical numbers, UPA moblises the animated medium for expressive purposes, abandoning diegetic consistency for the sake of heightening emotions and drama.

From a purely visual perspective, the superficially similar *Gay Purr-ee* and *The Aristocats* in fact mobilise the representational potential of animation in drastically different ways. While Disney's consistent, aesthetic approach depicts Paris with an assumption of 'objectivity', UPA allows its images of the city to modulate their relationship with photographic notions of reality in order to shape the film's dramatic arcs. With its marked aesthetic shifts, UPA's representation of Paris in *Gay Purr-ee* is highly subjective, prone to transformation in order to illustrate the emotional impact of a given scene. By contrast, Disney's version of Paris is just that: Disney's Paris, a city presented via the established studio's typical hyperrealist sensibility. If the pleasures of Disney's Paris lie in its resemblance to the real Paris, then UPA's pleasures may be located in its imaginative, oblique refractions of reality.

These films' contrasting approaches to representing the material world through the lens of animation are, as we have seen, indicative of their respective studios' prevailing aesthetic sensibilities. Yet while UPA's inconsistent representational strategies allow *Gay Purr-ee* to present a malleable, emotion-driven view of the world, the film's prismatic shifting also indicates a more profound sense of fracture. With its painterly style and its evident aesthetic shifts, the film draws attention to its status as a film crafted by artists. In the film's yellow skies, distortion of recognisable landmarks and polysemic character designs, viewers sense the presence of a host of animators, background designers and ink-and-painters creatively reinterpreting the world. Disney's dogged pursuit of consistently animated coherent diegeses has precisely the reverse effect.

It is not my intention here to value one film's visual approach over another. Although UPA's constantly shifting and blatantly artificial image systems stand at a marked distance from those of conventional live-action films, such splintering, subjective representational strategies have long been the typical domain of the animated medium. Conversely, by wrangling the theoretically infinite representational potential of the animated medium into a recognisable simulacrum of reality in *The Aristocats*, the Disney studio was carrying forth a set of aesthetic priorities that it had been pursuing for nearly half a century.

Song as fracture

Just as we have observed in their visual approaches, in their profiles as musicals these two films access and deploy the expressive register of song in very different ways, similarly aligning the studios' respective representational strategies with modernist fracture and organic cohesion. Broadly speaking, musicals are typically built upon an essentially splintered paradigm of expression, as characters modulate between the relative realism of spoken dialogue and the more conspicuously aestheticised mode of song. Scott McMillin (2006, p. 6) writes eloquently of the musical negotiating between 'two orders of time' – the direct, linear time of spoken dialogue and the more oblique and cyclical time of music and lyrics. While there exist a variety of strategies for creators of musicals to smooth over these theoretical leaps in logic, it is also possible to heighten the disjunctive experience of the speech-song dialectic.

Gay Purr-ee uses the majority of its musical numbers as spaces of heightened fantasy, even further distancing the film from its already tenuous relationship with reality. Though these songs find slim motivation in plot points, by and large they freeze plot in order to expand upon a character's emotional state, amplifying his or her reaction to a situation through the expressive tools of music and abstract animated images. Thus while the abstracted images in 'Take My Hand, Paree' work to mark this sequence as a fantasy, so too does the presence of song itself. In fact, the majority of *Gay Purr-ee*'s musical numbers in the film work similarly to halt narrative progress in order to explore and reflect upon a state of mind: 'Bubbles' motivates its transition out of speech as a diegetic drinking song, but upon suggesting this justification, the number quickly shifts to a freewheeling riot of colours and can-can debauchery. Later, Jaune Tom conjures an imaginary Mewsette to deliver 'Little Drops of Rain' as an extension of his misery before the screen revels in aquatic images, while the striking 'Paris is a Lonely Town' amplifies Mewsette's desperation into a hyper-expressive dramatic anti-climax. In each case, the film deploys song in order to disrupt the teleological progression of plot and inserts a moment of non-linear expression that emphasises feeling and desire rather than cause and effect.

While *Gay Purr-ee* primarily uses musical numbers to transcend diegetic continuity, *The Aristocats* takes a very different approach. Leaving aside for now the opening title song of Aristocats that acts as an introductory framing device, the Disney film's few musical numbers all grow directly out of narrative incident. Each song finds specific, causal motivation to justify its existence as a break in the register of dialogue into the heightened, aestheticised mode of musical expression. This device effectively minimises the formal gap between the registers of speech and song, contributing to the illusion of continuity from one mode to another.

Duchess literally summons the diegetic 'Scales and Arpeggios' as she commands her children to practise musical fundamentals. In so doing, the number further rationalises its presence in the film as an exercise, something other than a polished performance. The song thus appears rehearsed, perfunctory, even unemotional. Its emphasis on the building blocks of music rather than music itself – witness the references to scales, *arpeggios* and accurate classical vocal technique with the line 'Feel the music ringing from your chest and not your nose' – work to distance this number from the spontaneous welling into song exemplified by *Gay Purr-ee*.[4] Rather than serving the musical number's traditional function as a vehicle for sincere expression of feeling, 'Scales and Arpeggios' instead resembles a rehearsed regurgitation of received cultural artefacts.

Thomas O'Malley's self-titled introductory song largely works to counteract the clinical 'Scales and Arpeggios'. The song opens, unaccompanied, with apparently improvisatory scat syllables: it is as though we've encountered Thomas *in media res*, extemporising a song about himself. As the orchestra enters, brassy interjections from the horn section clearly associate alley cat Thomas with jazz, a popular counterbalance to the classical music of the pampered house cats. The song ends quite like it began, with the orchestra simply fading away leaving Phil Harris to deliver a plummy 'Yeah!' Starting and ending *a capella*, seemingly improvised vocalisations allow this number to appear spontaneous and unrelated to narrative events – and thus theoretically at odds with Disney's attempts at facilitating cohesion between speech and song.[5] Yet 'Thomas O'Malley' finds immediate justification when Duchess applauds and comments on Thomas's talent, thereby causing the audience to recognise the song as a song *per se* and retroactively delineating the entire performance as diegetic. Certainly, 'Thomas O'Malley' provides a dramatically and structurally important tonal balance to 'Scales and Arpeggios', replacing the restraint of elitist society with the earthy sincerity of the commoner and thereby setting the film's underlying romantic subplot into motion. Still, the fact that *The Aristocats* marks both of these songs as self-reflexive performances that spring 'naturally' from the narrative further demonstrates the film's commitment to integrated musical dramaturgy.

The strategy of counterbalancing the cold discipline of 'Scales and Arpeggios' begun by 'Thomas O'Malley' achieves its apotheosis in 'Everybody Wants to Be a Cat', an ecstatic, expansive jazz number composed by Floyd Huddleston and Al Rinker (Hischak and Robinson, 2012). Here, Duchess's family actively joins in a performance initiated by an ethnically diverse group of 'jazz cats', thus musically signifying the house cats' unreserved acceptance of Thomas's bohemian lifestyle. Where kitten pianist Berlioz once played a conventional Alberti bass pattern, here he offers a stride blues progression. Marie's earlier *solfège* syllables now become scat syllables as she mimics Scat Cat and Thomas's 'rinky-dinky-tinky' vocables.[6] The number ends with a New Orleans-style second-line special chorus, complete with cries of 'halleluiah', whose fade-out ending literally brings down the house and suggests an infinite expansion of infectious joy.

The classical/jazz dichotomy presented between 'Scales' and 'Everybody' effectively distils the high/low subtext underlying Duchess and Thomas's relationship. Yet even this sprawling, high-spirited number finds explicit justification as an

FIGURE 9.3 Scat Cat and his musicians point out that 'Everybody Wants to Be a Cat'.

Source: Photo provided by the editor.

organic outgrowth of the film's narrative. Dialogue frames the entirety of 'Everybody Wants to Be a Cat' as an answer to a question:

BERLIOZ: [hearing Scat Cat's gang performing jazz music] It isn't Beethoven, mama, but it sure bounces.
SCAT CAT: Say! This kitten cat knows where it's at!
MARIE: Knows where what's at?
SCAT CAT: Well, little lady, let me elucidate you:
　　[sings] Everybody wants to be a cat . . .

This spoken preamble effectively situates the entire expansive, multi-partite musical number as an elaboration of linear dialogue exchange. Though the song itself primarily reads as a reflection upon an attitude of jazzy coolness (anachronistic though it is to the film's putative setting) and as such largely halts narrative progress, its preceding dialogue works to smooth the transition from speech into song, again contributing to relative cohesion between two discontinuous modes of expression. As a showstopping number that revels in jubilant performance, 'Everybody Wants to Be a Cat' represents an emotional high point of *The Aristocats*, and yet the film is only permitted to access this illogical register of musical presentation when it is carefully aligned as a direct result of linear communication – a justification that is all but absent in a number like 'Take My Hand, Paree'.

All told, although all three of *The Aristocats*' narrative musical numbers fulfil distinctly different dramatic functions, and despite the fact that all three were penned by different composers and lyricists, the film deploys each song in a way that minimises the logical gap between the expressive registers of speech and song. Just as Disney's approach to visual representation embraces aesthetic continuity, so too do its musical numbers work to supply a relatively uniform aural impression of the world. By contrast, *Gay Purr-ee* embraces fragmentation through a logical dissonance that Disney avoids. Musical numbers here emerge with little to no diegetic justification and unfold in fantasy spaces that are clearly not of a piece with the rest of the on-screen world. This method of mobilising song falls in line with UPA's fractured approach to storytelling in its feature.

So far one significant musical number remains unexamined: the Sherman brothers' title song for *The Aristocats*. In many ways, this number presents something of a wrench in the gears of Disney's cohesive approach to the animated musical. The song occurs extra-diegetically, unfolding over the film's credits. What's more, as the credits roll the screen displays a montage of scenes from the upcoming film – Duchess preening, Berlioz playing the piano, Toulouse painting – and yet these characters appear as pencil sketches rather than as fully fleshed out and coloured images. Animators typically create such footage as so-called 'pencil tests', allowing them to check for fluidity of motion before sending a scene to the inking, painting and background departments where it is prepared to be photographed for the finished product (Furniss, 2007, p. 101). By revealing this pencil test footage to its audience, Disney appears, quite unusually, to be revealing the mechanics of its production, displaying the self-aware hand of the artist(s) that historically was anathema to the studio's sensibilities. In so doing, the opening number of *The Aristocats* seem to work against the film's prevailing paradigm of uninterrupted aesthetic continuity.

In order to make sense of this apparent disruption, it is imperative to examine the effect of the opening song's performer, Maurice Chevalier. To do so, we would do well to read Disney's use of Chevalier beside the presence of Judy Garland, the star of *Gay Purr-ee*. Though the size and scope of Garland's and Chevalier's roles in these films differ drastically, both performers exert similar effects on the animated diegeses to which they lend their voices. What follows should be considered a brief foray into rich territory, a series of gestures indicating the potential for future scholarship on Chevalier and Garland and on voice acting in animated film more generally.

Stars and the threat/promise of recognition

By the time they appeared in *Gay Purr-ee* and *The Aristocats* respectively, both Judy Garland and Maurice Chevalier had firmly established themselves as Hollywood superstars. Although Garland was more than 30 years Chevalier's junior, her long stint as an MGM-contracted child performer meant that their Hollywood film careers overlapped by several decades (DiOrio, 1973; Schechter, 2002). Both actors possessed a distinctive performance style, a trademark constellation of aural, visual and intertextual signifiers that not only distinguished them from other performers but indeed identified both actors as uniquely themselves. While the quality of being singularly recognisable through one's distinctive (if not inimitable) performance style is not unique to these performers, extant scholarship on Garland and Chevalier suggests that both of these actors exerted a similar phenomenological effect on their audiences. Building upon this literature, I contend that the ways in which *Gay Purr-ee* and *The Aristocats* deploy these two star personas extend their respective allegiances to fractured and integrated diegeses.

When he made his sound film debut in the late 1920s, Chevalier was already recognisable to many Americans as a theatrical entertainer. In the process of making the transfer from stage to screen, the consummate showman brought with him the mannerisms he developed as a live performer. Jane Feuer (1993, p. 2) explains that the recognisable image he carried from the stage allowed him to access modes of direct address that were atypical in film:

> Chevalier was even permitted to break a Hollywood taboo by looking directly into the lens to address the cinema audience. In *One Hour with You* [1932], Chevalier winked and leered into the lens as if letting the spectator in on a dirty joke.

Throughout the 1930s, as he became a mainstay of sophisticated film musicals, Chevalier regularly called upon these traits, codifying a style of performance that remained relatively consistent from role to role. As Chevalier biographer Michael Freedland (1981, pp. 104–105) writes,

> Unlike his mentor, Al Jolson, whom he so wanted to emulate, a Chevalier performance on screen [turned] out to be very much like Chevalier on stage . . . it soon became clear that Maurice himself didn't vary from one kind of performance to another. And with the same performance there was the same accent.

Chevalier typically portrayed variations on the same witty Frenchman, all smirks, deflating asides and cheerful demeanour. Audiences expected him to sing in his films, just as he had on stage, and in many cases he delivered these songs directly towards the camera. His costuming also became codified: white gloves, a bow tie, a cane and especially a straw boater hat came to stand as synecdochic signs for Chevalier. As early as 1932, the mere sight of a boater hat perched above a crudely drawn silhouette announces the performer's presence before he actually appears on-screen in the opening of *Love Me Tonight*.

Due to the regularity with which he relied upon a set of trademark performance mannerisms, Chevalier seemed to transcend the individual roles he played from film to film. Rather than disappearing into parts as a Stanislavski-trained actor might, Chevalier instead presented audiences with a single, identifiable persona thrown into a variety of circumstances. Because they were expected to sing, Chevalier characters seemed to need no justification to break into song. Audiences immediately identified each character as another extension of the Chevalier persona, and thus such diegesis-fracturing devices as songs and direct address became normative rather than disruptive strategies. Indeed, the mere presence of Chevalier in a film might be read as a breach of sorts, in that it is nigh impossible to separate the specifics of an individual role from the wide-reaching persona of the actor. Though frequent co-star Jeanette MacDonald, for instance, typically portrayed similar characters from film to film – variations upon a beautiful ingénue with a lovely singing voice – Chevalier's performance mannerisms were so specific as to make the characters he played inseparable from the performer himself.

It is through this sense of double recognition that we may link Maurice Chevalier and Judy Garland. Several writers have pointed out how Garland frequently took on roles that seemed to mimic her own 'real life' (or at least the public perception of her life), particularly after she was released from her contract with MGM in 1950. As Richard Dyer (1986, p. 143) puts it,

> much of her post-1950 career deliberately evokes and reworks her early career. Both *A Star is Born* (1954) and *I Could Go on Singing* (1963) are clearly based on Garland's life story, and 'Born in a Trunk' in the former is like a knowing précis of the image MGM had fostered.

Queer readings of Garland's reception have pointed to precisely this overlap between fiction and perceived reality as a key component of the performer's special appeal to gay men. Taking as his foundation the experience of *passing* – that is, the phenomenon of a queer person (in this case, a gay man) feeling forced to outwardly perform apparently normative heterosexuality in public in order to avoid potentially negative social repercussions – Jack Babuscio (2004, p. 126) writes that the attendant 'awareness of the double aspect of performance . . . goes a long way to explain why gays form a disproportionately large part of the audience of stars such as, most notably, Judy Garland'.

Like Chevalier, Garland's film acting promoted a double awareness of her characters as simultaneously diegetic and extra-diegetic. Unlike Chevalier, however, Garland's tendency to be recognised as herself stemmed less from an unmistakable performance style and more from a perceived system of intersections between her on- and off-screen personas. From a queer perspective, in Babuscio's (2004, p. 126) words, 'Garland's popularity owes much to the fact that she is always, and most intensely, herself'. Dyer (1986, p. 154) nuances Babuscio's take (first published in 1977), submitting that 'the sense of Garland performing herself, enacting her life on screen or stage, is a recognition of the theatricality of experience that the gay sensibility is attuned to'.

In a sense, the presence of a well-known star in a film, animated or otherwise, creates the potential for diegetic disruption. In the act of recognising a specific performer, viewers may be drawn out of the film's hermetic system of diegesis, if only briefly, as they locate the figures on screen as at once characters in a self-contained story *and* as 'real-life' stars playing parts. Yet the conceit that characters in film are necessarily identifiable as aspects of their live performers is so common as to nearly negate this double recognition as particularly disruptive. What's more, Dyer (1998, p. 20) articulates the inherent flaws in the notion that audiences recognise famous performers as 'real people', reminding us that stars

> serve to disguise the fact that they are just as much produced images, constructed personalities as 'characters' are. Thus the value embodied by a star is as it were harder to reject as 'impossible' or 'false', because the star's existence guarantees the existence of the value s/he embodies.

The system that creates and disseminates images of stars to the masses – in this case (and especially) Hollywood – in fact relies on audiences recognising on-screen figures as simultaneously fictional characters and actual people. This bifurcated mode of reception encourages the consumer to believe in the 'genuine persona' of a star, even as this image is typically just as artificial and constructed as the characters the actor portrays on screen.

While the visible presence of actors on screen in a live-action film all but assures a putative identification of actors with their roles, by its very nature the medium of animation redirects sound away from its actual source and relays it through imagined, artificially constructed bodies. Historically, accomplished voice actors like Mel Blanc were valued for their ability to carry out this very act of transformation themselves, concealing their real voice by metamorphosing it into a range of character-specific sonic traits (Lawson and Persons, 2004). Creators of animated

films can thus endeavour, with little effort, to mask the identity of their performers, subsuming their auras into an apparently seamless and self-contained diegesis.

As we have seen, however, the mere presence of performers like Garland and
Chevalier can be said to preclude the possibility of a hermetically sealed diegetic
construction. The act of recognition immediately draws attention to the star's
extra-filmic personality and thus towards the mechanics of the film's production:
audiences can picture the celebrity voice actor in a recording booth, contributing
to but ultimately distinct from the artificial on-screen world. As such, in attaching
the voice of a particularly well-known live performer to an animated character,
filmmakers can endeavour to promote the double recognition of character and star.
In this context Barbara Klingler (1989, p. 14) emphasises:

> Composed of animated characters, as opposed to actor's physical bodies, ani-
> mated films obviate the corporeality of the star performer from the image
> track. The stars' voices, however, remain inscribed on the film's soundtrack;
> the voice becomes the vehicle through which the animated image is 'indis-
> solubly attached to a star, becoming part of a star/character unit'.

Viewed through this critical lens, audiences can sense the presence of a star in
an animated film, even as the reality of the performer's physical body is effaced.
Donald Crafton (2013, p. 19) agrees, writing that, when an audience watches an
animated performance, 'it's as though viewers are in two places simultaneously,
within the fiction and outside it'. This paradigm would seem doubly true in cases
of a *singing* star – that is, a star known especially for his or her voice. How, then, do
UPA and Disney manage their star performers' voices with regards to this potential
for diegetic rupture?

The very first moments of *Gay Purr-ee* warrant close scrutiny. As the opening
credits begin, a few notes played by a solo accordion unfold over the Warner Bros.
logo, identifying the film's distributor while instantly and unmistakably evoking its
Parisian setting through familiar aural cues. After a mere three bars of introduction, an off-screen voice delivers the title line of the opening song, pleading 'Take
my hand, Paree' in a mellifluous contralto. Lest there be any confusion regarding
the source of this voice, the credits immediately make clear what most audience
members likely already knew: it is the voice of Judy Garland. A portrait of Garland
herself – smiling and wide-eyed, wearing a high collared Victorian blouse and a
brooch sporting the Tricolour – accompanies her name. By the next line of the
song, Garland's name and (human) portrait disappear, replaced by a labelled image
of Mewsette. The orchestra swells and Garland's voice drops out as the credits
reveal the film's title and studio. Though this entire process takes only 30 seconds, it reveals a wealth of information regarding *Gay Purr-ee*'s treatment of its star
performer. By immediately identifying its star – sonically through the distinctive
sound of her voice, but also visually via a portrait of the actress – the film fairly
commands the viewer to recognise Mewsette not as a self-contained character in
the filmic diegesis but rather as an explicit extension of Judy Garland herself.[7]

Gay Purr-ee's invitation for the audience to read Mewsette as an animated augmentation of Judy Garland extends far beyond its opening credits. Apart from her feline form, Mewsette in fact behaves very much like the types of characters for which Garland was best known. Like Betsy Booth in the Andy Hardy films, Dorothy Gale in *The Wizard of Oz*, Hannah Brown in *Easter Parade* (1948) and Esther Blodgett/Vicki Lester in *A Star is Born*, the character escapes her humble, provincial beginnings to pursue excitement, glamour and fame in the big city. Here, Paris becomes a stand-in for the endless magical possibilities of New York, Hollywood and Oz. Like Vicki Lester, Mewsette is primped and prodded, moulded into a beautiful form to be captured on screen in the former film and on canvas in the latter (see Figure 4). Also, like Lester, Mewsette ultimately achieves her goal of being celebrated and adored, but not without incurring devastating consequences along the way: one through the death of her lover, the other by narrowly escaping being forced into human (feline?) trafficking.

Likewise, Garland's performance as Mewsette is typically melodramatic, dealing in the extreme emotional shifts that Garland specialised in. Mewsette's large eyes (a physical feature further linking the character to Garland) burst frequently into tears; when Jaune Tom confronts her about her desire to move to Paris, she instantly transforms into a tragic figure, sobbing 'I wish I were dead!' The shattering blues

FIGURE 9.4 Judy Garland as a made-over Mewsette.

Source: Photo provided by the editor

number 'Paris is a Lonely Town' finds Garland at her dramatic best, delivering a wailing torch song that builds in intensity over its four-minute length. The climax of this sequence portrays the Seine splintering into a jagged line as Garland, in full belt, sings 'River, river, won't you be my lover? Don't turn me down!' The number ends with a shot of Mewsette perched on the edge of a bridge, peering despondently into the river below. What began as a torch song has now become a suicide scene, echoing Garland's own highly publicised attempts at suicide in the years leading up to *Gay Purr-ee*'s release (DiOrio, 1973; Dyer, 1986; Schechter, 2002). Though perhaps in poor taste, UPA's inclusion of a suicide aria here falls in line with the typical roles Judy Garland accepted post-MGM. The presumed connections between Mewsette's devastation and Garland's perceived real-life struggles makes the drama of the scene significantly more striking and immediate.

All of these instances of apparent alignment suggest that the studio hoped to encourage audiences to recognise the voice behind the cat. While constantly drawing attention to the actual source of Mewsette's voice may have the effect of revealing the character's (and, by extension, the entire film's) origins in labour and effort, the resulting recognition of *Gay Purr-ee*'s artifice lies neatly in line with the film's embrace of fractured aesthetic priorities. Coupled with the film's quicksilvery visuals and plot-halting discursions into fantastical song, the looming ever-presence of Judy Garland's persona permits UPA to explore extreme registers of emotion and drama. *Gay Purr-ee*'s complex and tenuous relationship with realistic depiction may thus be read as deliberate work towards exploiting the expressive potential of animated musical.

But what of Chevalier's appearance in *The Aristocats*, a film that relentlessly insists upon a cohesive diegetic construction? Although Feuer (1993, p. 39) warns against reading Chevalier's propensity for direct address as 'inherently subversive or radical' as they are in, for instance, the films of Jean-Luc Godard, she still recognises these breaks of the fourth wall as a diegetic breach – a strategy that would be antithetical to *The Aristocats*' carefully hewn diegesis.

Though brief, Chevalier's performance firmly asserts his presence in the film. The credits over which his song appears make no attempt to conceal his identity, prominently acknowledging the singer for his contribution at the very opening of the sequence. Belying his age, Chevalier delivers a typically charismatic performance of the Sherman brothers' jaunty tune, whose prominent accordion line and use of French lyrics reveal an overt vehicle for its intended singer. Chevalier even contributes a '*hanh-hanh-hanh*' chuckle before launching into the final verse, sung entirely in un-subtitled French. Although this stanza is simply a translation of the previous verse, it nevertheless represents the most prolonged deployment of the French language in either of the two films discussed here. Even as a disembodied voice, Chevalier's presence indelibly marks the opening of the film.

Nearly an hour after this opening scene, *The Aristocats* manifests Chevalier once again through visual signifiers. A brief shot in 'Everybody Wants to Be a Cat' displays Berlioz and Toulouse dancing atop an unmistakable straw bowler hat placed beside a pair of white gloves and a cane. On the line 'I've heard some corny birds

FIGURE 9.5 Berlioz and Toulouse dance on Maurice Chevalier's bowler hat; in the foreground can be seen the other accessories of his famous costume, the white gloves and the cane.

Source: Photo provided by the editor.

who tried to sing, but a cat's the only cat who knows how to swing' the kittens fall through their platform, shattering the hat. This fleeting sequence of events further asserts Chevalier's persona on the animated diegesis while simultaneously marking him (and, by extension, his performance style) as old-fashioned, passé and 'corny' in comparison to hep jazz.

Though the initial release of *The Aristocats* fell several years beyond the heyday of his fame, a great many of its audience members could be expected to identify the performer's singular persona. As with Judy Garland's presence in *Gay Purr-ee*, the viewer's unambiguous identification of the person behind the voice similarly enables a double recognition of performer *and* character, process *and* result, thereby calling attention to the inherent artifice of the animated realm on screen. And although UPA's mobilisation of Garland falls in line with the studio's expressively prismatic projection of the world, Chevalier's apparent breach seems to provide a striking exception to Disney's otherwise close and controlled relationship with reality.

Yet while in theory Chevalier and Garland may prompt similarly disruptive effects on their onscreen worlds, the ultimate results of these disruptions are quite different. Where Garland's presence constantly draws attention to Mewsette's origins in human labour, by placing Chevalier's disembodied voice over 'behind-the-scenes' pencil test footage Disney firmly locates the performer outside of *The Aristocats'* narrative world, situating the entire opening number as a sort of overture. Because the film works to safely contain Chevalier within an extradiegetic preamble, the singer's voice acts like a legitimising presence for *The Aristocats'* Parisian setting. That he sings a verse *en Français, sans sous-titres* doesn't matter: the mere sound of Chevalier's distinctive voice, later coupled with the image of his costume, evoke a nostalgic Gallic landscape that would be instantly recognisable to the film's initial audiences. We may thus understand Disney's use of Chevalier as a strategic tool for further creating an animated diegesis that would fall closely in line with viewers' expectations for the sights and sounds of the 'real' Paris.

Conclusion

In typically bold language, Paul Wells (2002, p. 2) summarises the history of American animation in the first half of the 20th century as follows:

> The great era of animation in United States from the late 1920s to the early post-war period is in itself perceived to be the summation of the form's achievement . . . the pre-eminence of the Disney studio and its output became synonymous with animation in a way that virtually marginalized any address of other work. This critical paradigm, which rightly elevated the work of the Disney studio to the status of 'art' while acknowledging its reassuring populist and ideological credentials, also managed to marginalize for many years the work of other pioneers in the field and the achievements in other areas of cartoon animation.

Although recent decades have seen the regular emergence of viable alternatives to the Disney model of the American animated feature film, Wells' positioning of the Disney Animation Studio at the epicentre of American feature animation can still be strongly felt today, and this was certainly true in the 1960s and '70s.[8]

The Aristocats' cohesive aesthetic strategies make the film conventional: conventional for Disney animation, and conventional in the sense that its efforts to collapse the distances between animation and live-action, musical expression and speech, allow it to resemble a recognisable version of reality with only moderate adjustments. This conservatism is particularly striking in comparison to *Gay Purr-ee*, whose abstract visuals and use of songs as plot-halting fantastical excursions work hard against the modes of visual representation that Disney had all but codified by the time of the film's release. Had Disney not maintained a stranglehold on audience expectations for the feature-length animated musical, *Gay Purr-ee* would likely have been received as conventional in its own way, given its blithe reliance upon subjective representation and exaggerated slapstick comedy that were familiar to nearly every other American studio's approach to the animated medium. Yet it is precisely *because* of Disney's centrality to audience expectations – not only for long-form narrative animated musicals, but for the representational strategies of animation itself – that *Gay Purr-ee* reads as an exception to the rule. Indeed, it is due to this very centrality that *Gay Purr-ee* exists in the first place.

Despite their superficial similarities, *Gay Purr-ee* and *The Aristocats* harness the animated musical's potential for representation to radically different ends. Still, by turning to this pliable, even volatile mode of expression, both films fundamentally allow their viewers to escape reality for an hour or so. Though their approaches may differ, both *Gay Purr-ee* and *The Aristocats* entertain, amuse and move us, all while giving us a cat's-eye-view of a multifarious Paris.

Notes

1 For extant literature on the animated musical, see Knapp, 2006, pp. 125–131; Smith, 2011, pp. 167–178; Rodosthenous, 2017; Bohn, 2017; Batchelder, 2018.
2 Thanks to Olaf Jubin for indicating these similarities.
3 See Disney's *Toot, Whistle, Plunk, and Boom* (1953) and *Pigs is Pigs* (1954).
4 The Sherman brothers also use form to carry forth this emphasis on practice. At first blush, the song falls into an awkward approximation of an AABA, with lopsided nine, eight, four and ten-bar phrases. Yet the first and final sections both open with a rote recitation of the triadic *solfège* syllables 'do-mi-sol-do'. Upon removing these utterances as 'extramusical' material set apart from the rest of the song, the tune now falls into a far more conventional eight-eight-four-eight system of bar distribution.
5 It is difficult to avoid comparison between 'Thomas O'Malley' and 'The Bare Necessities', a number performed by the bear Baloo in *The Jungle Book*. Both are Terry Gilkyson-penned vehicles for characters voiced by Phil Harris, and both serve as expository devices to introduce their respective, similarly laid-back personas. More strikingly, both numbers open with unaccompanied off-screen scatting. If 'Thomas O'Malley' appears derivative of 'Bare Necessities' – or, indeed, if Thomas reads as a facsimile of Baloo in a different form – this speaks to the Disney studio's creative paralysis upon the death of its founder.
6 Scat Cat and Thomas O'Malley are portrayed by Scatman Crothers and Phil Harris, respectively. Both of these performers enjoyed successful careers as jazz musicians outside of their work as actors.
7 The identification of a score composed by frequent Garland collaborators Arlen and Harburg further encourages this recognition.
8 See especially the work of Pixar, DreamWorks and Laika, along with numerous international and independent animators.

References

Abraham, A. (2012) *When Magoo Flew: The Rise and Fall of Animation Studio UPA*. Middletown: Wesleyan University Press.

Babuscio, J. (2004) 'Camp and the Gay Sensibility,' in H. Benshoff and S. Griffin (eds.) *Queer Cinema, the Film Reader*. Abingdon: Routledge, pp. 121–136.

Barrier, M. (1999) *Hollywood Cartoons: American Animation in Its Golden Age*. New York: Oxford University Press.

Batchelder, D. (2018) *American Magic: Song, Animation, and Drama in Disney's Golden Age Musicals (1928–1942)*. Cleveland: Case Western Reserve University.

Bohn, J. (2017) *Music in Disney's Animated Features: Snow White and the Seven Dwarfs to The Jungle Book*. Jackson: University of Mississippi Press.

Care, R. (2002) 'Make Walt's Music: Music for Disney Animation,' in D. Goldmark and Y. Taylor (eds.) *The Cartoon Music Book*. Chicago: A Capella Books, pp. 21–36.

Crafton, D. (2013) *Shadow of a Mouse: Performance, Belief, and World-Making in Animation*. Berkeley: University of California Press.

DiOrio, A. (1973) *Little Girl Lost: The Life and Hard Times of Judy Garland*. New Rochelle: Arlington House Publishers.

Dyer, R. (1998) *Stars*. New edition. London: BFI Publishing.

———. (1986) *Heavenly Bodies: Film Stars and Society*. New York: St. Martin's Press.

Feuer, J. (1993) *The Hollywood Musical*. 2nd edition. Bloomington, IN: Indiana University Press.

Freedland, M. (1981) *Maurice Chevalier*. New York: William Morrow.

Furniss, M. (2007) *A New History of Animation*. New York: Thames and Hudson.

———. (1998) *Art in Motion: Animation Aesthetics*. Revised edition. Eastleigh: John Libbey Publishing.

Gabler, N. (2006) *Walt Disney: The Triumph of the American Imagination*. New York: Alfred A. Knopf.

Goldmark, D. (2007) 'Before *Willie*: Reconsidering Music and the Animated Cartoon of the 1920s,' in D. Goldmark, L. Kramer and R. Leppert (eds.) *Beyond the Soundtrack: Representing Music in Cinema*. Berkeley: University of California Press, pp. 225–245.

Hischak, T. and Robinson, M. (2012) *The Disney Song Encyclopedia*. Updated edition. Lanham: Taylor Trade.

Klingler, B. (1989) 'Digressions at the Cinema: Reception and Mass Culture,' *Cinema Journal*, 28(4), pp. 3–19.

Knapp, R. (2006) *The American Musical and the Performance of Personal Identity*. Princeton, NJ: Princeton University Press.

Lawson, T. and Persons, A. (2004) *The Magic Behind the Voices: A Who's Who of Cartoon Voice Actors*. Jackson: University Press of Mississippi.

McMillin, S. (2006) *The Musical as Drama*. Princeton, NJ: Princeton University Press.

Newsweek. (1962) 'The Cat's Meow. Review of *Gay Purr-ee*,' *Newsweek*, 26 November, p. 92.

Rimler, W. (2015) *The Man That Got Away: The Life and Songs of Harold Arlen*. Urbana: University of Illinois Press.

Rodosthenous, G. (ed.) (2017) *The Disney Musical on Stage and Screen*. New York: Bloomsbury.

Schechter, S. (2002) *Judy Garland: The Day-by-Day Chronicle of a Legend*. New York: Cooper Square Press.

Smith, S. (2011) 'The Animated Film Musical,' in R. Knapp, M. Morris and S. Wolf (eds.) *The Oxford Handbook of the American Musical*. New York: Oxford University Press, pp. 167–178.

Thomas, F. and Johnson, O. (1981) *The Illusion of Life: Disney Animation*. Revised edition. Glendale: Disney Editions.

Watts, S. (1997) *The Magic Kingdom: Walt Disney and the American Way of Life*. Columbia: University of Missouri Press.

Wells, P. (2002) *Animation and America*. New Brunswick: Rutgers University Press.

———. (1998) *Understanding Animation*. London: Routledge.

PART IV
West End Paris

10

SHOCKWAVES AT A DISTANCE

Ellis and Herbert's *Bless the Bride*

John Snelson

One the most noted of the new British musical theatre works in London's West End in the immediate wake of World War II was *Bless the Bride*, an apparent throwback to mid-19th-century light opera distilled through early 20th-century musical comedy and influenced only to a limited degree by 1940s popular song.[1] It concerns the seduction in Victorian England of an innocent young woman by a visiting Frenchman. On the eve of her marriage to someone else, he awakens her heart to love and they run away to the French coast in defiance of the expectations of her rigid, even xenophobic family and to the dismay of her English fiancé. At the final curtain everyone is reconciled and the true lovers from two nations are set to be married. The script and lyrics are by A. P. Herbert, the music by Vivian Ellis, and the show was conceived and produced by C. B. Cochran. It opened at the Adelphi Theatre on 26 April 1947.

Cochran was a long-established and highly successful theatre impresario, in his mid-seventies by the time of this show. He was instrumental in providing the tone and location of the story, in continuation of his desire for something 'thoroughly English' as he had wanted with *Big Ben*, his show of the preceding year at the Adelphi, created with Ellis and Herbert (Pound, 1976, p. 199). *Bless the Bride* is set in just two locations, both semi-fictitious. The first is The Grange, a country manor house in the village of Mayfield in Sussex, which references the site of Cochran's own childhood at Lindfield in Sussex (Ellis, 1953, p. 228). As for the second, Cochran asked Herbert to 'find an excuse to go to Trouville for one scene, it would make a nice change': Trouville-sur-Mer in Normandy is adjacent to the more famously elegant holiday resort town of Deauville, which Herbert presented in the show as 'Eauville' (Pound, 1976, p. 205). This chapter is particularly distinguished from the others in this volume in that *Bless the Bride* has no scene set in Paris.

So what relevance could this British period piece have in a volume exploring the presentation of Paris in stage and screen musicals? The answer lies in an extraordinary, brief and even shocking speech on the penultimate page of the whole script. This final scene takes place at The Grange, where the twenty-first birthday celebrations of the young English woman at the centre of the plot, Lucy Veronica Veracity Willow, are under way. Dancing is stopped by the abrupt and unexpected appearance of a familiar character within the story, Suzanne Valdis, a French actress known to the family. Throughout the story she has been jealous of the mutual love between her fellow French actor Pierre Fontaine and Lucy. She regales them all, beginning 'En Angleterre the polka! In Paris, the hunger, the famine, the cold!' (Herbert, 1948, p. 62). Suzanne's intrusion, her anger, the reference to dancing and the contrast of the English domestic scene on stage with her description of Paris – this chapter explores how all of these come together in Suzanne's full speech and, as a consequence, what *Bless the Bride* reveals of the significance of evoking Paris at this time and in this place. The resonances that emerge account in part for the show's success immediately post-war as well as its subsequent neglect as those resonances have faded down the years in significance and particularly in recognition.[2] In the context of this volume, *Bless the Bride* contributes a rare example in a musical of how Paris is evoked not as a geographical setting for the story, but entirely for its symbolic significance to the show's home audience of the day.

French kisses

The story of *Bless the Bride* is predicated on an antithesis of character traits rooted in English and French national identities. Lucy's Victorian family is emotionally restricted and hidebound by convention, while Lucy's fiancé The Hon. Thomas Trout is unprincipled.[3] The point of that last name with its title is that Trout is *dis*honourable, happy to lie to suit his needs. In his establishing number 'I'm too Good to Be True', Thomas sings that 'I have found it proper to tell quite a whopper' and 'Too much of the truth is unkind and uncouth' (Herbert, 1948, p. 8). He is set up as an inappropriate husband for a young woman one of whose middle names is Veracity, the meaning of which 'has coloured all my life. To whatever other excesses I may be tempted, I have always detested, and resisted, any departure from the truth' (Herbert, 1948, p. 9). The discovery that her fiancé actively lies results in her introductory solo, whose lyrics make clear that she is marrying out of duty, not love, wishing it were 'Any Man but Thomas T' (Herbert, 1948, p. 10).

Enter Pierre Fontaine, the leading man, immediately after Lucy's expressed resignation to a wedded state of less than bliss. In contrast to the Hon. Thomas Trout, Pierre is emotionally open and genuine – a model of the charming, romantically motivated Frenchman. Importantly, Pierre stirs Lucy's heart to sincere emotion for the first time when he kisses her, then appeals to her not to marry but instead run away with him to France. Pierre's kiss sends Lucy spinning into the joyful waltz song 'I Was Never Kissed Before', whose title alone questions the relationship of Lucy and her erstwhile fiancé. The waltz is a genre associated with the Continent, which

FIGURE 10.1 The young English lady and the French actor: Lizbeth Webb (Lucy) and Georges Guétary (Pierre), the two stars of *Bless the Bride* (1947).

Source: Photo by Denis de Marney, courtesy of Getty Images.

imbues the song with a musical intimation of freedom and emotional charge.[4] Interpolated dialogue makes the dramatic meaning explicit.

PIERRE: Mademoiselle, I see you open like a rose. In two minutes you are grown up. Is there not a small bird fluttering inside you?
   [He places his hands on his heart.]
LUCY: *[. . . her hands on her heart].* That is perfectly true. What is it?
PIERRE: It is your heart. It is the first time you know you have a heart?
LUCY: My mother would never tell me where it was.

(Herbert, 1948, p. 18)

There is an archness, a conscious element of parody associated with the English characters, shown by Lucy's final comment above, in which a statement appropriate to her innocence is nonetheless designed to cadence with a laugh for the audience. But Pierre is characterised throughout as sincere, with no hint of parody. Lucy's values move away from those of her upbringing towards his, and she becomes a more rounded character, able to evoke empathy and gain sympathy from the audience when the story takes its darker turn.

The script does not state explicitly that Pierre is a Parisian, but the lyrics of 'I Was Never Kissed Before' invite such an association: he does promise to show

Lucy round Paris and visit his mother's house in the Bois d'Issy (a suburb in the southwest of Paris).[5] The charming Frenchman is a product of sophisticated Paris life, especially in 1870, by which time Paris had come to be viewed as the global city *par excellence*. Georges Guétary, who created the role, added an extra aura of apparent authenticity, with a personality and a voice – speech and singing – that exuded Paris seduction and sophistication (although, in fact, not a French citizen until naturalised in 1950).[6] He was cast in Paris, where Cochran, Herbert and Ellis held auditions. As Ellis recalled:

> The moment we met George Guétary at lunch, we both felt that he was our man. True, he knew practically no English, but being Greek, he would learn it, as he had learnt French. Guétary was one of the least troublesome and most hardworking stars I have ever had the pleasure of knowing.[7]
>
> *(1953, p. 231)*

There was an element of English/emerging – French/experienced reflexivity in the casting of Lucy and Pierre. Lizbeth Webb was the young English performing rose, creating her first leading role, written expressly for her, in the West End after being noticed in a minor role in her previous – and first – West End musical, *Big Ben*.[8] The ages of Lizbeth and Lucy neatly match at the time the time *Bless the Bride* opened. In contrast – suited to the more world-aware character of Frenchman Pierre – Guétary was an experienced, internationally rising cabaret singer-performer, having established himself as the leading member of the quartet known as 'Les Boys' who accompanied the French star Mistinguett in her revues at the Casino de Paris in the late 1930s. During the War, he developed a valuable performing relationship with the French songwriter Francis Lopez, with whose songs and shows he was to be associated for much of his career. Subsequently, Guétary became most widely known internationally for his performance in the film *An American in Paris* (1951), in duet with Gene Kelly in 'S'Wonderful', and epitomising the Parisian cabaret ideal in 'Stairway to Paradise' while playing out part of his own performance history.

Two discs of musical extracts from *Bless the Bride* were released on the Columbia label.[9] The recording took place in March 1947, in advance of the stage première, under the show's Musical Director Michael Collins and with the chorus and the theatre orchestra. Guétary sings in all four numbers. Two are performed with Webb as Lucy, where her English RP (received pronunciation) accent makes an evident contrast with Guétary's French accent in 'This Is My Lovely Day' and 'I Was Never Kissed Before'. Indeed, Guétary's accent dominates the recordings, not least with his two romantically directed solos, the pseudo-Gallic folk song 'Ma Belle Marguerite' and the tango 'Table for Two'. At the time of the opening of *Bless the Bride*, Guétary was being introduced to the British audience as a Parisian rising star, bringing native authenticity to the role in which he had been cast. This association was further made in a song recorded by Guétary the following month, again under Michael Collins and for which Vivian Ellis was composer-lyricist as well as a flamboyantly rippling pianist on the recording. The title of the song makes its character

FIGURE 10.2   A foreign actor making a splash on the post-war London stage: Georges Guétary is watched by theatrical manager C. B. Cochran as he cuts the cake to celebrate the one hundredth performance of *Bless the Bride* at the Adelphi Theatre.

Source: Photo by Anthony Wallace, courtesy of Shutterstock.

self-explanatory: 'I Dreamt I Was Back in Paris'.[10] The song annexes Guétary's promoted French identity with lyrics that name-check the familiar Paris attractions – especially clichéd to us many decades and so many more Paris songs later – that include such resonant locations as the Champs-Élysées, Montmartre, Montparnasse and the place de la Concorde. With the couplet 'Notre Dame, Vendôme, Mogador, I saw them all once more', the lyric references religion, politics and entertainment in a single line. The Théâtre Mogador is an especially appropriate reference for its operetta, musical theatre and revue associations. There is an association that makes Paris and France synonymous in Guétary's performance identity in a similar way to that of the older generations of notable performer Parisians-by-birth Mistinguett and Maurice Chevalier.[11] Like them, Guétary provides a shorthand for 'Paris'.[12]

An *Entente Cordiale*?

Act II of *Bless the Bride* opens in Eauville, to which Lucy has escaped with Pierre. To keep matters proper, Suzanne is present as chaperone to Lucy, although Pierre finds a way to have time alone with Lucy. The presentation of their new love is increasingly undercut by Suzanne, whose role within the entire show is to voice French scepticism of the English. In Act I, she tells Pierre in French what her opinion of his interest in Lucy will lead to: 'Veux-tu casser la tête contre une famille anglaise? Regarde autour de toi. Ils ressemblent au Rocher de Gibraltar' (Herbert, 1948, p. 23).[13] Suzanne's national stereotyping counterbalances that from Lucy's family of the French, throwing into relief Pierre and Lucy's open natures. Suzanne also voices the threat of war between France and Germany, undercutting seaside enjoyment, new love and the ignorant, flippant voicings of Lucy's family. Suzanne's role is to puncture the romantic bubble of Pierre and Lucy by speaking the unvarnished truth. Except on one life-changing point that emerges only at the end, Suzanne says it like it is. In the touching trio 'Mon Pauvre Petit Pierre' – musically wistful in its minor key and folk song structure with falling repetitions – Suzanne tells Pierre to leave Lucy and get ready: 'The King of Prussia makes attack – Vous allez à la guerre. . . . You must love only France to-day.' Pierre resists: 'To all the Emperors we say "There must not be a war to-day".' But by the end of the number, even Lucy sees the writing on the wall, now joining with Suzanne in telling Pierre 'Vous allez à la guerre' (Herbert, 1948, pp. 38–39). The Franco-Prussian war began on 19 July 1870, with the Siege of Paris beginning on 19 September; both Siege and War ended on 28 January 1871. The United Kingdom remained neutral throughout. Herbert's script brings together all of these historical events in its final scene.

When Lucy's family arrive to find her, what draws attention to them is their poor or non-existent command of the French language, ignorance of the most commonplace of activities and even the adoption of false beards as disguises by the men (father Augustus, cousin George and spurned fiancé Thomas). Their parody madrigal 'The Englishman' mocks a 19th-century clichéd view of the British Empire for its 1940s audience, who could thus laugh at themselves and recognise the unthreatening comedic tone in place of admitting any more serious intent in its lines. Lucy's mother, Mary declares:

> And I am tempted, I confess,
> To self-congratulation,
> When I reflect that I possess
> The virtues of my nation.
> And daily let my neighbours see
> How different their lives might be
> If they would but be ruled by me.

(Herbert, 1948, p. 42)

There is something of the wry smile of relief here from a victor's perspective, given that the same lyrics could be seen to apply to the designs of any nation on their neighbours, not least those of Germany on France.

Lucy's family end up at a restaurant table near to that of Pierre and Lucy. The waiters and Frenchmen in the ensemble 'The Fish' mix together the serving of the food, the impending Franco-Prussian war and suspicions that the strangers are Prussian spies: 'C'est la guerre! Au Rhin! Sept verres de vin. Vive la guerre. Deux champignons. Vive la guerre. Quatre jambons. . . . Anglais? Qui sait? Américains? Russes? Prusses? Quelques villains . . . Espions? Allemands! Espionage! Quatre fromage!' (Herbert, 1948, pp. 49–50). Lucy's father has been using a telescope in his search for his daughter, but one French local insists '[h]e examine the forts and defences'. Lucy and Suzanne together provide a convincing rebuttal, that Thomas is too stupid to be a spy and too big a liar to be trusted by anyone: 'In short, you see a pusillanimous, hypocritical, highly typical, English gentleman!'

With diverting affection *Bless the Bride* repeatedly mocks English stereotypes, but wartime situations and resonances cumulatively subvert this comic tone. Pierre enlists to fight for France, and Lucy is left with her family. The opening couplet of the romantic number Lucy sang earlier in the café scene with Pierre takes on a different connotation as the scene ends. The lines 'my lovely day, it is the day I shall remember the day I'm dying' linger behind Lucy's brief reprise of the song's conclusion, not quite completed as she 'breaks down and is led away by her parents' (Herbert, 1948, p. 56). It acts as a presentiment of what we will discover in the following scene, which is set at The Grange seven months later, in March 1871. By this time Pierre is believed to have been killed in action, and his death has affected Lucy greatly, we learn, such as to turn her attention constantly to fortune-telling cards which she picked up 'At the Church Bazaar – in aid of starving Paris', and which reveal to her 'Dark men. And France. Always France' (Herbert, 1948, p. 59). The musical bookends the Franco-Prussian War, showing the characters before and after it, but not during, which puts the focus not on the action and trajectory of war, but rather on the consequences it brings to individual lives.

Making a point

If it seems a stretch to read this affectionate, comic Victorian postcard as intentionally so redolent for a 1940s audience in London of the immediate legacy of wartime, support for such an interpretation comes from shows by the same creative team of Herbert, Ellis and Cochran: *Big Ben* the year before *Bless the Bride*, and *Tough at the Top* two years after.

On 17 July 1946, *Big Ben* opened at the Adelphi Theatre. It was the first of the post-war collaborations of Herbert, Ellis and Cochran. Herbert had first worked with Cochran in 1930–1931 when he provided an English translation and reworking of Offenbach's *La Belle Hélène* for a successful West End production that Cochran mounted. Herbert and Ellis first worked together on Cochran's highly popular revue *Streamline* (1934). The war had interrupted theatre work for all three: the privations of wartime hit Cochran's ability to produce new musicals, Ellis joined the Royal Navy and spent much of the time stationed at Devonport, while Herbert – also with a position as a Member of Parliament – used his own boat *Water Gipsy* on the Thames as part of the naval Civil Defence (he had been in naval service during World War I).[14] After the War, the three were reunited for *Big Ben*, in which themes of liberty and national identity come strongly to the fore. Indeed, the show emphasises its wartime influences throughout.[15]

The war had ended in 1945, when there had also been a General Election: ideals of democracy had been at the heart of the conflict. The sense of direction for national recovery socially, financially and not least politically was a theme Herbert turned into timely entertainment. His own description of the show indicates that his intended focus was on the contemporary and satirical:

> It was like no 'musical' that had gone before, and I do not know of anything like it since. It plunged into politics more boldly and deeply than [W.S.] Gilbert ever dared. The First Act contained a General Election and ended with an election meeting for all the candidates. The heroine became a Labour Member but married a Tory, and was locked up in the [Clock] Tower with him for obstructing the Sergeant-at-arms. Henry, the tenor, was red-hot. Grace's only electoral weapon was to sing, to one of Ellis's liveliest tunes, 'I want to see the people happy'.[16]
>
> *(Herbert, 1970, p. 118)*

The title *Big Ben* refers to the nickname of one character, but also to the nickname for the Clock Tower (now named the Elizabeth Tower) of the Palace of Westminster. In fact, Big Ben is the largest of the tower's five bells (the one that strikes the hour). The distinctive four-phrase chimes from the other bells that cumulatively mark the quarters of each hour are incorporated into both Herbert's text and Ellis's music, coming to a symbolic fruition in the closing moments of the show. Following a dramatic silence, the entire cast sing to the familiar Westminster chimes: 'Chime out Big Ben, Tell all the men, Say Eng-land will, Be Eng-land still' (Herbert, 1946, p. 102). The nationalistic assertion of identity is entirely of its time.

The show that succeeded *Big Ben* the following year was *Bless the Bride*, with the same production team: Cochran, Herbert, Ellis and director Wendy Toye. Herbert adopted a more distanced approach for this, following Cochran's desire for a 'Victorian period play' (1970, p. 118). Yet Herbert's own social proselytising remains in evidence. This is the crucial part of any reading today of *Bless the Bride*. As with *Big Ben*, *Bless the Bride* requires the mid-1940s mind set to appreciate the subtext. Associations the audience could draw from the work are crucial and bring this chapter back to its Paris significance. Herbert adapted the Victorian aspects as a decorative veil for his propensity for satiric, political contemporary comment. That *Bless the Bride* is set in 1870–1871 does not mean that it is solely about 1870–1871.

As further corroboration for this reading of *Bless the Bride*, a combination of European realpolitik and the appeal to national spirit is a defining factor of the third post-war collaboration of Herbert, Cochran and Ellis. *Tough at the Top* followed *Bless the Bride* into the Adelphi, with the expectation by its creators of a greater success than *Bless the Bride* had achieved. They were wrong; the show closed after some four months, with praise limited to performances and select music numbers. An imagined, distanced historical conflict of the early 1900s between a small Ruritanian country and its bullying Prussian neighbour evoked tensions pre-World War I. Nonetheless, Herbert acknowledged his contemporary purpose, 'a subtle satirical reference to Russia's way with small countries, but it was so subtle that nobody

FIGURE 10.3 The production team of *Bless the Bride* in rehearsal: from left to right, director Wendy Toye, actress Vera Ellis, designer Tanya Moiseiwitsch, actress Sonia Tylden and producer C. B. Cochran.

Source: Photo by Len Cassingham, courtesy of Shutterstock.

seemed to spot it' (1970, p. 127).[17] But as with *Big Ben* and with *Bless the Bride*, the concluding lyrics of *Tough at the Top* were intended to leave the audience with a reflection in the wake of World War II on moral purpose, national pride and a spirit of communal endeavour:

> They can wreck a man's happiness, but not a man's will:
>   Little lamps of liberty will smoulder still,
>   Till the trumpet sounds, and we break the chain
>   And the wings of the spirit ride the free air again!
> *(Herbert, 1970, pp. 128–129)*

Herbert acknowledged the enduring values behind these lyrics, describing them more than two decades later as 'A song for Czechoslovakia today – written in 1949' (1970, p. 129). With all this in mind, the concluding scene of *Bless the Bride* takes on added significance: its deconstruction in terms extrinsic to the drama's intrinsic references fits the pattern of Herbert's inclusion of the contemporary in an over-arching message behind a show's principal narrative: Herbert entertained, but also made his point.

The theatre of war

Dramatic presentations of war in film were legion both during and after 1939–1945 as part of the political and social bolstering of attitudes towards nation, allies and enemies. The popular routine of cinema-going allowed for the quick and wide dissemination of films and their associated messaging. Such British-made films as *In Which We Serve* (1942; naval warfare), *The Life and Death of Colonel Blimp* (1943; personal values in the context of the shifting imperatives of war), *This Happy Breed* (1944; domestic impact) and *A Canterbury Tale* (1944; the violation of the national idyll) reflected to a home audience the most desirable traits and values for a shared sense of national responsibility (Richards, 1997, pp. 85–110). The regular practice of screening newsreels by such names as British Movietone News and British Pathé News alongside features, supplemented information on radio with imagery that conveyed the power of home troops and the damage inflicted by enemy forces.

Wartime scenarios were overtly included on the musical stage too, but in dilution or in disguise through thematic and geographical displacement. This is hardly surprising. The marriage of the overt escapism of comedy, popular song and dance routines with sombre and real experience was a potential recipe for bad taste and even audience hostility immediately post-war unless played with unambiguous patriotism or with ambiguous interpretational potential.[18] Ivor Novello built critical commentary into his 1939 show *The Dancing Years*, whose premise he described as being inspired 'after the Nazis had occupied Vienna, and it occurred to me to wonder what would have happened to me if, as a composer of popular music, I had also been Viennese and of Jewish descent' (Noble, 1951, p. 228). The force occupying Vienna was not directly identified by uniform or named as Nazi, but the intended identity was clear.

In 1943, Harold Purcell and Harry Parr Davies's stage show *The Lisbon Story* dramatised a story of wartime intrigue. The leading character, a successful French singer in musical theatre, aids a resistance plot but at the cost of her life: she is shot dead in Paris by the Gestapo officer she has duped.[19] Such leading numbers in the show as 'Someday We'll Meet Again' and 'Never Say Goodbye' are part of a trope of parting and hope in the future that runs through the catalogue of popular songs of the time. The list is most famously headed up by 'We'll Meet Again' (1939) as performed by Vera Lynn.[20] It was established independently as a popular song in 1939, then incorporated into the film of the same name, released early in 1943, in which Lynn starred and by which time she was established as the 'Forces' Sweetheart'. The finale of the film shows Lynn singing the song in a concert for RAF troops, which creates an intensely powerful symbiosis of wartime iconography in sound, people and situation.[21]

Also in 1943, Novello's newest musical, *Arc de Triomphe*, was presented in London. Novello conceived the work as a showpiece for the singer Mary Ellis, a successful opera singer in her early years who moved into musical theatre and who had taken the leading female roles in Novello's *Glamorous Night* (1935) and *The Dancing Years*. Novello took as his starting point the biography of opera singer Mary

Garden, who rose to fame in Paris in the early 1900s, then reinvented elements of her life story as those of the fictitious French opera singer Marie Forêt who, while studying in Paris, falls in love with Pierre, a young actor. At the outbreak of World War I, Pierre is called up in a scene that plays out classic imagery 'ending with the male populace of Paris marching to war, accompanied by their female relations and the *Marseillaise*, whilst the silent and tragic figure of Mary Ellis stood, her hopes and dreams dashed around her' (Macqueen-Pope, 1951, p. 407).[22] Pierre is killed on the Western Front, and Forêt – now a great prima donna – performs in the title role of a new opera about Joan of Arc, during which she sings the patriotic song 'France Will Rise Again'. In both *Arc de Triomphe* and *The Lisbon Story* renditions of the *Marseillaise* contribute to dramatic climaxes, in the case of the latter at the end of the show in conjunction with the shooting by the Gestapo of the heroine.[23] The German Occupation of Paris, begun in 1940 but not to end until 1944, exerted its presence on both these works of 1943: that the capital city of Britain's European neighbour could be occupied was symbolic of how much was at stake.

Paris under German control was reported in newsreels and made its way into feature films, for example *Casablanca* (again, 1943). In one *Casablanca* exchange, Major Heinrich Strasser (Conrad Veidt) asks Rick Blaine (Humphrey Bogart): 'Are you one of those people who can't imagine Germans in their beloved Paris?' Another German officer, Col. Heinze (Richard Ryen), continues: 'Can you imagine us in London?'[24] Although the canonic status of the film began to develop in the decade after its release, it was nonetheless known – a Hollywood movie featuring established and rising stars, avidly watched along with the rest of the American film output in Britain and screened intermittently through the 1940s alongside new releases. The Paris flashback section of the film is only some nine minutes long, yet its imagery is striking, beginning with the establishing landmark of the Arc de Triomphe, progressing through a montage of German troops invading, and culminating with a tank in the street directly outside Rick's flat. Rick and Ilsa Lund may famously 'always have Paris', but in such circumstances just what Paris represents in its totality in *Casablanca* is a complex mixture of the personal, political, national and moral. The film is not unique in bringing together within the idea of Paris such meanings which were only to intensify in the remaining years of the War and well beyond. A short reference can be as packed with meaning as a long one.

Deconstructing Suzanne's speech

The predominant stylistic elements of *Bless the Bride* encourage reading it as inspired Victorian whimsy overlaid with an Edwardian musical comedy sensibility. But the prominent placing of Suzanne's short speech only minutes before the end of the show is consciously provocative. The stage directions indicate the intended impact: '*The music stops suddenly. At the big window stands Suzanne. She is pale and worn and thin. All turn and stare at her*' (Herbert, 1948, p. 62). Suzanne's following speech falls into two parts, the first defiant, with a startling statement drawn from her direct experience.

SUZANNE: Ah, ha, the polka! En Angleterre the polka! In Paris the hunger, the famine, the cold! In Paris we seek our bread in the streets – *dans la boite aux ordures*[25] – But here you have fine cake – with *sugar. Sugar!* [*She laughs horribly, looks about her and see THOMAS*][26] Ah, ha, le brave Capitaine Trout! A new uniform, too – *n'est-ce pas?* But you did not come to fight for France, I think. I did not see you in Paris – in the siege – when the Prussians hammer the gate – and the houses fall about us – and we eat RATS!

The second section turns towards regret and sadness (note the prevalence of exclamation marks in the first and their absence in the second).

SUZANNE: [*with a sudden change of mood*]. Ah, little Lucy, I am so sorry. I did not mean to speak so. The English have been good by us, and I have come with so different thoughts. But I come from Paris – [*She turns*] Suddenly, I see the dancing – and the happiness – and I remember – what I have seen – in Paris . . . [*She nearly breaks down – but recovers*]

The German Occupation of Paris began in 1940 and did not end until 1944, bringing to most Parisians severe hardship: 'the hunger, the famine, the cold'.

In respect of the first two deprivations, the supply of sugar and meat were two of the most acutely felt of wartime food shortages, and their formal rationing heightened the sense of perceived deprivation in the face of actual shortage. In Paris, many core foodstuffs were less available immediately after the War than during it, and their rationing was to continue until 1949 (Jones, 2004, p. 491). In the United Kingdom two years after the end of the War, when *Bless the Bride* was on stage, rationing was more stringent than it had been during the conflict, and was indeed to be relaxed only progressively until it was finally ended, as late as 1954. In 1947, bread was rationed, which it had not been during the War, and when personal rationing points were removed in April 1949 the overwhelming demand for chocolate and sugar confectionery in particular that followed was such that in August the rationing had to be restored to its previous level (Zweiniger-Bargielowska, 2000, pp. 83–85). Sugar supply per capita in the United Kingdom did not reach its pre-war level until 1954, so mentioning sugar shortages to a West End audience in 1947 hit home. The reference to meat did too. Present during the Siege of Paris, Victor Hugo noted in his diary entries in 1870 that 'Paris has been on a diet of salt meat for two days. A rat costs 8 sous' (23 November) and 'People are making rat pâté. It is said to be quite good' (27 November) (Robb, 1997, p. 454).[27] The historical detail in Herbert's libretto played to the British zeitgeist of 1947: the UK meat supply dropped below wartime levels in 1948–1949 and reached its lowest point in

1951 (Zweiniger-Bargielowska, 2000, p. 34). Indeed, the West End musical *Her Excellency* (22 June 1949–28 January 1950), a showcase for the performer Cicely Courtneidge, is predicated on the theme of a British ambassador in a country resembling Argentina being tasked with securing the beef supply for Britain rather than allowing it to be sold to America (Snelson, 2003, pp. 186–191). This continued a theme of the domestic experience of war presented in 1945, when Courtneidge had been the star attraction in the West End show *Under the Counter*, about obtaining black market ('under the counter') supplies during rationing restrictions. The show had opened in the West End on 22 November 1945, closing on 5 July 1947. It thus overlaps with *Bless the Bride* in both London performance and thematic reference.

When food controls were introduced in France on 17 September 1940, the adult ration began at 300g of meat on the bone per week and 500g sugar per month, and by 1943 Paris was receiving only just over half the necessary meat supply, which did not allow adults the allocated ration of 120g per week with many receiving none of it (Drake, 2015, pp. 125, 332–333, 481). That small but emphatic reference by Suzanne to rats and thus food shortages bridges historical and contemporary in London where the show was performed, but also within a Parisian context where queuing for food in Paris in 1940 sparked recognition with the illustration of such queues in Paris in 1870–1871 (Drake, 2015, p. 125). It was not such detail itself that was the point in London, but the knowledge that food shortage was a recent experience shared with Paris. One city could with little difficulty project the generalities of some of its own wartime experiences onto the other: shortages, underground stations as refuges from bombing raids, bomb damage, routine military presence, curfews, blackouts and so on.

Concerning Suzanne's third emphasis, cold, the difficulty of keeping warm during the severity of winters in the 1940s was a shared experience too, amplified by the hunger from food shortages. For the context of the show, the blizzards and power cuts during the severe winter of 1946–1947 had made the most recent impression on London's theatregoers. As in London, so in Paris too, which experienced severe winters during the German Occupation. Rosbottom documents that 'every winter seemed to last longer and be more frigid than the one before', and the oppression of cold could be palpable, as one Paris resident described: 'The enemy [cold] is there, who watches me behind the door in order to pinch and bite me' (2014, pp. 180–181). But in *Bless the Bride*, the reference is more to create a resonance with a recognized British experience than solely to specify the Parisian one.

The final message

Early in the last scene of the show, Augustus and Thomas have an exchange that can now clearly be understood as setting up the necessary past-present parallels crucial to the final section, from Suzanne's appearance. The 1870–1871 reading exists in reference to its 1947 significance.

AUGUSTUS: Peace terms are terrible and Paris is in a ferment. Those Prussians are too big for their boots: and one day we shall have to tread on their toes.

THOMAS: You're right, Sir. Poor old Froggies. [*He sighs*] Do you know, I often wish I'd done what the French girl said – and gone to fight for them.

MARY: You couldn't Thomas. We were neutral.

AUGUSTUS: And you held the Queen's commission.

THOMAS: I know, Sir. I know: but somehow – I wish I had.

(Herbert, 1948, p. 60)

Such making of amends continues with Suzanne. After her dramatic entrance and speech, she brings in Pierre. Out of jealousy, she had previously written to Lucy and lied that Pierre was dead. Next, Thomas Trout again relinquishes his returned fiancé Lucy to Pierre, this time willingly: 'Pierre, I salute you. I salute France' (Herbert, 1948, p. 62). The reunion of Lucy and Pierre at the end of the show is the inevitable happy ending for a light romance, as indeed the work can be interpreted from its surface. But the show has increasingly developed darker sides. The reprise of the lead romantic song 'This Is My Lovely Day' brings personal and political, historical and contemporary together. In Act II, Lucy and then Pierre both sing 'This is our lovely day. This is the day I shall remember the day I'm dying' (Herbert, 1948, p. 48). For the finale, Pierre leads the reprise with altered lyrics (p. 62):

> This is our lovely day . . .
>> I come to you from France, defeated, but never dying.
>> This is the better way,
>> The flag of France, the flag of England, together always flying.

The 'resurrected' Pierre has altered the message from 'dying' to 'never dying'. Given how prominent this simple change of words is as the conclusion of the show, and with Herbert's pattern of leaving his post-war audiences with a message that had contemporary resonance, the end of *Bless the Bride* also is more fully understood as a statement of 1940s post-war political and national conviction. It acknowledges the shared wartime history of France and England, using the neutrality of England in the Franco-Prussian war as a warning, with the correction of both World Wars implicitly acknowledging the importance of such an alliance. In 1950, Herbert was to recall of the outbreak of war that '[p]oor France was rolling down hill. . . . We were likely to be left alone, as we had not been for centuries, with a powerful enemy at Calais and Cherbourg' (1950, p. 150). Immediately preceding this finale, Suzanne's speech with its graphic, angry description of Paris during wartime has been placed to set up the context for this crucial recognition of shared interests and the need for international cooperation. Her dramatic intervention acts as the prism through which to focus the underlying post-war themes of the show as the catalyst for the final message and thus demonstrates what Paris could symbolise and summarise for its 1940s London audience.

Notes

1 The libretto designates the work a light opera (Herbert, 1948). The vocal score adopts the term 'musical show' (Herbert and Ellis, 1948).
2 The themes here expand on those explored in detail in Snelson, 2003, and outlined in Snelson, J. M., 2017.
3 Thomas Trout has something distinctly Gilbertian about him in his parody of Englishness, patter-based vocal style and character, playing with inherent contradiction of expectation.
4 For a summary of the significance of the waltz and especially its role in British musical theatre in the first part of the 20th century, see Snelson, J., 2017.
5 Herbert, 1948, p. 18. Issy was the name at the time of the show's 1870s setting; it was renamed Issy-des-Moulineaux, but only a couple of decades later.
6 He was born Lámbros Vorlóo in Alexandria, Egypt, to Greek parents on 8 February 1915.
7 One consequence of Guétary's lack of English was that he learned the text by heart, to which Ellis ascribed Guétary's wonderfully clear diction as Pierre (Ellis, 1953, pp. 231, 233–234).
8 Under the name Betty Webb, she had begun performing during the War as a singer with dance bands, not as an actress, establishing herself in particular through BBC radio broadcasts. Cochran cast her for her singing voice in a small role in *Big Ben* and as understudy to the lead, Carole Lynne. Cochran also gave her the new stage name of Lizbeth Webb. It was Lynne's pregnancy during the run of the show that gave Webb her opportunity to take the lead.
9 Columbia DB 2301 and 2302.
10 Columbia DB 2327. Ellis was an accomplished pianist and had also appeared as the featured solo piano player on a recording of melodies from *Bless the Bride*, recorded with the Adelphi Theatre Orchestra under Michael Collins on 18 July 1947 on Columbia DX1396.
11 In 1949, Guétary returned to London to appear at the Casino in the revue *Latin Quarter*. Guétary recorded songs including 'Clopin-clopant' and 'La-bas' (Columbia BD 2513), asserting a French identity even as they were sung in English. After London, he appeared on Broadway in the musical *Arms and the Girl*, winning a Tony Award as best foreign performer, which led in turn to his film role in *An American in Paris*.
12 For example, in the review of the show in *The Tatler and Bystander* (Kent, 1947a, p. 6), the caption alongside a cartoon of Guétary as Pierre describes him as 'the dashing and fashionable Pierre Fontaine, whose romantic attractions no maidenly mid-Victorian heart could possibly be expected to withstand'. The review of the show printed alongside makes Guétary's foreign star quality a point, describing 'an accomplished singer already well known to French radio listeners'. Through a pre-existing film commitment, Guétary played the role of Pierre until the end the year, having recorded the songs and established the identity of his character within the show. The part was taken over for the remainder of the long London run and the subsequent UK tour by Guétary's understudy, Edmund Goffron, who was English. The change of nationality was sufficient to be logged by *The Tatler* when, in August, Goffron went on for Guétary as understudy, a role for which the 'young English actor' had been picked by Cochran 'because he was able to sing in French' (Kent, 1947b, p. 261).
13 Translation given in the libretto: 'Will you butt your head against an English family? Look round you. They are like the Rock of Gibraltar.'
14 In the 1935 General Election, Herbert won the seat for Oxford University, holding it as an Independent until 1950, when such university seats were abolished.

15 For example, the opening scene takes place in the costume Showroom of the 'Colossal' department store, located in 'Little Britain, a Thames-side town', in which a 'Victory British Products Parade' is being rehearsed. The opening chorus is sung by the fashion mannequins (Herbert, 1946, p. 11): 'Come to Britain, for Britain's the best! / Here's where the Continent ought to be dressed. . . . We fashioned the Spitfire, and Germany fell: / We'll know how to make you a killer as well.'

16 The reference to the character of Henry being 'red-hot' is to his political views being on the extreme Left Wing. In a musicalised version of electioneering, his lines include the couplet 'A bright new beacon shines ahead / And all the world is thinking red'. Soon after he begins to sing *The Red Flag* (Herbert, 1946, pp. 23–24).

17 For a dramatic description of the work, see Gänzl, 1986, pp. 601–602, with contextual discussion in Snelson, 2003, pp. 152–156.

18 Mel Brooks demonstrates this point brilliantly with his 'Springtime for Hitler' parody show within the film *The Producers* (1967). The incongruity of wartime subject matter, genre and tone was amplified when the parody was actually incarnated through the film's adaptation for Broadway (2001) and the theatrically unstageable was indeed staged.

19 For a summary of story and music numbers see Everett, 2015, pp. 105–109. The choice of story and setting was thought in some reviews to be an uncomfortable mixture, 'neither a musical comedy nor a tragedy but a tinsel wartime drama' (*Daily Telegraph*), and the show provoked such headlines as 'Gestapo set to Music' (*Daily Mail*) and 'Too Much of a Mixed Show' (*Sunday Chronicle*) – but the public response was considerably more favourable, and the show became a success (Gänzl, 1986, pp. 528–529). That the World War II setting of the *The Lisbon Story* drew adverse critical comment but not those of the Franco-Prussian War for *Bless the Bride* and World War I for Novello's *Arc de Triomphe* (discussed later) is perhaps indicative that the boundary between 'good' and 'bad' taste was determined by the immediacy of memory: chronological distance could lend theatrical enchantment.

20 Recorded on Decca DR 3884, accompanied by Arthur Young on a Novachord, the earliest electronic organ, which had only been introduced the previous year.

21 For discussion of the tropes within Lynn's wartime films and songs, see Mundy, 2007, pp. 96–103.

22 In *Bless the Bride*, besides the scene in which Pierre departs for war leaving Lucy behind, the same trope was the subject of the second version of lyrics to what was to become in Herbert's third version the show's hit number 'Ma Belle Marguerite'. Cochran rejected Herbert's first lyrics (about a donkey) so Herbert 'wrote another song, all in French, about a tired soldier who was calling always upon his captain to halt: "Mon brave – e Capitain – e, Arrêtez, s'il vous-plait." But the Captain would never halt, even when Madelein – e [*sic*] was waving from the window. It was very sad'(1950, p. 381).

23 Purcell and Parr Davies, 1948, pp. 134–135. It is to be expected that the aural identifier of national identity, the French national anthem, should be widely and repeatedly used as the musical symbol of French patriotic defiance during the country's wartime occupation. For example, it was famously interpolated as the final bars of the Act II finale 'Salut la France' in Donizetti's *La Fille du régiment* at the Metropolitan Opera, New York, on 28 December 1940. The recording of the live broadcast, which included Lily Pons in her debut there as Marie, preserved the audience's applause in response as a display of solidarity with occupied France. There is an equivalent in *Bless the Bride* in the marching chorus 'To France!', led by Pierre as the finale to Act II scene as he departs with the other newly enlisted men to fight (Herbert and Ellis, 1948, pp. 153–157).

24 *Casablanca* (1943, directed by Michael Curtiz) [22:43 min.].

25 'In the rubbish bins.'

26 Earlier in the final scene, Thomas Trout is shown to have changed his ways and appears in the uniform of a Captain. Even Lucy's father, Augustus, notices the difference: '[H]e's a different man. Joined the Yeomanry. Takes the Army seriously. Given up that ridiculous betting' (Herbert, 1948, p. 59).

27 During the Siege, for meat Parisians also fell to consuming dogs, cats, birds and even zoo animals (Jones, 2004, p. 373).

References

Drake, D. (2015) *Paris at War: 1939–1944*. Cambridge, MA and London: Belknap Press of Harvard University Press.

Ellis, V. (1953) *I'm on a See-Saw*. London: Joseph.

Everett, A. (2015) *Accompanying Gracie: The Life, Times and Music of Harry Parr Davies (1914–1955)*. Bloomington, IN: AuthorHouse.

Gänzl, K. (1986) *The British Musical Theatre: Vol.2 1915–1984*. Basingstoke: Palgrave-Macmillan.

Herbert, A. (1970) *A.P.H.: His Life and Times*. London: Heinemann.

Herbert, A. P. (1950) *Independent Member*. London: Methuen & Co.

———. (1948) *Bless the Bride. A Light Opera in Two Acts. Libretto*. London: Samuel French.

———. (1946) *Big Ben. A Light Opera in Two Acts. Libretto*. London: Methuen & Co. Ltd.

Jones, C. (2004) *Paris: Biography of a City*. London: Allen Lane.

Kent, B. (1947a) 'At the Theatre Review of *Bless the Bride*,' *The Tatler and Bystander*, 14 May, p. 6.

———. (1947b) 'Backstage Theatre News,' *The Tatler and Bystander*, 27 August, p. 261.

Macqueen-Pope, W. (1951) *Ivor: The Story of an Achievement*. London: W.H. Allen & Co.

Mundy, J. (2007) *The British Film Musical*. Manchester: Manchester University Press.

Noble, P. (1951) *Ivor Novello: Man of the Theatre*. 3rd edition. London: Falcon Press.

Pound, R. (1976) *A.P. Herbert*. London: Michael Joseph.

Purcell, H. and Parr Davies, H. (1948) *The Lisbon Story. Vocal Score*. London: Chappell & Co.

Richards, J. (1997) *Films and British National Identity*. Manchester: Manchester University Press.

Robb, G. (1997) *Victor Hugo*. London: Picador.

Rosbottom, R. (2014) *When Paris Went Dark: The City of Light Under German Occupation, 1940–44*. London: John Murray.

Snelson, J. (2017) 'The Waltzing Years: British Operetta 1907–1939,' in M. Niccolai and C. Rowden (eds.) *Musical Theatre in Europe 1830–1945*. Turnhout: Brepols, pp. 241–266.

Snelson, J. M. (2017) ' "We Said We Wouldn't Look Back": British Musical Theatre, 1935–1969,' in W. A. Everett and P. Laird (eds.) *The Cambridge Companion to the Musical*. 3rd edition. Cambridge: Cambridge University Press, pp. 159–184.

———. (2003) *The West End Musical 1947–54: British Identity and the 'American Invasion.'* Unpublished PhD, University of Birmingham, Birmingham.

Zweiniger-Bargielowska, I. (2000) *Austerity in Britain: Rationing, Controls, and Consumption 1939–1955*. Oxford: Oxford University Press.

11

PERFORMING PARIS

Les Misérables, *The Phantom of the Opera* and *Aspects of Love*

John Snelson

If there is a city that embodies at its core the effects of the past on the present, it is Paris. The social and political upheavals in concentrated succession have been written into its landscape through everything from street patterns and street names to monuments, the juxtaposition of old and new and, in particular, where the new has swept away the past wholesale to create the absence of such visible contrasts.[1] In Michael Marrinan's phrase, this is 'the city as witness and battlefield', in which a 'geographical layering of events within the great monuments of Paris invested them with an aura of calm presence in the face of dramatic social ruptures. It gave them a special role in contemporary attempts to contextualize cataclysmic change' (2009, p. 45).

The musicals discussed in this chapter – following their source novels – reflect in different ways on the preoccupations behind the Revolutionary call 'Liberté, égalité, fraternité'. The French capital has been linked to these concepts from 1789 through to today. *Les Misérables* (novel 1862; musical 1985) is dominated by the macrocosm of Paris as a symbol of political and social change in the pursuit of the freedoms of the individual in relation to community and state.[2] This is the Paris of revolutionaries and ideals. *The Phantom of the Opera* (1909–1910; 1986) dramatises tensions around freedom of expression through the metaphor of art and within a specifically Parisian cultural microcosm, the Paris Opéra.[3] This is Second Empire-Third Republic Paris as the cultural and commercial centre of the world, a 'Hausmann landscape of power' (Jones, 2004, p. 384). And *Aspects of Love* (1955; 1989) draws from the associations of Paris with personal freedoms in relation to emotional expression within societal and artistic contexts.[4] This is Paris in the fall-out of the 19th century, in which the big ideas of political, commercial and societal revolution have become encapsulated within individual, quotidian lives.

More fundamental still, past-present interplay is crucial to all three novels, heightened in their adaptations to the musical stage through prologues that create contextual and historical reference points for the main events of the respective dramas. In *Les Misérables*, there is a temporal bifurcation in the character of its protagonist, Jean Valjean: he cannot escape his criminal past, however valiantly he reinvents his present. His back story is gradually revealed in the novel, but presented swiftly through the musical's 'Prologue' – chain gang and release, initial denial of work, example of charity and forgiveness – to reach the moment when Valjean concludes 'Is there another way to go? . . . Another story must begin' (Behr, 1989, p. 167).

At the start of the novel *The Phantom of the Opera*, an authorial Preface sets up the conceit of an extended reflection on the past through Leroux's own investigation of 'facts' from events some 30 years before at the Paris Opéra, drawing on archival documentation as well as those 'who would remember, as if it had happened just yesterday'. Leroux's detective work will show the truth behind 'the more or less legendary Phantom of the Opera' (1996, p. 22). The musical retains this framing through the equally 'theatrical' narrative device of an auction in 1905 of the contents of Paris's 'Opéra Populaire'. This scene is an exercise in memory above all else, with each item under the hammer a souvenir whose significance is to be revealed in the time-inverting flashback that makes up the substance of the drama.[5] The subsequent *coup de théâtre* of the rising chandelier, newly electrified, is intended to 'frighten away the ghosts of so many years ago', but plunges the audience back into a re-enactment of an episode in the theatre's history (Perry, 1987, p. 141).

While David Garnett's novel *Aspects of Love* begins with 17-year-old Alex in Montpellier in 1947, the 'Prologue' of the musical adaptation ('Love Changes Everything') takes place when Alex is 34. The body of the show is a time loop, running approximately 1964, 1947, 1949, 1959, 1961 and 1964: the show develops as one huge flashback appreciated only when it has run its course. The Prologue, conceived for the stage adaptation, amplifies at a fundamental structural level the theme of relationships across the decades.[6] In Garnett's novel, Alex thinks to himself of his first night with the actress Rose Vibert – slightly but significantly older and also more experienced – that 'She has changed the whole world and hung a curtain between the present and the past' (1989, p. 15). The next 20 years of Alex's life will show that any such clear division is illusory.

Each of the three musicals explored here evolved through different routes during a decade. There are some links that can be drawn between pairs – for example, the 'epic' theatricality that links *Les Misérables* to *The Phantom of the Opera*, the development of a musical style that leads from *The Phantom of the Opera* to *Aspects of Love*, or Trevor Nunn's directorial involvement with *Les Misérables* and *Aspects of Love* – but the geographical location of Paris *per se* was not in itself a principle generative force shared by all three projects.[7] While to differing degrees these shows are set 'in' Paris, they can be viewed more conceptually as 'of' Paris. They share a particular Paris preoccupation that has thus arisen independently from each literary source: that the past inexorably influences the present, refracting the symbolic identity of a city moulded *par excellence* from the ongoing reflexivity between states of 'then' and 'now'.

City landscapes

Victor Hugo's epic *Les Misérables* was first published serially in ten books.[8] It unfolds through times that re-defined the identity of France in the first part of the 19th century, beginning with an extended exposition outside of Paris: Jean Valjean's penal servitude at Toulon; release leading to his Damascene encounter with the Bishop of Digne and its brief but significant reinforcing coda with Petit-Gervais; his mayoralty at Montreuil; and his combined flight from Montreuil and rescue of Cossette from the Thénardiers at their inn at Montfermeil. Only a third of the way into the novel does the main action move to Paris, the centre of power and a symbol of the nation, where the manifestation of the iniquities of government and social inequalities are most in evidence. The novel is a political, social and philosophical commentary, its narrative the skeleton on which the Hugo's proselytising messages are fleshed out. As his preface states, 'as long as there are ignorance and poverty on earth, books of this kind may serve some purpose' (2013, p. 2).

Hugo embodies Paris through what he calls 'a sort of social epic' (2013, p. xxi): from the homeless street urchin Gavroche and the inhabitants of the Gorbeau tenement united in poverty if not morality, through to the destructively misguided Monsieur Gillenormand, wealthy and privileged grandfather to Marius and a relic of royalist, pre-Revolutionary values. Criminal classes (the Thénardiers), state authority (Inspector Javert) and a myriad of servants, shopkeepers, military men and prostitutes permit an exhaustive and forensic dissection of the condition of a city and, by extension, a nation.

But it is around events of historical significance that Hugo's focus circles. The opening chapter of Part IV of the novel – understatedly titled 'A Few Pages of History' – directs the reader to the events for which *Les Misérables* is especially known and which are at the core of its musical theatre incarnation:

> The two years immediately following the July Revolution – 1831 and 1832 – stand out as one of history's most distinctive and striking moments. Between the years that precede them and those that follow, these two years are like mountains. They have a revolutionary grandeur. Precipitous faces can be discerned. The social masses, the very foundations of civilization, the solid grouping of overlapping and tenacious interests, the age-old contours of the previous French landscape keep appearing and disappearing through storm clouds of systems, passions and theories.
>
> *(2013, p. 739)*

Everything revolves around the events on the barricades in 1832, where the coincidence of narrative lines and the fallout from their interaction is at its densest: in Graham Robb's precise evocation, 'the metaphorical and literal barricade at which all the strands and most of the characters converge like twigs floating up against a dam' (1997, p. 384). Hugo describes 5–6 June in inordinate detail. Appropriately, the musical makes them the centrepiece of Act II with the same dramatic

FIGURE 11.1   Enjolras (Michael Maguire) leads the students during the battle on the barricade in *Les Misérables*. Scene from the original 1987 Broadway production.

Source: Photo by Michael Le Poer Trench/Bob Marshak, provided by the editor.

counterpoints enhanced by what has become iconic staging as the barricade is formed. The novelist describes; the stage adaptation shows. This goes to the crux of the adaptation from political diatribe-as-epic-novel to performance piece.

John Caird, co-adaptor and director with Trevor Nunn of the 1985 stage show, summarised the key to its evolution from literary to dramatic form: 'For all its length, it is basically a story of intimate human relations, paralleled by the history of France' (Behr, 1989, p. 78). Hugo's lengthy digressions on, for example, convent life and street slang don't simply bring colour, but broaden the context of the Parisian experience, particularly in its evocation of the early 1830s. But strip these out and what is revealed is a set of universal family and community tensions. On stage, set and costume designs provide contextual detail, which allows the script to portray those specific Parisians as examples of shared human conditions. For example, Hugo takes seven sections at the start of Book 3 to establish Gavroche as a gamin, a street urchin (2013, pp. 519–536). Hugo's necessity is 'to explain how the Parisian populace, even when grown to manhood, . . . is ever the gamin. To portray the child is to portray the city' (2013, p. 535). Herbert Kretzmer's lyrics for Gavroche's introductory song 'Little People' turn observation to warning: 'So never kick a dog because it's just a pup/You'd better run for cover when the pup grows up' (*Les Misérables*, 1985). Consequences are inevitably played out down the years – and a couplet in the right context can do the work of several chapters.

There is a conciseness of adaptation too in those iconic numbers that act as emotional nodes in the show, in which Hugo's observational and lengthy dissections of character are transmuted into revealing soliloquies: 'What Have I Done' (Jean Valjean/24601); 'I Dreamed a Dream' (Fantine); 'Stars' (Inspector Javert); 'On My Own' (Eponine); 'Empty Chairs and Empty Tables' (Marius); and 'Dog Eat Dog' (Thénardier). Each encapsulates its character's unique experience and philosophy, transmitted primarily and viscerally in performance as emotional declaration not least through the artfully direct musical style. Meditations on past-present interactions dominate, with the two threnodies – Marius's to his friends and Fantine's to her own life – acutely resonant. These numbers of self-definition are carefully paced along the narrative line, which accounts for much of the cumulative emotional power of the characterisations. They are the dramatic equivalent of Hugo's lengthy soliciting of the social conscience of his readers, and they mirror too the novel's structural emphasis as signalled through Hugo's over-arching headings: Part 1 'Fantine', Part 2 'Cosette', Part 3 'Marius' and Part 5 'Jean Valjean'.[9]

Hugo weaves his own experiences into the novel to create the effect of a detailed historical narrative. It is, of course, a fiction made up of accurate and inaccurate memories, didactic distortions and creative flourishes. From Hugo's observations arose the arrest of Fantine (an incident on 9 January 1841), street uprisings and the building of barricades (witnessed in 1839 and 1848), the wedding night of Marius and Cosette (given the date of Hugo's first night spent with his mistress, Juliet Drouet). Hugo acknowledges that his Paris no longer exists:

> Since [the author] left it, Paris has been transformed. A new city has grown up that is, as it were, unknown to him. . . . As a result of the demolitions and rebuildings, the Paris of his youth, the Paris he religiously took away with

him in his memory, is now a Paris of the past. . . . he writes with the old Paris
before his eyes, treasuring that illusion.

(2013, p. 404)

Hugo's nostalgic perspective on the very identity of Paris has been hammered
into the public psyche repeatedly through the immediate success of *Les Misérables*,
globally reinforced more recently by screen adaptations and by the musical. Is it
possible today to think of Paris in response without automatically reflecting on
the passage of time, the changing environment and the flux of history? One detail
makes the point. In the novel, Gavroche has a 'home', a hiding place inside a large
plaster elephant near the Bastille. Hugo describes the elephant's origins in the creation of a plaster model for an intended bronze Napoleon had decreed should stand
as the centrepiece of a new fountain in the place de la Bastille. He also describes
its abandonment and decay, to be interpreted in Marrinan's analysis as 'a nostalgic emblem of Napoleonic ambition . . . a catalyst for the layered histories of the
Bastille – Old Regime, Revolution, and Empire – to become a volatile mix of
memories and fantasies that trigger political action' (2009, pp. 127–129). There is
no elephant in *Les Misérables* on stage, edited out as a distracting detail.[10] Yet in the
2012 film adaptation directed by Tom Hooper, the elephant – in the company of
Gavroche – features in the scene portraying General Lamarque's funeral cortège.
This political flashpoint is personalised through the ABC comrades and further
coloured by means of the elephant, incongruous were it not for the layered history
it embodies.[11]

This points to a key manner in which the film challenges a major contributory
factor in the success of the stage show. What is evocation and impression on stage is
shifted to 'reality', indicative of the persistent power of constructed historicism of
Hugo's Paris. The film's publicity stressed its authenticity as historically lived experience. The decision to have the actors' singing recorded in real time on set rather
than on a pre-recorded soundtrack for lip-synching is one of the most remarked
upon manifestations of Hooper's directorial aesthetic. For example, Hugh Jack-
mann's experience of location and weather: 'We were on a mountain top in the
Alps in the South of France . . . I was freezing cold and I felt vulnerable and you
could hear that' (Nightingale and Palmer, 2013, p. 86). Eddie Redmayne (playing
Marius) has emphasised that Hooper

likes to make it real. So we had that huge set of the Paris streets, all the shops,
the houses, and we had about forty students and about forty extras and five
cameramen all dressed as peasants, so they could be right in amongst us, and
then he said, 'Right, build a barricade. Action!'

(Nightingale and Palmer, 2013, p. 90)

Any such attempt to re-create historical Paris as presented by Hugo is a commitment to the realism of something that was to begin with a conflation of the
actual, the invented and the symbolic. The attempt to create an accurate Paris in

the film, through such inauthentic environments as film studios (the reconstructed street façades) and the Royal Naval College at Greenwich in London, cannot ring literally true, the consequence of an ever-present paradox of the techniques of film production. But such naturalism is not what a theatre performance is about. Proscenium arch, performing musicians, singers with amplified voices and the literal embodiment on stage of characters in the same physical space as the audience add to a focus on evocation, not re-creation. There is no pretence that the audience witness a 'real' event.

One example comes from designer Andreane Neofitou, whose costumes for the stage production drew on historical sources (Behr, 1989, p. 102). But for the ensemble 'Lovely Ladies', the negotiation of actual historicism and dramatic interpretation became an interpretational factor:

> Trevor [Nunn, stage director] at first wanted reality, he had visions of the whores in normal dresses of the period, but tattered and torn; I had stylised them in the erotic corsets of the time so the spectators had visions of whores, not necessarily as they looked in the 1820s but as they imagined them.
>
> *(Behr, 1989, p. 103)*

And of those defining cantilevering barricades, John Napier's approach on stage could not have been more different from Hooper's for film. Napier never read Hugo's novel. Instead, he spent a weekend in Paris with Trevor Nunn and John Caird:

> We visited the Victor Hugo museum, but also wandered the streets where the barricades, the revolutions had taken place. We soaked up the atmosphere of the old Paris, the Rue Saint-Antoine, the Bastille district. Like a shot out of the blue – that second morning in Paris, we were talking endlessly, about major problems: how do you achieve the barricades on stage? – an idea suddenly came to me. What you see on stage is basically that idea.
>
> *(Behr, 1989, pp. 98–99)*

What resonates as authentic may not necessarily be literal.

'Do you hear the people sing?'

Hugo created a truthfulness from his perspective through his mixture of fact, fiction and proselytising. Gaston Leroux's quasi-journalistic detective thriller *The Phantom of the Opera* is also a work of fact and fiction that revolves around memory for its narrative and temporal reflexivity with its original readership. The novel's Preface, in Leroux's own voice, establishes that the story is true, and that investigation through interviews with those involved alongside a mixture of private and public documentation has enabled him to piece events together (1996, pp. 21–26). The novel's action occurs mostly within the Palais Garnier, the home of the Paris

27. Théâtre National
de l'Opéra
L'Escalier d'Honneur   C. M.

FIGURE 11.2   The famous staircase of the Paris Opéra, the Palais Garnier. For an outside view of the building, see Figure 1.2 in Chapter 1.

Source: Postcard provided by the editor.

Opéra and a palatial centrepiece of the architectural transformation of Paris under
Baron Haussmann indicative of the dominant cultural status of French grand opera
in the 19th century.

Leroux's setting is more than location for it encapsulates values that define Paris
too. The first intertitle of the 1925 silent film – in comparison with most of the
60 or so film adaptations, this first surviving one is substantially faithful to the

novel – summarises the oppositions this presents with eloquent brevity: 'Sanctuary of song lovers, the Paris Opera House rising nobly over medieval torture chambers, hidden dungeons, long forgotten!' It is a guide to the oppositional forces upon which the narrative is built: ephemeral performance art embodied by physical structure, humanity's highest aspirations juxtaposed with its cruellest, spatial and temporal dialogue through the present literally built upon the past.

The factions and frictions that Hugo portrays on the Paris streets are internalised by Leroux such that the horizontal map of Paris through which Hugo has his characters move to elaborate upon the different socio-economic levels becomes a

FIGURE 11.3   The most liminal of spaces in *The Phantom of the Opera*: Carlotte (Rosemary Ashe) and Christine (Sarah Brightman) on stage of the Paris opera house, interrupted in their performance of 'Il Muto', the show-within-the-show, the eponymous character. Scene from the original 1986 London production.

Source: Photo by Clive Barda, provided by the editor.

vertically sliced map, from the roof of the opera house down through the stage and public spaces to subterranean levels, tracking the relationship between different strata of society. Elaborating upon Walter Benjamin's observations in his *Arcades Project* – 'The city is only apparently homogeneous' – Eric Hazan has described in detail the clarity with which the boundaries between one area of the city and another may be distinguished and at other points not, with the effect of city walls creating distinctions between quarters and between an 'old' and 'new' Paris 'like the growth rings of a tree' (2010, pp. 3–16). Spaces are defined in the theatre between public (foyer, auditorium, box), professional (dressing room, managers' office, scenery store) and transitional (foyer/staircase, corridor, passageway). The stage itself is the most liminal, linking all of them physically as well as articulating the essential purposes of the institution culturally and artistically. Old and new are juxtaposed vertically through the frictions between established and rising talent (the singers), contemporary and established composers (the repertory), aristocratic and bourgeois interests (financial sponsors and management). At its most stark, there is an aristocrat's wooing of a rising, beautiful young opera star high up on the Opéra roof in contrast to his chilling encounter with the rat catcher underground.

As with Valjean's rescue of Marius through the sewers of Paris, the underground nature of Paris has impacted on that overground repeatedly since the dramatic subsidence in the appropriately named Rue d'Enfer in 1774, which prompted under the direction of Charles Axel Guillamot the construction of an extensive sewer system (Robb, 2010, pp. 27–42). While the Paris Opéra is a symbol of 19th-century modernity in Paris above ground, Leroux's *The Phantom of the Opera* does not make a connection with modernity underground through modern sanitation. Rather, the privilege above ground is contrasted with socio-political exclusion below via the catacombs and the tunnels of the Paris Commune and, not least, a torture chamber (Hogle, 2002, pp. 94–95). In the Lloyd Webber musical, that contrast is extended to social-artistic interaction that implies complacency and convention above in the values of the Opéra as opposed to imagination and risk below represented in Erik as artistic visionary. To go a layer further down, the very conception of Leroux's story, and thus its iterations, can be found in the burying in 1907 of recordings of such opera stars (retired and rising) Francesco Tamagno, Adelina Patti, Emma Calvé and Enrico Caruso. The Paris press made a huge fuss of this internment under the Opéra to be dug up only after a century. Leroux, ever aware of his successful journalistic roots, takes this as the starting point for his story: in the process of digging to bury the recordings, 'the workmen's pics unearthed a cadaver. I was soon able to prove that this was the body of the Phantom of the opera!' (1996, p. 25). Leroux's story is a multi-layered exploration of that central image of buried voices and underground artists awaiting resurrection (Newark, 2011, pp. 136–166).

The notion of layers is relevant too in how the novel draws on the remembered and the forgotten to create complex resonances between past and present. In the novel, Christine's character is generated through constant acts of memory, given prominence in the musical through specific sections: the gala triumph 'Recall those days, look back on all those times . . . there will never be a day when I won't think of you'; her childhood friendship with Raoul in 'Little Lotte'; her dream-like description on waking for the first time in the Phantom's realm, 'I remember there was mist' (Perry, 1987, pp. 143–144, 147). Notably we have her dead father's words and music in many references that culminate in 'Wishing You Were Somehow Here Again', and which reaches the same acknowledgment of a turning-point to be found with Jean Valjean and Alex, seeking release from what feels like an ever-present past: 'No more memories . . . Help me say goodbye' (Perry, 1987, p. 160). The multiple identities of the title character rely on associations being made from past events with current ones. Indeed, having a track record requires that the past is correlated with the present, that patterns of events are established over time: the recall by Madame Giry of a freak in a circus years ago is possibly a memory of the hideous Erik; Christine's recall of her dead father creates her Angel of Music; the opera house staff's memory of previous accidents and visions conjures up the otherworldly Phantom of the Opera; and to the new managers the Opera Ghost is a long-established blackmailer. The other-worldly incarnations of the Angel/Phantom identities are shrouded with the undefined, extended time scales of memory-through-myth in contrast to the mortal life span of the contemporary, flesh-and-blood Erik/Opera Ghost figure who invokes them.

Hugo filled his novel with description and fact to bring alive what he viewed as historical truth. Leroux – with his professional background as a successful investigative journalist to the fore – uses that same technique but for the opposite purpose, mixing direct fact, distortions and parodies of known events, people and objects as a means of giving a total fiction (the Phantom's story) a sense of truth while providing a self-congratulatory frisson to any readers who picks up on his allusions. Genuine cultural memory on behalf of the reader is crucial for this to work. Who is to suppose that the doubly fictitious (work and composer) opera *Hannibal* by Chalmeau is not as genuine as those pieces cited in Chapter 2 as part of a gala programme, with Gounod conducting his own *Funeral March for a Marionette* and Saint-Saëns conducting his *Danse macabre*? Moreover, the substitution of an established prima donna by a new talent with drama behind the scenes parallels that in 1869 at the Opéra, when a reigning prima donna Caroline Miolan-Carvalho ('Carlotta') was replaced in *Faust* – a real opera around which the fiction of the novel weaves – by Christina [Kristina] Nilsson ('Christine') as Marguerite (Newark, 2011, pp. 163–164). In his human persona as Erik, the Phantom was involved in the building of the demonstrably genuine Palais Garnier – thus enabling him to build in his secret passageways, trap doors and sliding mirrors. And the fall of a counterweight of the famous chandelier into the stalls in 1896 during a performance killed one unfortunate person, as the press heavily reported at the time.[12] Maria Björnson's stage designs for Lloyd Webber's musical introduces such elements of the auditorium of the Palais Garnier as the gilt decoration on the theatre boxes. Similarly, Joel Schumacher's film adaptation (2004) of Lloyd Webber's musical introduces imagery whose historical resonances are co-opted for the creation of apparent rather than actual authenticity. To take just two prominent examples: Erik's appearance as the Red Death at the Opéra ball ('Masquerade') is not in the billowing cloak and plumed hat of the stage show (itself referencing the 1925 silent film with its still-striking colour sequence), but instead in the flattering, sleek lines of the suit of Ingres's portrait of Napoleon, *Bonaparte, Premier Consul* (1804), while the dress and distinctive diamond-star jewellery worn by Christine for her Gala debut copy Winterhalter's portrait (1865) of the Empress Elisabeth 'Sisi' of Austria.

Possibly the most important feature for Leroux that arises from Paris is led by what is heard. In the 19th century, Paris rose to become the capital of the world. One of its most striking exports was grand opera. For some 40 years from the late 1820s, this large-scale form dominated opera, and such composers as Wagner (unsuccessfully) and Verdi (successfully with commissions including *Les Vêpres siciliennes* and *Don Carlos*) sought the ultimate seal of approval that composing specifically for the Paris Opéra brought. From the ground-breaking *Robert le Diable* (1831) through to the posthumously premiered *L'Africaine* (1865), Meyerbeer's grand operas written with the librettist Scribe defined the genre's principal features as they have subsequently been extrapolated: long formats (often five acts); quasi-historical subject matter, individual relationships set against religious and political turmoil; impressive scenic and lighting effects; large-scale tableaux involving huge casts (chorus, dancers, supernumeraries, animals . . .) as participants in or witnesses of dramatised confrontations driven by emotions in conflict with power, often exemplified through class; star singers in roles written to show them off; substantial and obligatory ballet *divertissement*. Meyerbeer's operas *Les Huguenots* (1836) and *Le Prophète* (1849) in particular exemplify the archetype. Opera was at this time political as well as artistic, a bold statement to the world of power, wealth and influence. French opera's themes reflected a preoccupation with the role of the individual set against a state caught up in the sweep of history. Its extravagant scale of production provided a bold statement of French confidence and wealth. Significant here, the displacement of current political elements onto a dramatic narrative set in the past made it innately a form encapsulating subtextual, temporal dialogue.

Signifying itself most immediately through parody as grand opera is the chorus number 'The Trumpeting Elephants Sound', presented as from Chalmeau's *Hannibal*, in *The Phantom of the Opera*. It establishes a genre 'status quo' against which Erik's subsequent *Don Juan Triumphant* can be contrasted and enables the newness of Christine as a performer to be shown against a style set first by Carlotta (Snelson, 2018, pp. 244–246). Indeed, the operatic discourse in this musical is to the fore even in its title. The theatrical adaptation of Leroux's novel by Ken Hill that provided the springboard for Lloyd Webber's musical uses numbers from operas appropriate to French repertory at the time of the story but re-purposed with new lyrics.[13] Lloyd Webber went further in creating a new, near-continuous musicalisation. A parallel narrative to that of Erik Christine and Raoul in *The Phantom of the Opera* is that of genre identity: opera pitched against popular musical theatre.[14]

The list above of characteristics for grand opera readily map to those of the musical adaptation of *Les Misérables*. Operatic connotations through music in particular are present in a through-sung approach whose vocal lines require powerful, developed voices. The melodic overlays and alternations at the conclusion of Act I, expressing the perspectives of the different dramatic constituencies, adopts the classic *concertato* form of operatic climaxes. With multiple points of operatic signalling, 'Bring Him Home' follows the conventions of the operatic 'Prayer' (Christine's 'Wishing you Were Somehow Here Again' in *The Phantom of the Opera* does too) and puts a premium on vocal skill. It even states its operatic roots openly, being a reworking of the 'Humming Chorus' from Puccini's *Madama Butterfly*, and as a night-time vigil shares the same narrative function. The historical memory of 19th-century Paris brings with it cultural memory that naturally invites operatic modes of expression.[15]

Musical form contributes to memory through musical motif. Themes build up significance with each iteration, whether as direct restatement or modified. The abstract use of motifs in this way is fundamental to symphonic technique. In a work for the lyric stage, an additional layer of narrative and emotional cross-referencing is possible through associations with characters and events. To differing degrees, all three works of this chapter use motifs as musical memory, as historical landmarks in sound.

Les Misérables tends towards operatic reminiscence motif, in which a theme is restated in the same or a very similar way in order to connect present and past through shared music. A direct link is made between the opening prisoners' chorus on the chain gang, 'Look down, look down/Don't look 'em in the eye' and the later Paris Beggar's chorus 'Look down and see the beggars at our feet'. The music and lyrics pair the deprivations of the beggars and the prisoners. Other such repetitions include the mosaic of Act I's final chorus, in which the music delineates in an immediate, visceral way the idealism of the students, the grasping self-interest of the Thénardiers and the single-minded focus of Javert.[16] Similarly, in *The Phantom of the Opera*, the main theme of Act I's ensemble 'Prima Donna' is dominated by flattery to persuade the temperamental diva Carlotta to perform again. In Act II, Raoul uses the same music to persuade Christine to take part in the plot to catch Erik-Phantom through the performance of his *Don Juan Triumphant*. Raoul's quiet, initial restatement of the theme's opening is enough to prompt the associations of *prima donna* status with Christine and remind us of Carlotta's experience of returning to the stage. The use of reminiscence motif in *Aspects of Love* is most prominently carried by its opening number, but other examples are given below.

A more extended approach to thematic metamorphosis, developed from an operatic perspective more akin to leitmotif, runs through *The Phantom of the Opera*, and has been discussed in studies of the work.[17] Lloyd Webber's approach to thematic manipulation is of a different nature to that of Claude-Michel Schönberg, with multiple repetitions and developments of thematic motives more than restated extended melody. For example, the chromatically descending-ascending chords in the organ introduction to the title song (first heard as the chandelier rises at the end of the Prologue), are modified into the descending whole-tone descent of chords that accompany Christine's sensations around her Angel of Music as she first describes them to Meg.[18] Angel and Phantom are, of course, the same person, and the music lets the audience (if not at this point, Christine) know. Lloyd Webber's interest in such musico-dramatic presentation carries through in equally concentrated form into *Aspects of Love*, with distinctive melodic lines echoing through the score, blurring past and present musically. For example, in Act I during a trip into the countryside around Pau, Rose sings a folk song lodged in her memory, 'Pas de tendresse /Et pas de joie/Loin d'ici/Loin de toi' – the conclusion to a day such that 'Nothing is sweeter' (Gänzl, 1990, p. 141). In Act II, Alex retraces that day in the company of Rose's daughter, Jenny, who sings the same song in the same place: 'Mummy used to sing it to me/It was her love song/Her very first love song' (Gänzl, 1990, p. 153). The melody in that setting becomes a poignant symbol linking past and present as Jenny's musical reminiscence of her mother entwines with Alex's memory of Rose as his first lover.

'Take the journey of a lifetime'

At 138 pages, David Garnett's novel is hardly on the scale of Victor Hugo's, which for the author was 'a vast attempt . . . to make sense of his own life and its passing' (Tombs, 2013, p. xxiii). Yet it too concentrates on those same reflections, emerging in Garnett's fifth decade, between his own past and present: the title could well have been 'Aspects of Garnett'. A running textual motif is the phrase 'It will be a slight memory for you' (given in its French form, as 'Ce sera un souvenir léger pour toi'). What Garnett referred to as his 'French novel' has strong elements of actual biography, with Alex and George representing Garnett, the change-partners-and-dance relationships mirroring his own affairs within the Bloomsbury set and beyond, and the unconsummated relationship with Jenny a mirror of the consummated relationship of Garnett with Angelica Bell, who became his second wife and to whom *Aspects of Love* is dedicated. Since his youth, Garnett had been friends with Angelica's parents, the author Vanessa Bell and her husband, the artist Duncan Grant, with whom Garnett had had an affair. When Angelica was born, on Christmas Day in 1918, Garnett was present, writing in a letter to Lytton Strachey somewhat prophetically that Angelica was

> simply a very small very lovely naked human, with signs of great will power and intelligence. . . . Its beauty is the most remarkable thing about it. I think of marrying it: when she is twenty I shall be 46 – will it be scandalous?
>
> *(Knights, 2015, p. 138)*

Angelica grew up with him as a sort of uncle figure, developing a youthful crush on him, which turned into an affair. In the book and the musical, Alex resists Jenny's teenage romantic insinuations, as did Garnett of Angelica at a similar age. But whereas in fiction Alex ends up with Giulietta, former mistress of Alex's uncle George, in life David Garnett and Angelica Bell married in 1942, when she was 24 and he was 50. This is echoed too in the relationship between George and Rose, and the increasingly apparent differences in physical capability resulting from the difference between their ages.

FIGURE 11.4   One of several cross-generational love affairs in *Aspects of Love*: actress Rose Vibert (Ann Crumb) and her future husband, the artist George Dillingham (Kevin Colson). Scene from the original 1989 London production.

Source: Photo by Alastair Muir, provided by the editor.

Biographical elements are rife elsewhere. For example, Giulietta is in part modelled after the Italian artist Giovanna Madonia, a friend of Angelica and David Garnett, whom he described as 'extraordinarily beautiful with a classic beauty – very brown & thin'. Garnett knew France from teenage holidays with his mother, construction work during World War I to the north-east of Paris (as a pacifist he volunteered with the Friends War Victims Relief Committee in place of military service), and from many holidays as an adult. He stayed for several years running in the 1950s with his wealthy American friend Mina Curtiss at her Paris flat overlooking the Seine on the Isle St Louis, where in the novel Sir George Dillingham has his flat, and thus where Alex discovers the relationship between his former lover Rose and his uncle. The novel's description through Alex's eyes of the island and the location of the flat is Garnett's memory more than imagination:

> [T]imeless in the heart of the whirling, changing, kaleidoscopic city, the busy highway of the river hemming it in on each side . . . The room was as he remembered it, the most beautiful that he had ever been in. It was slightly asymmetrical with two great windows looking out over the end of the island and down the Seine.

(1989, pp. 40–41)

Through Mina, Garnett was entertained by wealthy, social and culturally prestigious circles that parallel those in the novel of Rose Vibert as celebrated actress (Knights, 2015, p. 397). Mina too enabled his financial support to research and write *Aspects of Love* in France. Even the break-in to George's house at Pau has a real source, when in 1916 Garnett and two friends broke into the Ashenham home rented by Vanessa Bell and Duncan Grant, who were away (Knights, 2015, p. 121). The act of remembering by Garnett through biography is seemingly stronger than the role of fiction in the book, and disentangling memory from imagination is as problematic as with Hugo and Leroux.

Garnett's biographer, Sarah Knights, considers that Garnett's upbringing within the sphere of the Bloomsbury set meant that he 'considered himself a congenital outsider, attracted to experimental living, to life beyond the mainstream' (2015, p. 4). The potential to view relationships as transgressive of societal norms provides the link to Paris, in association with artists in particular. Bizarre though it may initially seem, there is a link with the self-identification of Erik, the composer-phantom, and all he represents in pulling Christine away from safety and social respectability in marriage with Raoul towards an artistic life of challenge, non-conformity and self-expression. After all, Christine is at her most musically expressive when singing for her Angel of Music, not for Raoul. There is a long-established link between Paris and artistic freedom of expression – for writers, artists, performers. Archetypal examples are found in the 'Scenes of Bohemian Life' of Henri Murger (whose afterlife Puccini ensured through *La bohème*), the fictional artist William Bagot, nicknamed 'Little Billee', in George du Maurier's novel *Trilby* (1894), through to cinema with Hollywood's romanticised gloss in *An American in Paris* (1951) and the British satire of Tony Hancock in *The Rebel* (1961). Indeed, the musicals discussed throughout this volume make the point. But here, the most direct relevance comes through Garnett's novel of 1927, *Go She Must!*

In this early work in Garnett's output, the experiences and values of Anne Dunnock, the daughter of a vicar in a village in the Norfolk fens, are juxtaposed with those of Richard, the indulged son of the village grocer. The grocer subsidises his son's attempt to establish himself as an artist, and as Richard says, 'Paris is the only place for that' (Garnett, 1927, p. 60). The two young people meet in Norfolk, she develops feelings for him and follows him to the French capital, where her provincial ideas are challenged. For example, Anne eventually realises that a love letter by Richard she accidentally read was addressed to the other male artist in his Parisian ménage à trois with a female model. The role Paris plays as symbol of countercultural values and challenge to accepted norms is clear: 'It was no accident that the book's heroine acquired both personal and sexual freedom in Paris' (Knights, 2015, p. 215).

In the musical more than the novel, the few scenes in Paris present a wider world in an otherwise internally focussed drama. From Paris, in May 1953, Angelica Garnett wrote to her husband: 'Really Paris is the only place to live in you know, it's the only place you can do what you like in and enjoy it all at the same time' (Knights, 2015, p. 402). Things 'happen' in Paris: Alex's discovery of Rose with his uncle, his accidental shooting of her, the authentication of Rose's star status as an actress, the clash at the circus when the domestic focus is put into a larger landscape and its flaws are revealed. Paris remains the city that allows freedom of expression, particularly in cultural circles. After the opening 'Love Changes Everything' prologue, Act I opens with Rose's unsuccessful interpretation of Hilde Wangel in Ibsen's *The Master Builder* in 'a small provincial theatre in Montpellier, France' (Gänzl, 1990, p. 134). In contrast, the opening of Act II, 12 years later, presents Rose as Natalia Petrovna in Turgenev's *A Month in the Country*, received in the capital city such that she has 'Tumultuous applause ringing in her ears' (Gänzl, 1990, p. 148). The city can bestow status and acclaim in a way that a provincial town cannot. As Jenny exclaims, 'Weren't they wonderful reviews?/She'll be the toast of Paris!' George adds that success in Paris means success anywhere: 'How the work keeps flooding in,/With appearances in London/And movies in Berlin' (Gänzl, 1990, p. 149).

The city setting permits the activity and noise of the ensemble, where it is allied to personal ambition in the public sphere. In Act I, the visit by Alex to a Paris fairground two years after his first encounter with Rose provokes lyrics that stress trying your luck. Retrospectively they connect with Alex's 'having a go' in Montpellier and winning (if briefly) Rose. But the lyrics 'Everybody loves a hero!/Let's hear it for the man with a gun!' stress public approbation – Alex's success on a rifle range wins him a toy donkey – with some irony as the private gunshot in the scene to follow is far from heroic (Gänzl, 1990, pp. 142–143). In Act II, Jenny's 15th-birthday visit to the circus is linked through shared music and similarly aspirational lyrics. Again, the ensemble represents the wider world, shifting the lyrics to taking 'the journey of a lifetime./Every day's a high-wire-day'. And while the imprecation is 'part hymn in praise of daring, part invitation for a volunteer from the circus audience', it again places the key characters emotional risks and choices into a broader perspective, with the undercurrents in the increasingly easy intimacy of Jenny and Alex coming out in the anger of George. The participation as target by Alex in the knife-throwing act brings resonances of the gun in Act I, and if George does not literally throw a knife at Alex, the atmosphere suggests that he would like to (Gänzl, 1990, p. 154). Through each of *Les Misérables*, *The Phantom of the Opera* and *Aspects of Love*, some of the most significant dramatic flashpoints are created when private tensions are exposed in the public spaces of Paris. Symbolically, the city stands as a catalyst for change.

Paris changes everything

Each author's own biography to some degree is wound into the narratives, with a particular awareness of outsiders and rebels, insiders and conformists. There is a specificity about this biographical input in relation to Paris that fundamentally shapes aspects of each literary source, which becomes through selection and reinterpretation an important force in each of the three musical adaptations. Life is the source of art here through identifiably Parisian geography, architecture, politics, society and culture. It is difficult to imagine the musical *Les Misérables* remaining comprehensible set anywhere other than in France, specifically in Paris. While *The Phantom of the Opera* can be divorced from its Paris setting – numerous film adaptations globally have done so – Paris is essential to the richness of Leroux's conception. And if *Aspects of Love* does not need the constant physical presence of Paris to make its points, Parisian sensibilities towards emotional and artistic identity are an inextricable part of the novel's, and consequently the show's, DNA. There may not be an equal necessity for a literal Paris across these shows, but they do share a sense of appropriateness to a way of thinking around history and memory that ties them together. In reference to Victor Hugo and *Les Misérables*, Graham Robb writes: '[T]he sense of passing time, the undertow of memory, the unwholesome interference of the past with the present are impeccably rendered' (1997, p. 384). That this resonates so well with each novel and musical adaptation discussed provides an eloquent summary of how Paris – fact, fiction and symbol – permeates all three.

Notes

1   Eric Hazan describes such an effect in relation to the Opéra area of Paris, which provides geographical focus for Gaston Leroux's novel *The Phantom of the Opera*: 'The construction of the Opéra Garnier, the department stores, and eventually Boulevard Haussmann, brought the coup de grâce to this quarter of actresses and dancers, so that today only a few scholars are aware of its remnants, scattered among the traffic jams and perfumeries, shop-windows with Christmas toys and post-Christmas sales (2010, p. 141).

2   The musical *Les Misérables* had its première on 8 October 1985 at the Barbican Theatre in London. Immediately following its planned ten-week run there, it transferred to the Palace Theatre in London's West End on 4 December.

3   *The Phantom of the Opera* opened almost exactly a year after that of *Les Misérables*, in London's West End at Her Majesty's Theatre, on 9 October 1986.

4   *Aspects of Love* premiered at London's Prince of Wales Theatre, 17 April 1989.

5   Explicitly, the elderly Raoul, Vicomte de Chagny, muses to himself that a music box with a 'figure of a monkey in Persian robes playing the cymbals' has 'every detail exactly as she said . . . She often spoke of you, my friend' – note his use of the past tense (Perry, 1987, p. 141).

6   The temporal structure is reinforced by the music. 'Love Changes Everything' in the Prologue 'does not finish formally, but cuts into . . . [Scene 2]' (Gänzl, 1990, p. 134). It is deprived of Alex's climactic baritonal top A. The expected 'big vocal finish' does not happen until the end of Act I, in a scene set when Alex is some 15 years younger than in the Prologue. This Act I reprise mirrors the opening number as a retrospective analysis of an emotional journey by paradoxically completing it musically in its own narrative past. It is only with the very end of Act II that the musical-finish 'full stop' and chronological sequence meet.

7   *Les Misérables* emerged from a French spectacular via the Royal Shakespeare Company, which in turn shaped its dramatic development and presentational style. Among the provocations for his own works, Lloyd Webber has included the desire to address a romantic drama which he first attempted in the early 1980s through an interest in Garnett's novel, with ideas tried out during Lloyd Webber's Sydmonton Festival in 1983. But the 'major romantic story' he was attempting to create was in the event brought to the stage first in *The Phantom of the Opera* (Perry, 1987, p. 67). Moreover, there is no inherent contemporary fascination with Paris made manifest as a trope in London musicals in the 1980s. The two other shows that include a Paris setting in a similar period to those discussed here are relatively short-lived revivals: *Gigi* (1984) and *Can-Can* (1988).

8 The novel's ten instalments were published between 3 April and 30 June 1862.
9 Part 4 is ostensibly given a geographical focus as 'The Rue Plumet Idyll and the Rue St-Denis Epic', yet even this is the result of the focus on two individuals encapsulated in the street naming. Hugo's choice of title makes a conscious contrast between the societal quarantining of Cosette by Valjean (Rue Plumet) with the Paris of politics and factions, notably the ABC students (Rue St-Denis). This culminates in the clash at the barricade and Valjean's rescue of Marius on behalf of his 'daughter'. The 'idyll' becomes the 'epic' through the consequences of the love between Marius and Cosette.
10 Not so in *The Phantom of the Opera*, in which the use of the prop elephant in the extract from Chalmeau's *Hannibal* provides a witty and immediate symbol for the excesses of production at the Paris Opéra – what is real to the audience is hollow seen from behind the scenes.
11 The image of the huge Parisian elephant links through, too, to director Baz Luhrmann's vibrantly eclectic portrayal of Paris in the film *Moulin Rouge!* in 2001.
12 In the novel, Leroux makes an allusion to this when Erik denies to the Daroga (the Persian Chief of Police who has been pursuing him) any involvement in that event: 'I had nothing to do with the chandelier. *The chandelier was very worn.* . . . It fell by itself. It went boom!' (1996, p. 265).
13 Hill's *The Phantom of the Opera* was first produced in Lancaster in 1976. A production at London's Stratford East Theatre in 1984 led to Lloyd Webber's interest in developing the idea. Hill's adaptation draws on opera arias from composers including Mozart, Weber, Donizetti, Verdi, Bizet, Dvořák and Boito.
14 Extended analysis of the music and its genre significance can be found in Snelson, 2004, pp. 106–118.
15 For consideration of the reflection of Puccini's style in *The Phantom of the Opera*, see Snelson, 2004, pp. 176–180.
16 The idea of the reminiscence motif is characteristic of French and Italian opera, and a ready part of the techniques of, for example, Gounod, Massenet and Puccini. For discussion of recurring themes and motifs in *Les Misérables*, see Sternfeld, 2006, pp. 193–204.
17 See, for example Snelson, 2004, pp. 88–118; Sternfeld, 2006, pp. 241–263. This type of motivic transformation has roots in symphonic thematic development, taken to greater narrative levels through Wagnerian use and later into thematic associative devices in film scores.
18 Christine: 'He's with me even now', Meg: 'Your hands are cold', Christine: 'All around me', Meg: 'Your face, Christine, it's white', Christine: 'It frightens me', Meg: 'Don't be frightened' (Perry, 1987, p. 144).

References

Behr, E. (1989) *Les Misérables: History in the Making*. London: Cape, Includes Libretto, pp. 165–191.
Gänzl, K. (1990) *The Complete Aspects of Love*. London: Aurum Press, Includes Libretto, pp. 133–158.
Garnett, D. (1989) *Aspects of Love*. London: Guild Publishing. First Published 1955 by Hogarth Press.
———. (1927) *Go She Must!* London: Chatto & Windus.
Hazan, É. (2010) *The Invention of Paris: A History in Footsteps*. London: Verso.
Hogle, J. E. (2002) *The Undergrounds of 'the Phantom of the Opera': Sublimation and the Gothic in Leroux's Novel and Its Progeny*. New York and Basingstoke: Palgrave-Macmillan.
Hugo, V. (2013) *The Wretched* (C. Donougher, trans. and ed., R. Tombs, intro.). London: Penguin Books.
Jones, C. (2004) *Paris: Biography of a City*. London: Allen Lane.

Knights, S. (2015) *Bloomsbury's Outsider: A Life of David Garnett*. London: Bloomsbury Reader.

Leroux, G. (1996) *The Essential Phantom of the Opera: The Definitive, Annotated Edition of Gaston Leroux's Classic Novel* (L. Wolf, Ed.). New York and London: Plume.

Les Misérables [Original London Cast Recording]. (1985) London: First Night Records. Liner Notes, Including Libretto, unpaginated.

Marrinan, M. (2009) *Romantic Paris: Histories of a Cultural Landscape, 1800–1850*. Stanford, CA: Stanford University Press.

Newark, C. (2011) *Opera in the Novel from Balzac to Proust*. Cambridge: Cambridge University Press.

Nightingale, B. and Palmer, M. (2013) *Les Misérables: From Page to Stage to Screen: The Ongoing Story of the World's Longest-Running Musical* (C. Mackintosh, foreword). London: Carlton Books.

Perry, G. (1987) *The Complete Phantom of the Opera*. London: Pavilion Books, Includes Libretto, pp. 140–167.

Robb, G. (2010) *Parisians: An Adventure History of Paris*. London: Picador.

———. (1997) *Victor Hugo*. London: Picador.

Snelson, J. (2018) 'Controlling Voices: Singing in *Phantom* Films,' *Opera Quarterly*, 34(2–3), Spring–Summer, pp. 242–259.

———. (2004) *Andrew Lloyd Webber*. New Haven and London: Yale University Press.

Sternfeld, J. (2006) *The Megamusical*. Bloomington, IN: Indiana University Press.

Tombs, R. (2013) 'Introduction,' in *The Wretched*. London: Penguin Books.

12

THE COURTESAN AND THE COLLABORATOR

Marguerite

Clare Chandler

The 2008 musical *Marguerite* was conceived by a consortium of creators from theatre, musical theatre and film. Given their combined credentials and accolades (four Academy Awards, two Tony Awards, one BAFTA, three Grammys, two Olivier Awards and a Golden Globe) *Marguerite* should have been a rousing success, but the show never realised its full potential. Despite the best efforts of Alain Boublil, Claude Michel Schönberg, Michel Legrand, Herbert Kretzmer and Jonathan Kent, this transposition of *La Dame aux Camélias* (1848) by Alexandre Dumas *fils*, failed to resonate with British audiences. Subsequent revivals and revisions (all of which have had input from Boublil) have attempted to resolve the issues within the musical, with varying degrees of success.

This chapter considers the controversies, constructs and context that combined to undermine *Marguerite*'s potential success. It critically analyses the original 2008 West End production and the 2012 London revival, also touching on the more successful 2009 Tokyo and Osaka productions, as well as the 2010 Czech production in Ostrava. It argues that West End audiences' and critics' discomfort with the show was due to three major factors: British views of French collaboration during World War II; a general cultural unease with anti-heroes as musical protagonists; and an unease with female anti-heroes (especially older ones) in particular.[1]

'We're French. Why are we doing this?'

It is intriguing to note that in a book about musical theatre's association with Paris so few French writers are mentioned; of these, Michel Legrand, Claude Michel Schönberg and Alain Boublil certainly have the highest profile in the United States and the United Kingdom. The iconic duo of Boublil and Schönberg released their first concept album, musicalising *La Révolution Française*, in 1973; they then staged their own 'révolution française'[2] in the 1980s, when their epic 'poperetta'[2] musicals

Les Misérables (1980) and *Miss Saigon* (1989) reshaped ideas about content, style and scope of musical theatre around the world. Their most successful shows, as William Everett has noted, tend to be set somewhere France-related, against a backdrop of war, and include 'some sort of message of social edification' (2007, p. 230). Given their high-profile British collaborators (the Royal Shakespeare Company and Cameron Mackintosh) these shows are often grouped as part of the 'British Invasion' that swept Broadway during this decade. However, there is no denying their French heritage, both in subject matter and scope. The original French version of *Les Misérables* played in the 4,600-seater Le Palais des Sports, and, whilst it was later anglicised for British and American audiences, the show still bears the influence of its origins.

To date, the duo have written six musicals and two ballets. Together with Andrew Lloyd Webber, Boublil and Schönberg brought the so-called 'mega-musical' to spectacular life. This highly commercial musical theatre form, which repackaged the past (Eubanks Winkler, 2014, p. 279), combining sweeping operatic stylings with spectacle and borrowing heavily from preceding works,[3] was very much a product of the 1980s. Indeed, Vera Gottlieb labelled them 'Thatcher's Theatre' (1988) and theatre critic Michael Billington refers to them as 'Thatcherism in action' (2007, p. 284). As Amanda Eubanks Winkler has discussed, these works meshed well with the values of Thatcher and Reagan, synthesising 'values of traditionalism and capitalism' (2014, p. 279). They were also, as Stacy Wolf has noted, created during a period of antifeminist backlash, resulting in reinforced gender binaries and female characters that amounted to narrow and demeaning stereotypes (2011). These musicals tended to employ 'big themes, big sets and big music' (Wolf, 2011, p. 128), creating hugely popular shows which unconsciously reflected the misogyny of the period and which continue to dominate the West End.

Boublil and Schönberg have failed to repeat the success of *Les Misérables* and *Miss Saigon* in their more recent shows. These followed a similar formula of epic story and pseudo-operatic style and spectacle, but couldn't quite tap into the cultural zeitgeist. Audiences struggled to empathise with 16th-century catfishing (*Martin Guerre*, 1996) and with gender politics set against a backdrop of feuding Irish clans (*The Pirate Queen*, 2007). For their sixth musical the duo were inspired by a new collaborator, Michel Legrand, and brought things a little closer to home: reimagining Dumas *fils'* famous novel *La Dame aux Camélias* in war-torn World War II Paris.

'Queen of Paris after dark'

La Dame aux Camélias is a semi-autobiographical novel based on the brief love affair between Alexandre Dumas *fils* and Marie Duplessis, a renowned courtesan. Setting the standard for all the 'fallen women' in Romantic literature to follow, Dumas *fils'* tragic heroine (now named Marguerite Gautier) dies, purging her iniquitous life and ascending to a realm of romantic myth and cultural phenomenon.

Narrated by two male characters following Marguerite's death, the novel tells the tale of her doomed love affair with a man called Armand Duval. (It is highly unlikely that the author chose to give his protagonist his own initials purely by chance). Having been convinced by Armand to abandon her *demi-monde* existence for a life of pastoral bliss, Duval senior intervenes to persuade Marguerite to leave Armand, to save Armand's sister from taint by association. In what has become a generic tragic love story convention, Armand is unaware of Marguerite's self-less sacrifice until our heroine's death, believing instead that she has left him for another man.

Perhaps most famously and successfully adapted by Giuseppe Verdi as *La Traviata* (1853), the inaugural 'tart with a heart' story has been brought to the musical theatre stage in several guises. Baz Luhrmann and John Logan adapted Luhrmann's cult hit film *Moulin Rouge!* for Broadway, where it opened to a mixed critical response in 2019. Even more tepidly-received was Bryan Adams, Jim Vallance, Garry Marshall and J. F. Lawton's 2018 musical version of the 1990 film *Pretty Woman*. *Pretty Woman – The Musical* nods to its musical heritage when, as in the movie, Vivian and Edward attend a production of *La Traviata*, though in this iteration our heroine doesn't die tragically, thus subverting the Dumas *fils* romantic myth. Instead, she is allowed to achieve redemption; sex work unexpectedly leads to eternal bliss, as Vivien rides off into the sunset with her 'knight in shining armour', Edward.[4]

'How did I get to where I am?'

In the early 2000s, the soprano and actor Marie Zamora (Alain Boublil's wife) was touring the world and performing with the composer Michel Legrand. Legrand was inspired to write a musical for Zamora, so he approached Boublil to collaborate. At Schönberg's suggestion, Boublil and Legrand began to work on a retelling of *La Dame Aux Camélias* entitled *Marguerite et Armand*. As the piece developed, it was decided that the West End might be a good destination for the show. Schönberg came on board to collaborate with Boublil on the book, Herbert Kretzmer reclaimed his *Les Misérables* role as English lyricist and Jonathan Kent joined the quintet as director and additional book writer.

Once Boublil had made the decision to set this transposition of Dumas *fils'* story in the 'dark hours of Nazi-occupied Paris in 1942' (cited in *The Making of Marguerite*), he didn't think it was appropriate to use the sung-through format that had characterised his work with Schönberg. Having written a couple of versions of the script, which he felt were unsatisfactory, Boublil invited Schönberg to collaborate with him on the book. Reunited, the duo began working with Legrand and Kent to piece the show together in French (Kent later wrote the English book with Kretzmer providing English lyrics). This was a lengthy process; as Schönberg notes: '[Y]ou don't write a musical, you rewrite a musical' (quoted in *The Making of Marguerite*) and the pair wrote at least six drafts during this initial period.

This approach, referenced also by Jonathan Kent in his interview (2019), resulted in an overworked and somewhat cumbersome libretto; the clunky rhythms disrupt Legrand's melodies, rather than working in tandem with them. At other moments, Kretzmer's English lyrics juxtapose Legrand's emotive compositional sweeps with clichés: 'Lost are the songs we could have sung/Where are those melodies now?' (Bouberg, 2008, p. 29), or endless end rhymes: 'Intoxic*ation* . . . Imagin*ation* . . . Hallucin*ation* . . . Fascin*ation* . . . Compli*cation*' (italics added for emphasis) (Bouberg, 2008, p. 39).

Legrand's compositions are filmic in scope: they sweep through the narrative combining 'the big gestures of Europe's high romantics with the smoky, sexy sounds of after-hours Paris' (Obermüller, 2019). There is no concern that audience members will leave the theatre whistling the sets. Legrand's compositional trope (employed with Oscar-winning success in 'The Windmills of Your Mind') of repeating short phrases which oscillate between major and minor modes, creates some musical hooks, but also limits narrative development, as the songs keep returning to the same point. Unsurprisingly, most of the songs are 'A-A' songs,[5] expressing emotions rather than progressing the storyline.

The finale number is full of sweeping strings and soaring vocals building to an emotional peak as Marguerite and Armand declare their undying love, and our heroine accepts her tragic fate. As the final chords ebb away, the show's final scripted moment occurs as follows:

PIERROT: I couldn't find a doctor.
ARMAND: It's alright, she's going to be alright . . . She's asleep. Isn't she? She's asleep. Tell me she's asleep.

As an awkward silence falls, a plaintive piano variation of Marguerite's 'China Doll' theme is played, underscoring Armand carrying our fallen heroine 'through the collaborators, toward the light' (Bouberg, 2008, p. 94). The simplicity of these final eight bars succinctly evokes the tragedy of Marguerite's life and the inevitability of her fate.

Collaboration

The tone for *Marguerite* is established in the arresting opening sequence of the original production, which foreshadows the ending: Marguerite is attacked and stripped by a crowd for her crime of 'horizontal collaboration'.[6] As choreographer Nikki Woollaston notes, 'starting a show with an attack on the leading lady is a risk', but there was a desire to 'be brutal and keep it as real as possible' (Woollaston). Audiences might not understand the opening until they reached the end of the show (when the sequence was repeated in the run-up to the piece's tragic dénouement). However, Woollaston and the creative team felt it was important to open the piece in a way that presented the 'ugliness of war right there in a three minute sequence' (Woollaston). Opening the show with Marguerite's punishment at the hands of the mob might have presented Marguerite in a tragically sympathetic light, but this is complicated by the fact that she is soon revealed to be a collaborator with the Nazi occupiers.

Collaboration and its ambiguities provide one of the show's fundamental themes, but this in turn presented a problem for West End audiences; in particular, ambiguity and the resultant discomfort were not something that audiences familiar with Boublil and Schönberg's work were used to. Recent French historiography has worked to deconstruct the myth of 'good French' (resistors), 'bad French' (collaborators) and 'poor French' (everybody else) in order to create a more nuanced understanding of what happened between 1941 and 1945 (Gildea, 2002, p. 414). However, popular opinion in the United Kingdom hasn't moved beyond the collaboration/resistance binary prevalent in France until the late 1960s (Gordon, 2019): believing that the whole nation resisted, with the exception of a few evil collaborators. As the British Isles have not been invaded for several centuries, opinions about the German occupation of France tend to be very moralistic. Director and book writer Jonathan Kent observes that the United Kingdom was 'never occupied [during WWII] so can afford a kind of disapproval' (2019). Perhaps the historical antagonism between France and the United Kingdom, as manifested in continuing jokes about the spineless or flighty French, still colours opinions.[7]

In *Marguerite* the creative team initially chose not to shy away from addressing collaboration and its messy underbelly. The show's chorus navigates the audience through shifting feelings towards occupation, and there are some *bon Français* characters to provide a familiar narrative trope. The *Independent*'s critic Kate Bassett observed in her review of the original production that 'keeping the *amour fou* at the emotional centre, whilst introducing citizens, who are more valiantly engaged, as mere secondary characters, *Marguerite* actually makes itself look shallow' (2008). This perspective, wanting to focus on valiant resistance over the grey shades of collaboration, supports Jonathan Kent's contention that audiences reacted to the show with an 'odd sort of prudishness' (2019). This reaction wasn't limited to the musical; the 2015 film adaptation of Irène Némirovsky's posthumously-published and critically-acclaimed 2004 novel *Suite Française* also flopped at the box office.

Marguerite's ambiguities are highlighted by its tonal shifts; in its upbeat second song, 'Let the World Turn', celebrating the eponymous heroine's birthday, the Parisian high society sing:

> Screw this war.
> It isn't our war to fight
> Sweet surrender gave us a second chance
> Germany is putting our country right
> Germany is giving us back our France
>
> Out with the Reds
> Out with the Jews
> Take them away

Let the sky fall
Let the guns roar
Life gets rougher
Some will suffer
Some will quit

These are good times
It's a good war
Some eat foie gras
Some eat soufflé
Some eat shit

(Bouberg, 2008, p. 6)

The song also contains a nod to Marguerite's inevitable fate, when she sings 'Some women'd tear out my hair' (Bouberg, 2008, p. 7), as she enjoys the perks of passive resistance and active collaboration. At this stage, the audience had not developed empathy for the musical's characters, and so the quick shift in the positioning of the ensemble from the show's opening was destabilising.

FIGURE 12.1 Parisian high society enjoying itself during the Nazi occupation: Marguerite (Ruthie Henshall, centre) celebrates her birthday with lover Otto (Alexander Hanson, in uniform). At the piano sits Armand (Julian Ovenden), the man whom she will fall in love with and who will be her downfall.

Source: Photo courtesy of Donald Cooper/Photostage.

'It seems the British have decided to ruin your party.'

An audience inability to empathise with the complex dynamics of 'collaboration' (Gildea, 2002, p. 198) was felt by the teams of both the original production and the 2012 revival. Guy Unsworth, who directed the 2012 production, found the audience's lack of knowledge about occupation difficult to navigate and frustrating to behold:

> I found it very tricky to translate to a modern (British) audience the authentic context and experience of the occupation (for many Parisian citizens of class it was an easy, logical and ostensibly pleasant choice of life) alongside the danger and very real threat which many other groups of people experienced. By achieving the former, you release the danger and tension from the piece, but by increasing the latter, empathising with the lead character became harder and in fact seemed less authentic.
>
> *(2019)*

Kent also struggled to understand audiences' reticence to engage, stating that, as they couldn't 'sympathise with someone who is a collaborator with the Nazis', it meant the show was 'slightly unfairly treated' (2019). This apparent lack of audience empathy appears in many of the original production's reviews. These included ones branding the central protagonist an 'opportunist' (Billington, 2008), who 'never discovers much of a nagging conscience' (de Jongh cited in *Review Roundup*, 2008) and 'whose behaviour is totally abhorrent' (Fisher, 2008); far removed, critics felt, from Dumas *fils*' original tragic heroine. The central issue here appears to be Marguerite's collaboration, which takes her from 'tart with a heart' to 'heartless bitch'. This overlooks Marguerite's second act attempts to counteract her collaboration, colluding with the resistance to help them assassinate her lover (the Nazi General) Otto. This may be because she is now considered beyond redemption, or because this significant shift is overshadowed: at this point in the show, Armand's emotional journey is foregrounded. Later revisions have attempted to make Marguerite's resistance more evident.

Tepid critical reaction and a lack of audience engagement resulted in the original production closing in London two months earlier than planned, on 13 September 2008. A statement from Boublil and Schönberg released at the time reads:

> Despite high praise from audience members, critically acclaimed performances and the release of the much-anticipated cast recording, we have made the difficult decision to close the show in London a few weeks earlier than originally planned. Both the knock-on effect of the current economic climate, as well as disappointing ticket sales throughout the summer months have contributed to our decision to close early.
>
> *(Cited in Shenton, 2008)*

The economic climate undoubtedly had an impact. As had been seen following the Wall Street Crash in 1929 and the terrorist attacks of 9/11, audiences were attracted to 'safer' options, as the after-effects of the 2008 global credit crunch began to be felt. Therefore, jukebox musicals (such as *Jersey Boys* [2005]) and feel-good shows (like a revival of *La Cage aux Folles* [1983]) enjoyed economic success, whilst other shows bowed out earlier than expected. Writing in *The Guardian*, Matt Wolf dramatically declared that the posting of closing notices by *Marguerite* signalled the 'death of the West End Musical' (2008). Here was a show that had all the signifiers of success (successful creative team, talented cast, mixture of story and spectacle), and yet it was unable to join all the dots to become the success it looked destined to be. As jukebox musicals and star casting strengthened their stranglehold on the West End, Wolf felt that *Marguerite*'s failure signalled a crisis for original musicals. Where, he questioned, was the 'great new musical capable of galvanising both critics and the public?' (2008).

'Perhaps it loses something in translation.'

Despite the show's inability to connect with West End audiences, the creative team were hopeful about planned productions in Japan, Spain and France. The French and Spanish productions eventually fell through, but Kent recalls the success of the 'much liked' Japanese production (2019). Here, audiences were more readily able to engage with *Marguerite*. Subsequent productions have included Marie Zamora's thoroughly reworked version in Ostrava, and a 2015 amateur Spanish production by Spirale Asociación Cultural. Perhaps because of the historical experiences of these countries under authoritarian/totalitarian governments, the productions appear to have been better received than their UK counterparts.

The Japanese production starred Sumire Haruno (famous for her lead roles in Japan's all-female musical theatre Takarazuka Revue[8]) in the title role and was one of the most successful iterations of *Marguerite*; so popular that it achieved a second run. Despite a bumpy start – a huge earthquake hit on the day of its opening – the musical once again gained momentum and was 'very successful' (Kent, 2019). The production itself was a version of the London production, the main change being the positioning of the orchestra off stage. This gave the show a more filmic feel, which Kent felt suited the musical and Legrand's sweeping score.

The Czech reworking was produced at the National Moravian-Silesian Theatre in Ostrava and featured in the theatre's rep for two years. It marked an exciting moment for the theatre, which was able to claim that they were staging a 'world première', rather than their usual transfers of British and American musical hits, and speculated as to what this might mean for the future of Czech musical theatre (Valášek, 2010). Marie Zamora came on board as co-writer and director to provide the missing female viewpoint (Soldanová, 2011, p. 28). She and Boublil worked to revise the script working with the Czech creative team (Gabriela Haukvicová-Petráková, Radek Valášek, Michael Prostějovský and Patrick Fridrichovský) to make changes during the workshop rehearsal process. Boublil stated that they felt they 'didn't go deep enough in the original story' in the earlier versions as 'the character of Marguerite was not psychologically sophisticated, so my wife and I reworked the story' (Quoted in *Oprášená Marguerite měla světovou premiéru v Ostravě*).

In this production, the Parisian wartime setting was very much a backdrop to the central romance, with changes to characters and the plot intended to enhance the show's emotional punch. Marguerite was no longer a faded star, but a leading artist of the Tabarin Cabaret Club, a move that allowed for the inclusion of some light relief, in the tired stereotype of a camp choreographer. Otto, in this revision, was clearly the bad guy; phoning Hitler, killing an injured prisoner of war and strong-arming Marguerite. Because of these changes, Zamora felt that 'little by little [Marguerite] finds out what life she has actually lived [seeing] what a monster Otto, her German lover, is' (Cited in *Oprášená Marguerite měla světovou premiéru v Ostravě*). To further highlight Marguerite's instability, she now has a heart problem (*quelle surprise!*) and her death becomes the result of an accidental shooting rather than of a mob hungry for revenge. In time for the 2012 London revival Marguerite's cause of death had shifted again – to an overdose – but British audiences continued to appear unmoved.

'She's a whore – I knew it! I can smell them every time.'

Another theme evident from the West End reception of *Marguerite* is a resistance to a female anti-hero within a popular musical context. Writing in *The Guardian*, Michael Billington pondered 'can you have a musical with a heroine you don't learn to love?' (2008). Tellingly, Philip Fisher in *The British Theatre Guide* proposed that Marguerite was 'only rescued from her own terrible nature by love for a much

FIGURE 12.2 The older, 'compromised' woman in love with the younger, upstanding man: Ruthie Henshall as the title character and Julian Ovenden as Armand in the 2008 London production of *Marguerite*.

Source: Photo courtesy of Donald Cooper/Photostage.

younger man' (2008). Fisher reveals another underlying bias towards a female protagonist – her age. Boublil and Schönberg always thought Marguerite should be a 40-year-old woman (the show starts with her 40th birthday party) and envisioned Armand as half her age (WhatsOnStage, 2008a).

Whilst popular culture provides numerous examples of age-gap relationships, where the man is older, those with an older woman continue to be judged more harshly.[9] In the case of *Marguerite*, critics wondered at how quickly she fell in love with Armand and at the fact that she 'simply succumbs to brutal Nazi blackmail' (Billington, 2008), continuing to sleep with the enemy. Whilst it might be interesting to consider how the critics themselves would respond to brutal Nazi blackmail, it is more productive to compare Marguerite's tragedy with that of her fictional peers among Boublil and Schönberg's 'fallen women'.

'She drowns me in her song' – Boublil and Schönberg's fallen women

Boublil and Schönberg return regularly to the archetypal 'fallen woman' character. Their works contain three of the most well-known *demi-mondes* in recent musical theatre: Fantine (*Les Misérables*), Kim (*Miss Saigon*) and Marguerite (*Marguerite*). Each expresses loss and longing in a solo – although it should be noted that Kim's song is for and about her son, marking her difference from the other 'tarts with hearts'.

Marguerite is part of the group of fallen women in musical theatre whose songs sit towards the end of the show, around the 11 o'clock number.[10] These women disrupt convention by singing about themselves, by taking space on stage and in the story, and by being introspective. Charity ponders 'Where Am I Going' (*Sweet Charity*, 1966), Rizzo questions whether 'There Are Worse Things I Could Do' (*Grease*, 1971) and Marguerite considers 'How Did I Get to Where I Am?'. Their songs are still haunted by the men in their lives, but the shift in focus allows for a moment of self-reflection and a frisson of disruption. It is worth noting that Marguerite is the only member of this 'Disruptive Diva' group to suffer the tragic heroine's death, but her inclusion with the proto-feminist Charity and Rizzo feels appropriate.

The 2012 reworking of *Marguerite* replaced 'How Did I Get to Where I Am?' with 'No One Can Take His Love from Me', one of several attempts to make Marguerite more likeable; there was a concern that her original characterisation made empathy 'impossible' (Kent, 2019). This new song foregrounded Marguerite's love for Armand, but also developed into a choral number, drowning out Marguerite's voice at this pivotal moment – something that Schönberg (who wasn't involved in the 2012 revision) felt was a mistake. Indeed, musical adaptor Jude Obermüller recalls Schönberg telling him that he 'hated it' (2019). Later, Marguerite's 11 o'clock number became 'The Face I See', a song whose central focus is Armand, making this more of an 'Inevitable Tragedy' song but in the 'Disrupting Diva' spot.

Fantine and Kim are perceived to be truly tragic: desperate women, forced to pursue a life of prostitution. They are the moral centres of their respective stories, making the ultimate sacrifice for the love of their children. Marguerite's standpoint is more complex; she is seemingly happy with her situation before she meets Armand, and appears to have made conscious choices that have got her to this point. Woollaston had the impression that the audience 'felt Marguerite deserved the punishment. She didn't have a child, why was she choosing to behave this way?' (2019). Our perception of the situation is influenced by the class and rank of her lover and, as Woollaston observes, 'somehow Marguerite being a "kept woman" is worse' (2019), perhaps because it seems that she has the freedom to leave if she chooses. To further compound the situation, her lover, Otto, is presented as a three-dimensional character and given sonic space to articulate his feelings and elicit empathy – he is not the traditional popular culture Nazi (although later revisions moved him towards this stereotype).

Two decades after *Les Misérables* and *Miss Saigon*, *Marguerite* revisited the hackneyed gender stereotypes, representing its two female characters Annette and Marguerite, respectively, 'as the well-worn and limiting stereotypes of the virgin and the whore' (Wolf, 2011, p. 128). Marguerite is, as Woollaston observes, 'a woman who uses her sexuality to survive'. Her tragic fate epitomises Susan McClary's 'desire-dread-purge mechanism' (2002, p. 152), where a 'temptress' is killed to reinstate social order. Marguerite is an unmarried woman, who has failed to fulfil her socially accepted reproductive role and is flaunting convention by cavorting with a much younger man. In the original production, Marguerite's death is a direct result of her non-conformity, as Parisians (who we have also seen benefitting from collaboration) mete out their punishment.

'Count the teardrops as they fall/they won't wash her crimes away'

Perhaps the most fascinating part of the original production is Woollaston's opening choreography, which embodied a sordid moment in the history of the Resistance.[11] Following France's liberation in 1944, many of those who had collaborated or committed treason were tried and punished, in an effort to cleanse and heal the country. The fate of women who had committed so-called 'horizontal collaboration' was rarely decided by courts; instead, they were subject to the ritualistic and often violent punishment of having their heads shaved, becoming *femmes tondues*. Other punishments usually accompanied the head shaving, such as parading (often-naked) women through town with placards describing their crime and throwing things at them. These gendered punishments were meted out for a range of collaborationist crimes from cohabitation with, to cooking for the enemy. As the Historian Claire Duchen outlines:

> These women are targeted because they allegedly transgressed codes of patriotism and also codes of feminine behaviour. It is the latter part of their transgression that is highlighted or foregrounded. Women are seen as a body, and if women's bodies are the property of men and of the nation, then they must be punished in the body, by the nation.

(2000, pp. 216–217)

The blurring of the distinctions between public and private during the War meant that '[w]omen were punished for failing to recognise that, during war, private life was far from private and that the very personal had become political' (Duchen, 2000, p. 228). As Luc Capdevela et al. observe 'by repressing "horizontal collaboration" (or sleeping with the enemy), men affirmed their authority and regained their control over women's bodies' (2005, p. 57). This is suggested in the opening stage directions of the original production (the version that is licensed by Josef Weinberger). As the opening number ('Come One, Come All') starts, Marguerite is sitting in a chair as '[t]he silhouettes of bodies appear and engulf the woman' (Bouberg, 2008, p. 1). The uneasy transition from castigation to collaboration is suggested by the next stage direction, at the end of the opening number: 'The shadows segue into Marguerite's party guests' (Bouberg, 2008, p. 2). This highlights the unfairness in the treatment of the *femmes tondues* and also the complexity of the period where there was a need to play, as Gildea puts it, 'a number of roles at once, being ready to change direction as the occasion demanded' (2002, p. 414). What is most interesting is that the critical response of the theatre critics to *Marguerite* often echoed the sentiments of the *tondeurs* (headshavers), highlighting how far we still have to go in the quest for equality and to embrace female characters that explode the limitations of narrow stock characterisations.

Fallen women and the demi-monde

Marguerite's *demi-monde* status is suggested in the lyrics of the opening number and alluded to by Marguerite's former agent George: 'I knew her well. And I wasn't the only one. I should have taken a commission' (Bouberg, 2008, p. 11). However, it is Pierrot (a musician in Armand's band) who first labels Marguerite a prostitute, bragging to Lucien: 'She's a whore – I knew it! I can smell them every time. It's this talent I have' (Bouberg, 2008, p. 12). As Capdevila et al. note, *fille publique* is the French term for prostitute, 'with the adjective *publique* underlining the crossover from the private to public sphere' (2005, p. 53). Marguerite understands the realities of her situation and the lack of agency she has. In 'China Doll' she sings: 'Someone turns the key/And the china doll must dance' (Bouberg, 2008, p. 15) and later she explains to a naïve Armand that 'love has never been an option' (Bouberg, 2008, p. 20).

'Someone turns the key and the china doll must dance'

'China Doll', Marguerite's signature song, is a diegetic number; performed, prompted by Armand, in the opening scene. This 'sad little song' (Bouberg, 2008, p. 14) highlights the parallels between prostitutes and performers, who have 'no choice' but are just 'there to amuse' (Bouberg, 2008, p. 15), suggesting the Nazi occupation as the reason behind the change to Marguerite's profession.

'China Doll' is reprised twice; first by Armand, demonstrating his understanding of Marguerite, before allowing our lovers their first duet. Later, it marks the end of Marguerite's journey, as Armand carries her broken body through the streets of Paris. Like much of the writing, the china doll metaphor for Marguerite is not particularly subtle. Whilst there is no suggestion that Marguerite wrote the song, it does have an autobiographical feel. China dolls are, by their very nature, fragile and brittle. They adorn rather than engage. Whilst these are characteristics that can be seen in Marguerite, it is evident that she views herself as more than a mere decorative object that men use as a status symbol. More poignant is the image of the never-ending carousel that Marguerite is unable to escape, suggesting more depth than her fellow collaborators. This is the part that Armand connects with, pondering 'who will set her free' (Bouberg, 2008, p. 18) in his reprise of the song. Unfortunately for Marguerite, Armand's chipping away at her protective casing results in her ultimate destruction.

By making the private public and blurring the distinction between the two Marguerite has, in the eyes of society, lost the right to dignity. This is articulated by the other collaborators in their final number, the reprise of 'Come One, Come All'. Here they taunt Marguerite from their own morally and politically vacuous standpoint, singing:

> Turned her back upon her own
> Without regret
> This tart who had a heart of stone
> We won't forget
>
> There were
> Brave honest Frenchmen
> Resisting and dying
> Where was her pride?
> Selling herself to whoever was buying
> Now, Marguerite where can you hide?
> (Bouberg, 2008, p. 36)

The audience are deliberately placed in an uncomfortable position: those singing were benefiting from Marguerite's 'false embraces' (Bouberg, 2008, p. 35) earlier in the show, but now they are denouncing them. The singers have appeased the enemy in different ways, but Marguerite's 'horizontal collaboration' is deemed to deserve a harsher punishment. Her brutal fate contrasts with the sentimental death of *Les Dame aux Camélias*, allowing the creative team to highlight the changeable morals of Parisian society: its members shift from celebration to censure depending on their personal gains. Marguerite makes the ultimate sacrifice for her misdeeds, but we witness the usual corrupt factions of society continuing to flourish. Perhaps this inequality didn't sit right with British audiences, whose image of the War was one of romanticised (if historically inaccurate) 'Blitz spirit'. Maybe Boublil, Legrand, Schönberg and Kent were making a wider point: that punishment is often decided by class, and that some bad people get away with their misdeeds.

In contrast, Annette – originally Armand's sister, but promoted to secondary love interest for Armand in the Ostrava revision – is punished for her good deeds both at the hands of the Nazis and by Armand, who prefers the less heroic Marguerite. By making Annette Lucien's sister and having her be secretly in love with Armand, (rather than having Armand's sister fall for Lucien) the original version's secondary romantic pairing was lost. As previously noted, the relationship between Annette and Lucien was seen by some critics as a more appropriate central love affair than that of tarnished Marguerite and youthful Armand. It also created a second love triangle, offsetting the triangulation of Armand, Marguerite and Otto. Zamora not only directed the Ostrava production but worked with Boublil to rewrite the libretto, so it is perhaps her influence that results in a feistier and more influential Annette.

'Take Good Care of Yourself', originally a love duet for Annette and Lucien, was rewritten by John Dempsey for the Ostrava production to become 'The Questions of Your Heart', exploring the love triangle between Armand, Annette and Marguerite. In the 2012 revision Obermüller, Unsworth and Boublil transformed the second half of this song into a larger solo for Annette in order to 'give her character more time to explore her love for Armand' (Obermüller, 2019). In making her feelings for Armand so central to her characterisation, the revisions removed Annette's political engagement and created a character similar to Marguerite; sharing motivations, but inhabiting the binary opposites of virgin and whore respectively. All versions of the show encourage comparisons between Annette and Marguerite, which often find the eponymous anti-heroine wanting. As Unsworth observed in a recent email correspondence:

> [T]here's a resistance to anti-heroes in musicals anyway, let alone female ones, and although societal views towards women's stories are finally changing (particularly in younger generations), we're only just getting towards a stage where these characters can be accepted by the general public as mainstream viewing.
>
> *(2019)*

'Paris . . . it corrupts us all'

Discussing French cinema,[12] Nicoleta Bazgan highlights that 'through a dual metonymical relationship, the city and the female star can stand in one for one another' (2010, p. 96): the women become icons of the city, embodying Parisian femininity. This is certainly the case with Marguerite. She is presented as flawed, her glory dimmed and, in what appears to be a consensual relationship with a German officer – evoking 'the image of France (so often represented as a woman in the figure of Marianne) as a willing partner of Nazi Germany' (Duchen, 2000, p. 218). Paris during World War II was, as Woollaston observes, a 'faded demolished beauty, almost like Marguerite herself' (2019). Susan Hayward has discussed how – in contemporary French cinema (1950s–1990s) – 'Parisian women are mainly typified in roles of excessive and "deviant" femininity' (Hayward quoted in Bazgan, 2010, p. 97); this is also evident in the musical. Marguerite's female deviance is central to the show's story. Subsequent revivals and revisions have attempted to soften her edges to evoke empathy but her central flaw, that she is a 'fallen woman' with minimal self-sacrifice,[13] is inescapable.

FIGURE 12.3   For German officer Otto (Alexander Hanson), his domination of faded star Marguerite (Ruthie Henshall) is synonymous with his control over both Paris and France.

Source: Photo by Nigel Norrington, courtesy of ArenaPal.

If the audience doesn't draw the obvious parallels between Marguerite and Paris then several songs make these explicit. In his solo number 'I Hate the Very Thought of Women',[14] Otto outlines how his mistress and Paris are synonymous to him. Here he sings about his unrequited love for Marguerite but as the number progresses, she comes to represent not only Paris but France as well, with Otto declaring:

> With half the world in our possession
>> She still commands me with a glance
>> Until I'm free of this obsession
>> I still have not defeated France
>>> (Bouberg, 2008, p. 15)

Here, images of occupation, dominance and obsession reinforce gendered and national stereotypes, as Otto portrays France as beautifully feminine and subservient in comparison to Germany's aggressive masculinity: 'Great Germany supreme in power/And France in Beauty, side by side' (Bouberg, 2008, p. 15).

By providing Otto with a solo number (he also emotes beautifully in 'Intoxication', alongside Armand and Marguerite, and 'Day by Day (Part Two)') he is marked as an important character in the musical's hierarchy, able to position himself as the show's jilted lover and given a platform to elicit the audience's empathy. 'I Hate the Thought of Women' was cut from the 2012 revival as the creative team unanimously agreed that 'the song felt perhaps a little glib for a character as dangerous as Otto' (Obermüller, 2019). This and other subsequent revisions reduced Otto to a stereotypical melodramatic villain, robbing the musical of some of its original complexity, whilst attempting to give the audience what the creative teams felt they wanted.

'What you read is not my voice'

The original production of *Marguerite* struggled to connect with critics and audiences, so subsequent revisions tweaked the script and story to try to liberate the successful musical within. Discussing the 2012 revival Unsworth felt the pared down-interpretation allowed for 'a more human story, driven by Marguerite, rather than the political situation at large' (2019). However, the changes made to mollify the audience raise questions about why musical theatre audiences can't be challenged. By removing the references to *femmes tondues* and creating a more binary representation of occupation and collaboration, this revival became historically vague; an apolitical love story that once again failed to ignite.

In every version of *Marguerite* the central female character's focus is Armand. Marguerite may be the show's protagonist, but she is undermined by the story's gender politics and weakened, as she spends much of her stage time chasing her 'saviour' (the irony being that Armand is actually her downfall). As Obermüller observes: 'This action ultimately means Marguerite is written to get in the way of Armand's work as a resistor, in pursuit of her own desire' (2019), which makes it even harder for the audience to empathise with her. However, their ability to empathise with Armand highlights the gendered double standards at play. Rather than reading Marguerite as a wanton distraction to Armand's more important work resisting the Nazis, a closer reading highlights that he only fully engages with this course of action once Marguerite rejects him. Prior to his encounter with Marguerite, Armand tells us he has just been 'drifting. Holding my breath, waiting for my life to happen' (Bouberg, 2008, p. 19).

Jude Obermüller has often wondered how shifting the narrative focus from Marguerite to Annette might allow the audience to engage more readily with the show. As he notes:

> The setting of World War II Paris has the potential for endless dramatic possibilities of a fem-led piece . . . Annette's struggle and nobility against the backdrop feel like really fascinating conflicts to me. And, for my money, would still have offered Michel the same opportunity to write the gorgeous, gushy score he did.
>
> *(2019)*

Whilst Obermüller's proposal presents some interesting narrative opportunities, the movement of Marguerite away from the heart of the show avoids – rather than addresses – the issues with her character. The change would create another young virtuous female lead and lose a complicated middle-aged female protagonist. It would have been interesting to see the inclusion of a 'collaborative duet' between Marguerite and Annette in the later versions of the musical. This might have given the two women something tangible to discuss beyond Armand (at the moment this musical is nowhere near passing the Bechdel-Wallace test[15]) and provided the different relational possibilities that Wolf writes about (Wolf, 2011, pp. 26–27). Perhaps by giving Marguerite a moment where she doesn't have to pine over Armand, the audience might have found space to connect with her and engage more fully with the piece.

Marguerite has the feel of a piece that missed its moment, musically and thematically. It failed to find its niche amongst the jukebox musicals of the noughties, and the tinge of the wrong kind of nostalgia haunted the show. As Obermüller observes 'it was a near perfect European-style score written too late in the musical theatre canon; accompanying a story less resonant to a post-millennium audience' (2019). The story of Dumas *fils'* tragic lovers may have survived countless revisions and re-imaginings, but perhaps it needs to evolve in order to engage with a contemporary audience and explore the story more effectively from Marguerite's perspective.

The original staging, with its political framing and reference to the *femmes tondues*, feels all the more resonant in the current political climate, so maybe there is a way to revive and revitalise the show once more. Musical theatre has come a long way since *Marguerite's* 2008 première; perhaps now there is space in the canon for a flawed female protagonist at the heart of a complicated situation. As musical theatre writer Georgia Stitt recently observed: 'When you write strong, complicated female characters, you get strong, complicated male characters' (2019) and there is definitely space in this epic love story for further development to achieve this, rather than pandering to increasingly dated ideas about perfect protagonists in popular culture.

Notes

1 The following analysis would not have been possible without the generosity of members of *Marguerite*'s various creative teams, who have very kindly shared materials and recollections to help shape a picture of the musical's journey, and explore why it never quite achieved the success that the calibre of its creators and the popularity of its source material suggested it should.

2 A portmanteau of 'pop' and 'operetta'. It references the sung-through nature of these works and their combination of both operatic and pop sensibilities and styles. Ben Macpherson identifies the 'Poperetta Voice' that such musicals require which 'evokes operatic sensibilities of full-throated, serious vocal production combined with "more of a 'pop' or commercial sound"' (2019, p. 72).

3 Webber's tendency to 'recycle' has been much discussed (Snelson 2001, 2004; Coulson 2014; musical comedy duo Kit and the Widow also explore Webber's contrafacta in their song 'Somebody Else'). There is also a strong echo of Puccini's 'Dawn Chorus' from *Madame Butterfly* in 'Bring Him Home' from *Les Misérables* which is ironic considering that the Boublil and Schönberg musical based on that opera is actually *Miss Saigon*.

4 These deviations from the Dumas templates were not the reason for the stage musical's poor critical reception. This had more to do with the dated script and storyline which, as Alexis Soloski noted in her one-star *Guardian* review, have 'aged about as well as a carton of milk left on a radiator forever' (2018).

5 Usually a musical theatre song in a book musical tends to drive the plot of the show forward by providing a small shift in the onstage drama; the number helps movie the narrative to progress from 'A to B'.

6 Marguerite is the mistress of a Nazi officer, General Otto von Stadt.

7 Interestingly, many of these terms are gendered, painting the French as effeminate. Saskia Huc-Hepher suggests that 'contemporary microaggressions are the by-product of residual rancour left over from the Second World War', stating that 'anti-French xenophobia has been embedded and generationally reproduced in British society for so long that its very historicity fuels an "epistemology of ignorance"' (Hepher, 2019).

8 This all-female troupe stages lavish productions of Western-style musicals and Japanese works where women play all of the roles. In Japan, where its audience is predominantly female, it has cult status.

9 Compare for example the press reaction to French President Macron and his wife, Brigitte Trogneux, who is 24 years his senior, to the treatment of the American President Trump and the First Lady Melania Trump – there is a similar age gap, but with the man as the older party.

10 A number which usually involves a final decision or moment of realisation and which propels the musical's central character (and the audience) to the show's finale.

11 This opening was changed for the 2010 and 2012 revisions. For the 2012 revival Boublil outlined to Obermüller in email correspondence that he wanted the show to start 'beautifully, not aggressively, and personally, not politically'.

12 In her exploration of the ways that female protagonists embody iconic Parisian femininity and the city itself Bazgan looks at the following films: *Une Parisienne/La Parisienne* (Boisrond, 1957), *Ascenseur pour l'échafaud/Elevator to the Gallows* (Malle, 1957), *Le Fabuleux destin d'Amélie Poulain/Amélie* (Jeunet, 2001) and *Chaos* (Serreau, 2001) (Bazgan, 2010).

13 Forsaking love to save Annette, however, doesn't rank her sacrifice as high as that of Fantine or Kim, especially when we have been repeatedly told that Marguerite is incapable of love.
14 Characters who sing in musical theatre are elevated because they have an opportunity to let the audience into their world and to gain their understanding. Otto is clearly marked as the musical's 'bad guy' but here has an opportunity to elicit the audience's sympathy. This resonates with the creative team's decision to portray Otto as a more nuanced character than the traditional stereotypical Nazi characters British audiences are used to.
15 This test measures whether a show has more than one female character, whether they talk and (importantly) whether they discuss something other than a man. It was conceived by Alison Bechdel and Liz Wallace, and first appeared in Bechdel's 1985 *Dykes to Watch Out For* comic strip.

References

Bassett, K. (2008) 'Marguerite Theatre Royal Haymarket,' *The Independent*, www.independent.co.uk/arts-entertainment/theatre-dance/reviews/marguerite-theatre-royal-haymarket-londonthe-long-road-soho-theatre-londonthe-pitman-painters-833849.html, accessed 29 September 2019.
Bazgan, N. (2010) 'Female Bodies in Paris: Iconic Urban Femininity and Parisian Journeys,' *Studies in French Cinema*, 10(2), pp. 95–109.
Billington, M. (2008) 'Marguerite,' *The Guardian*, 21 May, www.theguardian.com/stage/2008/may/21/theatre2, accessed 29 September 2019.
———. (2007) *State of the Nation: British Theatre Since 1945*. London: Bloomsbury.
Bouberg. (2008) *Marguerite: Libretto*. London: Josef Weinberger Ltd.
Capdevila, L., Rouquet, F., Schwartz, P., Virgili, F. and Voldman, D. (2005) '"Quite Simply Colonel . . .": Gender and the Second World War,' in H. Diamond and S. Kitson (eds.) *Vichy, Resistance, Liberation: New Perspectives on Wartime. France*. Oxford: Berg, pp. 51–59.
Coulson, W. R. (2014) 'They're Playing Our Song! The Promise and the Perils of Musical Copyright Litigation 13 J. Marshall Rev/ Intell. Prop. L. 555,' *Review of Intellectual Property Law*, https://repository.jmls.edu/ripl/vol13/iss3/4/, accessed 20 September 2019.
Duchen, C. (2000) 'Opening Pandora's Box: The Case of the *Femmes Tondues*,' in M. Cornick and C. Crossley (eds.) *Problems in French History*. London: Palgrave-Macmillan, pp. 213–233.
Eubanks Winkler, A. (2014) 'Politics and the Reception of Andrew Lloyd Webber's *The Phantom of the Opera*,' *Cambridge Opera Journal*, 26(3), pp. 271–287.
Everett, W. A. (2007) 'From French to European to Global: The Saga of Schönberg and Boublil's *Les Miserables*,' in D. Mayer-Dinkgrafe (ed.) *European Culture in a Changing World: Between Nationalism and Globalism*. Newcastle: Cambridge Scholars Publishing, pp. 229–236.
Fisher, P. (2008) 'Marguerite,' www.britishtheatreguide.info/reviews/marguerite-rev, accessed 29 September 2019.
Gildea, R. (2002) *Marianne in Chains: In Search of the German Occupation of France 1940–45*. London: Palgrave-Macmillan.
Gordon, D. (2019) Interview with the author, 17 May.
Gottlieb, V. (1988) 'Thatcher's Theatre – Or after *Equus*,' *NTQ – New Theatre Quarterly*, 4(2), pp. 99–104.
Huc-Hepher, S. (2019) '"Sometimes There's Racism Towards the French Here": Xenophobic Microaggressions in Pre-2016 London as Articulations of Symbolic Violence,' *National Identities*, www.tandfonline.com/doi/abs/10.1080/14608944.2019.1649250?journalCode=cnid20, DOI: 10.1080/14608944.2019.1649250, accessed 7 May 2020.

Kent, J. (2019) Phone interview with the author, 2 June.

MacPherson, B. (2019) 'Sing: Musical Theatre Voices from *Superstar* to *Hamilton*,' in J. Stern-feld and E. L. Wollman (eds.) *The Routledge Companion to Contemporary Musical Theatre*. London: Routledge, pp. 69–77.

McClary, S. (2002) *Feminine Endings: Music, Gender, and Sexuality: Music, Gender and Sexuality*. Mineapolis: University of Minnesota Press.

Obermüller, J. (2019) Email correspondence with the author, August.

'Review Roundup: Critics Unmoved by Marguerite?' (2008), https://www.whatsonstage.com/west-end-theatre/news/review-round-up-critics-unmoved-by-marguerite_19498.html, accessed 29 September 2019.

Shenton, M. (2008) 'New Musical *Marguerite* Closes in London Sept. 13', www.playbill.com/article/new-musical-marguerite-closes-in-london-sept-13-com-153216, accessed 29 September 2019.

Snelson, J. (2004) *Andrew Lloyd Webber*. New Haven: Yale University Press.

———. (2001) 'Webber [Lloyd-Webber; Lord Lloyd-Webber of Sydmonton], Andrew Lloyd', *Grove Music Online*, www.oxfordmusiconline.com/grovemusic/view/10.1093/gmo/9781561592630.001.0001/omo-9781561592630-e-6002278217, accessed 16 January 2020.

Soldanová, S. (2011) *Muzikál Marguerite: The Musical Marguerite*, Thesis, Janáček Academy of Performing Arts in Brno, Faculty of Theater, https://is.jamu.cz/th/cifbh/, accessed 7 May 2020.

Soloski, A. (2018) '*Pretty Woman* Review – Broadway Romcom Transfer Is a Tasteless Disaster', *The Guardian*, 16 August, www.theguardian.com/stage/2018/aug/16/pretty-woman-broadway-musical-review, accessed 29 September 2019.

Stitt, G. (2019) '25 September,' https://twitter.com/georgiastitt/status/1176905623478394880, accessed 29 September 2019.

Unsworth, G. (2019) Email correspondence with the author, April.

Valášek, A. (2010) 'Alain Boublil Visited the Workshops of the Musical *Marguerite* in Ostrava,' www.musical-opereta.cz/alain-boublil-v-ostrave-navstivil-worshopy-muzikalu-Marguerite/, accessed 7 May 2020.

WhatsOnStage. (2008a) 'The Making of *Marguerite*,' www.whatsonstage.com/west-end-theatre/news/the-making-of-Marguerite_19543.html, accessed 29 September 2019.

———. (2008b) 'Review Round-Up: Critics Unmoved by *Marguerite*?' www.whatsonstage.com/west-end-theatre/news/review-round-up-critics-unmoved-by-Marguerite_19498.html, accessed 29 September 2019.

Wolf, M. (2008) '*Marguerite* and the Death of the West End Musical,' *The Guardian*, 29 August, www.theguardian.com/stage/theatreblog/2008/aug/29/margueriteandthedeathofth, accessed 29 September 2019.

Wolf, S. (2011) *Changed for Good: A Feminist History of the Broadway Musical*. Oxford: Oxford University Press.

Woollaston, N. (2019) Email correspondence with the author, August.

PART V
Naughty Paris

13

GAY SHAME IN 'GAY PAREE'

Re-contextualising gender progressiveness in two film versions of *Victor/Victoria*

Florian J. Seubert

Gay shame as cinematic discourse in 20th-century representations of Paris

The various film and theatrical versions of *Victor/Victoria* have often been used as a playground for queer and feminist readings (Arnold-de Simine, 2012; Thompson, 2002; Kael, 2009). These works and interpretations have in common that they contrast conservative plot components such as the main heterosexual romance with more progressive elements of same-sex love and double cross-dressing, foreshadowing the gender fluidity of contemporary LGBT+ performances. A staple of 20th-century pop culture, the films are often considered in the light of gender *laissez-faire*, sexual ambiguity and the liberated *savoir vivre* of 20th-century Parisian nightlife.

Throughout cinema history, there have been various remakes of the original 1933 German film each of which shows subtle nuances in its reworking of gender politics: shortly after the first *Viktor und Viktoria*, a British version called *First a Girl* (1935) hit the market. The British film relied on a similar concept of double cross-dressing to the German original, which also was remade in 1957 as part of the more conservative *Papas Kino*[1] of post-war West Germany. In the United States, the subject matter was picked up by Blake Edwards for his 1982 film *Victor/Victoria*. The slash in the title perhaps already indicates a cultural climate that was more likely to deconstruct the clear binary separation between the genders. A 1995 screen-to-stage adaptation, again starring Julie Andrews, marks another intriguing manifestation of the subject matter.

For the purpose of this essay, however, I want to focus on two cinematic versions and their gendered filmic language. (I will use *Victor/Victoria* or just one of the names with the year of release to indicate the German or US film.) *Victoria* 1933 and 1982 bookend 20th-century cultural history and make for a rewarding contrast. The two 'original' versions for the German and American market allow for useful close readings that link similarly conflicted cultural contexts across the Western hemisphere and develop a matrix that can easily be related to the other film versions.

The concept of gay shame, which has recently emerged as a potent discourse in cultural theory, helps to shed new light on the intricate relationship between the progressive and more conservative elements in *Victor/Victoria* and bring disparate observations together as two sides of the same coin. Some academic articles on the films describe the seemingly contradictory tension between anti-feminist repression and queer (post-)modernity. The New Woman movement in the 1920s and 30s, the anti-feminist backlash in the 1980s and a straight Hollywood regime that exploits gay play as commercial fix seem to be at odds with each other (Arnold-de Simine, 2012; Thompson, 2002; Kael, 2009).

This chapter wants to continue that discussion by pinpointing individual examples of gay shame and awareness in the visual language and style of the two *Victoria* films. Aesthetic and directorial choices beyond the content level will ground a conceptual discussion around gay shame in a wider understanding of filmmaking practice. A close comparative analysis of framing techniques shows how queer shame is invoked and, by doing so, also partly processed in the two films. This will refocus the discussion on subtle stylistic moments that contribute to the discourse around gender and morals in the films by looking at how they also tell the story in non-verbal ways. 'Queer' is used in this context to identify a whole spectrum of non-normative sexual identities that shine through the performance acts of travesty and backstage goings-on in the films by Reinhold Schünzel and Blake Edwards.

Comparing their two film versions of *Victor/Victoria* investigates the implications of a conservative visual language from a non-binary perspective and shows how films about cross-dressing, travesty and queer role-play can be perceived as homo-conservative when scrutinised carefully, but at the same time also as gender-progressive,[2] though arguably more in their subject matter than in their compositional language. The progressive element can also emerge as an aesthetic choice that reveals gender as a performance act. This process exposes moral judgements around how to behave 'properly' with regards to same-sex attraction and will be explained more closely with reference to Judith Butler and Susan Sontag's theory of 'camp'.

In a succession of representative examples, the essay problematises how the editing, cinematography and composition of the frames can undermine the partly progressive content by sending mixed moral signals. Detecting the performative contrast between what is said and what is shown exposes a significant tension between the different filmic sign systems when depicting queer affection. It is only because the films feature excessive gay performance that they allow underlying gay shame to come to the surface and be consciously processed. Carefully deconstructing their representation of queerness shows how the two canonical films about 'Gay Paree' can exhibit rather traditional sexual politics as well as progressive intentions as part of the same psychosocial process.

The following piece of film criticism examines how gay shame is created by the filmic language of the *Victoria* films in their presentation of non-mainstream gender and how this connects to subliminal cultural strategies, which contribute to creating a moral superstructure. I will briefly clarify the concepts of homo-negative portrayals in the context of what has been labelled 'gay shame', but this essay is not intended as a 'politically correct' polemic against homophobic art from the last century. It shows a way of delving into and understanding the problems gay shame has produced on an unconscious plane, even in pop cultural products that promote gender openness and sexual liberation against the backdrop of the Parisian *demi-monde*.

Discursive intimacy in the city of liberal love and heterosexual romance

Gay shame as a psychosocial discourse is linked to the historical prosecution and ostracising of homosexual and queer identities as a transnational phenomenon with special prominence in the 19th to mid-20th century. The concept translates into a bundle of aesthetic choices that communicate the feeling of (sexual) deviance, wrong-doing and guilt within a dominant heterosexual social discourse. The recipient or victim of gay shame consequently feels his/her behaviour is perceived as 'strange' or 'alien' as a result of showing 'attraction to someone of the same gender' (Todd, 2016, p. 49). This perception can be extended to gender fluidity in general and cross-dressing in the case of *Victor/Victoria*.

The aesthetic discourse passes judgement in non-verbal form, which may subliminally be picked up by the viewers. In this way, they absorb behavioural patterns around gay shame or simply internalise judgement through the media portrayal (Todd, 2016, pp. 49–56). This sensation of gay shame which accumulates around the social responses to a particular pattern of unconventionally-gendered behaviour can be reinforced through a variety of filmic means, such as editing techniques. The audience's responses – which might involve moral judgements – can be influenced by choices in the cutting room, because these go hand in hand with what is socio-culturally believed to be shameful, not decent or just illegal in a certain historical era.

Another visual strategy to communicate sexual indecency non-verbally involves the arrangement of bodies within the frame, for instance when depicting physical intimacy. Depending on the gender constellation, the movie's characters may be blocked differently – two men may not touch during a dance routine in order to imply what is socially acceptable/unacceptable.

Gay shame as a cinematic discourse in the two versions of *Victor/Victoria* spanning 50 years of 20th-century representations of Paris shows different nuances of same-sex awkwardness. In this context it is important to point out that whenever 'aberrant' gender constellations occur in the films, the audience is well aware that it sees a comic, even carnivalesque scenario that uses dramatic irony to excuse the deviant sexual behaviour of travesty, cross-dressing and same-sex interest. Straight audiences are safe from shame and never in real danger of witnessing gay romance. Beneath multiple layers of costumes and performance, the heteronormative order is still unashamedly intact. Gay shame as a cinematic discourse translates into the visualisation of the social policing of same-sex love or gender-fluid sexuality as 'not right' and therefore produces feelings of emotional arrest in a character. By extension, this can also be absorbed by the viewer through their mirrored emotional involvement (Todd, 2016, p. 50).

Paris as the cultural *topos* of liberal love accumulated throughout the 19th century various socio-historical associations: at the heart of the French Revolution, the city formed the epicentre of demands for liberty and equality, though of course more in terms of politics and class structure than with regards to gender. Over time, however, the foundations of cultural liberalism merged with the transgressive and free spirit of the artistic quarters from Montmartre to the Quartier Latin and with Paris' famous cabaret culture. In the 19th century, when new arrivals to the cities discovered the leisure industry, cabaret was a much seedier, more pornographic version of today's variety entertainment. The 1982 version references this hedonistic cultural history in Toddy's musical number 'Gay Paree'. *La Bohème* (1896) and other works promoted ideas of outsider romance from the *fin de siècle* onwards and located a free and lascivious lifestyle among the artists of Paris.

The existence of non-conformist love affairs in Paris is often acknowledged as part of a libertine Parisian *demi-monde*. Consequently, the gender avant-garde is associated with the social periphery. Depictions of Paris contain both romantic happy endings and the dark romanticism of the shamed outsider. In this context, cross-dressing allows the testing of normative moral virtues as much as it plays with identity free from social constraints.

In a socio-critical reading, it is possible to see the 'city as a space conducive to self-reinvention' as well as space for 'self-dispersal rather than self-discovery' (Sheringham, 2013, p. 228). The fluid play with identity creates a sense of comfort, but also allows for stripping oneself of feelings of identity discomfort, ultimately evading a process of self-acceptance. There is noticeable identity discomfort in both versions of *Victor/Victoria*. In this context, using witty identity play so as not to confront but instead to accept (gay) shame can be seen as a symptom of internalised queer-phobia as well as of liberal relief. Matthew Todd describes escaping into entertainment and camp performance as one of the ambivalent coping mechanisms for gay shame, intended to generate a different form of acceptance or validation from others as a stage performer (Todd, 2016, p. 53).

Crossing cultural contexts: Berlin in the 1930s; Hollywood in the 1980s

The tracing of the intimate link between seemingly opposed discourses of a liberal and tolerant Paris on the one hand, and an exclusive and censorious one on the other, highlights how the emergence of transnational narratives around urban modernity has been accompanied by a discourse of queer shame. Weimar Berlin of the 1920s and early 1930s, against which the first *Viktoria* film is set, was (in)famous for its inclusive nightlife and pockets of sexual openness. Its film industry was hailed for its queer output (Arnold-de Siminie, 2012, pp. 379–384) and for promoting new female role models such as the woman cross-dresser, in the case of Viktoria as a version of the flapper. But the celebration of queer content did not necessarily lead to a celebratory representation of queer identities on screen. In the mixed social climate of the 'sexual crisis of Weimar Berlin' (Arnold-de Siminie, 2012, p. 383), diverse gender role models coexisted with laws that criminalised homosexual activity: the notorious Paragraph 175 criminalised homosexual activity between two men and remained a topic of political debate from its inception in the late 19th century until its abolition in 1994. The contradictions in public opinion about homosexuality are also reflected in the cultural output of the times. The Berlin film industry produced successful 'queer' films that upheld Prussian discipline, heteronormative order and reinforced queer shame at the same time as they promulgated alternative gender roles.

The early sound film *Mädchen in Uniform/Girls in Uniform* (1931) is a good example of this ambivalent depiction of queer love. Critics often describe the budding affection between a governess and her student as a lesbian '*Urtext* of the schoolgirl genre' (Mennel, 2012, p. 6). However, the affair is severely criticised by the headmistress and framed as shameful by a system that punishes queer or alternative sexual behaviour. The 1933 version *Viktor/Viktoria* was produced in this very cultural climate and exhibits the same social values. The contrast between the content of the film and the visual representation of the theme echoes the psychosocial confusions promoting queer shame in 1930s Berlin.

Just as the 1930s *Viktor/Viktoria* reflects the harsh laws and conflicted queer politics of the Weimar Republic, Blake Edwards' *Victor/Victoria* (1982) is set against a similarly repressive media discourse around gay behaviour. Arguably, film production had evolved slightly to allow for more radical depictions of deviant gender identities after the 1960s and New Hollywood. But, the youthful liberalism of Kennedy, the hippie movement and Nixon's Watergate had also led to a new conservatism that celebrated straight masculinity. The Hollywood studios remained strictly commercial and therefore conservatively minded, especially given their fear of TV competition. In 1981, Republican Ronald Reagan was elected president, re-igniting dreams of stable traditional families, picket fences and suburbia. Therefore, it can be argued that the fragmented liberties of Weimar Berlin are also echoed in the complex media discourse around non-normative sexualities in the unfettered capitalistic politics of 1980s America. The suspicion of 'deviant' sexuality seemingly was confirmed – and found its ultimate justification – when the first five AIDS victims were discovered in June 1981 in the United States and 'the aberrant' practice of same-sex love attained a shocking newsworthiness. Once more, associations of same-sex attraction with punishment, shame and stigma were reinforced in the public's mind. The media discourse around queer identities became harsher, and the reception of queer art works became tainted by the emerging stigma of AIDS (Todd, 2016).

Though conceived in a different spirit, Blake Edwards' movie eerily fore-shadows this struggle with gay shame and points to the conflicted moral values of its time, while also revealing the underlying sociocultural narratives of Hollywood heteronormativity it was produced in. Its ideological ambivalence – the film veers between homo-positive conversations between Toddy and Victoria, which are short but outspoken, and a general frame of straight romance – reflects the imbalance between budding gender-progressiveness and homophobia in US society.

Either cultural context, therefore – that of 1930s Germany and of 1980s United States – results in a conflicted portrayal of queerness, allowing for a detailed analysis of gay shame and queer acceptance as a cross-cultural tendency. In both cases, the diverse sociocultural climate is mapped out in the modern metropolis of Paris. In these filmic representations of the city's cabaret scene concepts of gay shame and Gay Paree overlap within the same space and can be seen to influence each other across the 20th century and Western Hemisphere.

'There should be a law': the visible language of being embarrassed

Cross-dressing comedy as a genre heightens the idea of presenting the markers of one's identity as fluid or changeable as befitting the needs of a specific context:

> Cross-dressing is only one aspect of a broader comedy concept based on disguise, role reversal, and mistaken identity in which all social variables used to define individuals – gender and sexual orientation, race, ethnicity, nationality, class, age – can be switched.
>
> *(Arnold-de Siminie, 2012, p. 379)*

However, just as the play with different roles of self can facilitate processes of self-discovery which are beneficial for the role-player, the masking of one's identity can also hide the emotional reality of not feeling accepted as a result of hegemonic social attitudes. Read from this perspective, a cross-dressing comedy such as *Victor/Victoria* therefore emerges as a Foucauldian *panopticon* of observation and adjustment as well as a playful rebellion. It triggers emotional processes of resistance, through exaggeration, but also of shame and embarrassment. This seemingly contradictory blend is mirrored in the aesthetic of each film.

Toddy of the 1982 film corresponds to Viktor Hempel in the 1933 version, while the character of Susanne Lohr is turned into Victoria Grant. Both films tell the story of how Victor has to come up with a travesty act in order to earn a living. When he is unable to perform due to illness and coincidentally meets an equally hapless Susanne, he ingeniously reconceives his act by double cross-dressing Susanne as his understudy so that she can fulfil his performance duties. Victor/Victoria becomes a huge star across Europe as hugely successful female impersonator. (In the earlier version, Susanne becomes a sensation in London.)

In both films, a rich man who embodies the macho stereotype, named Robert (1933) and King Marchand (1982), respectively, is immediately attracted to the lady he sees on stage and is shocked when he discovers that he has actually fallen for a 'man'. Being secure in his cis-gendered straight identity, he puts hers to the test and wins her over. Whereas the initial discovery sends King through moments of identity crisis and soul-searching, in the German version, the crisis gets interspersed with late 19th-century duel culture and the farcical humour of a comedy of mistaken identities. In order to explore the way in which the two films introduce themes of same-sex attraction, I will look at how they delineate the main character in close detail as those early sequences set the intricate tone of the films regarding themes of gender performance against the urban backdrop.

The opening scenes of the 1933 *Viktor und Viktoria* illustrate the twin processes of social regulation and performative exaggeration. Before we see Viktor Hempel desperately trying to convince an audition panel by giving a highly theatrical performance, he is visually and verbally framed with a conservative preamble. An elderly lady and man waiting for their audition in the hallway complain: 'Was aber heute alles zum Theater geht' ('The kind of people – in German this translates into 'what' – who nowadays appear on the stage'). The response is: 'Es müsste ein Gesetz geben' ('There should be a law'). Not only do these two actors represent

FIGURE 13.1   The heterosexual man desperately confirming his cis-gendered straight identity through 'masculine' activities: mobster King Marchand (James Garner, right) and his bodyguard 'Squash' Bernstein (Alex Karras, left).

Source: Photo provided by the editor.

the binary voices of man and woman, but they may also be seen as giving voice to a general public opinion reminiscent of Prussian values. The visual language links these lines to the next person we see as the pre-empted voice-over primes the viewer.

What we observe is thus already framed within a set of moral judgements and with a pejorative use of a neutral gender pronoun 'Was' (what/what kind). The fluid movement of the camera pans to the whimsical audition of Viktor, thereby providing an image the viewer can associate with 'what' should be banned from public visibility by law. Tellingly, the German pronoun used here ('Was') does not communicate either a male or female identity but shows disgust through its use of a colloquialism that turns Viktor into a mere object. The movie implies that the two old actors are motivated by jealously, but they also give voice to a social discourse which communicates a right and a wrong kind of behaviour regarding what constitutes a proper appearance and a decent representation of social performance on stage and what it means to be a 'man'.

Though this 'lawful' standard of theatrical behaviour is not explicated, the dialogue exchange sets up a dynamic that shames behavioural difference in connection with a gender-neutral pronoun which is, likewise, used in a pejorative way. Therefore, a directorial strategy that is used to provoke comic contrast and sympathy for the character of Viktor Hempel in his pathetic audition attempt, also promotes value judgements when it comes to behavioural norms. The question remains of how much a historical – or contemporary – audience might have been/might be able to distance itself from the subtle workings of this montage. This question, however, is of secondary relevance to the observation that shaming deviant gender-behaviour is at the core of this joke at the expense of Viktor.

Likewise, in the next audition room – connected to the first one via an elegant long take that shows how all-encompassing the power dynamic between acceptance and shame is in the Parisian theatre agency portrayed – the future Viktoria recites a song in front of an older actress and her husband-producer. Here, conventional, heteronormative signs of lecherous sexuality exhibited by the male are reprimanded immediately by his domesticating wife, the archetype of a Prussian mother. Consequently, the couple's interaction reveals a discourse of shaming any overt portrayal of sexual desire regardless of orientation.

What is visibly in place, in the film's world, is a system of control that is apparent when behaviour is not deemed to be decent, 'lawful' or in line with the 'civilised' norms of disguising sexual desire in public, be it for the purpose of freeing comedy or castigating regulation; then, such overt sexual behaviour or gender deviance is surrounded by signals of shame. For our argument, the focus lies on the consequences this acquired control mechanism has for non-normative gender identities; however, the sequence also shows how such cultural conditionings are perpetuated consciously or unconsciously.

The fluidity of the camera movement that connects different levels of the social hierarchy, from the high stakes of an audition process to the social performances in the vestibule, not only illustrates how pervasive the sanctioning of a certain gender-related behaviour is in this diverse urban space – it is also used as an aesthetic representation of modern urbanity in itself. The long pan perceives the modern city, such as Paris or (later in the film) London, as a melting pot where different identities and social roles can come together in a display of technical virtuosity. The complex matrix of social interdependence and competing value judgements in Weimar Germany is held together by the movie's cinematic style.

Viktor Hempel's opening audition is also striking with regard to the version(s) of masculinity he performs – with obvious emotional commitment. He performs a speech from Schiller's *Don Carlos*, a play that interestingly frames an anti-conventional protagonist within classical Aristotelian conventions. Carlos as a character is still heavily influenced by the rebellious anti-movement of *Sturm und Drang* which ushered in a new type of sensitive, emotional masculinity in the form of the *Kraftkerl* ('robust man of action') at the end of the 18th century who places spontaneous feelings over politics and accepted sexual manners.

It is remarkable that the audition panel presses the button to show Hempel's performance is not welcome at exactly the moment when Viktor, in character, talks of himself as a 'Memme' ('sissy') and after a performance which has shown genuine emotional vulnerability. His attempt at a committed and – in Stanislavskian terms – 'truthful' performance of an agitated self is recognisably detrimental to his mental health. This is shown through close-ups that communicate desperation and emotional pain after he is rejected for his more sensitive portrayal of revolutionary masculinity.

What makes this scene additionally relevant for a gender-focused analysis that distinguishes between shameful and accepted 'male behaviour' is Viktor's reaction to the blunt panel decision: he counters by showing them a photo gallery of the more conventional masculinities he can play, hoping that his display of heteronormative archetypes will lead to acceptance. The lovesick young Carlos is replaced with pictures of Karl Moor (a bandit from Schiller's play *Die Räuber/The Robbers*, with excessive beard and over-sized, phallic gun in hand), Romeo (the romantic, straight lover despite his youthful sensitivity), the virile Othello (a character in which discourses of race and masculinity intersect) and then with a picture of a generic knight in armour whose face isn't even visible. These depictions tend towards masculine stereotypes. By immediately setting his record 'straight' and thus by disavowing his emotional performance, Viktor proves that he can play more 'acceptable' male characters.

Visual silences, defined here as moments when something is noticeably missing from a logical shot-to-shot succession, are another stylistic means which indicate that the film addresses some form of shameful or even traumatic reality in connection with questions of gender: a prominent example is the elliptical cut away from Viktor when he reveals his drag work to Viktoria by showing her another picture from his photo gallery that features him dressed as a woman. Though this cut is used to create tension, it aesthetically constitutes an embarrassed look away and a disruption in the editing – a visual silence in the form of an invisibility. This conversation between the two luckless actors takes on an aura of the illicit: they whisper and are shown in a more intimate framing which suggests a secret being shared. The closer Viktor comes to revealing his 'secret job' of playing a woman, the more hushed his tone becomes.

A more overt policing occurs when Viktoria loses her female wig in front of a policeman when already in disguise as young gentleman Viktor. The officer gives her a suspicious look which creates an atmosphere of spying on illegal behaviour and thus criminalises queer attributes. Viktoria's reaction to this encounter reveals discomfort, anxiety and the shame of being found out: 'Ich habe schreckliche Angst' ('I am terribly afraid'). Hempel interprets this as stage fright; however, the editing suggests a different reading with regard to Viktoria's psychology. In a Freudian interpretation, her admission points to the unconscious response to sexual taboo: the German word 'schrecklich'/'terribly' is in close semantic proximity to 'unheimlich'/'uncanny' – thus referencing emotional tremors that emanate from the psychosocial id of sexual deviance and its internalised terrors.

In the context of the film, the reaction of the policeman as a representative of the state marks the carrying of non-masculine attributes as 'unlawful' behaviour for a 'man', just as the conversation opening the film shows disdain for an all-too emotional male performance. The irony of the film lies in the fact that Susanne voices her shame as a double cross-dressed 'third gender'.

We can now take a look at how an even more complex dynamic around double-cross-dressing is framed within this discourse during Viktoria's stage show at the cabaret. The backstage area and the changing rooms of her first nightclub engagement reveal telling mechanisms of camp gender exaggeration. But these spaces also visualise psychosocial strategies of feeling shame and repressing body openness.

On the one hand, Viktoria's first flamenco-style performance as double-drag artist appears like an early form of *voguing* with its blurring of feminine and masculine body and voice. Furthermore, 'typical' male performers reveal backstage that their virile attributes are more show than masculine essence: to Viktoria's surprise, they remove their beard, hair and flat-chests along with their stylised repetitions of performative man-acting. The humorous play with gender attributes pre-empts in a non-verbal way Susan Sontag's and Judith Butler's concept of gender as performative and being-as-role-playing. In her seminal essay 'Notes on Camp', Sontag (2009, p. 280) explains: 'Camp sees everything in quotation marks. . . . not a woman, but a "woman". To perceive Camp . . . in persons is to understand Being-as-Playing-a-Role.' Butler (2007, p. 175) later developed this awareness of gender stylisation into a theory of 'performative subversions' to confuse, and ultimately undermine, established role models.

In 1933, not fitting into the expected binary of male or female in the wardrobe area, however, produces moments of cognitive irritation and expressions of discomfort on Viktoria's face. The increasing awareness that gender is just show does not prevent her from appearing visibly ashamed to be in the male changing room. In her case, under the disguise, the binary, based on 19th century discourses of decency and civilisation, seems to be still in place. All this is communicated in a wordless scene which is presented in the mode of silent movie comedy. Therefore, personal shame within a setting of ambivalent gender is expressed almost entirely in the non-verbal filmic text. On a non-intellectualised level, the conservative binary still controls the queer actions and emotions of the protagonists in this Weimar cross-dressing comedy.

It not only affects the performers but also the audience within the film. Male spectators who have been left in the dark about Viktoria's 'real' identity during her London tour are reprimanded twice by a female chaperone that they are voicing desire for a drag performance and hence a male body. When Viktoria reveals her identity theatrically, the two men show the body language and coping mechanisms of embarrassment: the expressions on their faces turn to disbelief; one covers his face in personal humiliation then diverts the unpleasant emotion of shame into jocular repartee. Their female companion laughs out loud to further alleviate the unpleasant situation for her male friends. These reaction shots are intercut with Viktoria's drag performance and gender reveal. Again, editing helps to reinforce the message of what is socially acceptable, and of what should provoke shame and therefore needs to be relieved by comedy – of what cannot be accepted straight-forwardly as desire.

FIGURE 13.2   The double cross-dressing woman as civilising influence: Renate Müller as Susanne Lohr and Hermann Thimig as Viktor Hempel in Reinhold Schünzel's 1933 *Viktor und Viktoria*.

Source: Production still provided by the editor.

Many more examples could be given to illustrate how in *Viktor und Viktoria* queer public performance and potential same-sex attraction are critiqued on a visual, performative level, which ultimately aims to defang the film as 'merely a harmless comedy'. The gender-subversive concept of a woman who double-cross-dresses, therefore, ultimately acts as a civilising process, a means to emphasise the dénouement's safe heteronormative resolution. This unthreatening outcome is implied to the audience from the beginning: struggles of personal acceptance are resolved into playful laughter around mistaken identities, even if the movie at the same time opens up the gender arena for progressive play.

The way it is depicted here through cutting to perplexed male spectators, same-sex attraction in the end appears to be no more than surface confusion. The gay tit-illation does not succeed in upsetting the 'real' biological intuition of straight men. Cinemagoers who identify as straight and male are protected from falling into this 'trap' as they are let in on the gender masquerade right from the start. In contrast, when Susanne enters a glamorous London restaurant as star Viktor, female guests cast appreciative glances at the young 'gentleman' – without any noticeable signs of discomfort about this moment of female-female attraction. Their 'misinformed' desire is not resolved. Thus, the film limits moments of same-sex attraction to the realm of female kinship and lesbian desire. Interestingly, this form of deviant sexuality seems to be deemed less threatening to the patriarchal, heteronormative order and here remains surprisingly unreprimanded in comparison to *Mädchen in Uniform* with its strict Prussian codes.

'If you are not happy with the arrangement': *Victor/Victoria* 1982

Rick Thompson (2002) points out that Blake Edwards' remake of the Weimar version is franker in its portrayal of same-sex attraction. Thus, at the beginning of the new millennium, he praised the remake as more accepting of queer gender roles: 'Edwards . . . goes for the throat, 1982 offering more latitude than 1933 – Edwards wanting to make a much more confronting film than Schünzle.' At a time when the canon of gay films and literature was still being formed, Edwards' sympathetic portrayal of Toddy and gay love may have stood out positively.

However, reviewing the movie in 1982 for *The New Yorker*, Pauline Kael (2009, pp. 333–334) was much less enthusiastic: she saw the musical's sentimentalisation of homosexuality, which to her was exacerbated by 'prejudicial old gags' and gay clichés, as hugely problematic: turning Toddy into Victoria's stereotypical 'gay best friend' removes any sexual tension between the two characters, even when they represent the same gender; it keeps their relationship 'pure' and preserves the female body as an exclusive object for alpha-men. Since the film thus avoids any potential discomfort for straight audiences, Kael was astonished by its reception in the gay community, posing the question: 'Why are homosexual spokesmen celebrating the film?'

Reviewed through the lens of gay shame at the beginning of the 2020s, *Victor/Victoria*'s visual discourse does indeed reveal strategies of reinforcing gender conventions. However, I would argue, these strategies become apparent exactly *because* of the film's conflicted message; identifying its stylistic problems thus can help to further aesthetic discussions. In addition, Edward's remake overtly addresses the psychosocial complex of gay shame – it takes part in identifying the processes of gay-shaming as much as it endorses them.

As shown above, 1920s and '30s European city culture was much less liberated than it is often assumed nowadays; in fact, Weimar cinema was anything but straightforwardly queer. Featuring reflections between Toddy and Victoria about gay shame within this earlier historical setting, therefore, illustrates an ongoing conflicted discussion rather than radical confrontation. In this sense, the 1930s become a metaphor for the 1980s, rather than the realisation of historical alterity:

TODDY: Shame is an unhappy emotion invented by pietists in order
    to exploit the human race.
VICTORIA: Who said that?
TODDY: I said that.
VICTORIA: You don't believe in shame?
TODDY: I believe in happiness.

This blunt dialogue (78:55 min.) about queer shame and religion in 1930s Paris is an interesting anachronism, as it seems more informed by the gay liberation movements of the 1970s than by historical accuracy. It also continues an Americanised glorification of the free and anti-conventional lifestyle of Paris' bohemia. At the same time, it presents that lifestyle as a potential for US society, even if it does so at a remote distance and in disguise. Toddy's claim to happiness as a gay man is striking because it instrumentalises an established cultural rhetoric and points to the absence of equal rights for gay men at a time when the male American role model once again became more and more conservative with Reagan as the political leader.

The wording of this short exchange is interesting since it juxtaposes the positive and potentially inclusive cultural embodiment of a 'pursuit of happiness' with the exclusive and learned psycho–moral construct of shame. A 1980s audience that had been exposed to roughly two decades of the revaluation of American social myths in the wake of the 1960s social movements would have been especially sensitive to such allusions. In the progressively more restrictive social climate of the early 1980s, Toddy's awareness of moral judgement comes across partly as wishful thinking; in addition, it is safely relocated in the distant past by a film that tries to work through its own subconscious depictions of gay shame within Hollywood's straight mainstream. What we see is an idealisation of gay pride that is confined by its own conservative filmic language.

The struggle with deviant male happiness is illustrated by King Marchand's reaction to his discovery that he might be attracted to a 'man' such as Viktor. We see King, the self-declared straight male lover (and future husband of Victoria), struggle forcefully to accept even the slightest implication that he might be gay; for instance, he auto-destructively provokes pub fights to confirm his heterosexuality. The film's editing creates moral critique in a similar way to the 1933 version – numerous reaction shots capture King's discomfort at being perceived as gay by the cabaret audience: 'Well, if you think I'm worried about everybody thinking I'm a fag, you're right.'

The 1982 film also brings to light the homophobia implicit in the mobsters' code of masculinity, voiced by one of King's friends: 'Eventually, I'd ask you to stop being a gangster because I was worried about everyone thinking I was your moll.' *Victor/Victoria* exposes the dynamic of gay shame, but it doesn't resolve gay shaming by means of genuine acceptance. Similar to the earlier film, it trivialises the conflict that has been caused by these multiple layers of social guilt: the dénouement reinstates heteronormative gender roles. Queer love is kept in the realm of comedic make-believe. The budding love affair between Toddy and King's bodyguard is visually unconfirmed as they remain spatially separated whereas Victoria and King stand united.

It is important to point out that the alpha-male King only proceeds with his pursuit of 'Viktor' once he has confirmed that she is in fact a woman by sneaking into her bathroom. Obviously, the film didn't dare suggest that King might

FIGURE 13.3 Two happy couples which are not equal in visual terms: whereas the heterosexual pair Victoria and King sit next to each other, the gay lovers Toddy and 'Squash' are situated at opposite sides of the frame. Scene from Blake Edwards' *Victor/Victoria*; in the front, from left to right: Robert Preston, Julie Andrews, James Garner and Alex Karras.

Source: Photo provided by the editor.

be attracted to an effeminate man, although it was comfortable with having him desiring a boyish woman. Within a more liberal stage context, Edwards changed this for the 1995 stage adaptation of the musical. Here, King is not sure that Viktor is female before embarking on an affair.

Victor/Victoria as a whole shows moments of awareness of how shame is a consequence of a set of moral values which are constructed by those in power while at the same time relying on a visual discourse that regularly still speaks the language of straight framing. The heteronormative social reality of the audience and queer stage travesty can co-exist within Blake Edwards' Paris mainly because they are embedded within a straight romance plot between of the primary couple.

The scene which introduces Toddy in 1982 marks a useful point of comparison between the two film versions, because like Viktor Hempel in 1933, the gay actor recites famous lines from the theatrical canon: 'Love looks not with the eyes, but with the mind, and therefore is winged Cupid painted blind' from Shakespeare's *A Midsummer Night's Dream*. Interestingly, Toddy quotes Helena's lines here, introducing the film's playful approach to mixing up and layering binary gender concepts in gleeful confusion. Yet unlike in the previous version, the character is not shown in a public space but in the private space of his bedroom in a post-coital morning scene.

The intimate environment contrasts with the audition stage of 1933, where Hempel is pushed to switch to a more clearly defined masculine role in order to reframe his dramatic rendition. Stylistically, the space of Toddy and his lover's queer intimacy is clearly set apart from the main sphere of Parisian society: with a fluid pan echoing the earlier movie's opening sequence, Edwards links diverse realms of the city space. Languidly, the camera watches the world go by from the Bohemian setting of Toddy's flat on the top floor of a multi-story house. The apartment is cluttered with symbols of queer subculture, such as a photograph of Marlene Dietrich.

Same-sex attraction, therefore, is confined to a room in a different stratum, literally closeted, located at the vertical periphery of society, out of sight. Yet the architectural marginalisation does not result in a safe haven of free morals, since the visual depiction of Paris is permeated with the sound of nearby church-bells which accompany the intimate scene and might remind the viewer of a competing set of moral values associated with attending services and with weddings, subtly suggesting the omnipresence of Christian beliefs – the ones later alluded to by Toddy. Again, in the diverse spaces of a modern urban centre such as Paris, a capital synonymous with liberty and carefree romance, a demonstration of Bohemian gender progressiveness is inseparable from discourses on 'decent', 'proper' Sunday morning behaviour.

The visual plane in this scene nevertheless reinforces judgement, self-doubt and shame in very straight terms for the gay character: when Toddy's lover points out that their relationship is *de facto* that of a rent boy and his client, we see Toddy close the closet door and watch himself reflected in its mirrored front. Observing oneself in a mirror is a traditional visual motif of self-reflection and self-confrontation, derived from the mythological Narcissus. Autonomously, with the moral authority of a narrative means, the camera zooms in on Toddy's reflection, creating the impression of penetrating self-scrutiny. The psychological blank space created through this cinematographic strategy allows the audience to project their own feelings and inherited moral standards onto Toddy, who has just been shamed by his lover's condescending suggestion that Toddy is free to change their affair if he doesn't like 'this arrangement'.

The independent zoom (i.e. a zoom which does not represent a character's point of view) is a potent visual strategy of observation, often used in thrillers and spy movies, as it draws attention to being watched and judged by a controlling outsider similar to a panopticon. The film's visual language, therefore, externalises a double-edged 1980s psychological discourse on morality, which introduces alternative forms of intimacy, but then links them to the need for being scrutinised by an impersonal super-ego, followed by a heteronormative moral judgement. Though this scrutiny seems to be triggered by the act of (male) prostitution as much as by any deviant gender behaviour, it nevertheless implies that judgements on what constitutes a 'decent' relationship are delivered in heterosexual terms.

Set against the church bell on the soundtrack, the camera movements suggest that the sexual 'other' (which in this context could be casual sex, queer sexuality or sex for money) is incompatible with the unspoken norms of romantic love, such as monogamy or heteronormative marriage. Thus, the situation troubles the protagonist psychologically and pushes him to investigate his intimate arrangement. The non-verbal subtext of the church bells in combination with the visual plane depicts gay shame in the moral struggle for self-acceptance even in the more progressive 1980s version of 1930s Gay Paree.

Conclusion: towards a renewed visual language

In my analysis, I explored how moments of gay shame have been cinematographically expressed in the 1933 and 1982 versions of *Victor/Victoria*, and how their queer subject matter made the presentation of gay shame possible. The filmic dissection used heightened awareness as a starting point to re-investigate how competing cinematic sign systems of the two cross-dressing pictures depict alternative moral codes within the intimate and diverse urban space of 20th-century Paris. Various visual techniques, such as autonomous camera movements or emotional engineering through editing, contribute to creating the cinematic stylistics of gay shame in the two *Victoria*-films. However, the non-verbal moral scrutiny of gay behaviour could only become apparent in tandem with the films' occasionally forward-looking depiction of gender and their aesthetic of camp subversion.

It is through their audiovisual devices that the two versions also partly expose the struggle with moral norms from a queer perspective; especially, when they clash with an awareness of gender roles as performative acts (1933) or moments of gay pride (1982). Though this arguably constitutes a modern reading of the films beyond their troubled sociocultural context, it also shows creative potential.

Increased awareness of those codes may help directors to depict free love in Paris and elsewhere, without shame. It seems time for another remake.

Notes

1 *Papas Kino* is a term used by the young directors of the New German Wave in the late 1960s and 1970 to denounce West-Germany's post-war commercial cinematic output after 1946. It refers to light-hearted genre filmmaking which was extremely popular with audience, but was also defiantly apolitical on the surface while endorsing conservative values such as the heteronormative family and an often homespun ideology with close links to rural identities. It was literally produced by 'the fathers' of the post-war generation with the artists in front and behind the camera showing a lot of continuity with film production under the Nazi party. Therefore, the generation of filmmakers coming up from 1962 onwards defined *Papas Kino* in political as well as aesthetic opposition to their own cinematic movement.
2 By 'gender-progressive' I mean any accepting portrayal of sexual or gender identity that tends towards questioning binary constructs.

Bibliography

Arnold-de Simine, S. (2012) 'Crossdressing, Remakes, and National Stereotypes: The Germany-Hollywood Connection,' in T. Ginsberg and A. Mensch (eds.) *A Companion to German Cinema*. Chichester: Wiley-Blackwell, pp. 379–404.

Butler, J. (2007/1990) *Gender Trouble: Feminism and the Subversion of Identity*. Reprint. New York and London: Routledge.

Kael, P. (2009/1984) *Taking it All in*. Reprint. London and New York: Marion Boyars, pp. 331–335.

Mennel, B. (2012) *Queer Cinema: Schoolgirls, Vampires and Gay Cowboys*. New York: Wall-flower Press.

Sheringham, M. (2013) 'Paris: City of Disappearances,' in A. L. Milne (ed.) *The Cambridge Companion to the Literature of Paris*. Cambridge: Cambridge University Press, pp. 228–243.

Sontag, S. (2009/1964) 'Notes on Camp,' in *Against Interpretation and Other Essays*. Reprint. London: Penguin Books.

Todd, M. (2016) *Straight Jacket: Overcoming Society's Legacy of Gay Shame*. London: Black Swan.

Thompson, R. (2002) 'He and She: Weimar Screwballwerk,' *Sense of Cinema: An Online Film Journal Devoted to the Serious and Eclectic Discussion of Cinema*, 22, http://sensesofcinema.com/2002/cteq/viktor/, accessed 30 April 2020.

Victor/Victoria. (1982) Directed by B. Edwards. DVD. Hamburg: Warner Home Video.

Viktor und Viktoria. (1933) Directed by R. Schünzel. DVD. Hamburg: Koch Media Gmbh.

14

À LA RECHERCHE DE QUEL *TEMPS?* CAN-CAN AND THE FLUIDITY OF PARIS *PERDU*

Raymond Knapp and Mitchell Morris

> *Ev'ry time I look down*
> *On this timeless town,*
> *Whether blue or grey be her skies,*
> *Whether loud be her cheers*
> *Or whether soft be her tears,*
> *More and more do I realise*
> *I love Paris*★
> (Porter, 1953, pp. 102–103)

Paris has long seemed to exist in a symbolic space that appears at once timeless and a kind of time machine, allowing access in the operative present to a lost past that was both innocent and naughty, both Oriental and Western, eternally both then and now and aspirationally both past and future. As such, it was not only the ideal birthplace for operetta in the 19th century, but also, by the early decades of the 20th century, the most congenial portal between the United States and Europe, between the erstwhile New World and the Old, standing usefully between the primitive and the ultra-sophisticated, between (and merging) *Les Apaches* and *Les Avant-gardes*.

But all of this is much too figurative and abstract. That Paris became a beacon for Americans after the Great War was by roughly equal parts owing to circumstance, reciprocal accommodation and romanticised notions attaching to a 'timeless town' that had managed to emerge from that grim episode not only mostly unscathed but also developing its own romanticised notions about the freshness of American art, especially its music and most especially its music with African-American roots. And in the wake of its even more miraculous physical survival after the even grimmer episode of World War II, those connections were reinscribed through a second layer of romanticisation while others were added – most saliently centring around music, dance, film, a re-labelled operetta (the 'integrated musical'), an evolving but still closeted camp sensibility and the birth-struggles of a not-yet-fully emergent sexual revolution.

It is in these more specific contexts that certain post-war stage and film musicals traded on the fluidity between timeless Paris and much more localised recreations of its symbolic freedoms. Thus, *Gentlemen Prefer Blondes* (Broadway, 1949, film 1953), *An American in Paris* (film 1951), *Can-Can* (Broadway, 1953, film 1960) and *Gigi* (film 1958) provide paired, apparently opposing approaches to the dynamic between Paris and Americans: in the earlier two forthrightly showing Americans interacting with Parisians in 1920s Paris, in the later two ostensibly recreating an even earlier Paris, predating the important cultural intersections after World War I. But, of course, this dichotomy is only apparent. *Can-Can* and *Gigi*, while both ostentatiously about recreating Paris *perdu*, *sans* Americans, are vibrantly engaged with their historical moments of creation. Indeed, with *Can-Can* we must distinguish carefully in this regard between a stage show conceived and mounted during the McCarthy era and a film made in the shadow of *Playboy* and *Gigi* for an audience on the brink of the 1960s' sexual revolution. And, for both works, there are two particularly relevant versions of Paris *perdu* in operation: the official recreation of *fin-de-siecle* Paris and, in intriguing patterns of interference, the quite different Paris between the Wars, the Paris that all Americans will 'always have' as a first port of call, thanks to fictional characters such as Humphrey Bogart's Rick, songwriters such as George Gershwin and Cole Porter, and the persistence of Maurice Chevalier, from the hero of 1930s film operettas to post-war *grand homme*, as a Parisian for all seasons.

Two tales of a city: *Can-Can* (1953) and its film adaptation (1960)

Abe Burrows conceived, wrote and directed *Can-Can* at the height of the McCarthy era, and the stage musical shows how well the conventions of musicals could be brought to bear on serious issues. In this case, those issues – relating in obvious ways to then-current political events – are censorship and the cruel hypocrisy involved in prosecuting inhumane and unjust laws. Substantial effort was put into researching how these issues played out in *fin de siècle* Paris, some of it conducted on site. Separate typewritten reports were submitted to Burrows on key historical figures who provided important models for many of the principals, including dancer Jane Avril, artist Henri de Toulouse-Lautrec and Senator René Bérenger – the latter clearly being seen as a precursor to US Senator Joseph McCarthy. Other research addressed institutions such as the Parisian courts, Montmartre *bals* and *cafés* (especially Le Chat Noir and Moulin Rouge), and the *Bal des Quat'Z'Arts*, the latter an often scandalous annual event that started in 1892. Various aspects of public and private life were also researched, including censorship, sexuality, pornography, prostitution, duels, laundries, public dancing, public nudity, the art world (including critics), and prisons.[1] Through following the conventions of the 'well-made

TABLE 14.1 Can-Can song deployments in the 1953 stage version and the 1960 film version

Stage Version 1953	Film Version 1960
★ = changed deployment/**Bold** = deployed similarly but with some changes/*Italics* = not used in film version	★ = changed deployment/**Bold** = deployed similarly but with some changes/*Italics* = interpolated into film version
Act I	★I Love Paris Chorus (over opening credits)
★Maidens Typical of France Claudine & Laundresses (to judges), joined by police	**Montmartre** François, Paul, & chorus
Never Give Anything Away Pistache (with laundresses)	★Maidens Typical of France Claudine & female dancers (as staged number)
★C'est Magnifique Pistache (& Aristide)	★Can-Can (dance only, interrupted) Claudine & female dancers
Quadrille[1] Dance: Claudine, Laundresses, Friends & Dancers	★C'est Magnifique François with Claudine & other dancers (to Philippe)
★Come Along with Me Hilaire Jussac and Boris (to Claudine)	★Apache Dance Pistache & male dancers
★Live and Let Live Pistache (to Aristide)	★C'est Magnifique (reprise) Pistache (to Philippe)
I Am In Love Aristide	★Can-Can (reprise; dance only, interrupted) Claudine & female dancers
If You Loved Me Truly Claudine, Boris, Bohemians & girlfriends	★Live and Let Live Paul & Philippe
Montmartre Singing ensemble, framing ballet	*You Do Something to Me* [from *Fifty Million Frenchmen*, 1929]
Garden of Eden Ballet Eve (Claudine), Snake ("Aristide"), & other animals	Philippe (solo)
Allez-Vous En Pistache (to Aristide)	*Let's Do It* [from *Paris*, 1928] François & Pistache
Act II	★It's All Right with Me François (to Claudine)
Never, Never Be an Artist Boris, Bohemians, & Model (to Aristide)	− Intermission −
	★Live and Let Live (reprise) Philippe & Paul
★It's All Right with Me Aristide (to streetwalker)	★Come along with Me Pistache (to entertain Philippe's party guests)

Stage Version 1953	Film Version 1960
Every Man Is a Stupid Man Pistache	*Just One of Those Things* [from *Jubilee*, 1935] Paul (to Philippe)
★Apache Dance Claudine & male dancers	**Garden of Eden Ballet (**renamed **Adam and Eve)** Eve (Pistache), Adam, Snake (Claudine), & other animals
★I Love Paris Pistache (with chorus)	
★C'est Magnifique Aristide (to & with Pistache)	★It's All Right with Me (reprise) Philippe (to Pistache)
Can-Can (song with dance) Pistache & Laundresses	**Can-Can** (dance only) Pistache, Claudine, female dancers, male dancers
Finale (Montmartre) Entire Company	★I Love Paris Chorus (over closing credits)

[1] 'Quadrille,' while not used as the basis for a musical number in the film, launches both the pre-credit overture and the post-credit exit music.

musical', as detailed just below, *Can-Can* advances its serious themes, grounded in serious research, without surrendering its commitment to either entertainment or the prurience promised by its title (also duly researched). Given the concerns of the original show, not to mention the care taken and craft exercised by Burrows and his collaborators to advance those concerns, it can seem appalling that almost none of those specific investments are on display in the film made just seven years later, despite its adherence to the basic plot outlines of the stage show and its retention of at least the highlights of the original score, if drastically redeployed (see Table 14.1, discussed more fully later).

But more seems to be involved in this case than the wholesale makeovers that had in the past mangled stage shows as they were adapted for film. However much the film disappointed fans of the stage show, it evidences considerable care and craft devoted to concerns of its own. The disconnect between stage and screen versions – particularly jarring due to their shared material – along with related notions that the film is a failure and the stage show not a particularly viable candidate for revival, derive from the fact that neither version is completely true to its themes. The stage show undermines art's prestige – a central pillar of its larger argument – by making its artists comically pretentious, while frequently indulging a generic tendency to favour quick laughs and gaudy spectacle over serious themes – acting, half a decade after *Kiss Me, Kate* (1948), as though *Can-Can* were just a typical Cole Porter show of old, its story little more than convenient scaffolding for songs, dances and jokes. To be sure, this assessment not only unfairly slights *both* pre-'integration' Porter and *Can-Can* itself, but also conveniently ignores the practical issue of deniability, since comic deflection was especially useful cover during the McCarthy era.[2] Nevertheless, *Can-Can*'s invitation not to take its themes too seriously was blithely accepted by the film adaptation, which had other fish to fry (see below), but whose most interesting conceits too often and crudely run up against, or simply seem to reflect, the negotiations of star power. Whatever the film's own claims to seriousness, they were swamped by Hollywood's tendency to pander, which could thus easily be blamed for the film's apparent failure to take the full measure of the stage show.

Following the conventions of the 'marriage trope',[3] the main romantic couple in *Can-Can* is introduced in diametric opposition, each half to the other. La Môme Pistache is the owner of *Bal du Paradis*, a café and dancehall notorious for performing the can-can, which Aristide Forrestier, as an idealistic young judge, is bound by the 'Public Morals Law of 1790, 1876, 1878, 1880, and 1881' to regard (in the language of the official charge) as unlawfully 'lewd and lascivious [with] exhibitionistic and indecent posturing and movements calculated to inflame, disturb, arouse and debase the minds, souls, moral fibres and characters of the spectators' (1–1–4).[4] In advancing their relationship while resolving the musical's main plot, both characters must compromise professionally: she as a businesswoman on the outskirts of respectability must look past immediate financial gain and overcome her distrust of him and the nature of his concern for her, and he must judge not only humans who contravene the law, but also the law itself, which he – unlike Senator Bérenger, on whom he seems at least partly based – comes to realise can be unjust and hypocritical. Their progress in love and requisite growth as individuals are charted through their interactions with sidekicks and confidantes, primarily fellow judge Paul Barrière for Aristide and a succession of associates (employees, patrons, police, etc.) for Pistache.

Much of the serious thematic work, as noted, is consigned to a more comic plane, as an extension of the secondary, comic couple – laundress/dancer Claudine and penniless sculptor Boris Adzinidzinadze – whose romance is threatened by the triangular entanglement of Hilaire Jussac, a lecherous and opportunistic art critic. Specifically through Claudine's and Boris's other associates, the close relationship between the dancers' disreputable display and the Bohemian art world is brought into immediate focus. Thus, Claudine's fellow laundresses/dancers and Boris's band of artists – whose studio employs a nude model to serve as simultaneous inspiration to a painter, sculptor and poet – are similarly committed to feminine display. Significantly, as well, neither dancers nor artists are paid for their work, so that, in essence, it is Pistache's continued employment of the dancers as laundresses that supports both them and their *beaux artistiques*.[5] At the climax of the first act, this economic arrangement becomes an artistic collaboration within the balletic entertainment they devise for the notorious *Bal des Quat'z'Arts*: 'The Garden of Eden', in which Aristide is overtly parodied as the Snake who despoils the innocence of the Garden, where the 'beasts were not beastly' and all were 'happy and gay' as they 'loved and drank their fill . . . Until . . .' (1–10–70).

FIGURE 14.1   The 'Garden of Eden' ballet in the 1953 stage version of *Can-Can*; third from the left is Eric Rhodes (Hilaire Jussac), at the centre, playing Eve, is Gwen Verdon (Claudine) and recumbent right of centre is Lilo (La Môme Pistache).

Source: Photo courtesy of Photofest NYC.

The songs, too, follow many of the conventions that became entrenched during the 'integrated musical' era, even if some types (such as the list song) were associated more specifically with Cole Porter than with Broadway generally. Thus, 'Maidens Typical of France', 'Montmartre' and the instrumental dance number 'Quadrille' act as establishing numbers. 'Never Give Anything Away' and 'Live and Let Live' together serve as Pastiche's 'I Am' songs, establishing her character attitudinally, first as a businesswoman and then in rejecting Aristide's blind devotion to the law.[6] As a speculative love song, 'C'est Magnifique' follows convention by charting the progress of the central relationship both through its internal narrative and in its deployment, with Pistache singing the song in Act I to Aristide, who first rejects it but then serves it back to her as a second-act reprise.

Following a related convention, each romantic lead sings of their love in soliloquy (he with 'I Am in Love' in Act I and she with 'I Love Paris' in Act II), so that the audience, but not the singers' *objets d'affection*, knows their true feelings. 'Apache Dance' serves as a second-act novelty number, framed – like 'In Dahomey' in *Show Boat* – as a bit of staged (that is, faked) 'authenticity' but which also helps validate the artistic pretensions of the dancers. Porter's most characteristic moments come with the playfully multi-linguistic 'C'est Magnifique' and 'Montmartre'[7] as well as with the verbal dexterity of his list songs, especially 'Come along with Me', 'Live and Let Live'

FIGURE 14.2   The romantic couple at the centre of *Can-Can*: La Môme Pistache (Lilo) and Judge Aristide Forrestier (Peter Cookson). Scene from the original 1953 Broadway production.

Source: Photo courtesy of Photofest NYC.

and 'Can-Can' (also, if less pervasively, in the ensemble numbers 'Maidens Typical of France', 'If You Loved Me Truly', 'Montmartre' and 'Never, Never Be an Artist'). But perhaps most memorably 'Cole Porter' are the poetic indirections of Pistache's 'I Love Paris' and Aristide's 'It's All Right with Me' – the latter a love-song to Pistache sung to a streetwalker, astonishing from several perspectives.

Almost none of this finds its way into the film, in some cases not even the characters' names, which are angled, like the cast, towards their American audience (thus, *Simone* Pistache, *Philippe* Forrestier). The only artist in the film (beyond a few cartoon images during the opening credits) is Toulouse-Lautrec, who has no lines but provides the occasion for two throwaway jokes (7:20, 1:05:45).[8] The dancers are laundresses not in real life but only for the duration of a stage number at the *Bal du Paradis*. The only gesture towards art criticism occurs when society ladies discuss the relative worth of the poets De Musset, Verlaine and Baudelaire in front of Simone, who has never heard of them (1:34:15). A new character – François Durnais, Simone's lawyer, played by Frank Sinatra – derails the marriage trope that structures the stage show, leaving behind a conventional love triangle and an enfeebled treatment of the intertwined themes of artistic freedom and legal injustice. The issue of censorship along with the abusive and discriminatory potential of law enforcement are deflected in many other ways, as well, for example by beginning in Montmartre instead of in court (as in the stage show; later stage revivals follow the film in beginning in Montmartre)[9] and by making respectability and class the decisive issues between Simone and Philippe (played respectively by Shirley MacLaine and Louis Jourdan); this leg of the triangle thus becomes, not a meeting of adversaries engaging the story's main theme, but – aspirationally, at least – a version of Cinderella, a reverberation of not only *Gigi* two years earlier but also its partial model, *My Fair Lady* (Broadway, 1956), both musicals by Lerner and Loewe.

That there were so many changes, so pervasively implemented, suggests that there must have been a guiding principle of some sort behind them. But what? A snarky summation by a staff writer for *Variety*, writing about the film two months before its première, may hold the key to answering that question: 'It's Las Vegas, 1960, not Montmartre, 1896'(Variety Staff, 1959). Indeed, many of the changes do suggest a conscious determination that the easiest way to evoke *fin de siècle* Paris for Americans would be to show them modern Las Vegas. There is, however, more to it than that, with at least three separate, intertwined rationales.

If we take the snarky literal meaning to heart, we are led directly not to an intentional strategy but to Frank Sinatra and his deployment of star power. Sinatra's early involvement in the project – not only as actor but also as a key stakeholder – along with his recruitment of Shirley MacLaine and the invention of a new character in the story for him to play (with an inside track in the central love triangle), already guaranteed a palpable geographic shift. The seven intervening years had seen Sinatra – whose first film was set in Las Vegas (*Las Vegas Nights*, 1941) – rejuvenate his film and singing careers while settling in as a Las Vegas fixture. Thus, he opened at The Sands in late 1953 and emerged in late 1960 as the new leader of the 'Rat Pack', whose principal members (including an uncredited Shirley MacLaine) all played in *Oceans 11*, Sinatra's next film after *Can-Can*, set in Las Vegas. And, even apart from the deployment of songs in the film, the choice of orchestrator Nelson Riddle, a frequent collaborator of Sinatra's, also guaranteed a sound world closer to Vegas than Broadway's version of Paris.

But the deployment of songs for the film also displays a recognisably Vegas sensibility in ensuring a correlation of stars to major hits. Sinatra, as lead singer, had most of the best-known tunes, including 'Montmartre' (which became the opening number), the interpolated 'Let's Do It', and the first versions of 'C'est Magnifique' and 'It's All Right with Me'. MacLaine, lacking Sinatra's star positioning, actually lost several songs that Pistache sang on stage: 'Live and Let Live' (taken over by Chevalier), 'Allez–Vous En' and 'Every Man Is a Stupid Man' (both dropped), 'I Love Paris' (sung by Sinatra and Chevalier in a late reprise that was cut after previews) and the sung version of 'Can-Can' (which is danced, but not sung). But as lead dancer, she did manage to take over the central dancing roles in 'Apache Dance' and 'Adam and Eve' (danced on stage by Gwen Verdon's Claudine) and performs 'Come along with Me' as a staged number with beefed-up dancing (rescuing it from being dropped along with Hilaire Jussac, who sings it onstage as a book song), while retaining a reprise of 'C'est Magnifique' and joining Sinatra for 'Let's Do It'. While Sinatra's songs are not outright thefts, as MacLaine's dance roles are, they are in two cases pre-emptive, as he gets a crack at both 'C'est Magnifique' and 'It's All Right' before they are sung by those who first sing them on stage, thus undercutting Pistache's initial engagement with Philippe in the former (who in the film complains, 'No, no, please, not again . . . why must I be bombarded by this song?'; 40:40), and eclipsing Philippe in the latter, in terms of both performance and situational richness, so that Sinatra's version comes across as one of the film's best moments, and Jourdan's as an afterthought.

But we might also shift the snarky comment's literal meaning by observing that *Can-Can* presents *both* Las Vegas, 1960, *and* Montmartre, 1896, again partly on the basis of casting and song deployment. In such a process of deep Americanisation, the film participates in a wider cultural moment in Hollywood cinema: over a dozen US films from the 1950s and early 1960s take up Paris of the *fin de siècle* as a setting and source of thematics (Schwartz, 2007, pp. 8–55). Although Sinatra wanted Cary Grant for Forrestier, Grant declined, and although Barrie Chase was chosen for Claudine, she withdrew when she learned that much of the role's dancing would be taken over by MacLaine – which set the stage for Louis Jourdan and newcomer Juliet Prowse (then working in Paris) to assume those roles, joining Maurice Chevalier among the leads and thus swinging the balance, with help from some of the supporting cast, to something more recognisably Parisian, even without Sinatra's or MacLaine's cooperation.[10] Moreover, although Jourdan's singing was reduced to his joining in two iterations of 'Live and Let Live' (with Chevalier), the interpolated 'You Do Something to Me' and the reprise of 'It's All Right with Me', Chevalier – as a star with a distinctive vocal style and as sidekick to both male sides of the triangle – was given several songs, even though his character did not sing on stage: he sings the interpolated 'Just One of Those Things' having already joined with François in 'Montmartre' and with Jourdan in 'Live and Let Live' (twice). Moreover, the three song interpolations themselves seem calculated to remind us of Cole Porter's own attachment to Paris. 'You Do Something to Me' and 'Let's Do It' come from Porter's first two Broadway successes, each about Americans encountering Paris: *Fifty Million Frenchmen* (1929) and *Paris* (1928), respectively, whereas 'Just One of Those Things' begins by citing Madame du Barry (instead of Dorothy Parker, as in the original). But 'Let's Do It', sung as a duet by the two American stars, ends up being the most French of the three, thanks to a series of revisions: thus, 'In Spain' and 'waiter' from the original lyrics are replaced with 'In France' and 'garçon', and a new chorus (apparently written for the film) includes several French references: *sans regret*, Marie Antoinette, Napoleon, *Mam'selles*.[11]

To take the full measure of the odd merger of Las Vegas and Paris in *Can-Can*'s filmic transformation, however, we must first consider with more specificity both how the stage show's recreation of Paris is itself strategically incomplete, and how and why its elisions mattered for American audiences.

The fluidity of *Can-Can*'s Paris *perdu*

The particular piquance of French in *Can-Can* is a complex result of multiple frames of historical and cultural reference encoded in overlapping, only semi-coherent ways, and this rich context deserves a little unpacking. Take a small detail of material culture: the culottes exposed in the skirt-hiking kicks of the dance were not always closed. For reasons of hygiene, culottes had mostly been split at the crotch, and the split breeches were sometimes employed in the dance rather than closed *pantalons*. (This was controversial enough that the Moulin Rouge, for instance, made a point of insisting on no revealing undergarments.) This uncertainty over underwear meant that any performance might offer spectators a chance for more than a display of limbs, adding a prurient *frisson* to the febrile, sexualised intensity of the kicks and gestures themselves, and guaranteeing that the can-can would always retain a heavy erotic vibe (Maruta, 2014).

As mentioned earlier (see note 4), the name of our romantic lead, 'La Môme Pistache', is not only a quaint little sobriquet ('The nutty gal'?), but is also a specific

FIGURE 14.3   The notorious can-can, the scandalous, sensuous dance deemed to be 'lewd and lascivious' by the French judiciary. Scene from the 1960 film version; at the centre of the image Juliet Prowse (left, as Claudine) and Shirley MacLaine (right, as Simone).

Source: Photo provided by the editor.

recollection of a historical can-can dancer-cum-acrobat. A notable percentage of the most famous women cabaret performers in Montmartre during the *belle époque* were openly involved with both male and female partners – La Môme Fromage and La Goulue were well-known as lovers, and to more denizens of the scene than Toulouse-Lautrec alone; the most famous dancer of them all, Jane Avril, courted women as well as men. Colette, escaping her first husband for a stage career as an acrobat and mime, embarked on a series of relationships with women that merely intensified the lesbian affairs her husband had encouraged. Such relationships were relatively open in Montmartre – although they may have provoked scandals in polite society, the milieu of the *avant-garde*, with its rallying cry *épater la bourgeoisie*, offered cover for heterodox affections.

It is also worth comparing the Sapphic situation in Paris with that of New York at the time. After all, the most powerful theatrical agent in America at the turn of the last century was Elisabeth Marbury, who lived for 30 years in a public relationship with the actress, socialite and interior decorator Elsie de Wolfe. Or consider the career of Mercedes de Acosta: daughter of a socially-prominent Cuban-Spanish family and brought up in New York, she became a notorious seducer of actresses, on Broadway and in Hollywood – and the affairs were considered worthwhile as a means of expanding the emotional range of the actresses involved.[12]

Whether in Paris or New York, dissident and unseemly sexual liaisons were a typical part of the theatrical world. Their explicit representation was, however, anything but ordinary. It is rather commonplace to observe that homosexuality, like all non-normative sexual expressions, has usually suffered from a ban on representation in cultures of the West. Not only must those loves not dare speak their name, but they have to hide from public view as well – even while that public is peering everywhere in the hopes of seeing them. In the context of film, critic D. A. Miller notes that such bans on representation mean that homosexuality, to take a pointed example, must work by connotation rather than denotation. But connotation always solicits support, precisely because it is NOT what it is. Needing corroboration, finding it only in what exhibits the same need, with no better affordance for meeting it, connotation thus tends to light everywhere, to put all signifiers to a test of their hospitality (Miller, 1990, p. 120).

In Paris, the ban on representation that exists so strongly in Anglophone nations was considerably relaxed; from at least Gauthier's *Mademoiselle de Maupin* (1935) onwards, French literary culture was pleased to portray lesbians in more or less open terms. Verlaine and Rimbaud conducted their scandalous relationship in the public eye. The Napoleonic Code famously omitted same-sex relationships from the Criminal Code (such matters were left to the Police Code, but in Anglophone eyes that distinction tended to be lost). The very openness to the public appearance of sexual dissidence made Paris seem innately hypersexual to prudish American eyes. Paris, then, afforded not only the openness of a peep-show to anxious Babbitts and Puritans, but also a rogues' gallery of persons available for prurient speculation.

Moreover, Las Vegas itself has a Parisian pedigree; it is worth registering here the origins of the showgirl in cabarets such as the Moulin Rouge but most crucially at the Folies Bergère. Located in a more respectable arrondissement (the 9th) and catering to a self-consciously international and expensive crowd, the Folies Bergère specialised in various forms of nudity; Josephine Baker featured her banana skirt dancing and other routines in the venue's music hall revues. More than any other club, perhaps, the Folies Bergère offered the model pioneered in Vegas by the El Rancho casino in 1941.

Mention of Baker also calls up the history of African Americans in Paris, which inflected the ongoing history of the 'American colony' based in Paris. From the 1880s onward the expatriate community developed a division between the staid businessmen and respectable people who lived on the Right Bank and the raff-ish Bohemians and artists who quickly gravitated to the Left Bank, especially to Montparnasse in the 14th and 15th arrondissements; but Montmartre, at the north edge of the city limits proper, also flourished as a site of openly disreputable art-istry and entertainment. By far the most risky and déclassé area, Montmartre had been the site of the most influential early cabarets: Le Chat Noir opened in 1881, for instance, and Le Lapin Agile, transformed from its earlier incarnation as Cabaret des Assassins, rollicked along beside it in the 1890s. After 1919, Montmartre seemed especially hospitable to African-Americans, and the clubs became a centre for the per-formance of jazz. To take a significant case, Ada 'Bricktop' Smith, a mixed-race jazz performer from West Virginia, was performing in Paris from 1924 and quickly caught the eye of Cole Porter, who hired her to teach the Charleston and the Black Bot-tom to his friends in the 'smart set'. She prospered to such an extent that by 1929 she operated her own cabaret, Chez Bricktop, at 66 rue Pigalle in Montmartre.[13] Already overtly sexualised in white American ears because of its racial and social origins, jazz acquired a kind of hypersexual sophistication from its time in the Parisian cabarets. Indeed, that was part of its attraction to artists like Porter, who from the '20s onward participated in the creation of an urbane trans-Atlantic culture defined by riotous liv-ing and celebrity. What would become 'the jet set' and 'café society' was established in this convoluted milieu of the idle rich, dissipated nobility, Bohemians, artists, stranded émigrés and jazz musicians, with all of it celebrated by the new organs of mass media, such as radio or the Condé Nast magazines.

This is the world that Burrows and Porter wished to evoke and bowdlerize. Careful self-censoring was all the more crucial because of the way not only Hol-lywood but also Broadway was rapidly being incorporated into the new TV econ-omy. As a form of low-cost domestic entertainment, television was subject to more stringent official and unofficial standards than even film at the height of the noto-rious Hays Code. (Consider the ban on female navels, which led shows such as *I Dream of Jeannie* or the original *Star Trek* into peculiar costume designs to hide the offending umbilici.) Already in the early '50s, TV hosted innumerable stars from Vaudeville and the 1920s who necessarily cleaned up their acts to appeal to the folks gathered around the set in the living room. One reason for the success of a 'personality' such as Ed Sullivan was his weird, stodgy humourlessness (no double entendre could enter his head), always on hand to underwrite the blandest, most anodyne interpretations of stars' onscreen antics. Connotation indeed: the vast majority of the lubricious perversity that a good chunk of the cognoscenti knew about remained invisible to the mainstream, only showing up as a connotational *frisson* here and there. If Broadway still had more license – and licentiousness – than TV or Hollywood, as well as an arguably stronger claim, specifically, to *artistic* license at the height of Broadway's belief in the eminent domain of the integrated musical in its ongoing quest for higher artistic status, its commercial setting, as well as Burrows' political agenda, dictated a 'cleaner' version of Paris than history – even the history uncovered by his researchers – would indicate.

The Americanisation of *Can-Can*

Although surely to some extent the result of casting happenstance, the blend of Las Vegas and Paris that emerges in the film version of *Can-Can* functions for American audiences much like the depiction of Salzburg in the film version of *The Sound of Music*.[14] In both cases, the taint of Nazi association is papered over by familiarity, by the notion that what we are seeing, rescued from the 'bad Europe' of World War II, is a version of 'us', reassuring Americans then immersed in the 'Cold War' that there had been, after all, a Europe worth fighting for. This function seemingly sidesteps the important historical circumstance that allowed both Salzburg and Paris to survive the War more or less intact: their quick acquiescence to Nazi rule, supported (undoubtedly to much different degrees) by local sympathy for some of their aims. But if both Salzburg and Paris were cast as Nazi victims, Paris played that role more vividly during the War, both because it fell under threat of arms rather than political maneuvering and because the long-standing animosities between France and Germany had more bite, historically, than those between, for example, Austria and Germany. Indeed, the fall of Paris took on much of the character of feminine submission to the threat of masculine violence, making it an immediate and lasting symbol of Europe's need for rescue.

The latter association is reinforced throughout the film, especially in the sexualised violence simulated in 'Apache Dance', which depicts street thugs brutally abusing a woman as they fight over her, until she – betrayed even by her apparent allies – turns the tide, in the end stabbing the last of her attackers, who dies at her feet just as he is about to stab her with the same knife she used on him. This narrative dance occurs with much the same contours in both stage and film versions, although with a different character as lead dancer: Claudine (Gwen Verdon) on stage, and Simone (Shirley MacLaine) in the film. But the deployment and significance of the number is entirely different, quite apart from this recasting. In the stage show, the number is a self-contained scene, bracketed off as a 'novelty' and already described as 'fake' by Pistache in the previous scene (2–2–21), whereas in the film the number appears much earlier, when, without preamble, an *Apache* attacks Simone while she is in conversation with Philippe, grabbing her and tearing off her skirt, so as to create the shocking illusion of a genuine attack before the violence becomes more stylised and the movement more balletic. We are, if only briefly, invited to see the violence as real (28:35).

Undercurrents of violence and betrayal run throughout the film and are especially evident within the machinations of the love triangle. Philippe threatens both Simone and François with incarceration, if at different times. François tricks Simone by getting her drunk and talking her into performing a vulgar and scandalising number at a fancy party ('Come along with Me', sung much earlier on in the stage show). Simone then tricks François into assuming legal responsibility for the 'lascivious' dance she plans to stage in defiance of the law. And Philippe brings all of their behaviour back to the *Apache* context by assuming the character of a street thug in a last-ditch effort to win Simone, even if his imitation of Sinatra brings him closer to an American gangster than Parisian *Apache*.

The film's enhanced emphasis on sexualised violence, perhaps inevitably, reorients the film version towards relationships as such, which takes definitive form in the refashioning of the 'Garden of Eden' into the 'Story of Adam and Eve' (1:51:40). The ballet, which occurs near the end of the film instead of midway through as in the stage show, recasts the Snake, who originally represented Forrestier, as a female seductress, danced by Claudine, who after successfully tempting Eve turns her attention towards seducing Adam away from Eve.[15] The resulting triangle, itself a gender reversal from the film's main romantic triangle, devolves into a gender reversal of 'Apache Dance', supported by *Apache*-like behaviour from the formerly benign creatures (with related reversals; e.g. the rabbit walloping the fox). By the end of 'Adam and Eve', its parallel with 'Apache Dance' is obvious (in a way that would not have been possible in the stage show, where 'Garden of Eden' comes much earlier), as Eve drags a supine Adam upstage in direct recollection of key choreographic tropes from 'Apache Dance', highlighting the fact that Simone wins both conflicts.

If reorienting the film's emphasis towards relationships as such flows from the more basic reorientation towards Las Vegas, it also has a more obvious point of reference, already noted, in the Cinderella story of *Gigi*, from which it also borrows not only its prince and his main confidante (Louis Jourdan and Maurice Chevalier) but also the function of precious jewels as basic currency in what we might today think of as a courtesan economy.[16] The stage version of *Can-Can* had no place for this element, recently parodied in *Gentlemen Prefer Blondes*, and was in fact at great pains to make it clear that the dancers had a legitimate profession and were not being accused of prostitution despite the origin of the complaint from the 'League against Sidewalk Licentiousness' (renamed the 'League against Filthy Dancing' in the film; 1–1–5 and 17:00, respectively). In the wake of *Gigi*, the film version of *Can-Can* restores that economy, with François early on ostentatiously presenting a bejewelled garter to Simone while indicating that this is an ongoing practice between them, regarded as an exchange ('Oh, François! You'll never know how grateful I am!'/[to himself] 'Yes, I will' [11:45]), and with Philippe, much later, offering her a cat named the 'Duchess de Grimont', adorned with a 'diamond necklace' (2:01:35), just before François offers her a second bejewelled garter.[17]

That the film version of *Can-Can* was meant to cash in on the success of *Gigi* is of course well-known, but less explored is its relationship to *Playboy* and the still-nascent sexual revolution. *Playboy* first appeared in December 1953 with a cover and centrefold featuring Marilyn Monroe, who had just that summer enjoyed her definitive success as Lorelei Lee in the film version of *Gentlemen Prefer Blondes*, less than two months after the premiere of *Can-Can* on Broadway. She was thus a natural choice for Pistache in the film version of *Can-Can*, and she was in fact offered the role before MacLaine (Vogel, 2014, p. 191).[18] Had she accepted it, the film's connection to *Playboy* might have been more explicit, but the magazine's values are nevertheless quite vividly on display in the film, specifically in the latter's projection of a sophisticated 'swinger' as its male principal (newly invented for the film), its positioning of blatant feminine display as a form of Art (as already in the stage version), its encouragement of a more casual attitude towards sexuality (thus interpolating 'Just One of Those Things' and the added verse to 'Let's Do It'; see note 11), and its evocation of *Playboy*'s fundamental gambit of encouraging and celebrating the sexual liberation of women through their crudely systematic objectification.[19] It is in this regard that the film's redeployed songs play an especially important role, particularly those performed by Sinatra.

The choreography of Sinatra's version of 'C'est Magnifique' — a song that traces the beginning, lapsing, and rekindling of a single love affair — reshapes the song to suggest dalliances with three different lovers, gradually reconstituting the photograph being posed just before the song (with four dancers whose hairstyles subtly suggest those of Vegas showgirls) and culminating in Durnais breaking character ('Ring-a-ding-Ding-ding!') in response to Claudine's 'Mon amour' (23:40).[20] Even Forrestier's rehearsal, just before the song, of clichéd enticements proffered by Durnais's lifestyle plays a part in re-setting the song's purpose, while reinforcing that lifestyle's natural habitat as quintessentially Parisian ('wine from a lady's slipper, dawn in a strange bed, intoxicating intrigue, . . . romance in "Gay *Paris*"'; 21:35).

'Let's Do It', which is already designed to work well as a duet with each participant trying to outdo the other, is set up by François as an alternative to Simone's suggestion of marriage: 'Look, why should we get married and lose each other? Let's just be in love. It's more fun that way. Everybody does it' (1:02:30). Again, choreography is key: having lured her into the song, and into a progressively assertive danced interlude, he tangoes her into the boudoir, from which they shortly emerge, him disappointed, to sing a chorus probably added for the film (see note 11):

SIMONE [EMERGING FROM THE BOUDOIR]: The royal set *sans regret* did it,
FRANÇOIS [EMERGING AFTER HER, WRYLY]: And they considered it fun.
SIMONE [DANCING SEDUCTIVELY]: Marie Antoinette did it,
FRANÇOIS [STRIKING A POSE BY HER SIDE]: With or without Napoleon.

Significantly, Sinatra gets not only the lines most suggestive of casual sexual indiscretion (thus, also from this chorus: 'Mam'selles, every time they're short of rent, did it'), but also the earlier sophisticated turn of 'garçon, the shad roe' (1:02:40).

By having François sing 'It's All Right with Me' not to an anonymous streetwalker but to Claudine, whom he has told Paul he is 'saving for a rainy day' and with whom he has already flirted (after 'Maidens Typical of France' and during

'C'est Magnifique'), the sexual tension is already much elevated. In Sinatra's gorgeous, intimate rendering of the song, the movements are subtle but telling, especially apt for the filmic setting (1:18:20). He pours her a drink before the song, she lights his cigarette during it, they toast, he leaves the bar but she follows him to his table, placing one hand on his shoulder and the other over his, which he then lifts to her face before again taking her hand. As the song ends, they share a kiss that seems to suggest both goodbye and future promise. Conveniently, the lyrics in the final chorus also point to Vegas, as well as to their inevitable kiss:

> It's the wrong game with the wrong chips,
>> Though your lips are tempting, they're the wrong lips,
>> They're not her lips but they're such tempting lips

If Sinatra's songs allow him to embody the 'man about town', the sophisticate open to sexual adventure, Pistache's performances conform no less to *Playboy*'s sway. As she is stripped to her tights in 'Apache Dance', appears in a towel in a scene with Philippe, and dances 'nude' (with full-body tights) as Eve, she seems always on display. But she is also 'liberated', as sole proprietor of *Bal du Paradis* with two quite eligible suitors, holding her own against multiple male attackers in 'Apache Dance'

FIGURE 14.4   Frank Sinatra (as François Durnais) and Shirley MacLaine (as Simone Pistache) perform 'Let's Do It' in the 1960 film version of *Can-Can*.

Source: Photo provided by the editor.

and against both Snake and Adam in 'Adam and Eve', and – whatever the disastrous consequences for her betrothal to Philippe – delivering a saucy 'Come along with Me' that takes every opportunity to make the gender flip from the original tell, as she flirts with several men in the presence of their wives. Moreover, she even outdoes François in legal maneuvering, nearly leading to his disbarment and balancing the scales for his earlier manipulation of her.

But despite all this, the terms throughout belong to the men. In taking over 'Montmartre' as the opening song, François and Paul assert proprietorship of a private 'hunting ground'. All positions of official power – police, judges, lawyers – are held by men and, in the end, access to that power allows François to spirit Simone away from a potential re-blossoming of her relationship with Philippe through instigating her false arrest. It even matters that it is not Pistache in this version, but two men – two magistrates, in fact – who argue to 'Live and Let Live'. Critically, the failure of Pistache's 'Come Along', despite her bravura performance, comes down not just to issues of class deportment, but also to her presumption, as a woman singing as a man might (and did, in the stage show), albeit without the specifically gendered interjections of 'woof woof' for which the stage song was known.[21] While the *Gigi*–Cinderella story holds credibility almost to the end, despite Simone's (and, eventually, Philippe's) failures to surmount their class differences, its foreclosure is predetermined by the very presence of Sinatra in the cast, within a film that celebrates male prerogatives from beginning to end, without the softening touches of human frailty that the comic subplot offered in the stage version.

For *Can-Can*, Paris thus has multiple charms: as a realm in which prudishness does not keep sexuality apart from Art, and as a city that has not only learned to "Live and Let Live" but also, for the film version, provided viable models to show Americans how to break free of their Puritan prohibitions, symbolized first by its appeal to the sinful side of Broadway, but extended from there through Hollywood and Las Vegas in order to entice the kind of man who reads *Playboy*. For the film version, especially, Paris represents the eternal feminine of the *demi-monde*, the ideal playground for the sophisticated man and the quintessential town for such a man to be about. This greatest of all Old-World models of luxurious commodities, the home of newly revamped *flâneurisme*, was thus the perfect courtesan of hedonic dreams, endlessly available and accommodating. Its timeless charms, as *Can-Can* treats them, testify to the luminous spectacle of passions and their purchase.

Notes

* Verse to "I Love Paris," words and music by Cole Porter, sung by La Mome Pistache in *Can-Can* (Broadway, 1953). As given in *Feuer and Martin present Cole Porter's Can-Can*, Abe Burrows and Cole Porter, New York: Chappell & Co. Inc., 1953, 1954, pp. 102–103.
1 These reports and related material are preserved in the New York Public Library Archives & Manuscripts: Abe Burrows Papers, Box 25, Folders 1–15. Our thanks to the library personnel, especially Doug Reside, for facilitating access to these and other materials in this collection relating to the show, and to Zelda Knapp, who helped work through them. The information about Jane Avril (one of the era's most famous dancers) provided much basic information for the show, including the fact that in many venues women danced for free, at least at first, while earning their livings as seamstresses, laundresses (as in *Can-Can*), or

related trades; Avril herself married a painter, in parallel to *Can-Can*'s comic couple, dancer Claudine and sculptor Boris (F1). Toulouse-Lautrec was the most famous of the artists who frequented Montmartre during this period and so was apparently not researched beyond including an elaborate souvenir-style brochure detailing his life (F11). René Bérenger was longtime Vice-President of the French Senate, serving as President from 1894–97, just after the 1893 date of *Can-Can*'s action; Bérenger took part in the First National Congress against Pornography (1905) and authored a 'Practical Guide for Fighting Pornography', a lengthy document that Burrows's researchers tracked down in Paris and translated (F2 and F9). Besides typed notes, the research preserved in Box 25 of the Abe Burrows Papers includes several souvenir programmes (F6 and F10) and a special issue of *Le Crapouillot*, titled *La Sexualité: A Travers les Ages* (May 1950), which includes several articles, each on the histories of specific practices starting with prostitution (F4). Some of this research became the basis for articles in *The New York Times Magazine* (Skinner, 1952) and *The New Yorker* (Boal, 1952); that those articles and another on Toulouse-Lautrec were saved as press clippings (F15) strongly indicates that they were 'planted' as a kind of advance publicity for the show. Additionally, Burrows wrote a newspaper piece prior to the Philadelphia tryout in which he describes 'falling in love' with the research accounts of daily life, which he describes as 'translations of stories from the French papers of 1893'; he then relates his (surely feigned) surprise in learning 'that in the 90s in Paris, there was censorship' (Burrows, 1953, clipping from the Abe Burrows Papers, B27, F11).

2 Wariness about the show's politics seems the most plausible explanation for an unusual degree of advance secrecy surrounding its plot. Thus, in a clipping preserved in the Abe Burrows Papers announcing the Philadelphia tryout run (B27, F11), *The Evening Bulletin* reports 'For reasons best known to themselves . . . the entrepreneurs of *Can-Can* are being mighty chary of plot details of their new opus' (Harris, 1953). That the threat was indeed real, especially for playwrights, is reflected by the front page of the *New York Times* on the day before *Can-Can*'s Broadway première, which reported on Jerome Robbins's testimony at the McCarthy hearings (Kihss, 1953).

3 Regarding the 'marriage trope', see Knapp, 2005, p. 9; Altman, 1987, p. 50.

4 All dialogue quotations from *Can-Can* (stage show) are from the 1950s' working script (including handwritten corrections and changes) preserved in the Abe Burrows Papers, B23, F12. The *nom de guerre* of the character is undoubtedly a sly reference to La Môme Fromage, a hoydenish, openly lesbian cabaret performer who was the lover of legendary can-can dancer La Goulue [Louise Weber], called 'The Queen of Montmartre'. The couple were the subject of portraits by Toulouse-Lautrec.

5 While one might assume from the film version that dancers earning their livings as laundresses was a mere fancy or pretense, it was supported by research (see Note 1) and was to have been supported, as well, through eventually excised scenes in the laundry and songs that were unused or cut from the show ('Nothing to Do but Work', 'I Shall Positively Pay You Next Monday', 'Rub, Rub' ['Laundry Number'], and 'Her Heart Was in Her Work' [Abe Burrows Papers, B25 F21–23; see also Anon., undated]).

6 Aristide once had an 'I Am' song of his own in the opening scene – 'The Law', eventually cut – launched as an argument between him and Paul (Abe Burrows Papers, B25, F22).

7 In its original version, 'Live and Let Live' – preserved in the Abe Burrows Papers, B25, F22 (lyrics) and F23 (sheet music) – was also multi-lingual, ending with the song's key phrase rendered in French: 'Live and let live, and repeat now and then:/ *Tes affaires sont tes affaires et mes affaires sont les miennes'*.

8 All timings for the film version of *Can-Can* are derived from the 2007 DVD release from Marquee 20th Century Fox Musicals, which is also the source for transcribed quotations.

A possibly related change concerns the year of the show's action. *Can-Can* was originally set in 1893 – exactly 60 years before its première and the year of the second and most notorious of the *Bals des Quat'z Arts* – but the film changes the setting to 1896. While the specific rationale for this change may be unclear, it does deflect the scandal associated with the earlier date (for those who might be aware of that history) while remaining plausible historically.

9 See documents in the Abe Burrows Papers B23 F13 and B24 F1.

10 Prowse was actually South African, though then working in Paris. But her foreignness is sufficiently palpable, and her spoken lines sufficiently minimal, that she easily passes as French by Hollywood standards. Although Pistache and Durnais are ostensibly French, neither MacLaine nor Sinatra attempts a French accent, and Durnais seems to take the position of an outsider in arguing with Forrestier: 'But how can you possibly ignore love when so many of your countrymen have died for it?' (21:55).

11 Besides this chorus not being part of the original lyric (Porter, 1983, pp. 72–73), it seems too inept to have been written by Porter, given its lyrical awkwardness ('Parliament pleasure bent did it') and, in the part quoted in the text below, its inelegance in referring to the 'royal set' after the song opens with 'the best upper sets' and its hilarious historical lapse in linking Marie Antoinette and Napoleon. The supposition that this chorus was added specifically for *Can-Can* is supported not only by its references to the film's Parisian setting (reinforcing the substituted lyrics already noted), but also by its more explicit references to casual sex, which Porter's original only hinted at (thus 'it' is 'considered . . . fun' or done when 'short of rent'), and its support for the number's choreographed narrative (see subsequent discussion).

12 For more on the fascinating career of Mercedes de Acosta, see Cohen, 2013.

13 In later years Bricktop asserted that Porter had written 'Miss Otis Regrets' especially for her. Opinions differ on her claim, but what matters most is that she felt entitled to make it. For additional perspectives on Americans in Paris during the '20s and '30s, see Green, 2014; Morris, 2016, pp. 73–85.

14 Regarding Salzburg and *The Sound of Music*, see Knapp, 2004, pp. 133–144) and Knapp, 2005, pp. 230–239.

15 Adam is not even identified in the list of characters in 'The Garden of Eden' until revivals staged after the film. The Snake was originally danced by Bert May.

16 This economy is delicately on display in Colette's novella *Gigi* (1944), where the title character is being trained as a courtesan by her grandmother and great-aunt. Of particular importance in this process are lessons on appraisal – how to judge jewelry and metalwork, for instance. Courtesans were not paid in cash, but in expensive gifts. (Lorelei Lee's diamonds in *Gentlemen Prefer Blondes* are another product of the courtesan economy.) The primary remnant in the film musical of *Gigi* comes from the pointed comments about pearls being 'dipped' to improve their appearance.

17 The Duchesse de Grammont – the obvious referent for the film's 'Duchess of Grimont' – was a prominent *salonnière* and contemporary of famous courtesan Madame du Barry, referred to just earlier in the revised verse to 'Just One of Those Things' [1:45:45]); both Grammont and du Barry were executed during the Reign of Terror. Yet another reference to the role of jewels in this 'courtesan economy' occurs in the lead-up to 'Just One of Those Things', as Simone's letter to Philippe, read out by Paul, ends 'PS, this is the first piece of jewelry I ever returned to a man' (1:45:15).

18 Had Monroe accepted the role of Simone Pistache, *Can-Can* might have been a very different film, but without directly affecting the basic 'Frenchness' of the film as discussed above.

19 The attention to a highly-sexualised consumerist lifestyle is part of an ongoing project in this era of Hollywood film-making. See Worland, 2018, pp. 156–168.

20 This narrative is supported in part through the convention of extending the song by repeating the second half or the chorus, which in this case conveniently adds a second episode in which the 'loved one drifts away'.

  The flash photography featured in this scene is central to the plot of both stage and screen versions (to provide legal documentation of the can-can's performance), and its historical accuracy was researched through direct inquiries to Eastman Kodak. The reply from the Curator of George Eastman House, dated 5 January 1953, explains: 'Flash powder was invented in Germany in 1887 and was almost immediately adopted for press photography so Mr. Burrows need have no fear of anachronism' (Abe Burrows Papers B26, F8).

21 A review from the Philadelphia preview predicts the song will become known as the 'Woof Woof' song (Sennenderfer, 1953).

References

Note: the 'Abe Burrows Papers' are stored at the New York Public Library Archives & Manuscripts. The authors refer to a number of boxes (B) and folders (F) in this collection, especially Box 25, Folders 1–15; Box 26, Folder 8; and Box 27, Folder 11. When an item of the following list derives from this source, it is marked in square brackets at the end of the entry.

Altman, R. (1987) *The American Film Musical*. Bloomington: Indiana University Press.
Anon. (undated) 'Can-Can: Original Broadway Production,' www.sondheimguide.com/porter/cancan.html, accessed 12 October 2019.
Boal, S. (1952) 'The Girls of Paris,' *The New Yorker*, July, pp. B[25], F[15].
Burrows, A. (1953) '*Can-Can* – Musical Genuinely French in Spirit (Burrows Says),' *Clipping*, pp. B[27], F[11].
Can-Can. (1960). Directed by W. Lang. DVD. Los Angeles: Marquee 20th Century Fox Musicals.
Cohen, L. (2013) *All We Know: Three Lives*. New York: Palgrave-Macmillan.
Green, N. L. (2014) *The Other Americans in Paris: Businessmen, Countesses, Wayward Youth, 1880–1941*. Chicago: University of Chicago Press.
Harris, H. (1953) 'Living Theater: Cole Porter-Abe Burrows Musical, Odets Drama Open Here Tomorrow,' *The Evening Bulletin*, 22 March, pp. B[27], F[11].
Kihss, P. (1953) 'Robbins, Showman, Admits He Was Red: Dance Creator Says He Quit in 47 – Lists Playwrights Among Party Members,' *The New York Times*, 6 May, p. 1, https://timesmachine.nytimes.com/timesmachine/1953/05/06/issue.html, accessed 12 October 2019.
Knapp, R. (2005) *The American Musical and the Formation of National Identity*. Princeton: Princeton University Press.
———. (2004) 'History, *The Sound of Music*, and Us,' *American Music*, 22, pp. 133–144.
Maruta, N. (2014) *L'Incroyable histoire du cancan*. Paris: Parigramme.
Miller, D. A. (1990) 'Anal Rope,' *Representations*, 32, p. 120.
Morris, M. (2016) 'Lists of Louche Living: Music in Cole Porter's Social World,' in D. Randel, M. Shaftel and S. Forscher Weiss (eds.) *A Cole Porter Companion*. Urbana, Chicago and Springfield: University of Illinois Press, pp. 73–85.
Porter, C. (1983) *The Complete Lyrics of Cole Porter* (R. Kimball, ed.). New York: Alfred A. Knopf.
———. (1953) 'I Love Paris,' in A. Burrows and C. Porter (eds.) *Feuer and Martin Present Cole Porter's Can-Can*. New York: Chappell & Co. Inc., pp. 102–103.
Schwartz, V. R. (2007) 'The Belle Epoque That Never Ended: Frenchness and the Can-Can Film of the 1950s,' in *It's So French! Hollywood, Paris, and the Making of Cosmopolitan Film Culture*. Chicago: University of Chicago Press, pp. 8–55.
Sennenderfer, R. E. P. (1953) 'Can-Can,' *The Evening Bulletin*, 24 March, pp. B[27], F[11].
Skinner, C. O. (1952) 'Paris in the 90's: Guys and Dolls,' *The New York Times Magazine*, 2 March, pp. B[25], F[15].
Variety Staff. (1959) 'Can-Can,' *Variety*, 31 December, https://variety.com/1959/film/reviews/can-can-1200419730/, accessed 30 September 2019.
Vogel, M. (2014) *Marilyn Monroe: Her Films, Her Life*. Jefferson, NC: McFarland & Co.
Worland, R. (2018) 'Original Swingers: Hollywood's Postwar Bachelor-Pad Cycle,' *Journal of Popular Film and Television*, 46(3), pp. 156–168.

15

ART, ARTIFICE AND ARTIFICIALITY

The various versions of the Musical *Gigi*

Olaf Jubin

'I don't understand – they're *Parisians*!': a Rehash of *My Fair Lady*?

How close is too close?

It has become customary in film studies to categorise the 1958 MGM musical *Gigi* as a near relation to *My Fair Lady* (1956) – that earlier smash hit by Alan Jay Lerner and Frederick Loewe. Various scholars have detailed where they detect similarities in the works' narrative, characters, score, song placement and setting (Mast, 1987, p. 289; Harvey, 1989, p. 145: Levy, 2009, p. 304; Griffin, 2010, p. 212), to the point where some have denigrated *Gigi* as a mere 'imitation' (Gottfried, 1973, p. 191).

The endless comparisons between the two musicals are not surprising, considering that they were initiated by the movie studio itself. It was the film's producer Arthur Freed who decided to stress the screen musical's kinship to the still-running stage success as 'the best way to showcase *Gigi*' (Harvey, 1989, p. 143). The film's director, Vincente Minnelli, found this tendency to draw analogies bewildering: 'But they were completely different stories, as I saw them, the one we were involved in showing the manners and morals of the French aristocracy at the time' (Minnelli, 1975, p. 310). For Minnelli, who won an Oscar for *Gigi*, 'the story's attitude was French' (Minnelli, 1975, p. 306), by which he meant that in contrast to the 'antiseptic' *My Fair Lady*, the later work 'teemed with nuance and possibility' in regard to sexual relations (Minnelli, 1975, p. 317). Although the film may have packaged the subject – as Minnelli puts it – 'discreetly' (p. 317), it *does* approach it, not least through its setting, sensual décor and mise-en-scène.

How important the backdrop – Paris at the beginning of the 20th century – is for the narrative is underlined by the personification of the city in the novel;[1] the metropolis appears less a location than a mind-set that observes and judges every step of its more prestigious citizens. The capital's obsession with the private affairs of the rich and famous is given physical evidence in publications such as the specialised weekly, *Paris en amour* (Colette, 2001, p. 27).

For Alan Jay Lerner, 'Paris was as much a character as Gaston and Gigi themselves' (Lerner, 1994, p. 156), which is why the screenwriter-lyricist insisted that the songs for the movie were written in the French capital, because 'unquestionably it was bound to help the atmosphere of the score' (Lerner, 1994, p. 148). Producer Freed in turn 'was dead set against manufacturing France at the studio and decided to shoot all of the exteriors and some of the interiors in Paris and the surrounding area' (Fordin, 1975, p. 459); the city was expected to also inspire Minnelli who was sent to Paris well in advance of actual filming to scout locations (Levy, 2009, p. 297).

With his creative team, the director accomplished something remarkable; in the words of Farran Nehme, he 'made Paris look even more beautiful than it is' (Self-Styled Siren, 2014). The *fin de siècle* was a preferred period of Minnelli's, who imagines it here and in other films such as *Meet Me in St. Louis* (1944), as 'a utopian space of vivid colours, deviant eroticism, and leisure time' (Hext, 2014, p. 69). Yet in *Gigi*, the director never lost his critical faculties – he did not succumb to nostalgia, but instead 'scrubbed the sentimentality with a bracing astringent' (Als, 2015, p. 91). Minnelli presents the world of the Parisian *haut monde* of 1900 as 'one of ostentatious artifice' (Hext, 2014, p. 52). It has even been argued that 'artifice is *Gigi*'s one and true subject' (Levy, 2009, p. 206) – and what genre is better suited to reveal the unnatural and calculated than the musical, 'an unrealistic form of expression' (Lerner, 1994, p. 142), which is by its very nature stylised?

In fact, an intriguingly strong sense of both artifice and artificiality imbues all three major incarnations of the musical *Gigi*: the 1958 film, the 1973 stage musical and the 2015 Broadway revival. Yet the form of these stratagems and ruses varies overtly from version to version, partly in response to changes in the movie's reputation. With the help of a carefully calibrated colour scheme, Minnelli depicts a stilted society averse to bodily spontaneity. When the film musical moved to Broadway 15 years later, the creative team was at pains to make up for the loss of the movie's location shooting and French cast; its attempts to replace the sensuous ambiance of the screen version with several additions to the Oscar-winning score only underlined that the property seemed contrived outside its 'natural' habitat. Lastly, the 2015 rewrite of the stage musical overlays the story with a 'modern sensibility' that goes against the core of the source material and thus creates its very own type of disingenuousness.

'In this fixed, fixed world': rigidity vs physical abandon

The year 1900 not only marks the beginning of the 20th century, but also the very end of the Victorian period when European society has become fossilised and industrialisation has started to encroach on all areas of life – in just one generation, Honoré Lachaille's 'prince of love' has been replaced in the public eye by the 'sugar prince' Gaston – a lothario praised for his skills at seduction is succeeded by somebody who is celebrated for adding sweetness to life via a processed product. In spite of his 'scandalous' behaviour, Honoré's nephew does not really have the reck-lessness and daring of the older relative – even his attire is less audacious than his uncle's as Madame Alvarez notes when complimenting Gaston on his suit: 'Just the sort of thing Honoré used to wear. A bit more conservative, perhaps' [15:12 min.[2]].

The movie opens in the Bois de Boulogne where Honoré introduces the audi-ence to Parisian society and their mores. What is noticeable straight away is the languid way the visitors of the park move about – they stroll or ride in carriages – which is met by Minnelli's measured camera movements. These are flâneurs, both male and female, taking in the environment and each other in regular paces. Yet there is one exception to this gathering of town folk at its more proper and deco-rous: dashing about in the background are little girls, enjoying both the outdoors and the chance to run around. The onlookers in the park seem less to be sitting calmly than petrified into posture. That this exquisitely clad upper class is in danger of ceasing to move altogether and to fall victim to *rigor mortis* is wittily illustrated in the two scenes at Maxim's where the patrons actually *do* freeze.

The striking contrast between adult propriety and the uninhibitedness of chil-dren is underlined by the eponymous character: we first see Gigi at the centre of a game of tag. The young girl's complaint that she doesn't understand 'The Parisians' in their obsession with the other sex sees her traversing the city with large strides, waving her arms about in irritation in clear contrast to the elegant miniscule move-ments of society's elite. Aunt Alicia is exasperated by Gigi's lack of lady-like bearing and gestures, but the sequence in Trouville only reinforces the girl's enjoyment of her own physicality. Here, Minnelli crosscuts between a society couple playing tennis and the two Parisians doing the same [57:10–57:52 min.]. While the former observes strict gender norms – the woman is not meant to exert herself and thus is not prepared to move even one inch to the left or right to hit the ball – Gigi com-petes for every single point, racing around the tennis court; she tries her hardest to be a real opponent to Gaston. Yet there is no question which couple has more fun, and that extends to the viewer.

French society is bound to deform flexible young girls once they reach a certain age as is emphasised by the stilted movements of the guests at Maxim's, especially the girl in yellow sitting next to Gaston on the left side of the frame [32:58–33:24 min.], and the unnatural deportment of the model at the dressmaker's where Alicia and her niece shop for clothes [68:56–69:38 min.]. It is this overwrought control of the body that sophisticated society prizes: 'Gigi has to learn how not to be natural, how to calculate her movements and judge the meaning of each gesture' (Elsaesser, 2009, p. 94). Throughout the movie, Leslie Caron beautifully modulates her body language, subtly delineating the journey from gawky teenager to potential mistress with perfect posture. But even at the end of this process Gigi does not possess the stiffness of the typical Parisian society dame.[3]

The lack of traditional dance numbers in *Gigi* has been highlighted by scholars (Mast, 1987, p. 289)[4] and by the director himself, who argued: 'Since Gigi was essentially a dramatic story, there was no reason to mount production numbers' (Minnelli, 1975, p. 313). 'The Night They Invented Champagne' possibly comes closest, but even this burst of merriment is limited: it doesn't feature any complicated steps since two of the actors (Louis Jourdan and Hermione Gingold) aren't trained dancers, so only Caron gets to show off some can-can kicks. Once again, it is Gigi who exerts herself the most. The quickstep was staged by Charles Walters, who maintains the movement patterns established by Minnelli; consequently, the action is limited to the private sphere (Mamita's living room). As was his custom, Minnelli uses one long take with neither the action nor the actors ever leaving the frame.

The film comes full circle when we return to the Bois in the final sequence; that the continuous game of love will continue is emphasised by the girls playing Badminton in the background of the frame in a visual echo of the Trouville tennis game.

Another attractive feature that – although also not encouraged by the French fashionable milieu – attracts the opposite sex, is full-throated laughter. It is telling that Honoré twice abandons his plans for a *tête-à-tête* with a much younger woman when he hears Mamita chuckle with merriment, first on the beach and then on the terrace. Lack of inhibition – both when exerting your body and when succumbing to a fit of hilarity – of course, also has sexual connotations. The rush of instant enjoyment, of letting go and of reacting spontaneously without consideration of what others think are all elements that the Parisian affairs of the heart do not allow – they are conducted with calculation and with both eyes on public perception.

'I never want monochrome again': colours in *Gigi*

For Alan Jay Lerner, Minnelli's genius 'lies in his faultless sense of style' (Lerner, 1994, p. 147). This style is on ample display in *Gigi* – as conceived by the director and his extraordinary design team, led by costumier Cecil Beaton, the musical offers 'the best kind of sensory overload' (Griffin, 2010, p. 216). The sets and costumes of the 1958 film are testament to Minnelli's 'singular preoccupation with bright, striking colours' (Hext, 2014, p. 60). Yet in contrast to many other works of the director such as *Yolanda and the Thief* (1945) and *Lust for Life* (1956), which feature whole sequences dominated by yellow (Hext, 2011), Minnelli's favourite colour plays no major part in *Gigi*.

He also goes against what one might expect by steering clear of the city's most famous landmarks in exterior shots, thus avoiding visual clichés; even the Eiffel Tower is only seen from below. According to *Gigi*'s screenwriter, Minnelli wanted to showcase 'the green of Paris – the Parks, the trees, the gardens' (Lerner, 1994, p. 157). However, the colour only appears in both outdoor and indoor scenes via flowers, plants and trees. Otherwise its conspicuous absence in both costumes and décor emphasises how far Parisian society in 1900 is removed from nature.[5]

Thomas Elsaesser has interpreted the film's colour symbolism as 'a story of degradation, with Gigi's red and green becoming a merely fashionable mauve and pink'

TABLE 15.1 Colour Scheme for the Costumes in *Gigi* (1958)

Character	Main Colour(s)	Additional Colour(s)
Gigi	shades of dark blue white	red black
Mamita	black	white
Gaston	shades of beige and brown light grey	dark blue black (for evening wear) white (shirts)
Honoré	shades of beige and brown	red light grey black (for evening wear) white (shirts)
Alicia	shades of pink	black light blue dark blue beige white (lace)
Liane	powder blue brown	[multicoloured]

(Elsaesser, 2009, p. 94). I would like to offer an alternative reading of how their clothes and surroundings characterise the protagonists. Before going into details, it should be pointed out that in 1900 specific items of clothing were *de rigeur* in certain situations, and so a number of design decisions complement the dominant colour scheme without undermining it. For instance, men of the upper class mostly wear white shirts as well as black tailcoats when going out in the evening, while Aunt Alicia's wealth is displayed in the various pieces of expensive white lace she wears.

During her jewellery classes, Gigi's aunt displays one of her most cherished possessions – a flawless emerald, one of the rare ones to show a ray of another colour, darting about deep within the green. What makes the stone so priceless is 'that miracle of elusive blue' [21:54 min.],[6] a line which is later repeated when Gigi admires the emerald bracelet Gaston has chosen as a gift for their first outing in society.

Throughout the film, hues of dark blue are mostly employed for its eponymous heroine. On the one hand the movie thus equates Gigi with a valuable gem, to be bought and/or gifted, but on the other hand it gives her the status of one of nature's most precious creations, a collectible to be treasured for its exquisite beauty, more than just as a decorative ornament.[7] Gigi's costumes often combine dark blue and white. We first spot her wearing the Scottish dress – dominated by red, but also featuring white and blue – to which Gaston is so partial. However, when the girl is sent off to her weekly lessons with Aunt Alicia, she puts on a Prussian blue coat, which she also sports during 'The Parisians'.[8] Another prominent garment is her navy blue sailor dress; Mamita mends it during Gaston's first visit to her flat; it later makes another appearance in the scene featuring 'The Night They Invented

Champagne'. Gigi's bathing costume is blue with some white stripes; at the dress-maker's she is clothed in a berry blue skirt and white blouse. She wears a similar combination – white blouse and (midnight) blue skirt with matching small bows on the blouse and a big bow in her hair – when she discusses with Gaston the terms of their relationship. We next see her preparing for her big night out with her new suitor in a white (night?) dress with Persian blue flowers as she implores 'Say a Prayer for Me Tonight'.

Apart from the opening sequence there are only three scenes where Gigi does not wear something in a dark blue: when she plays tennis and frolics on the beach in Trouville, she is clad in summery white. Her first adult dress is also completely white; it may be less the cut of the creation with its high collar that stuns Gaston, but its colour: it not only speaks of her virginal innocence, but also hints at mar-riage, both topics which are bound to make the bachelor uncomfortable. Finally, the stunning gown she puts on for her date with Gaston is white with black feath-ers on the sleeves. This colour combination twins her with Mamita on the terrace in Trouville and suggests that Gigi could also wind up on her own, once the affair with Gaston is over, with wistful memories and a few regrets.

That Gaston is the perfect partner for the girl is already implied at the beginning of the movie: during his first scene he changes from his red dinner jacked into a

FIGURE 15.1 Gigi (Leslie Caron) stuns Gaston (Louis Jourdan) in her first adult dress, while her grandmother (Hermione Gingold) looks on.

Source: Photo provided by the editor.

midnight blue one, thus following the colour shift already observed with Gigi. Later, the 'sugar prince' wears a royal blue suit celebrating his 'first suicide'. Gaston who usually is clothed in beige, brown or bluish-grey suits, chooses to come to his masked ball as a black and white *pierrot*, a clear outsider to the colourful proceedings. The only other people to wear black and white (or rather white and black) are Mme Alvarez and Gigi, which underlines the extraordinary status of both: Mamita confirms that she was unusually principled for a courtesan during 'I Remember It Well', while Gigi proves at Maxim's how well she can render the services of a courtesan, only to make Gaston realise that his feelings for her go beyond those for a mistress.

The final moment to associate Gaston with the 'elusive blue' of a prized jewel occurs right after he has dragged a bewildered Gigi back to her apartment; he leaves the flat in a daze and – in a visual reprise of the title song – takes another walk to investigate his feelings. On this occasion, it is night-time; the sky is of the darkest blue and the cobblestones and façades glitter like blue gemstones. Our last glimpse at the couple show Gigi in pink and Gaston in brown, indicating that – their love story brought to a satisfying close – they have finally entered the world of their aunt and uncle, respectively; the couple must now move aside for another generation to be hit by Cupid's arrows. But although Gigi has followed Alicia's trajectory of upward social mobility, a huge sapphire brooch symbolises that even as a young wife she has retained her uniqueness.

The supporting characters of the older generation are usually always dressed in the same colours, with a few noticeable exceptions: Mamita wears black, Alicia is clothed in shades of pink[9] and Honoré's world – both his suits and bedroom – are dominated by beige and browns. The one occasion when the latter appears in something more striking is during Gaston's costume ball, which his uncle attends as a red devil – a fittingly eye-catching and dramatic attire for an extravagant festivity where Honoré tries to live up to his notorious youth. It is in Trouville that Mme Alvarez exchanges her black dress for a white one with a black bow and white hat with black hatband, a combination which foreshadows the creation Gigi will sport to Maxim's. Here, white serves as a visual reminder of the marriage that Honoré, hopelessly in love with Mamita, contemplated and then fled from; it triggers their song of nostalgic memorising, 'I Remember It Well'.

Throughout the movie, the colour most consistently associated with Alicia is pink, variations of which, including fuchsia, mauve and rosé, can be found in her wardrobe, scarves, furniture and bedroom wallpaper. When she hears of Gigi's refusal to become Gaston's mistress her sky blue jacket twins her with Liane (see below) and the world of constantly changing sexual relationships – notice the cornflower blue curtains and the occasional azure dress at the Palais de Glace where the younger courtesan's affair with her skating instructor is displayed for all to see.

Only twice is Alicia's apparel dominated by dark colours; both mark important turning points in the narrative: firstly, when she announces to her sister her plan to prepare Gigi for a liaison with Gaston. This is the moment when the siblings recognise how high their protégé might ascend and so, fittingly, both of them wear dark blue, with Mamita in an indigo cloak and gloves in the same hue but in a lighter shade, and

FIGURE 15.2   A song of wistful memories: Mamita (Hermione Gingold) and Honoré (Maurice Chevalier) perform 'I Remember It Well'.

Source: Photo provided by the editor.

Alicia in a dress that combines a bright pink with black and navy blue stripes. Secondly, on the extraordinary occasion of Alicia leaving her apartment to intervene on Gaston's behalf, thus appearing in public, her Prussian blue gown (trimmed with red and lace) signals to whoever sees Gigi's aunt her elevated social standing as a famed courtesan – a singular gem to be appreciated by those in the know.

The dresses of Liane d'Exelmans attest that she fits perfectly into the world of Honoré and Alicia with its unwritten rules on how to conduct your life as one long series of love affairs. She wears brown at the Palais de Glace[10] and powder blue when she continues her tryst at the inn, while the elaborate gown she has chosen for Maxim's is a rather overpowering riot of black, yellow, purple and strawberry. In Minnelli's refined world that combination comes across as positively garish – additional proof (if proof were needed) that Liane is a very different breed of courtesan from the always impeccably dressed Alicia.

'Thank heaven for little boys': examples of arrested development

Rick Altman has shown conclusively how the society depicted in *Gigi* is strictly organised according to gender – a rigid distinction that is set up right from the opening line of the movie ('Bonjour Monsieur, Bonjour Madame') and then straight away is confirmed by its opening number, 'Thank Heaven for Little Girls' (Altman, 1989, pp. 31–22). The film's dual-focus editing continually 'reinforces the notion that men and women alike play predetermined parts in an already written scenario' (Altman, 1989, p. 24).

For Altman, Gigi and Gaston also signify another contrast since '*she* is a child and *he* is a man' (Altman, 1989, p. 25; emphasis in the original). I would like to question this particular reading. While the movie presents 'little girls', spearheaded by Gigi, in Honoré's words as 'the future', it more or less completely ignores their male equivalents, who are conspicuously absent.[11] But then, can either Gaston or his uncle count as truly grown-up? Based on their behaviour, it seems more apt to classify them both as 'little boys'.

In the tones of a mopey teenager, the younger Lachaille complains that in spite of all his possibilities 'the world is round, but everything on it is flat'. Gaston may bring champagne and duck as presents, but at Gigi's apartment he stuffs himself with biscuits and caramels. Like a kid at a grown-up party, he falls asleep in the middle of his own festivities. Just as his nephew is easily swayed by both Gigi and her grandmother, Honoré is quickly distracted from his pursuit of potential love objects by one burst of laughter from Mamita; like a puppy, he loses interest in whatever he was about to do and refocuses his attention. The two bachelors also share a teenage insecurity about their masculinity, always fearful of being replaced in their lovers' affections by a physically stronger and thus more 'virile' specimen: working class he-men who usually gain access to the bored upper classes as instructors of leisure pursuits like skating or swimming.[12]

In his overview of how the French are portrayed in Hollywood movies, Pierre Verdaguer comes to the conclusion that, in most American films, the female population of France is shown in a more positive light: 'Unlike French males, French women do not need to be redeemed' (Verdaguer, 2004, p. 446). *Gigi* could serve as a prime example of this stance; for Minnelli the former and future cocottes at the centre of his narrative may defy traditional morals, but it is these women who with their style and standards outsmart the immature males naïve enough to play with them.

'Paris is cardboard again': Hollywood becomes Broadway

One of the biggest challenges when adapting the movie musical *Gigi* to the stage – the first ever such transfer – was how to make up for the loss of the location shooting that gave the 1958 film such distinction. Yet it wasn't just the sun-drenched 'real' backdrop that set the movie apart; its small cast of eight may not have been entirely 'authentic', but it undoubtedly had a special flair in being wholly *European*: in addition to the three Gallic leads and a fourth French actor (Jacques Bergerac) in a supporting role, there were three English thespians (Hermione Gingold, Isabel Jeans and John Abbott as Honoré's servant Manuel) as well as one exiled Hungarian (Eva Gabor).

The 1973 Broadway ensemble was made up of musical theatre stalwarts like Alfred Drake and Maria Karnilova, four-time Oscar nominee Agnes Moorehead and 28-year-old Karin Wolfe in the title role, of whom not much more was heard. (The cast recording reveals her as no more than serviceable.) The only non-American in the cast was British actor Daniel Massey as Gaston who returned to

FIGURE 15.3 *Gigi* moves to Broadway: Karin Wolfe as the eponymous character and Daniel Massey as Gaston in the 1973 New York production, the first ever screen-to-stage transfer of a Hollywood musical.

Source: Photo courtesy of Photofest NYC.

the Great White Way ten years after playing the male lead in another play-turned-musical, *She Loves Me* (1963).

Lerner and Loewe contributed seven new songs to the stage version, three of which – 'All about Gaston', 'Da Da Da Da' and 'Everything French Is Better' – were cut before the New York opening (Suskin, 1999, pp. 8–9), while the rest are mostly not on par with the best of Lerner and Loewe or, indeed, the original score.

Instead of the real Bois de Boulogne, the Broadway musical opens in 'the Pre-Catelan Restaurant in the Bois' (*Gigi*, 1973, p. 1). In an obvious attempt to reassure the audience that the stage production *will* manage to recreate the flair of the French capital, Honoré leads the ensemble in 'Paris Is Paris Again', a number that was added during the try-out in San Francisco to give audience favourite Drake another chance to shine (Suskin, 1999, p. 9). The song offers verses and internal rhymes of explicit lasciviousness, all in synch with the less prudish and prohibitive United States of the early 1970s, referencing 'the rooster in search of the hen', 'the sweet/Intertwining of women and men', and promising a 'spicely, vicely', 'gallicly, phallicly', 'gaudily, bawdily/Physically,/Aph-er-o-disically/ Paris' (Gigi, 1973, pp. 1–4A-25–1–4B-25). Maybe because the creative team was painfully aware that recreating any 'real' French-ness on stage was impossible, the 1973 stage adaptation ends Act One with the perplexing 'I Never Want to Go Home Again'. In a work so closely associated with the French metropolis it seems inapposite to have the female protagonist praise the seaside at expense of the city. This and the tepid critical reception of the number might explain the surprising decision not to include it on the Broadway Cast Recording – cuts to the musical material when preserving a theatrical score usually involve reprises or songs by minor characters, not the Act One finale, especially when performed by the eponymous heroine.

In New York, the show struggled to make the small-scale story at its centre emerge on the enormous stage of Broadway's biggest theatre, the Uris (now the Gershwin). The full-voiced delivery of the score, especially by the male leads, also results in a loss of intimacy. The unaffected intonations in the movie, often close to the microphone, were more apt for a Parisian society that doesn't shy away from extravagant gestures but is not given to exuberance. In spite of 'atmospheric settings by Oliver Smith, costumes by Oliver Messel, new orchestrations by Irwin Kostal' (Jablonski, 1996, p. 168), the true spirit of the French capital proved elusive, as Douglas Watt confirmed: 'But the magic and, more particularly, Paris have all but disappeared' (Watt, 1973, p. 190). What was missing was the secure hand of Minnelli, whose singular 'touch' (Jablonski, 1996, p. 261) had imbued the movie with that most elusive of qualities, the one which simply cannot be manufactured – charm. The theatrical *Gigi* limped along for 103 performances, before closing on 10 February 1974; although it was re-staged once in a while, it never became a staple of the musical theatre repertoire.

FIGURE 15.4   What goes around, comes around: Louis Jourdan, the former Gaston, playing Honoré in the 1984–1985 national tour of *Gigi*, which featured Lisa Howard as the title character.

Source: Photo by Richard Brodzeller, provided by the editor.

'It's a whore': *Gigi* turns from screen classic to improper intellectual property

The 1944 novella *Gigi*, Colette's last published piece of fiction, became the most popular of all the author's works (Davies, 1961, p. 100), maybe because for once 'the bleak erotic wisdom that suffuses most of [Colette's] writing is filtered, in *Gigi*, through a gaze of nostalgia for quaint French naughtiness' (Thurman, 2015). Yet that naughtiness – after all, the story revolves around a young girl being trained to become a courtesan – caused MGM a lot of headaches, since everybody involved with the making of the 1958 movie was aware of the potential problems the source material might encounter with the Hays Production Office. *Gigi*'s arduous way to the screen, involving several years of negotiations with the censorship institution, have been chronicled in detail (Fordin, 1975, pp. 454–456). But as a reward for their efforts, the creative team had an enormous hit on their hands. The 'biggest moneymaker of all the Minnelli-Freed collaborations' (Harvey, 1989, p. 139) swept the Academy Awards and won eight of the coveted statuettes.

Gigi is the only one of Colette's heroines to be granted a happy ending; but what Nicole Ward Jouve describes as 'a fairy tale fate' (Jouve, 1987, p. 79), has irked many a viewer. It is difficult to pinpoint the exact moment when the movie first drew the ire of 'well-meaning', 'progressive' cultural critics, predominantly in the United States. Over the years, more and more 'flaws' of the movie were highlighted, starting with Honoré's paean 'Thank Heaven for Little Girls' which was retrospectively attacked for notions of paedophilia, while the movie itself was accused of promoting teenage prostitution (Weinman, 2015, p. 57). The age difference between Gigi and Gaston was also questioned, with the former labelled 'jailbait' (Thurman, 2015).

The first stirrings of these resentments may have been formulated by Minnelli scholars; it took several years longer for them to be propagated in popular media. As early as 1993, James Naremore expressed his disdain for the movie: in his book on the director, he refused to discuss *Gigi* in detail, because the film 'strikes me as a patently sexist fantasy about "little girls"' (Naremore, 1993, p. 5). Then in the mid-2010s, several journalists publicly directed their indignation against the movie, with Kate Arthur, editor of *Buzzfeed*, denigrating it as 'the creepiest, most paedophiliac movie ever to win Best Picture', and critic Andrew Parker calling it a 'leering sexual predator's dream' (quoted in Weinman, 2015, p. 57). Parker continued: 'The sexual politics in the film are positively revolting', reserving especially harsh words for the movie's director: '[I]t needs a true pervert to make it work' (quoted in Weinman, 2015, p. 57).

'Why remember it well?': blinkered readings of the past and present

Faced with an online community which declared *Gigi* 'terrifying, the worst, chauvinist, and hateful', Farran Nehme proceeded to mount a spirited defence of the movie in her blog, asking why a musical, 'which ends with its vivacious heroine happily married to a rich man who loves her the way she is' (Self-Styled Siren, 2014) was deemed so offensive.

Most of the criticism reveals a wilful disregard of the historical context of the story and a striking ignorance of the current law. The film is set in 1900 in a city with its very own view of the relations between the sexes. To retrospectively impose contemporary ethical standards onto that society is unlikely to yield illuminating insights, as Nehme emphasises: 'Scowling at the sexual morals of an earlier time is fun and all, but it's not an especially rewarding critical approach' (Self-Styled Siren, 2014). Such an ahistorical reading pays no heed to the reality of Parisian life at the turn of the century, where marrying at a young age was not the norm, but occasionally did happen.[13] Under-age nuptials are also not inevitably a thing of a less-enlightened past: in the United States, more than 200,000 American minors were legally wed between 2002 and 2017 (Syrett, 2017). So a 16-year-old (like Gigi) marrying a man in his early thirties (like Gaston) would not necessarily be uncommon even in the United States of 2020.

While we today may frown at an upbringing that prepares a young girl for a life of exchanging sexual favours for money (although this takes the form of expensive gifts and paying for living expenses), at the turn of the 19th century this form of prostitution presented one of the few options for women to move up in society and to gain prominence as well as influence. One should also not forget that in French society of that time '[m]any marriages within the bourgeoisie were pure business ventures' (Harvey, 2003, p. 193). Faced with alternatives such a factory work or taking in laundry, the women in *Gigi* use what nature gave them and what they have cultivated to secure a life and living standard far above that of the average Parisienne – they may not decide how society is run, but they participate on their own terms: 'These are not, perhaps, the rules these ladies would prefer to play by. . . . But it is . . . 1900. In any era, you play the hand you're dealt.' (Self-Styled Siren, 2014). The film thus honours and reflects Colette's admiration for 'female autonomy – sexual and financial' (Thurman, 2015); like the author, it does not condemn consensual sex work.

Whether or not one agrees with this *laissez-faire* attitude is a matter of personal opinion, but it seems rather sanctimonious for cultural critics, especially those working in popular media, to take the moral high ground. Vanessa Hudgens, star of the 2015 Broadway revival, may have been on to something when she compared the courtesans of the early 20th century with the Reality TV stars of the 21st: around 1900, 'a courtesan wasn't a hooker. She was very sought after. She had a level of class. She was like a reality star' (quoted in Thurman, 2015). In this context it should be remembered that both Paris Hilton, probably the first woman to cement her celebrity status via the new television format, and Kim Kardashian, the ubiquitous super nova of Reality TV and social media who followed in her wake, first gained notoriety with a sex video. Thus, like cocottes, they reached their elevated visibility in society via sexual indiscretions everybody was aware of, but chose to overlook once they had acquired admirers, cultural influence and (especially in case of the Kardashian clan) enormous wealth. In other words, there may have been less change over the last 120 years then we may wish to believe – modern society is certainly no less morally fickle when it comes to who we designate arbiters of taste and who we admire. The Paris of 1900 may simply have been less hypocritical.

'The night they diluted champagne': undermining the *auteur* or collaboration?

At first sight, it is astonishing that not more film scholars have argued against that ahistorical, reductive reading of the movie, especially since Minnelli is one of the key figures in the pantheon of great film directors as built by supporters of the *auteur* theory. Yet a closer look at the monographs published about the filmmaker reveals *Gigi* to some degree exempt from the status of a classic masterpiece in true Minnelli fashion in the eyes of cinema specialists. The movie's deliberately loose plot and lack of narrative urgency, brilliantly rationalised by Altman (pp. 21–26), its paucity of dance numbers and its long takes have led to accusations that *Gigi* as a whole 'isn't very cinematic' (Harvey, 1989, p. 145). Harvey declares that the movie amounts to no more than 'an illustrated soundtrack' (p. 148), apparently unaware that one could define any film musical in these terms – after all, the songs are usually written and recorded *first* and constitute the work's main *raison d'être*.

The Minnelli expert then blames studio politics during post-production for what he calls the film's 'stylistic lapses' (Harvey, 1989, p. 148): MGM had ordered to stop location shooting in August 1957 and to film the rest of the musical in Hollywood, at a point when the movie was already $500,000 over budget (Levy, 2009, p. 302). Because contractual obligations forced Minnelli to abandon post-production of the movie,[14] in Hugh Fordin's view the finished film shows that the director 'was unable to protect his intention of making a truly French story' (Fordin, 1975, p. 495), i.e. that his original (*auteurist*) vision was diluted by interference of the Hollywood machinery in the guise of producer Arthur Freed and the creators of the movie's score. Lerner and Loewe reportedly stepped in to save the movie after its first disastrous preview in early 1958 (Lerner, 1994, pp. 174–175). It was Lerner who insisted on major changes once the film was assembled, which included the addition of close-ups to 'She Is Not Thinking of Me', thus breaking up Minnelli's elaborate long shots (Fordin, 1975, p. 488). Those changes 'were finally agreed upon but executed without Minnelli's supervision' (Levy, 2009, p. 303). That Freed ceded control to the songwriters led Gerald Mast to characterise *Gigi* as less director-shaped than a traditional movie since their tampering documents 'the swallowing of the old Hollywood by the new Broadway' (Mast, 1987, p. 288). From an *auteurist's* point of view these interventions weaken any claim of sole authorship and compromise the director's artistic vision.

Because of its stubborn insistence that one artist alone is responsible for a work's greatness, Thomas Schatz has criticised the *auteur* theory for 'effectively stalling film history and criticism in a prolonged state of adolescent romanticism' (Schatz,

1988, p. 5). As an analytical approach it seems particularly contrived in the context of the musical, a genre that, both on film and on stage, like no other requires collaboration to thrive. In the theatre, what happened to *Gigi* once Minnelli left, would be construed as a prime example of a joint effort – all members of the creative team pulling together for the benefit of the work. That Minnelli in his autobiography does not mention or criticise any artistic decisions made by others, could of course indicate that, in contrast to many of the scholars who dissected his oeuvre, the director might simply not have categorised the changes and additions as meddling, especially since they did not negatively impact *Gigi*'s public reception. Perhaps Minnelli's did not object to this kind of working together – he did come to Hollywood from Broadway, after all.

'I'm glad she's not young anymore': removing the 'objectionable'

Aware of the critical discourse surrounding *Gigi*, the producers of the first major New York revival hired a writer, Heidi Thomas, famous for female-centric narratives (such as *Call the Midwife*), to attune the intellectual property to modern sensibilities. The new production came about in a cultural climate which made remounting the musical a particular challenge – Judith Thurman has drawn attention to the 'paradox that Americans are, more than 50 years [after the movie's release], after a revolution in mores, less prudish yet more moralistic than their parents' (Thurman, 2015).

Before revising the 1973 libretto, the 1958 film was shown to focus groups, so that Thomas could adapt the stage musical based on their reactions or their misconceptions: the rewrite goes out of its way to avoid any suggestions of paedophilia and teenage prostitution, irrespective of whether any of these elements are actually present in the film (Thurman, 2015). The new version was intended as a family show, as is attested by the casting of Hudgens, famous for the squeaky-clean *High School Musical* trilogy (2006–2008). Therefore, in the attempt to remove any objectionable material, the revival artificially foists a wholesomeness and 21st-century feminist awareness onto *Gigi* which are completely alien to the source material and so distort it out of its prior shape.

Colette's novella presents Gigi as 15½ years old (Colette, 2001, p. 33), but advanced for her age[15] (p. 8), whereas her suitor Gaston is 33 (p. 23), but 'youngish-looking' (p. 10). In the movie, their age difference is not specified; however, Leslie Caron was 26 at the time of shooting, while Louis Jourdan was ten years her senior. Thomas pre-empts any accusations of a May-September romance by reducing the age gap between the couple: Gigi is no longer a minor as she 'came of age three months ago' (Gigi, 2012, p. 36a), and the part of her future husband (whose age is not specified in the libretto) was filled by 27-year-old Corey Cott, who is actually three months *younger* than Hudgens.[16]

In order to give Gigi more agency, the revised libretto makes her acutely aware of her limited choices as a woman in a society dominated by men. But still she doesn't despair, assuring him and the audience that 'I'll find something I can do' (Gigi, 2012, p. 62), probably following in the footsteps of her grandmother who had hoped to become an artist but had to settle for teaching calligraphy. Thus, the girl, as Heidi Thomas is keen to point out, 'is writing her own rules' (quoted in Thurman, 2015).

'She is not thinking of men': to each her own agenda

The librettist's attempt to give every single female character agency puts a damper on things, as empowering women as a gender seemingly prohibits them from being silly. This may be a promising approach to drama, but it is severely limiting in (musical) comedy.

Liane d'Exelmans is changed from a brainless, luscious decorative object into a woman with 'real feelings'[17] and a lovely singing voice, who berates Gaston that '[b]ored people are boring' (p. 33). Like any good grandmother, the 2015 Mamita merely wishes to protect Gigi from harm; she decidedly does not want the girl to become a courtesan. Thus, she reminds her sister: 'I did not send Gigi to you so she could follow in your footsteps!' (Gigi, 2012, p. 36). That Gigi doesn't share the values of her great-aunt is made clear right from the beginning: when Alicia insists 'There is nothing more romantic than a nice stroll to the bank', her warden responds with 'This is just depressing' (Gigi, 2012, p. 13).

Yet when and how is Gigi – and by extension, Mamita – supposed to have acquired these convictions, so very much outside the value system of her environment and her society as a whole? Incorporating feminist ideas which 'would have horrified Colette' (Thurman, 2015), the revival is less a revision than a revisionist retelling that retrospectively imposes contemporary cultural pre-occupations onto its source material instead of exploring what the 1944 novella and the 1958 film can mean to a modern audience in the current context. Minnelli's movie sets the stifling comfort of the leisurely lifestyle in the Paris of 1900 against the irresistible allure of the natural instincts exhibited by the young girls who constitute the city's greatest asset. The 1973 stage adaptation cannot recreate those elements and winds up mimicking their surface features. The 2015 revival stumbles for a different reason: it aims for a 'progressive' attitude that is incongruous with the story at its centre and therefore comes across as laboured and affected.

The production tries to recalibrate the basic parameters of the character interactions while still retaining the famous score and some of its later additions – with limited success: 'Paris Is Paris Again' makes for a fine opening number and gets proceedings off to a sprightly start, but reassigning 'Thank Heaven for Little Girls' does not really solve what some people find problematic about it. That notorious number is given to Alicia and her sister in a vain attempt to remove any notions of impropriety and to allow the siblings to praise their own sex in an act of solidarity. Yet if one is determined to detect an unlawful lusting after minors when a man performs the song, what prevents one from doing the same when two older women sing it? When assuming the worst, one might as well go all the way.[18]

FIGURE 15.5 The ensemble during the opening night curtain call of the revised version of *Gigi*; the Broadway revival premiered on 8 April 2015 at the Neil Simon Theatre.

Source: Photo by WENN, courtesy of Alamy Stock Photo.

The critics' response to the new *Gigi* was mostly dismissive, not least since some of them were unconvinced that the movie was really that questionable to begin with.[19] Others decried the rewrite as 'aseptic' (Stasio, 2015, p. 136) and 'disconcertingly wholesome' (Winer, 2015, p. B4). The theatregoing public seemed to share that opinion – the revival closed after 20 previews and 86 regular performances.

'The flair and other minor things': conclusion

There have recently been attempts to refashion Colette as a proto-feminist (most strikingly in the 2018 bio-pic that bears her name). Yet however one sees the author's role in the fight for women's rights – a movement she did not condone[20] – her female protagonists, even those that do not get their happy ending, are consistently independent of mind as well as means; they are also often stronger and wiser than the men.

When the 2015 Gigi lectures Gaston on the advantages he has as a beneficiary of patriarchal society, Heidi Thomas fails to understand that the character as conceived by the French writer does not need to rebel against the limitations put upon her by society, because Colette's women best men at their own game. The novella's fairy tale solution comes about because its eponymous heroine outmanoeuvres everyone, including her older relatives – it is she who gets Gaston to the point where all he can do is propose marriage. How else to interpret Alicia's retort to her sister: 'Leave well alone. Don't meddle anymore. Can't you see she is far beyond us?' (Colette, 2001, p. 57).

This hint at pure calculation in Gigi's handling of her own affair(s) is still present in Anita Loos' 1951 stage adaptation,[21] but it is missing from all the musical versions. Minnelli doesn't need it, because in the world of artifice he creates, Gigi's main quality is her naturalness – she captivates Gaston because of her immediate access to responses which are spontaneous and without ulterior motive. Her emotional directness represents a way out of an environment that holds neither stimulus nor challenge. When every show of affection, every gesture and every move is deliberately planned, life becomes dull in spite of its gorgeous trappings (and nobody's trappings are more gorgeous than Minnelli's – has there ever been a film where the flowers have been more carefully arranged first in their vases and then within the frame?). It is Gigi's spark and sparkle that set her apart, and so far, imbuing the character with the same qualities on stage has failed, because they cannot be faked when the Paris of 1900 is not present in either atmosphere or spirit.

Notes

1 Reporting on Gaston's various liaisons, 'Paris mistakenly proclaimed', before 'Paris later remedied the mistake' (Colette, 2001, p. 27).
2 All tracking numbers refer to the Blu-ray release of the film (i.e. *Gigi*, 1958).
3 No doubt Caron's classical ballet training came in handy in this context.
4 'Throughout the film, the principals often perform their songs while seated' (Griffin, 2010, p. 218).
5 The montage covering the festivities celebrating Gaston's 'first suicide' wittily illustrates how alien nature is to most of Parisian upper-class society: his 'Queen at the Battles of the Flowers' is allergic to the bouquets which fill their carriage.
6 This remark comes directly from Colette's novella (Colette, 2001, p. 35).
7 When Gigi rushes through the parks of Paris, she literally is the dark blue darting around the green.
8 Identifying the exact shades of blue in *Gigi* is difficult without having access to a proper print of the original Metrocolor negative. The indifferently manufactured Blu-ray of *Gigi*, released in 2008, was clearly made without the necessary attention to chromaticity – for instance, the colour of the suit Gaston wears during the title number varies from shot to shot. To some degree, the earlier DVD release is better calibrated, although it also does not allow one to draw definite conclusions. Therefore, the following remarks should be seen as indicative, not conclusive.
9 That Alicia initially plans for Gigi to follow in her and – to a lesser degree – in Mamita's footsteps is symbolised by the dress she chooses for her ward: it is bright pink with black applications.
10 As Vanessa R. Schwartz has pointed out, that brown dress is actually a reproduction from the one depicted in a 1894 poster by Jules Chéret advertising the Palais de Glace (Schwartz, 2007, p. 37).
11 The only time the camera captures male children is when Honoré first addresses the audience; at the moment he starts talking, a woman holding the hands of two boys passes behind him [2:48–2:54 min.].
12 The 2015 Broadway revival replaces the ice-skating teacher with a singing teacher and consequently loses the connotation of working class with sexual prowess; a rival from the

art world seems unlikely to trigger the same self-doubt in men of Gaston's and Honoré's background.

13 The average age for women to marry in France between 1900 and 1909 was 24.1 years; for men it was slightly higher at 27.8 years (Henri and Houdaille, 1979, p. 413).

14 The director had to move on to his next feature, *The Reluctant Debutante* (1958), which started shooting two weeks before *Gigi*'s first preview (Harvey, 1989, p. 143).

15 The girl is first described as a 'great gawk looking at least eighteen' (Colette, 2001, p. 8).

16 Although in fine voice throughout, Cott was seriously miscast as Gaston; utterly unbelievable as a ladies' men, he came across as an over-eager schoolboy.

17 After Gaston ends their relationship, she watches him go 'surprisingly vulnerable and utterly alone' (*Gigi*, 2012, p. 33).

18 Marilyn Stasio opined that the 'ludicrous choice' of reassigning that song makes Mamita and her sister 'seem like a couple of madams sizing up the next crop of courtesans' (Stasio, 2015, p. 136).

19 For instance, David Noh called 'Thank Heaven for Little Girls' 'baselessly notorious' (Noh, 2015, p. 28).

20 In 1910, the French author told a journalist that suffragettes deserved 'the whip and the harem' (quoted in Thurman, 2015).

21 Alicia: 'Let the child go! Can't you see she's got method in her madness?' (*Gigi*, 1951, p. 2–3–42).

References

Als, H. (2015) 'The Theater: *Gigi*,' *The New Yorker*, 20 April, p. 91.

Altman, R. (1989) *The American Film Musical*. Bloomington, Indianapolis and London: Indiana University Press, BFI Publishing.

Colette. (2001) *Gigi and the Cat* (R. Senhouse, trans.). London: Vintage.

Davies, M. (1961) *Colette*. Edinburgh: Oliver and Boyd Ltd.

Elsaesser, T. (2009) 'Vincente Minnelli,' in McElhaney, J. (ed.) *Vincente Minnelli: The Art of Entertainment*. Detroit: Wayne State University Press, pp. 79–96.

Fordin, H. (1975) *MGM's Greatest Musicals: The Arthur Freed Unit*. New York: Da Capo Press.

Gigi. (1958) Directed by V. Minnelli, Blu-Ray. BD-03-DIM1 64988. Hamburg: Warner Home Video Germany.

Gigi by Lerner, A. J., Loewe, F. and Thomas, H. (2015) Directed by Eric Schaeffer. New York: Neil Simon Theater, 26 March.

Gigi: A Comedy in Two Acts. (1951) Dramatized by Anita Loos, from the Novel by Colette. Typescript. New York: Public Library for the Performing Arts, RM928.

Gigi: A Musical Comedy in Two Acts (2012) Book and Lyrics by A. J. Lerner. Music by F. Loewe. Revised Book by H. Thomas, 1st Draft (Polish), 12 March. Unpublished Manuscript. London: Bethan Evans – The Agency.

Gigi: A Musical Play. (1973). From the Musical Film Adaptation of the Novella *Gigi* by Colette. Book and Lyrics by A. J. Lerner. Music by F. Loewe. 11 July. Typescript. New York: Public Library for the Performing Arts, RM#1960.

Gottfried, M. (1973) 'Theatre: *Gigi*,' *Women's Wear Daily*, 15 November; *New York Theatre Critics' Reviews*, XXXIII, p. 191.

Griffin, M. (2010) *A Hundred or More Hidden Things: The Life and Films of Vincente Minnelli*. New York: Da Capo Press.

Harvey, D. (2003) *Paris, Capital of Modernity*. New York and London: Routledge.

Harvey, S. (1989) *Directed by Vincente Minnelli*. New York: The Musical of Modern Art, Harper & Row.

Henri, L. and Houdaille, C. (1979) 'Célibat et âge au mariage aux XVIIIe et XIXe siècles en France. II: Age au Premier Mariage,' *Population*, 34(2), pp. 403–442. DOI: 10.2307/1531570.

Hext, K. J. (2014) '"Somehow This Crazy World Has Taken on a Wonderful Design": Vincente Minnelli's Neo-Victorian Utopias in Hollywood,' *Neo-Victorian Studies*, 7(11), pp. 52–78.

———. (2011) 'Minnelli's Yellows: Illusion, Delusion and Impressionism on Film,' *Wide Screen*, 3(1), June, pp. 1–18.

Jablonski, E. (1996) *Alan Jay Lerner: A Biography*. New York: Henri Holt and Company.

Lerner, A. J. (1994) *The Street Where I Live*. New York: Da Capo Press.

Levy, E. (2009) *Vincente Minnelli: Hollywood's Dark Dreamer*. New York: St. Martin's Press.

Mast, G. (1987) *Can't Help Singin': The American Musical on Stage and Screen*. Woodstock and New York: The Overlook Press.

Minnelli, V. and Arce, H. (1975) *I Remember It Well*. London: Angus & Robertson.

Naremore, J. (1993) *The Films of Vincente Minnelli*. Cambridge: Cambridge University Press.

Noh, D. (2015) 'Gigi,' *Gay City News*, 14 May, p. 40.

Schatz, T. (1988) *The Genius in the System: Hollywood Filmmaking in the Studio Era*. New York: Henry Holt and Company.

Schwartz, V. R. (2007) *It's So French! Hollywood, Paris and the Making of Cosmopolitan Film Culture*. Chicago and London: University of Chicago Press.

Self-Styled Siren [aka Nehme, F]. (2014) '*Gigi* (1958): A Defense,' http://selfstyledsiren.blogspot.co.uk/2914/02/gigi-1958-defense.html, accessed 17 March 2014.

Stasio, M. (2015) 'Review: *Gigi*,' *Variety*, 14 April, p. 136.

Suskin, S. (1999) 'Liner Notes,' in *Gigi: The Original Broadway Cast Recording (1973)*. CD 09026-68070-2. New York: RCA Victor, pp. 6–10.

Syrett, N. (2017) 'Child Marriage Is Still Legal in the US,' *The Conversation*, 12 December, https://theconversation.com/child-marriage-is-still-legal-in-the-us-88846, accessed 15 February 2020.

Thurman, J. (2015) 'Good, Clean Fun: A Revival of *Gigi*,' *The New Yorker*, 7 April, www.newyorker.com/culture/culutral-comment/good-clean-fun-a-revial-of-gigi, accessed 4 June 2019.

Verdaguer, P. (2004) 'Hollywood's Frenchness: Representations of the French in American Films,' *Contemporary French and Francophone Studies*, 8(4), pp. 441–451.

Ward Jouve, N. (1987) *Colette*. Brighton: Harvester Press Ltd.

Watt, D. (1973) '*Gigi* Returns as a Stage Musical,' *New York Daily News*, 14 November; *New York Theatre Critics' Reviews*, XXXIII, p. 190.

Weinman, J. J. (2015) 'A Creepy, Pervy Family Classic Is Back,' *McLeans*, 128(11), p. 57.

Winer, L. (2015) '*Gigi*, Prettied up for a New Age,' *Newsday*, 9 April, p. B4.

APPENDIX: TABLE 15.1 Musical Numbers in the Various Versions of *Gigi*

Film 1958	Stage Version 1973	Broadway Revival 2015
	◘ = changed deployment; ♫ = added song	
	Act I	Act I
'Overture'	'Overture'	'Overture'
'Thank Heaven for Little Girls' – Honoré	'Thank Heaven for Little Girls' – Honoré	'Opening' [= 'Paris Is Paris Again'] – Honoré and Ensemble
'It's a Bore' – Gaston and Honoré	'It's a Bore' – Gaston and Honoré	'It's a Bore' – Gaston and Honoré
'The Parisians' – Gigi	♫ 'The Earth and Other Minor Things' – Gigi	'The Parisians' – Gigi
		♫ 'À Toujours' – Liane
'The Gossips' – Honoré and Guests at Maxim's	♫ 'Paris Is Paris Again' – 'Honoré and Ensemble	'The Gossips' – Guests at Maxim's
'She Is Not Thinking of Me' – Gaston	'She Is Not Thinking of Me' – Gaston	'She Is Not Thinking of Me' – Gaston
	♫ 'It's a Bore (Reprise)' – Gaston	◘ 'Thank Heaven for Little Girls' – Mamita and Alica
'The Night They Invented Champagne' – Gigi, Gaston and Mamita	'The Night They Invented Champagne' – Gigi, Gaston and Mamita	◘ 'Paris Is Paris Again [Reprise]' – Honoré, Liane and Ensemble
'I Remember It Well' – Honoré and Mamita	'I Remember It Well' – Honoré and Mamita	'I Remember It Well' – Honoré and Mamita
		'The Night They Invented Champagne' – Gigi, Gaston and Mamita
	♫ 'I Never Want to Go Home Again' – Gigi and Ensemble	'I Never Want to Go Home Again' – Gigi and Ensemble
	Act II	Act II
'Gaston's Soliloquy' – Gaston	'Gaston's Soliloquy' – Gaston	'Gaston's Soliloquy' – Gaston
'Gigi' – Gaston	'Gigi' – Gaston	'Gigi' – Gaston
	♫ 'The Contract' – Alicia, Mamita and Gaston's lawyers	'The Contract' – Alicia, Mamita and Gaston's lawyers
'I'm Glad I'm Not Young Anymore' – Honoré	'I'm Glad I'm Not Young Anymore' – Honoré	◘ 'I'm Glad I'm Not Young Anymore' – Honoré and Mamita
'Say a Prayer for Me Tonight' – Gigi	♫ 'In This Wide, Wide World' – Gigi	'The Letter' [= 'In This Wide, Wide World'] – Gigi
'Thank Heaven for Little Girls (Reprise)' – Honoré and choir	'Thank Heaven for Little Girls' (Reprise)' – Honoré and Ensemble	◘ 'Say a Prayer for Her Tonight' – Mamita
		♫ 'In This Wide, Wide World [Reprise]' – Gigi and Gaston
		♫ 'Finale' – Ensemble

PART VI
Artistic Paris

16

'ARTISTS IN ART'S CAPITAL CITY'

Americans in Paris on screen and stage

Robert Gordon

Music, love and the love of music

The major Hollywood players responsible for the 1951 movie *An American in Paris* were united by their love and admiration of George Gershwin. Producer Arthur Freed, director Vincente Minnelli, pianist and actor Oscar Levant, the MGM musical directors Johnny Green and Saul Chaplin and the orchestrator Conrad Salinger were all good friends of Ira Gershwin, so it was to be expected that Ira would play a significant role in shaping the approach to the musical material by his famous brother. When Freed first asked his permission to use the name of the 1928 composition *An American in Paris* as the title for a movie, it was Ira who suggested the film use only Gershwin music (Fordin, 1996, p. 306).

In fact, both the movie and the 2014 stage adaptation utilise not only large sections of the 'tone poem' but also colonise a number of popular Gershwin songs, some of which are incorporated as underscoring: in the film, Oscar Levant even performs part of the 'Concerto in F'. Eight Gershwin songs are performed on screen. In the stage version, there is almost continuous underscoring of dance sequences masking scene changes, from *An American Paris*, the *Concerto in F*, the *Second Rhapsody*, the *Cuban Overture* and other Gershwin material as well as 12 songs.

Vincente Minnelli: the aesthete in the factory

From its opening montage of stock MGM shots of Paris [1:25–2:23 min.[1]], *An American in Paris*, like other Hollywood movies from the 1950s set in Paris,[2] elaborates what became a ubiquitous cinematic trope reflecting the way newly accessible forms of European tourism were being promoted to Americans – the tourist or foreign visitor's relationship with the city s/he is looking at and/or photographing. Director Minnelli deepens this focus, complicating the motif of visual perception to involve the transformative gaze of the artist and lover; in this perspective the act of looking becomes the cue for the film's interconnected strands of imagery. Paris, in the director's vision, is not so much the 'City of Light' as the city of art.

Insofar as the film represents the unifying vision of Minnelli as *auteur*, it is highly self-reflexive, an assemblage of visually articulated epistemological discourses on the pleasures of looking and the discipline of artistic viewing. The perceptual collision of the high arts of French painting and architecture with the popular art of American/Hollywood entertainment that Minnelli was employed by MGM to create, provides the sensuous grounding of the intentionally unsettling narrative construction that foregrounds parallel dramas of identity experienced by three young friends (Gene Kelly and Oscar Levant as two American artists and Georges Guétary as a French *artiste*). The inevitable conflict of the harsh and solitary regime of artistic creation with the ecstasy of love and its attendant suffering determine the trope of art versus the 'real life' it portrays.

Reaching its apogee at MGM between 1939 and the early 1950s, the studio system determined that filmmaking was an industrial process of collaborative work. Minnelli explained how the two opposing factors paradoxically drove the creation of *An American in Paris*:

> As no one sets out to make a bad picture, rarely under the old studio system did anyone set out to make a classic. *An American in Paris* certainly wasn't designed as such. Arthur [Freed] and I . . . were planning a solid commercial entertainment aimed at a mass audience. Yet all the elements meshed so perfectly that what was planned as another slick musical became a standard by which all such pictures are measured.
>
> *(Minnelli and Arce, 1974, p. 215)*

Taking account of the choreographic ambition and star persona of Kelly, who had worked closely with him on *The Pirate* (1948), the popularity and artistic reputation of the Gershwin music as well as the commercial and artistic aims of the Freed Production Unit at MGM, the usually reticent Minnelli nevertheless categorically asserted his status as the movie's *auteur*:

> Some erudite types point to *An American in Paris* as the perfect example of the studio-as-auteur theory. I disagree. Though I don't minimize anyone's contributions, one man was responsible for bringing it all together. That man was me.
>
> *(Minnelli and Arce, 1974, p. 228)*

The notion of Minnelli's authorial vision as a filmmaker is supported by the film's art director, who believed that Minnelli 'had everything preconceived in his head' (quoted in Knox, 1973, pp. 162–163) and that his Paris, rather than attempting a photographic compilation of well-known urban views, should be a composite of artistic images that comprehended the city as a series of art works in the making. The new Hollywood convention of visual authenticity, celebrated as a defining strength of MGM's *On the Town* (1949) shot partly on location by directors Stanley

Donen and Gene Kelly, was to be challenged.[3] In its place Minnelli would evoke 'Paris' through the inter-animation of compelling images constituted in the eye of a viewer's mind from the web of visual and kinetic symbols constructed in the film, until finally in the 17-minute ballet sequence, this 'virtual Paris' would disappear to be reconstructed in expressionistic terms through dance and painting/scenography in the oneiric space of Jerry's dream.

As the eponymous American in the Paris of the symphonic 'tone poem' in 1928, which he had called 'a rhapsodic ballet' (Jablonski and Stewart, 1958, pp. 138–141), George Gershwin was an apt choice, his career representing the preeminent American paradigm of the conflict between concert music (high-brow art) and popular music ('low-brow' entertainment). In the role of would-be composer Adam, concert pianist and MGM contract player Oscar Levant was a kind of surrogate for Gershwin, elaborating the high-brow/low-brow trope that can be seen in a number of musicals since Judy Garland (swing) was first pitched against Deanna Durbin ('classical') in *Every Sunday* (1936).

Film scholar James Naremore, in his monograph on Minnelli's career, refers to the director as an 'aesthete in the factory' (Naremore, 1993, p. 7), reinforcing the well-documented evidence of his abiding interest in the visual aesthetics of the Impressionists, Symbolists, Decadents and other avant-garde art movements of the late 19th century (Hext, 2014). Minnelli's obsessive pre-occupation with the use of colour as a primary compositional tool in the art of filmmaking was a significant aspect of Symbolist art. In Angelo Bertocci's formulation, Symbolist painting, opera and drama deployed colour as a metaphor for the unity produced by the reciprocal relationship of its component art forms:

> *Symbolisme* . . . may be seen as the aspiration . . . toward a thoroughgoing poetic unity conceived in terms of the metaphor of 'colour' (which, as we have seen, also has its 'music') in a philosophical context which permits interflow and interglow of meaning.
>
> *(Bertocci, 1964, p. 77)*

Bertocci concludes that the 'import' or comprehensive meaning of an art work cannot be derived merely from one structural element (e.g. the shape of its narrative), but 'comes together' as a response to the interaction of all its component strands. While Minnelli's long-standing absorption in late 19th-century aesthetic praxis counterposed his experience in the MGM 'dream factory', he espoused the Symbolists' aesthetic ideal of the Wagnerian *Gesamtkunstwerk* to generate a satisfactory artistic whole from the heterogeneous mixture of artistic modes and technical tools of cinema:

> A film that means anything at all . . . is made up of hundreds of hidden things. Things that the audience may not be aware of unless it's pointed out to them but nevertheless help to involve them and haunt them a little.
>
> *(Minnelli and Arce, 1974, p. 59)*

A British ballet choreographer in Paris and New York

Christopher Wheeldon, possibly the most accomplished international ballet choreographer to have emerged since the late 1990s, has been celebrated among other things for his ability to construct narrative ballets, initially at the New York City Ballet (NYCB), home of Georges Balanchine and Jerome Robbins, key figures in the development of the Broadway musical.[4] According to Wheeldon, 'Gene Kelly was one of the reasons I first wanted to dance. Of all those MGM stars, he was my favourite. I loved him in *An American in Paris*' (quoted in Mackerell, 2014). With NYCB star Robert Fairchild in the 'Gene Kelly' role of painter Jerry Mulligan, Wheeldon was nevertheless able to create a more completely balletic alternative to the film that utilised a theatrical language as effectively as Minnelli had used his filmic vocabulary.

Where Minnelli's inspiration was primarily visual art, Wheeldon's was ballet, the rationale for his and book-writer Craig Lucas' addition of a subplot in which the main characters stage an experimental new ballet for the (fictional) Châtelet Ballet Company. This subplot allowed Wheeldon to choreograph several additional dance scenes. According to dance critic, Judith Mackerell, 'Dance is . . . the driving language of the show – a fluid mix of tap, jazz, mime and ballet that links the naturalistic action and the more formal dance numbers'; she also quotes the director's view that nowadays 'audiences are comfortable with the idea of a dance-driven musical' (Mackerell, 2014).

Gene Kelly's star persona under the female/queer gaze

The athletic, open and assertively masculine persona that Kelly elected to project as a screen hero who was also a dancer, was a profoundly anxious response to the general public's prejudice against male ballet dancers as effeminate – and, by implication, homosexual.[5] Thus Kelly is often quoted as saying that it was his mission to prove to moviegoers that dance as an art form was not just for 'sissies'.[6]

> *An American in Paris* is probably the most complete expression of the star image Kelly strained so hard to project – the lovable, regular guy who just happened to be a genius . . . If Jerry Mulligan's painterly prowess underwhelms, the variety and virtuosity of Kelly's dancing fulfills the metaphor of star-as-artist . . . Everybody in the world of this movie except perhaps heiress Nina Foch is the lucky recipient of Kelly's Yankee goodwill.
>
> *(Harvey, 1989, pp. 99–100)*

Many today would feel sympathy with this somewhat cynical critique of Kelly's narcissistic star persona. 'As in most Kelly pictures', opines Harvey 'he's happiest when he's carousing with his chums, even if his joy is prompted by the new love in his life. Kelly and pals do a powerful lot of male bonding' (Harvey, 1989, p. 100).

Both screenplay and direction undermine Jerry's smugly masculine persona in his relationships with the woman he woos (Lise) and the one he is wooed by

(Milo), exposing him as immature, insecure, narcissistic and sexist. As artists, both Kelly and Minnelli had strong motivations to prove that a Hollywood musical featuring a hugely popular song-and-dance man in tandem with a classically trained French ballerina might aspire to the aesthetic sophistication of a high art work. Minnelli's own bisexuality would have instinctively countered Kelly's anxiety in allowing the camera to transform a famously attractive male body into an object for the male and female 'gaze'.[7] In fact, Minnelli anticipates the post-1990s reconfiguration of gay cultures as 'queer' by establishing a queer perspective on the identity of the characters embodied by Kelly, Levant and Guétary as an axis of the film's intersecting themes of artistic, sexual and social identity explored in this chapter.

The politics of identity: dramas of artistic as well as national allegiance, sexuality and gender

One of the crucial differences between the film and the more socially and historically oriented approach of Lucas and Wheeldon's stage version is in the representation of Jerry. In 2014, Jerry and Adam's argument soon after they meet Henri in the café concerns whether art should be escapist or existentially dark; and in one delicious innovation, Adam plays his first version of 'I Got Rhythm' at an angst-ridden, funereal pace, to have the apparently more 'cultivated' Henri improve it by recommending he take it at the zippy 4/4 beat in which the piece has become familiar.

Wheeldon and Lucas' approach to the problem of how to vary the time-honoured trope of 'young artist meets mystery girl and must propose to her by the final moments of the play/movie', is very different to that of Minnelli and Lerner. In her provocative essay comparing the film with the new stage version, Natalia Cecire addresses the conundrum:

> How to establish that Lise (Bouvier in the film, Dassin in the musical), the aforementioned girl, does not belong with her dorky French fiancé is a question that each production must address. Like the film, the stage musical resists making any of the decoy lovers (whether Henri Baurel, Lise's fiancé, or Milo Davenport, Jerry's rich American sponsor) into enemies; the musical goes further still in attempting to complicate the film's economy of value (American/French, modern/old-fashioned, 'jazz'/waltz, matches of convenience/matches for love).
>
> *(Cecire, 2016)*

Both Kelly and ballet star Robert Fairchild play Jerry as a would-be painter. Ballet references tease audiences on the unconscious plane to entertain discourse of contemporary social media in speculating whether the performer/character is gay.[8] In keeping with current more relaxed notions of sexual orientation/image, Fairchild does not possess either Kelly's confident grin of machismo aggression or embody the putative effeminacy/homosexuality that is often homophobically ascribed to male ballet dancers. Fairchild is fleet and suave; taller than Kelly, he is also less obviously muscular, his strength apparent through his highly acrobatic agility rather than indicated by his sheer physical presence. The impression he creates is kinetic rather than corporeal. The passionate enthusiasm of his wooing is that of a youth, having no overlay of cocksure masculinity about it. Jerry's desire here is impulsively romantic rather than compulsively sexual.[9]

Unlike a majority of Hollywood films, *An American in Paris* positions the three male figures as objects 'to-be-looked-at' some time before Leslie Caron's Lise is situated in the classic cinematic position of woman as object of the male gaze (9:30–12:04 min.).[10] The trio's affectionate and at times palpably physical homosocial admiration for one another, vividly if comically sung and danced in 'By Strauss' at the Café des Amis, verges on homo-eroticism.

Whereas the film does not editorialise on the topics of gender identity and sexual orientation, instead incarnating them wholly in the bodily aura of its three central male figures, the stage script has recourse to a more limited and paradoxically conservative conception of gender/sexuality, which identifies Henri's 'secret' as a key to the resolution of the plot. Henri is no longer the mature and successful singer represented by the famous Georges Guétary, the character being invited by an American agent to perform in New York; he is a shy, repressed would-be cabaret singer who is afraid to reveal his ambition to become a Broadway star to his wealthy and snobbish parents. His inability to propose straightforwardly to his intended bride, Lise, prompts even his repressed mother to ask him directly: 'Do your romantic interests lie beyond the fairer sex?' [46:04 min.]. By contrast the film registers the pulse of the unconscious more forcefully: it is of no consequence whether Henri is gay or bisexual. He certainly does not appear to exhibit powerfully sexual feelings for Lise, but appears to reach his own peak of pleasure in a sublimation of sexual drive by way of a performance in which he quite unambiguously seduces the audience.

From early on in the film, Minnelli and Lerner carefully chart the uneven trajectory of Jerry's emotional development. At first he and Adam are deliberately revealed as narcissistic babies, Jerry being observed through his mansard window lying in a foetal position in bed (2:54 min.), then waking up and moving in a spontaneous dance-mime to look intently at his own self-portrait in charcoal, only to wipe it out a moment later (4:20 min.), his voice-over narration being taken up in almost identical fashion by the comically self-hating Adam, who buttonholes the viewer with his words 'It's not a pretty face, I grant you, but underneath this flabby exterior is an enormous lack of character'(5:22–5:31 min.).

Adam then introduces his friend Henri Baurel who picks up the voice-over narration, tricking the film viewer in a similar manner to his predecessor into mistaking him first for an unsuitably older man, then for a very pretty younger man, whose face appears momentarily in a mirror (6:08 min.) in which Henri himself appears immediately after (6:22 min.) as a handsome, vain and well-dressed but slightly more mature man,[11] whose reflection on his age parallels his vanity as a French music hall star with the narcissism of the two immature American artists. Minnelli's interpretation of this thematic motif is more complex still, ironically allying Kelly/

Jerry's Neanderthal American masculinity with brutal industrial modernity, while counterposing Jerry's attitude with the sophisticated 'femininity' of Henri as a representative of French culture and artistic refinement – old-fashioned, perhaps, but also the sign of a less mercenary and more highly advanced civilisation.

At the start of the film the narcissism of all three men is deliberately manifest: the stage adaptation embodies none of the unconscious 'masculinity panic' of the film.[12] Minnelli implies that Adam's dream/fantasy of conducting and performing his own concerto (62:46–67:22 min.) – Gershwin's *Rhapsody in F* in fact – is actually a form of masturbation. Levant's character is unchanging throughout the film, by contrast with Jerry, whose maturing as a lover allows him ultimately to accept the possibility that though he loves art he may never become a great painter.

Jerry's need of approval is revealed in 'I Got Rhythm' (24:08–28:00 min.) where he self-consciously 'performs' to entertain Parisian children who regard him as their American friend. Kelly's brash masculine charm is at its most attractive as he jokingly explores American/French cultural relations through the medium of a song-and-tap dance routine. But the tap dance which accompanies '*la chanson Américaine*' serves yet another function: Jerry's deployment of fractured French to explain his English words directly compares France and America in the terms of popular culture. Jerry gives the children American bubble gum; his compendium of vaudeville routines comprises parodies of a number of American icons – a cowboy the kids identify as 'Hopalong Cassidy' and a clown they recognise as 'Charlot' (Charlie Chaplin). The onscreen audience of children, who also participate in the performance, enhances Kelly's carefully cultivated charm.

Sandwiched between two rather brittle dialogue scenes with Milo (Nina Foch), the number humanises Jerry's otherwise unpleasant egoism, contrasting with the distinctly misogynistic attitude to the wealthy woman whose sexual attraction to him he exploits for mercenary gain. When Kelly/Jerry performs, he is charm personified, wooing old ladies and younger men with the promiscuous abandon of the professional exhibitionist. When dealing with women however he appears as a practiced seducer: with Lise, this encompasses everything from casual pickup routine, aggressive stalking strategy to song-and-dance performance and with Milo, a calculated gigolo out for what he can get from a wealthy woman, while insisting on his superior status as a man.

In response to Milo's pretence of throwing a party to trick him into an evening-*a-deux*, his reaction is disproportionately furious – as though she had hired him as a paid escort; after an initial encounter with Lise in the nightclub he visits with Milo, he becomes obsessed with the younger woman and cruelly tries to pick her up under Milo's nose in retaliation for being treated as the kept man he is in fact becoming. Conventional Hollywood misogyny represents as moral Jerry's rejection of Milo's assumption of the patriarchal male role of seducer, overlooking his complete hypocrisy in his rude staring at Lise (34:43–35:31 min.). Coupled with the moment when he literally pulls her onto the dance floor (35:36–37:00 min.), Lise is objectified in a manner that goes beyond even the normalised reification of the male gaze in mainstream cinema (Mulvey, 1975).

Jerry's aggressive attitude when he later gets out of Milo's car in a fit of hurt pride demonstrates the toxicity of his patriarchal notion of masculinity at its worst. When Milo later tracks him down to the café the point is made that he has done to Lise exactly what he earlier accused Milo so angrily of having done to him. Jerry's conservative gender politics implicate the gaze of art with the gaze of the male sexual predator yet Milo's assertion of her right to 'gaze' at both art and men establishes an opposed feminist perspective on modern gender relations. Unfavourably contrasting the spiteful behaviour of the American with the *savoir faire* exhibited by the French Henri, the film thereby elaborates its comparison of New and Old World cultures as well in respect of love and sex as in its many other tropes. In 2014, no echoes of such male chauvinism persist: Jerry is as respectful as the most gallant young lover, while even the frustration of the lovesick Adam is never misogynistic but presented as a paradigm of the male artist who sublimates his unrequited passion in his music.

One of the iconic songs from the movie, Henri's 'I'll Build A Stairway to Paradise', comes just before the Beaux Arts Ball scene. It is an elaborately staged and baroquely decorated number, the last before the long ballet, which is a pivotal

FIGURE 16.1 Georges Guétary performing 'I'll Build a Stairway to Paradise' as the confident and famous Henri in the 1951 film version.

Source: Production still provided by the editor.

FIGURE 16.2   The shy Henri of the stage version (played by Haydn Oakley in the 2017 London production) can so far only fantasise about starring in a big Broadway show.

Source: Photo by Bettina Strenske, courtesy of Alamy Stock Photo.

moment in its plotting because Henri is performing in a French music hall for the benefit of his fans and in particular an American producer who will offer him a contract to appear in New York, thereby making it possible for him simply to relinquish Lise to Jerry at the end of the film.

While the popular singer Georges Guétary portrays Henri as an experienced performer who personally greets fans from the runway on which he makes his entrance, in the stage show Henri is a novice making a debut in a small café. His performance begins shakily but as he gains in confidence, he imagines the song as a huge Broadway showstopper that includes Adam and the staging reinforces this with a neon backdrop to match. The stage show therefore places a different narrative emphasis on the resolution of the ballet, which in the movie is a psycho-sexual resolution that substitutes for plot.

The post-war setting: art and politics

The MGM film is set in a Paris contemporaneous with the time of its making (1951). Although Gene Kelly had wanted to film on location in Paris (the film's studio-based mise-en-scène must at first have seemed old-fashioned after the pioneer location filming of the earlier Kelly-Donen *On the Town*), Minnelli exploits the additional level of control possible by filming on MGM's Hollywood backlot, the artificial design of every interior and exterior shot allowing him to evoke post-war Paris as a series of paintings, which expresses the thematic motif of art – and Paris as the visual art capital of the world. Kelly/Jerry is an ex-GI in France who, once demobbed in 1945, had chosen to remain in Paris in order to pursue his artistic ambitions. Jerry's decision is grounded in the historical fact that '[i]n the aftermath of the Second World War, there were still 250 American artists living in the capital thanks to the GI bill' (Higonnet, 2002, p. 418). Since the film was released only six years after VE-day, Minnelli assumed his audience would immediately grasp the post-war context.

In 2014, on the other hand, with World War II no longer even a distant memory, Wheeldon and Lucas set their stage version immediately after the liberation of Paris in order to emphasise the harsh realities of the recently ended war. As Adam Hochberg lights a cigarette, he is established as the narrator: 'When you think of Paris what do you think of? The Champs-Élysées, romance, cheese. Well it wasn't always like that; for four years the City of Light was dark.' After his brief introduction a party seems in swing as we watch gigantic banners with swastikas torn down as a symbolic act of liberation, the start of a balletic jazz dance, which establishes a convention that frames the entire show as a kind of jazz ballet. So while the movie's aesthetic key is filming as an analogy of painting, the theatre performance is keyed to the staging of dance. All the action in the streets of Paris is danced from the first appearance of Jerry until his meeting with Adam at the café when they realise they are both Americans.

The shadow of Nazi occupation falls sombrely over a number of scenes in the show, with wounded soldiers and beggars on the streets and accusations of collaboration hanging in the air. The theme of the stage show is identified by Adam in his opening speech as the struggle for the light of creativity and love to emerge from the darkness of destruction represented at its starkest by the Nazi regime. The dramaturgy of the latter is fairly traditional in its deliberate 'tidying up' of the unconventional shape of Minnelli/Lerner's screenplay to produce a narrative that more naturalistically maps the motivation of all the characters by means of expository and didactic explanation. Lucas therefore avoids the more equivocal attitudes of the actors/characters in the film, with all the resonances of unconscious impulse that Minnelli is at pains to put in play.

The stage production has recourse to the rather old-fashioned device of composing letters aloud to fill in quite a large amount of expository material concerning Henri and Lise's relationship, as well as Adam's voice-overs and direct address to the audience regarding his infatuation with Lise, a more overt and clichéd historical and psychological rationale for the characters' behaviour. They have made explicit the fact that Lise is Jewish; they've played with the possibility that Henri Baurel might be gay (letting it 'bubble under the surface' of his awkwardness with Lise); they've given Jerry traumatic war memories and Adam a leg injury. This complicates the character exposition considerably, necessitating a number of additional scenes with Madame and Monsieur Baurel as sponsors of the Châtelet Ballet in order to underpin Lise's career as star of the new ballet with a backstory that involves their having hid and protected her during the War, in turn supporting the idea of her as the obvious choice of wife for their sexually ambivalent son.

This represents an oddly literal approach to storytelling in view of the choreographer's stated inclination to create a show that appeared to be a jazz ballet with interpolated dialogue scenes. In an interview with Mackerell, Wheeldon revealed his genuine interest in the actuality of Paris itself as a location:

> [T]he choreographer is in Paris himself, . . . and he admits . . . he made a pilgrimage to the exact spot by the Seine where Kelly and his co-star Leslie Caron had their great love scenes:[13] 'I needed to see it for myself,' he says, 'and I sent my actors there, too. It makes such a difference to be working on this in Paris, to soak up the atmosphere where it all takes place.
>
> *(quoted in Mackerell, 2014)*

The medium: painting/film vs scenic spectacle/dance

The 2014 production is far from being a simple transference from screen to stage. For Wheeldon the film is 'a perfect, one-of-a-kind period piece. 63 years later, there's no point attempting a replica' (quoted in Mackerell, 2014). Yet of course, the film never actually represents the banks of the 'real' Seine because it was not actually filmed on location. The opening montage of second unit shots of picture-postcard Paris with Kelly's 'I am a painter' voice-over establish the theme of Paris as art work: 'Brother, if can't paint in Paris, you better go home and marry the boss's daughter.' The painterly views through Jerry's window accentuate the act of looking from the point of view of both the tourist/voyeur and the art-lover.

The filmic property that prompts an envisioning of the subject's perspective through the identification of his gaze with the view of the camera cannot be simply translated to the stage but needs to be deconstructed as a trope and re-assembled in theatrical language. In the film, Jerry's identity as a painter is expressed directly in the voice-over in which he names his profession; by contrast the stage show demonstrates his work as a painter from the moment he produces his sketch pad in the ballet rehearsal and begins to draw ideas for his set design. Thus Wheeldon has also moved beyond the mediated Paris familiar to fans of the movie, replacing the picture-postcard or art references of Minnelli with Bob Crowley's virtuoso digital rendering of Paris in the act of being sketched and painted – a technically sophisticated stage device to remind the viewer literally that the artist Jerry is painting the Paris of his imagination as well as illustrating vividly how any place is always partially constructed through the eyes of its viewers. Although Mackerell believes that Lucas, Wheeldon and Crowley made the topic of art and creativity much more central, this appears wholly to miss the subtlety of Minnelli's screen version, which is deeply imbricated in a dialectical discourse about Paris in art and artists living in Paris. In keeping with Wheeldon's own emphasis on dance as key compositional instrument Lise needed to be an aspiring ballerina, thereby motivating the ballet rehearsals- and performances-within-the-show that might foreground his kinetic composition as opposed to Minnelli's filmic analogy of painting.

Imagistically, the red of the Nazi conflagration at the start of the piece is immediately replaced by a gigantic *tricolour* – the red, white and blue with aircrafts superimposed on it signifying both the French flag and the red, white and blue of the American flag. The theme of American and French culture re-asserting their identities in *détente* after the German Occupation is figured in the plot by Milo Davenport who tries to sell her financial sponsorship of the new ballet as a Franco-American collaboration, celebrating 'French and American youth side by side marching ahead into the future together'.

In spite of Kelly's earlier male bravado, his wooing is very gentle by the Seine: he calls her 'a girl of mystery', then she hums a few bars of 'Our Love is Here to Stay' to introduce the song surreptitiously before he sings it. The banality of American suburbia is contrasted with the romance of the Seine ('Sunday night in America – everybody catches cold'), but when they dance somewhat balletically, Caron is seen to have elevated Kelly from hoofer to ballet dancer until they kiss in the dance, which finally elides into walking. Such a subtle segue into and out of dance enhances the dreamlike quality of the moment, illuminating the characters' desire in oneiric terms as they dance out the joy of their 'love affair'.

Both Fairchild and Cope are professional artists looking for jobs with the Châtelet Ballet Company. The stage version of the scene at the Seine exposes the asexuality of Henri's wooing in its stark contrast with the ardour of sexual desire in both Jerry/Robert Fairchild and Eliza/Leanne Cope in 'Liza', added for the 2014 production, a song in which he Americanises her French name by way of seducing her in dance to the rhythm and melody of the Gershwins' famous song. As a dancer she reacts almost immediately, her bodily response authenticating the truth of her attraction. In a way Crowley effectively parallels the film's second-hand rendering of Paris through the painters' images, with sketches of a putative visual landscape that is further removed from the photographic realism of cinema and more in line with the self-referential discourse of the designer/artist. The view of the bank of the Seine where Kelly and Caron dance repeatedly and which Wheeldon claims to have visited to 'soak up the atmosphere of the place' is even more artfully rendered than in Minnelli's film; it is self-evidently a stylised, cartoon-like drawing of the river with two silhouettes of rowing boats, whose artifice is rendered yet more extreme when Jerry jumps into the water and pops up completely dry 10 seconds later.

On screen, the Beaux Arts Ball psychoanalytically presents Jerry's major crisis of interior life (82:56–92:14 min.), its monochromatic visual motif dovetailing a representation of the self-conscious abstractions of modern art with the trope of the heightened self-awareness of archetypal psychology within Jerry's consciousness as analysand. On stage, an imagined sequence of ballet rehearsal and Jerry's process of design succeeds a brief scene in which Milo tries to get Jerry to dance: it appears as a fantasy, a parallel to the Ball in the stage version and eventually morphs into a masked ball, luridly lit in red and pink to represent the sensual pleasures of modern art and dance in carnival mode rather than with any degree of interiority in the protagonists' psyches. Whereas Irene Sharaff dresses Kelly in a joker outfit split down the middle between white and black with black lozenges on white thereby emphasising the oppositions in his personality, Crowley and Wheeldon do not concentrate on the interior life of the protagonists, except as a means of delineating their infatuation/aggression and its resolution.

Instead they highlight the prominence of modes of art – both painting and dance – and bourgeoise social conventions in determining the destiny of the individuals they circumscribe. In this and earlier sequences the physical manifestations of the design on stage comprise framed mirrors and numerous window and empty picture frames, reminding the audience of the blank canvases which Jerry is expected to fill with designs and paintings. Significantly the carnival dance (most directly comparable with the Beaux Arts Ball sequence) begins with a devilish Milo, entering from the upstage left in red and black, to dress Jerry in a white tuxedo as her party begins. A nun in a black sequined wimple is hoisted aloft, as is Lise who has been dancing with Henri in a black dress with red flowers. As opposed to the monochrome of the movie, the colour scheme is red, white and black, a highly eroticised manifestation of the material luxury afforded by Milo, climaxing with Jerry unmasking and kissing Milo as his diabolical partner.

The musical number that follows, Mrs Baurel's society presentation of the brief ballet concert, the pretentiously avant-garde 'The Eclipse of Uranus',[14] a still-born creation which provides a vivid contrast to the aliveness of 'Fidgety Feet', whose syncopated jazz rhythms attempt to allay the boredom of the spectators in a spontaneous outburst of irritable energy that reveals the human instinct to move/dance. Instead of an inner psychological crisis, Wheeldon and Crowley create kinetic images of a crucible of modern art, with projections on the cyclorama and on moveable screens employed for the creation and destruction of artworks in the factories of modern art institutions.

Minnelli and Kelly's development of the film ballet

Beth Genné has brilliantly illustrated the process by which Minnelli and Kelly developed a unique type of 'film-dance-drama' at MGM, which came to be known as the 'film ballet' (Genné, 2018). Starting with Minnelli's partnership on Broadway with Georges Balanchine in *Ziegfeld Follies of 1936*, then continuing in film with Astaire in MGM's *Yolanda and the Thief* (1945) and *Ziegfeld Follies* (1946), before culminating in his collaboration with Kelly on *The Pirate* (1948) and *An American in Paris*, the process became progressively enriched. Genné defines these film ballets as dance dramas concerning the vicissitudes of courtship, in which 'the lover and beloved investigate new aspects of their emotional lives by entering a dream world in which they are free to reveal their deepest and most contradictory feelings' (Genné, 2018, pp. 193–194). Where earlier directors, such as Busby Berkeley, had piled lavish effects upon already spectacular dance sequences,[15] Minnelli's approach instead co-ordinated 'dance, décor, music, and camerawork to play out the stylised drama of seduction which is at their core' (Genné, 2018, p. 194).

Minnelli's innovation was to manoeuvre the 'mobile boom or crane camera in such a way that it participates in the dance' (Genné, 2018, p. 194). In the 'Limehouse Blues' number from *Ziegfeld Follies*, Minnelli introduced 'fantastic, dreamlike settings and dramatic lighting and colour effects' for the first time (Genné, 2018, p. 197). *Yolanda* introduced a Freudian concept of dream in a surrealistic style of ballet, while in *The Pirate*, Kelly and Minnelli worked so closely that 'Minnelli would co-ordinate that moving body with light and shadow, colour and texture, like a painter creating a visual world within the boundaries of a canvas' (Genné, 2018, p. 205). What was new in *An American in Paris* were the tableaux that presented pastiche versions of the work of French Impressionist painters, in particular Renoir, Rousseau, Dufy and Toulouse-Lautrec, Utrillo and Van Gogh.

An anagnorisis of art and love

Minnelli and Kelly's 'American in Paris' ballet (92:14–107:30 min.) is directly predicated on the black-and-white abstraction of the Beaux Arts Ball, an antithetical resolution in dance and scenography of Jerry/Kelly's fractured psychological identity; it also resolves the plot in which Jerry must finally woo and win Lise/Caron to consummate the onscreen romance that has been so long delayed by the narrativisation of music, painting and dance. The ballet constituted a revolution in the art of Hollywood screen dance. Deliberately setting itself up as a competitor to the British film *The Red Shoes* (1948),[16] which was much admired in the United States[17] and whose 14-minute ballet was the longest dance sequence ever presented within a narrative film, Kelly/Minnelli's eponymous ballet lasting almost 17 minutes was quite possibly the most complex attempt on screen to date in terms of its mise-en-scène, exploiting all the spectacular effects of lighting and travelling boom camerawork Minnelli had perfected in filming the dances in his earlier works discussed above.

Phenomenologically one might view the sequence as an act of 'world-creation', the existential gesture by which an artist confronts the conflictual, contradictory and incomplete world in which s/he has been historically immersed to remake it through a series of experiments of the imagination. In Lise's presence Jerry rips up a sketch of Paris destroying his own vision of the city. Yet as Kelly emerges in daydream into the monochrome sketch to pick up a red rose, red, white and blue are splashed on the canvas and his dancing sketches in the outlines of a new world of sensuous experience embodied in the colours he (Jerry) conceives as a painter and the shapes he (Kelly) invents as a dancer-choreographer. Yet like his progenitor, Minnelli the filmmaker, Jerry/Kelly does not create in a void but manufactures a bricolage of image and kinesis by quoting from the great paintings of Paris by artists of the *fin de siècle* and the movement vocabularies of (French) ballet and (American) jazz dance. What the film has throughout been hinting at in hesitant yet suggestive stabs is now finally achieved: the patchwork of second-hand expression – in mimicry and pastiche – is given unique screen form.

What the film accomplishes in the ballet is a psychic integration of the fragmented personality of Jerry Mulligan, implying his resolution of the conflict between dark and light (unconscious/female and conscious/male) aspects of his nature in a process that demands he relinquish his masculine desire to triumph as an artist, who in turn tames financially powerful/phallic women (Milo) in order to possess the feminine woman (Lise) he desires. In doing so he surrenders to his feminine unconscious, allowing himself to love and be loved by Lise without protecting the masculine privilege that has prevented him from being vulnerable to the demands of his deepest self. Starting from a staged battle with anonymous female dancers represented in white ballet gowns as harpies, who soon appear again to menace him in red, before other men and women including a platoon of dancing French soldiers (embattled men) appear, Lise enters to the fountain as the first female figure who is not phallic and the scene transforms to a flower market, lit for the first time in sunlight, with a brilliant range of colours.

Finally, a quartet of American servicemen appear as Jerry's allies/friends, who assume the brightly coloured striped blazers and straw boaters they take from a shop window display, emblematising the swagger of American masculinity in competition against the French 'feminine'. The quintet of male dancers then perform American-style choreography in which Kelly deliberately incorporates the George M. Cohan 'strut' and there seems to be a kinetic conversation between masculine and feminine factions. As men and women dance in their striped costumes the air turns amber and becomes smokey as Jerry lifts Lise tenderly and carries her to the fountain (blue) for a romantic *pas de deux* among the statuary, which subsequently

FIGURE 16.3   Gene Kelly (Jerry) and Leslie Caron (Lise) in the Madeleine flower market section of the 'American in Paris' ballet, with set and costumes inspired by the paintings of Auguste Renoir and Édouard Manet.

Source: Production still provided by the editor.

turns red and blue.[18] Then a 16th century-style painting of Paris architecture suffused with orange, amber and brown ushers in the joke figure of Toulouse-Lautrec with a sandwich board and the famous painted figure of his Le Chocolat,[19] a black dancer whose position Kelly adopts in a highly sexualised dance that reveals him as a homo-erotically charged object. In the café, are seated Oscar Wilde, Aristide Bruant and other denizens of the Parisian *demi-monde* of 1896.[20]

According to Wheeldon, the 2014 stage version 'is very much about how love and art inform each other' (Mackerell, 2014), yet that is in fact precisely what the MGM movie is about. Some critics have commented on what appears to be the film's perfunctory ending, but this is part of the artistic intention. The resolution comes in the ballet-within-the-film; the marriage proposal in the frame narrative is merely a formality. Rushing down the long staircase to kiss Lise, Jerry comes down to earth, to the real world in which his true love must be grounded just as she ascends to the plane of his artistic vision. As the film ends, the camera pans upwards to leave the viewer a panoramic view of Paris as the 'City of Light' – the underlying subject of the film.

In the stage version, abstract painting and design keys the dancing in the 'American in Paris' ballet: suggestive of paintings by Mondrian and other pop artists,

FIGURE 16.4 The final moment of the 'American in Paris' ballet in the 2014 stage version of the film, as choreographed by Christopher Wheeldon and designed by Bob Crowley. Held aloft at the centre of the image in front of a stylised Eiffel Tower is Leanne Cope as Lise. Scene from the 2017 London production at the Dominion Theatre.

Source: Photo by Johan Persson, provided by ArenaPal.

Crowley and Wheeldon's scheme evokes the ways in which modern art and dance interact to transform Paris into the pre-eminently modern city of the 20th century. Not as much concerned with Jerry's psychological identity as with Lise's choice, Wheeldon has created a charming ballet in the modernist style of the Stravinsky ballets sponsored by Diaghilev's *Ballets Russes* at mid-century. When the ballet-within-the-show begins, Lise is dancing with a ballet partner in a Mondrian-inspired costume, but later Jerry enters the dance (of Lise's unconscious) in black, taking the place of her partner: he has a red belt; she has a red décolletage. The ballet ultimately demonstrates the liberation and reconstruction of Paris by Americans and French working together so that the red, white and blue/tricolour of their national flags combine in the projections with a stylised image of the Eiffel Tower at the conclusion of the dance.

While Minnelli taps into his deep understanding of visual art and design to fully exploit the aural and visual imagery of the cinematic medium in investigating the unconscious interrelationships of music, painting, dance, personal and national identity, Wheeldon's stage musical more consciously historicises its source narrative to provide rational explanations of each strand, using dance and digital scenography to explore its key themes of destruction (war) and creation (art) with more conscious intent. Yet each in its own way is an art work that pays homage to Paris, Gershwin, ballet and French art of the *fin de siècle* and mid-20th century.

Notes

1 The tracking numbers refer to the DVD release of *An American in Paris* and the cinema broadcast of the 2017 London stage production, respectively.

2 For instance, *Gentlemen Prefer Blondes* (1953), *Funny Face* (1957) and *Silk Stockings* (1957).

3 For more information on the location shooting of *On the Town*, see Fordin, 1996, pp. 263–267.

4 For the NYCB, Wheeldon choreographed a 21-minute ballet based on *An American in Paris* (2005). He is currently Artistic Associate at the Royal Ballet in London.

5 'The television series *Omnibus* invited Kelly to create a documentary about the relationship between dance and athletics. He gave them *Dancing: A Man's Game* (1960), where he complains about widespread effeminacy in male dancing which he felt stigmatized the art form, alienating boys from entering the field. Kelly said: 'Dancing does attract effeminate young men. I don't object to that if they don't dance effeminately. I just say that if a man dances effeminately he dances badly. Unfortunately, people confuse gracefulness with softness. John Wayne is a graceful man and so are some of the great ball players. But, of course, they don't run the risk of being called sissies. You can spot many of these male dancers by their arm movements: they are soft, limp, and feminine' (quoted in Rutledge, 2020).

6 'Sissy' is a barely disguised code word in the first half of the 20th Century for a homosexual man.

7 According to Steven Cohan, Kelly's 'solo numbers work as straightforward exhibitionist displays. As they underscore the dancer's awareness of being watched, however, they make more visible the choreography's camp inflection of Kelly's "showing off" as a self-conscious performance of manliness that teeters between exhibitionism and parody in the erotic display' (Cohan, 2005, p. 176). For an incisive analysis of Kelly's eroticised dance representation of masculinity as queer or camp, see Cohan, 2005, pp. 166–183.

8 Fan blogs, Twitter and other means of social media are often obsessed with knowing whether a male ballet star is gay, see for instance Gramiliano, 2013.

9 Although technically irrelevant to his self-presentation as a stage performer, the duet *Us* (2019) by Christopher Wheeldon, which Fairchild performed at the Fire Island Festival with the openly gay Travis Wall, explains the ease with which he registers masculinity onstage without recourse to the heavy-handed machismo that undermines the performances of so many American leading men in musicals.

10 Since the publication of Laura Mulvey's seminal essay, 'Visual Pleasure of Narrative and the Male Gaze' in 1974, feminist criticism has assumed that the spectatorial position in classic film is a woman as object subjected to the male gaze.

11 The greying of his dark brown hair may have been a signal to the audience that Gene Kelly (38 years old), not Guétary (35 years old), was the romantic lead in the film.

12 According to Natalia Cecire, 'Joel Dinerstein has pointed out how tap, in its heyday, signified the modernity of what Kristin Ross has called "fast cars, clean bodies," a technological modernity strongly associated with Americanness, especially in postwar France: "Similarly, the tap dancer took the speeded-up machine-driven tempo of life and the metallic crunch of cities and factories and spun it all into a dazzling pyrotechnical display of speed, precision, rhythmic noise, continuity, grace, and power"' (Cecire, 2016).

13 Ironically, 'Our Love Is Here to Stay' was not shot on real location, but on a carefully manufactured studio set on MGM's Hollywood backlot.

14 The Greek god Uranus, who was castrated, gave his name to the Uranian, a 19th-century idea of homosexuals as constituting a third sex – women in men's bodies.

15 See also the musical numbers in MGM's own *The Great Ziegfeld* (1936) and *Ziegfeld Girl* (1941).

16 Freed, Kelly and Minnelli have acknowledged their direct competition with Powell and Pressburger's Oscar-winning classic, which had proved an unlikely box office success shortly before they began production; see Genné, 2018, p. 212.

17 It had been called 'the most ambitious – and probably the most dazzlingly successful – use of traditional – type ballet in any motion picture to date' (Scheuer, 1949, p. 19).

18 The costume designer Irene Sharaff, designed both sets and costumes for the 'American in Paris' ballet, working closely with Minnelli in referencing the appropriate painters for the ballet (Fordin, 1996, pp. 317–219).

19 *Chocolat Dancing in Bar Darchille,* 1896.

20 In the ballet, Leslie Caron references the dancer Jane Avril, whom Lautrec painted a number of times.

References

An American in Paris. (2019). Directed by C. Wheeldon. Cinema Broadcast, 7 May.

———. (1951). Directed by V. Minnelli. DVD. Los Angeles: MGM Home Video.

Bertocci, A. P. (1964) *From Symbolism to Baudelaire.* Carbondale: Southern Illinois University Press.

Cecire, N. (2016) 'He Just Wants to Sing,' *Arcade,* https://arcade.stanford.edu/ blogs/he-just-wants-sing, accessed 29 March 2020.

Cohan, S. (2005) *Incongruous Entertainment: Camp, Cultural Value, and the MGM Musical.* Durham, NC: Duke University Press.

Fordin, H. (1996) *MGM's Greatest Musicals: The Arthur Freed Unit.* New York: Da Capo.

Genné, B. (2018) *Dance Me a Song: Astaire, Balanchine and the American Film Musical.* New York: Oxford University Press.

Gramiliano. (2013) 'In and Out: Bolle. Gomez, Stiefel – How Easy Is It to Be an Openly Gay Ballet Dancer?' 7 July, www.gramilano.com/2013/07/in-out-bolle-gomes-stiefel-how-easy-is-it-to-be-an-openly-gay-ballet-dancer, accessed 27 June 2020.

Harvey, S. (1989) *Directed by Vincente Minnelli.* New York: Harper and Row.

Hext, K. J. (2014) '"Somehow This Crazy World Has Taken on a Wonderful Design": Vincente Minnelli's Neo-Victorian Utopias in Hollywood,' *Neo-Victorian Studies*, 7(1), pp. 52–78.

Higonnet, P. (2002) *Paris: Capital of the World* (A. Goldhammer, trans.). Cambridge and London: Belknap Press.

Jablonski, E. and Stewart, L. D. (1958) *The Gershwin Years*. New York: Doubleday.

Knox, D. (1973) *The Magic Factory: How MGM Made an American in Paris*. New York: Praeger.

Mackerell, J. (2014) 'Return to Rive Gauche: How Christopher Wheeldon Adapted an American in Paris,' *The Guardian*, 8 December, www.theguardian.com/stage/ 2014/dec/08/an-american-in-paris-christopher-wheeldon-gene-kelly, accessed 29 August 2019.

Minnelli, V. and Arce, H. (1974) *I Remember It Well*. New York: Doubleday.

Mulvey, L. (1975) 'Visual Pleasure and Narrative Cinema,' *Screen*, 16, October, pp. 6–18.

Naremore, J. (1993). *The Films of Vincente Minnelli*. Cambridge: Cambridge University Press.

Rutledge, S. (2020) '#Queer Quote: "Any Man Who Looks Like a Sissy While Dancing Is Just a Lousy Dancer." – Manly Man, Gene Kelly,' *The Wow Report*, 23 August, https://worldofwonder.net/queerquote-any-man-who-looks-like-a-sissy-while-dancing-is-just-a-lousy-dancer-manly-man-gene-kelly, accessed 3 July 2020.

Scheuer, P. K. (1949) 'Co-Producer Explains *The Red Shoes* Success,' *Los Angeles Times*, 19 December, p. 19.

17

PARIS AND THE CURSE OF CHICAGO IN STEPHEN SONDHEIM'S *SUNDAY IN THE PARK WITH GEORGE*

Robert Lawson-Peebles

'The last time I saw Paris'

'Reich Tanks Clank in Champs-Elysees.'

The anonymous sub-editor at the *New York Times* may never have flexed his prosodic muscle to greater effect than on 15 June 1940. The despatch, from Associated Press in Berlin, was necessarily more subtle in suggesting the rape of Cockaigne, describing German mechanised forces advancing down the famous 'tree-lined' avenue, 'at the head of Nazi units occupying the "City of Light"' (Anon, 1940a, p. 1). Two weeks later, the *New York Times* devoted a page to photographs of the German occupation, one of them contrasting a large foregrounded Swastika with the distant Eiffel Tower (Anon, 1940b, p. 96). Oscar Hammerstein II viewed the reports with dismay, and in response he wrote 'The Last Time I Saw Paris':

> The last time I saw Paris, her trees were dressed for spring,
> And lovers walked beneath those trees and birds found songs to sing.
> I dodged the same old taxicabs that I had dodged for years.
> The chorus of their squeaky horns was music to my ears.
> The last time I saw Paris, her heart was warm and gay,
> No matter how they change her, I'll remember her that way.
>
> *(Hammerstein II, 2020)*

The refrain is an example of modern pastoral, integrating nature and culture (birds and taxis) to create a dream of leisure and pleasure. The first verse initiates the theme of nostalgia for a golden age, represented by a feminised Paris whose spirit has departed, with drab streets now stalked by 'lonely men with lonely eyes'. The second verse extends the refrain by sketching familiar sights. Both verses close with blighted images: Paris 'has left the Seine' and the 'City of Light' has plunged into darkness (Hammerstein II, 2020). The song, composed by Jerome Kern, won the 1941 Academy Award for Best Song, confirming the belief that the Nazi occupation of Paris brought a chapter in the city's history to a close.

'The Last Time I Saw Paris' begins this essay for two reasons. Firstly, Hammerstein and Kern are important influences on Stephen Sondheim's career. It is well known that, in addition to acting as a surrogate father, Hammerstein supervised Sondheim's initial training as a lyricist (Banfield, 1993, pp. 13–14). Sondheim later regarded Hammerstein as little more than a boot-camp instructor (Sondheim, 2010, p. xix). His appreciation of Kern endured, based not on gratitude but rather on his awareness of the composer's technical mastery (Sondheim, 2010, p. 232). For this he was indebted to Milton Babbitt. Babbitt was an unrepentant serialist composer who later became a pioneer in electronic music; he was also a closet songwriter for musicals and therefore a perspicuous choice for Sondheim's postgraduate fellowship (Secrest, 1998, pp. 84–88). So they spent their time subjecting Kern to musicological analysis on an equal footing with Bach and Beethoven. Babbitt's teaching became the core of Sondheim's praxis. When he was chosen in 1990 as the first Cameron Mackintosh Visiting Professor at St. Catherine's College, Oxford, Sondheim made his students analyse Kern's 'All the Things You Are' with the same stringency that he had experienced with Babbitt. He also took them to rehearsals (see Figure 17.2) of his 1984 musical, *Sunday in the Park with George*, at London's National Theatre (Sondheim, 2010, p. 303; Lipton, 1997, p. 264). This duplex pedagogic strategy gave the students a privileged insight into Sondheim's working practice, which had in this case a self-referential outcome. Sondheim indicated the importance of *Sunday* (as I shall henceforth call it) by naming his two volumes of annotated lyrics after its song about the process of artistic creation, with the first, *Finishing the Hat* (2010), taking its title and the second, *Look, I Made a Hat* (2011), referencing two key lines: 'Look, I made a hat/Where there never was a hat' (Sondheim and Lapine, 1990, p. 45). To create something out of nothing is fundamental to many artistic endeavours. As the narrator remarks in John Banville's *roman à clef* about the art historian-cum-spy Anthony Blunt and his love of the French painter Nicolas Poussin (1594–1665): 'Why did he paint it? – Because it was not there' (Banville, 1997, p. 343).

Sunday opens with a stage that is entirely white, a blank canvas on which the artist George must paint a number of figures, most of them wearing hats (Sondheim and Lapine, 1990, p. 1). That form of adornment appears in many shapes and sizes in the painting upon which *Sunday* is based. Georges Seurat's *Un dimanche après-midi a l'Île de la Grande Jatte/ Sunday Afternoon on the Island of La Grande Jatte*, portrays a suburban park in Paris and its occupants as the material for creating an ordered design. In turn, Sondheim uses the painting as a means for exploring the demands and costs involved in that endeavour. The two acts of *Sunday* explore the relation of aesthetics and the mundane, the conflict between the isolating demands of artistic production and the needs of human beings for love and reproduction. The tree is an important image in *Sunday*. It functions as a natural event (as it does in 'The Last Time I Saw Paris'), as a pliant art object and – with the metaphor of

FIGURE 17.1 Georges Seurat's *Un dimanche après-midi a l'Île de la Grande Jatte/Sunday Afternoon on the Island of La Grande Jatte* (1884–1886), which can be seen at the Art Institute of Chicago. Oil on canvas.

Source: Photo provided by the editor.[1]

the family tree – as a symbol of the taxonomy (and regeneration) of kinship. This is the second reason why 'The Last Time I Saw Paris' is a helpful entry point to this discussion. It represents both the halfway stage and the pivot between two modes of examining Paris in *Sunday*. In Act I, set in the 1880s, Paris is the source of the artistic imagination. Act II is set in 1984. It is briefer and, because the same cast play different roles,[2] is sometimes regarded as an appendage to the first. However, Act II introduces a new dimension into the musical, with Paris in 1984 as a residuum of creative and personal integrity, embellished by a memory of the pre-war city that has been almost but not quite overwhelmed by a monetary view of art, symbolised by Chicago.

La belle époque: Seurat's Paris and Sondheim's tourists

The Cast Page of *Sunday* states that Act I takes place between 1884 and 1886, to correspond with the period that Seurat's was painting *La Grande Jatte* (Sondheim and Lapine, 1990, n.p.). Seurat began work in May 1884, and the painting was shown at the 8th Impressionist Exhibition in May 1886 (Herbert et al., 2004, pp. 22, 68). However, two other paintings by Seurat make an appearance in Act I, expanding the time period. Early drafts for *Une Baignade à Asnières/The*

Bathers were begun around 1882, and the completed painting was exhibited in May 1884 (Leighton and Thomson, 1997, pp. 54, 125). *La Poudreuse/Young Woman Powdering Herself* was painted somewhere between 1888 and 1890 (House, 1994, pp. 160–161). Furthermore, in *Sunday*, the Old Lady's dismay at the construction of the Eiffel Tower (Sondheim and Lapine, 1990, pp. 54–55) suggests that the third Sunday might occur between 1887, when work on the Tower started, and 1889, when it was completed in time for the International Exposition of that year (Harison, 2020, pp. 179–180).

The dating of the play places Paris at the height of the (posthumously named) *belle époque*. Venita Datta's chapter in this volume explains that Paris was at that time the tourist capital of Europe, a city of (electric) light, with glittering department stores and a boulevard culture bustling with cafés, music, theatre and cabarets. In addition, there was a plethora of opportunities for those with lascivious inclinations. Before the Moulin Rouge was opened in 1889, the naughty epicentre of tourist Paris was the Jardin Mabille, in the Faubourg Saint-Honoré, parallel to the Champs-Élysées (Harison, 2020, pp. 197–198).

On the second Sunday of Act I, two American tourists, identified simply as Mr. and Mrs., wander into the riverside scene at La Jatte. They are not impressed. 'Paris looks nothin' like the paintings', sneers Mr. Mrs. agrees. The Parisians are 'placid'; they lack 'passion' and 'style'. So Mr. and Mrs. will return early to Charleston, South Carolina, after visiting the galleries. But they love the pastries of Paris, so they decide to take a pâtissier back home with them (Sondheim and Lapine, 1990, pp. 40–41). The tourists make three brief appearances in Act I of *Sunday*. They do not sing, and they are not amongst the figures in *La Grande Jatte*. They are a plot device, luring Louis the baker from Paris, and with him his new lover, Dot. Dot's pregnancy has failed to distract George from his painting; and so Marie, their child, is taken to the United States to become the grandmother of the second George. (Let's follow Olaf Jubin, and call him George II [Jubin, 2014, p. 202, Note 2]). In Act II, George II presents his latest art installation in the un-named gallery where *La Grande Jatte* is displayed. The tourists, therefore, are largely hidden ligatures in a musical where the imperative for both Georges is, precisely, to 'connect' (Sondheim and Lapine, 1990, pp. 59, 101). To resort for a moment to the language of medicine, they operate as the autonomic nervous system in the body of the text.

The American tourists have other, more ironic, functions in *Sunday*. Despite their disappointment, they are determined to fulfil their roles as patrons and consumers of Paris, whether it is pastry or art. But they are in the wrong place. The work of Baron Haussmann had by 1870 turned a central area of Paris, including the Étoile, the Champs-Élysées and the Avenue de l'Opéra, into a magnet for tourists, a vast arena of straight avenues and squares. Beyond that arena, Paris developed as a set of concentric rings radiating out from the original city walls, with the poor banished to the margins of the city that could be unsafe for tourists (Hazan, 2010, p. 7 and *passim*.; Sante, 2015). To the north-west, beyond the Boulevard Périphérique (built between 1958 and 1973), is La Jatte, the last island as the Seine snakes northward towards Le Havre and La Manche (or the English Channel, as the Brits would have it).

La Jatte was one of the parks where various ranks of the bourgeoisie[3] gathered at the weekend, boated on the Seine and engaged in the pastime of *flânerie* (Harison, 2020, pp. 103–104). 'Paris', wrote Edmund White, himself a noted practitioner, 'is the great city of the *flâneur* – that aimless stroller who loses himself in the crowd, who has no destination and goes wherever caprice or curiosity directs his or her steps' (White, 2001, p. 16). The cost of transatlantic travel in the 1880s would mean that *flânerie* would not be an activity for purposive American tourists. They would have restricted themselves to the centre; and those interested in 'passion' would have ventured to Montmartre.

Seurat's painting of La Jatte portrays several *flâneurs*. It also includes other Parisians, most dressed in their Sunday best, walking, sitting or lounging; two soldiers; a musician playing a horn (or merely an amateur practising, for there is no sign of a collection box); one child running while another demurely holds her mother's hand; three dogs (one, perhaps a Jack Russell Terrier, is towards the centre background); and a monkey. The pets, suggesting stability and fidelity, are indicators of bourgeois status (Harison, 2020, p. 167). The pug and the monkey in the foreground of *La Grande Jatte* are more exotic examples of pet kind, indicating perhaps that their owners are of higher status than most of the others, or are willing to spend more of their disposable income for the purposes of display. This is particularly apparent in the male, who sports a cigar as well as a top hat. The soldiers and the nurse (on the left, with her back to the viewer and next to her elderly charge), are permitted entry because of their roles (House, 1989, p. 124). In sum, *La Grande Jatte* displays 'elegance and pretension, current fashion and social parade' (Herbert et al., 2004, p. 163), but within a limited social range. This, I suggest, is the interpretation that Sondheim and Lapine adopted, for it allows them to emphasise the ironic contrast between the frozen order of art, emphasised by Seurat's formalist structures, and the seething chaos of life to be found (as we shall see) in their presentation of the (often indecorous) activity on the island.

La Grande Jatte lends itself easily to social-iconographic readings, and it has been argued that there are exceptions to this sunny bourgeois scene. If the males were indulging in *flânerie*, the females could be loitering for other purposes. There has been a debate about the status of the women in *La Grande Jatte*. Arguments by some critics that some of the women are prostitutes have been rejected by others.[4] There has also been much debate about the status of the reclining man, in the left foreground of the painting, dressed in oarsman's clothes and smoking a churchwarden pipe (Clark, 1984, pp. 265–267; Clayson, 1989, pp. 162–163, 244, footnote 43; Herbert et al., 2004, p. 162). Similar remarks may be made about the black dog loitering close to, if not associated with, the athlete; for it is counterpointed against the leaping pug wearing a dainty bow. It has been suggested that this is a working-class dog (Herbert et al., 2004, p. 164), and has even been called a 'mongrel' (House, 1989, p. 124).

If the athlete and the dog are not bourgeois, they are in the wrong place, and on the wrong day. They would be more at home in *The Bathers*, on the far bank in Asnières. Despite their similar large scale, *The Bathers* and *La Grande Jatte* were not designed as a pair of paintings, but when brought together on the page seem to take part in an ironic discourse, where the stares of the men on the bank at Asnières, and the call by the boy in the water (on the right of the painting), are met with studied indifference by the bourgeois on La Jatte.[5] For the two paintings portray differing social circumstances. *The Bathers* portrays lounging males and a dog (probably a spaniel), taking time off during a working day, against a backdrop of the railway bridge at Asnières, the gasworks and factories of Clichy (on the opposite bank to Asnières), and the giant sewer, designed by Haussmann, which ejects its contents into the Seine some metres (happily) downstream of the bathers in Seurat's painting (Leighton and Thomson, 1997, pp. 53, 56; Fenton, 2000, p. 154).

The varieties of paintable pleasure

According to Robert Hughes:

> Around 1870, the field of paintable pleasure dramatically widened. . . . all these painters had, broadly speaking, something in common. It was the feeling that the life of the city and the village, the cafés and the bois, the salons and the bedrooms, the boulevards, the seaside, and the banks of the Seine, could become a vision of Eden – a world of ripeness and bloom, projecting an untroubled sense of wholeness. One might look at this world with irony, but never with the eye of despair.
>
> *(Hughes, 1980, p. 113)*

All this thanks to the expansion of the railways, which allowed easy access for Parisians to the suburbs and – of course – for foreign tourists to Paris from the coastal ports. Baedeker's *Handbook for Travellers* noted that, as it was just three-and-a-quarter miles from Paris, Asnières was 'a favourite resort for boating and other amusements in summer' (Baedeker, 1900, p. 291). And where the Parisians went, the painters followed. Claude Monet painted twelve views of the Gare Saint-Lazare, the station from which passengers could reach Asnières in ten minutes (Rathbone et al., 1996, p. 60; House, 1994, pp. 120–121; Fenton, 2000, p. 152). Asnières was portrayed by Van Gogh, Émile Bernard and Paul Signac as well as Seurat, integrating the bridge and trains with the surroundings to create a balanced image of industry, nature and leisure. A 'schematic map' of the area, marking the points of view adopted by the painters, shows that Seurat, unusually, restricted his perspective so that *La Grande Jatte* excludes any sign of industry (Leighton and Thomson, 1997, pp. 138–144). Baedeker ignores La Jatte; it had no railway station. The two Americans are therefore way off the tourist track, literally and metaphorically.

As Robert Hughes has shown, there are many different scenes available to painters. *La Grande Jatte* draws on a tradition that records the activity known (in the vernacular phrase) as 'mucking about on the river' – and also on the banks of it. This trope is largely indebted to Charles Daubigny's *Voyage en Bateau* (1862), illustrated with his own etchings. Probably the most celebrated painting in this tradition is Auguste Renoir's *Le déjeuner des canotiers/Luncheon of the Boating Party* (1881), revered, together with *La Grande Jatte*, 'as pillars of the modern move- ment . . . icons of modern art, modern life, and popular culture of the twentieth century' (Rathbone et al., 1996, p. 154). Maybe so; but Henry James, the pioneer of literary modernism, was not impressed with the Impressionists. He also cast a censorious eye at the hanky-panky on the banks of the Seine. He 'took a penny steamer' down-river, and was alarmed by 'the frantic pursuit of pleasure' that he observed (James, 1957, p. 190).

'Ripeness and bloom' (to use the phrase of Robert Hughes) – in the centre of Paris, on the suburban Seine and as recorded in the paintings – may for now have been too ripe for James. (The lessons of Paris would later be absorbed into James's fiction.) Unlike their seemingly staid Northern compatriot, the two American tourists in *Sunday* are not shocked but bored. The island is too 'placid' for them, so they continue to search for 'style' and 'passion' in Paris. They did not have to look too far. At this time, according to Roger Shattuck, Paris 'had become a stage, a vast theater for herself and all the world . . . where everyone wore a costume and displayed himself to best advantage'. It was, he added, 'this theatrical aspect of life, the light-opera atmosphere, which gave *la belle époque* its particular flavor' (Shat- tuck, 1968, pp. 5–6). For Julian Barnes, *la belle époque* 'was a time of great triumph for French art' but also a time when its reputation for casual sex was at its height, where even its pioneering gynaecologist, Samuel-Jean Pozzi, mixed his practice with pleasure (Barnes, 2019, pp. 31, 131–132). So the tourists could have found much to satisfy them. Instead of Seurat's *La Grande Jatte*, Manet's *Le Déjeuner sur l'herbe* (House, 1994, pp. 104–105) might have been more to their taste. Or, if they confined their search to urban delights, they could have sought Renoir's *Bal du Moulin de la Galette* (Nochlin, 1989, pp. 139–140); Degas' *Two Dancers on the Stage*, a leggy spectacle barely obscured by gauze (House, 1994, pp. 104–105); or – most likely – the saucier works of Toulouse-Lautrec, such as the suggestive *In the Private Dining Room* (House, 1994, pp. 174–175).

In 1929 the English painter and critic, Roger Fry, compared Toulouse-Lautrec with Seurat:

> Both frequented Montmartre and saw similar sights . . . Toulouse Lautrec would have seized at once on all that was significant of the moral atmosphere, would have seized most of all on what satisfied his slightly morbid relish of depravity, with just too little of detachment for irony but not for an amused and half-disdainful complicity. . . . But Seurat, one feels, saw it almost as one might suppose a visitant from another planet would have done . . . with this penetrating exactness of a gaze vacant of all direct understanding . . . that refused to see any implications other than visual elements in a scheme of fixed and abstract perfection. . . . however precise and detailed Seurat is, his

passion for geometrizing never deserts him – enclosed so completely, so shut off in its partition, that no other relation than a spatical [*sic*] and geometrical one is any longer possible. The syntax of actual life has been broken up and replaced by Seurat's own peculiar syntax.

(Fry, 1929, p. 290)

Fry recognised that Seurat had revived the formalist vision of an Old Master like Poussin. In his 'Foreword' to Fry's essay on Seurat, Anthony Blunt emphasised Fry's almost 'religious enthusiasm' for the painter's formal structures. Of *La Grande Jatte*, Blunt noted that 'here is still a hot afternoon on the Seine, but the subject has been frozen into a sort of Egyptian frieze'. He also drew attention to the politics of Seurat's contemporary artists (Blunt, 1965, pp. 3–6). Fry, for his part, recognised that the syntax of Seurat's vision was 'peculiar', and in 1926 he set out the process by which that vision was constructed:

With him [Seurat] the stages of perception, analysis, and synthesis were clearly separated, and at each stage was carried through with a methodical precision and exactitude to which the history of art hardly affords a parallel. So perfectly were his sensational data reduced to method that in the end he was able to work as easily by night, and with very imperfect illumination, as he was by day. Every touch had been prearranged by his synthetic system.

(Fry, 1926/1994, p. 244)

Seurat's rage for logical form (analysed in painstaking detail in Herbert et al., 2004, pp. 178–195) made him the perfect subject for *Sunday in the Park with George*.

Act I of *Sunday* sets out the steps that George took to create his masterpiece and destroy his love-affair. It begins with George announcing his 'method': 'design . . . composition . . . balance . . . light . . . and harmony'. Geometry abrogates naturalism. The statement of method is accompanied by arpeggiated chords and complex rearrangements of flies, tracks and lighting. It is only when George is satisfied with the setting that 'the music coalesces into a theme', and Dot is allowed to appear on set (Sondheim and Lapine, 1990, pp. 1–2). He treats her as an object, despite the discomforts expressed in her first song, 'Sunday in the Park with George' (Sondheim, 1984, No. 3), and he moves her in accord with the continued changes in the scenery.

When George has finished his on-site sketches, he returns to his studio with Dot, but now he has no use for her. They are on different sides of the stage, separated by a scrim through which can be seen a draft of *La Grande Jatte*. (The use of soft focussed lighting confirms Fry's description of Seurat's nocturnal practice.) George's *pointilliste* style of execution is influenced by Eugène Chevreul's *The Law of Simultaneous Colour Contrast* (1839)[6] and is replicated in the scintillas of Sondheim's music, derived (as he acknowledged) from the minimalist music of Steve Reich and Philip Glass (Banfield, 1993, pp. 357–358).

Dot now represents a different Seurat painting, *La Poudreuse*, of a plump woman before a dressing-table. She regrets that she is the wrong size to qualify for alternative

FIGURE 17.2   The artist completely oblivious to the needs and wishes of his model/lover: Maria Friedman as Dot and Philip Quast as George perform the title song of *Sunday in the Park with George*, the musical's opening number. Scene from the first British production (1990) at the National Theatre in London.

Source: Photo courtesy of Donald Cooper/Photostage.

employment at the Follies. Her powdering is initially synchronised with George's painting, and the music changes briefly into a love-duet until, needing to 'finish the hat', he refuses to accompany her to the Follies (Sondheim and Lapine, 1990, pp. 15–23; Sondheim, 1984, Nos. 8–8C). So another stake is driven into their love affair.

The fundamental conflict between George and Dot has its counterpart on the island. A 'commotion' heralds the sudden appearance of a *tableau vivant* of a third Seurat painting, *The Bathers*. The geo-social contrast noticed earlier in this essay is caricatured in the behaviour of the males in the painting. The boys jeer at the bourgeois and make derisive comments about George ('kinky beard . . . kinky beard'), while – in the 1984 televised performance – the reclining man in the foreground is masturbating. The scene, in all its crude vitality, is frozen at George's command and, separated by a frame, reverts from a *tableau* excessively *vivant* to the original painting. Jules, a more conventional artist, and his wife Yvonne, engage in patronising banter about *The Bathers*. They finally agree that it has no 'life', at which point the tableau refutes them, with the boys blowing off 'a loud Bronx cheer' (the British would call it a 'raspberry') (Sondheim and Lapine, 1990, pp. 10–15).

The bourgeois on La Jatte, meanwhile, grumble and fumble as if they were in a French farce. They complain and bicker, friendships fall apart and proposed dalliances are stillborn – with one exception, when Jules is exposed 'tonguing'

FIGURE 17.3 The Act I finale of *Sunday in the Park with George*: the artist begins moving his subjects to their final positions. The male tourist, dressed in white at top right, will be ejected. Scene from the 1984 Broadway production, starring Bernadette Peters and Mandy Patinkin (at the centre).

Source: Photo by Don Perdue, provided by the editor.

with his servant in the long grass by his daughter Louise (Sondheim and Lapine, 1990, p. 61). The spitefulness of Louise and the animosity of the oarsman (transformed to a foulmouthed one-eyed boatman) infect everyone on the island, and the scene becomes 'one big fight' (Sondheim and Lapine, 1990, p. 63). The conflict is arrested by George who, preceded by an arpeggiated chord, repeats the design principles enunciated at the start of the Act. He resolves the conflicts by moving the characters to the positions they will assume in Seurat's painting. George and the company come together to sing the lovely melody of 'Sunday', compared by Banfield (1993, p. 360) to the 'passionate control' of French art song. 'Sunday' closes with a flourish, exultantly proclaimed by a horn (Sondheim, 1984, No. 24, p. 134). Order has been restored, and the painting is complete.

Entr'acte: interwar Paris and the art market.

On the third Sunday of *Sunday*, Mr. appears on La Jatte, 'carrying a big steamer trunk', together with Mrs., who is bearing 'a number of famous paintings, framed, under her arm' (Sondheim and Lapine, 1990, p. 57). The tourists have acquired a taste for masterpieces as well as pastry. This stage-instruction is a joke, an impossible demand on the tourists, and it is not followed in the 1984 televised performance.

It is, though, an indication of the growing status of French painting. By the 1880s the leading dealer for modern paintings was Paul Durand-Ruel. He maintained a gallery in London between 1870 and 1875 and was displaying works by impressionists, including Monet and Pissarro (Zarobell, 2015, p. 82; Robbins, 2017, pp. 60–61). Durand-Ruel's breakthrough came in 1886, when he organised the first group show of impressionists in New York and sold 49 paintings for some $40,000 (Thompson, 2015, pp. 142, 146). Between 1886 and 1898, Durand-Ruel visited New York nine times, and he was largely responsible for the growing appreciation of impressionism amongst wealthy collectors in Philadelphia as well as New York (Thompson, 2015, pp. 136, 279, footnote 69).

According to Julian Barnes, the demise of *la belle époque* may have been the only benign result of the World War I (Barnes, 2019, p. 135). After the War, the nature of the American presence in Paris changed. There were, of course, still the tourists, but now there was a contingent of writers, amongst them Ernest Hemingway, Janet Flanner and F. Scott Fitzgerald. The aims of the two groups were different. The tourists were there for the sights, and their involvement with Paris ended with the return trip. In *Sunday*, Mrs. tells the Boatman, 'we are alien here'. As you would expect, his response is vicious (Sondheim and Lapine, 1990, p. 46). The writers, in contrast, had exiled themselves (sometimes temporarily, sometimes not) from their homeland.[7] Gertrude Stein conveys an urgent sense of flaming youth, 'everybody was twenty-six . . . it was the right age apparently for that time and place' (Stein, 1933/1961, p. 212). For American interwar writers, escaping from Prohibition, Paris was an aesthetic, sensual and often sexual paradise.

Another push-factor for the writers was their distaste of capitalism; and it was, ironically, capitalism that brought the United States into competition with London as a major site for modern French painting. The British textile magnate, Samuel Courtauld, found himself hunting over the same ground as Albert C. Barnes, the American manufacturer of patent medicines, and Frederick Clay Bartlett, the son of the president of an American wholesale company (House, 1994, p. 29; Brettell, 1986, p. 104). The consequence was the dispersal of Seurat paintings. Barnes bought *Les Poseuses/ The Models*, an enigmatic painting which reproduces, in the background, the right-hand portion of *La Grande Jatte*. It is in the Barnes Foundation in Philadelphia (Cachin, 1991, pp. 174–177). Courtauld acquired *La Poudreuse* for an unknown price in 1926 and gifted it to the Courtauld Institute in 1932 (House, 1994, p. 160). He purchased *The Bathers* for the National Gallery in 1924; it cost almost £4,000, including tax (House, 1994, pp. 14, 222). Bartlett purchased *La Grande Jatte* for $20,000 in 1924. He bought it for the Art Institute of Chicago, where it still hangs (Brettell, 1986, p. 104). If you wish to experience at first hand the geo-social contrast of *The Bathers* and *La Grande Jatte*, you will have to undertake a 4,000-mile shuttle.

1984: Chicago and the retreat to Paris

Act II of *Sunday* is organised into four segments. The first begins as Act I ended, with the completed canvas of *La Grande Jatte*. The canvas lifts to reveal the *tableau vivant* of the occupants of the park. They are not happy, for they have been held in position for a long time, and their complaints are recorded in 'It's Hot Up Here' (Sondheim, 1984, No. 25). Their griping and sniping is moderated by Dot's thanks to George for her prominent position and for the hat that had once been the subject of contention (Sondheim and Lapine, 1990, p. 70). The characters understand that they are part of a masterpiece, but even their gratitude is tempered by their awareness that they are fading. In fact, some pigments of Seurat's palette deteriorated quite quickly, diminishing the luminous affects achieved by his *pointilliste* technique (Herbert et al., 2004, pp. 208–209). The *tableau vivant* then disintegrates, with the characters exiting and the scenery disappearing. The boatman, the last to leave, remarks wisely that the figures hated Seurat because they relied on him for their existence. The stage reverts to a blank canvas, its state at the beginning of Act I (Sondheim and Lapine, 1990, pp. 72–75).

Act II therefore continues the theme of conflict between the demands of art and the needs of the mundane. Now, though, the nature of the conflict changes with the beginning of the second segment. It is 1984 – the present, when the musical premiered – which is signalled by the arrival of the successor to *La Grande Jatte*, George II's Chromolume #7. In the 1984 production, Chromolume #7 resembled a Dalek. Whether or not Tony Straiges, who designed the set, had seen the British science-fiction TV series, *Doctor Who*, the atmosphere of threat is nevertheless deftly created. For we are in Chicago, a city with a bruising tradition (think Al Capone, Mayor Daly), that has often been regarded as the epitome of the United States. Perhaps with this in mind, Sondheim and Lapine do not identify the site, but it cannot be anywhere else because *La Grande Jatte* has become the most charismatic painting of its permanent home, the Art Institute. It has become so recognisable that it is open to parody. Recently, the front cover of the British news magazine, *The Week*, inserted a puzzled policeman into *La Grande Jatte* to indicate the confusions over social distancing during the COVID-19 pandemic (*The Week*, 2020, p. 1).

Saul Bellow's Tanner Lectures 'on Human Values,' given in Oxford in 1981, indicate why Chicago is such a significant site for *La Grande Jatte*. Although for much of his life Bellow was a resident and regarded himself a Chicago writer, he was explicit about his city. The novelist understood that the metropolis was created for the sole purpose of making money. Phillip D. Armour was a leading figure amongst 'Chicago's nineteenth-century founding capitalist fathers' (Bellow, 1981, p. 186). Armour made his millions with an enormous meat-packing plant, established in Chicago in 1868, with his products distributed nationwide using refrigerated railroad cars. Bellow thought that the taint of Armour's enterprise remained even after the introduction of Federal food standards:

> The old yards, the 'killing beds' now are gone, but until the Second World War Chicago was an animal-flavored city. You knew what its big industry was when the wind blew from the Yards. . . . red cattle cars waited in the sidings, cows and sheep staring through the slats in brute ignorance, death-bound.

The odor of blood, manure, bacon-making, soap- and fertilizer-manufacture became a weight lying on your heart. Indeed it was a smell which seemed to have the power to enter into the light . . . adding itself to the air as a sort of broad-daylight blood gloom.

(Bellow, 1981, pp. 187–188)

The miasma generated a permanent structural division in Chicago.

According to Bellow, 'money was a vital substance . . . the final product of a vast system of bloodshed, labor, sacrifice, and nutrition'. The system was characterised by a 'struggle with subhumanity', with the well-off living in triple-locked, security-protected apartment blocks, while the streets below were ravaged by a violent underclass (Bellow, 1981, pp. 183, 187). Forms of art-expression, like Chicago's social structure, were infected by, subordinated to the vitality of money. Philip D. Armour is, once again, an exemplar. When asked if he had any interests apart from money, Armour responded: 'My culture is mostly in my wife's name' (Bellow, 1981, p. 186). Cultural pursuits were, to use a modern business term, outsourced. Chicago, of course, is not without culture. It has several world-class institutions: universities, a fine symphony orchestra, an opera-house and the Art Institute. It also has, as Bellow pointed out, 'a "Culture Bus" . . . to take out-of-towners, suburbanites, and school children to points of interest' (Bellow, 1981, p. 178). Art-expression, then, in Bellow's view, is not integrated into the life of Chicago, but rather a by-product, like animal waste.

I suggest that the Bellovian view of Chicago dominates the second and third segments of Act II of *Sunday*. The Chromolume, which alludes to Seurat's term for his style of painting, *chromo-luminarisme* (Herbert et al., 2004, p. 116), may originally have been an inspired conception by George II. But now we have reached the seventh iteration, commissioned by the museum to commemorate the centennial of *La Grande Jatte*. It is a multi-media production, combining a light show, video projections of sketches for *La Grande Jatte*, electronic music and a memoir of Seurat's life read by George II and Marie, who is now 98 years old. The presentation breaks down. George II suggests that 'the surge from the musical equipment has created an electrical short' and therefore 'no electricity, no art' (Sondheim and Lapine, 1990, p. 78) – perhaps an ironic comment on the electronic experiments of Sondheim's former teacher, Milton Babbitt.

While George II and his assistant, Dennis, attend to the Chromolume, the head of the museum steps forward. His name is Bob Greenberg. This is perhaps another ironic comment, this time about Clement Greenberg, the leading American formalist art critic, roughly contemporary with Babbitt. Greenberg announces that he has sold the 'air rights' above the museum, and the 27 floors of apartments, built above the museum, will be available later for inspection by the audience. The Chromolume has meantime been repaired, and the presentation proceeds to its close.

The third segment is the succeeding reception. It takes place in front of *La Grande Jatte*, but the guests ignore the painting for they are more interested in networking. The extended musical sequence that dominates this segment, 'Putting it Together' (Sondheim, 1984, No. 27) concerns the problems of artistic production in a money- and fashion-dominated society. As Redmond, a curator visiting from Texas, laments to Greenberg, 'tomorrow is already passé'. They then sing in duet the pun: 'That is the state of the art' (Sondheim and Lapine, 1990, pp. 81–82). George II has embraced the monetary requirements of artistic production, adding the names of his contributors to the side of each Chromolume. His solo in 'Putting it Together' notes that 'every little detail plays a part', but the details are no longer open-air sketches. Instead it is 'a little cocktail conversation' that leads to finance from 'a good foundation' (Sondheim and Lapine, 1990, pp. 86–87).

A comparison with the Barbra Streisand version of the song, rewritten by Sondheim for *The Broadway Album* (Streisand, 1985), is helpful. Streisand begins the song hesitantly, discomfited by the overbearing commercial concerns of the recording executives. But she gains strength as the song progresses, brushing aside the plaintive question, 'do we really need all these musicians?' with the triumphant interpolation 'yes, we do'. George II, in contrast, has become a creature of the system. The company conclude that 'the state of the art' is 'a matter of promotion', and George II agrees. Putting his Chromolumes together involves a form of prostitution, 'Drink by drink/Mink by mink' (Sondheim and Lapine, 1990, p. 96).

The company, still gabbling about money and art, are called to dinner, leaving Marie and George II alone in front of *La Grande Jatte*. Marie's touchingly simple solo, 'Children and Art' (Sondheim, 1984, No. 30), in stark contrast to the superficial chatter of the company, goes to the heart of the problem concerning the musical: the relation of aesthetics and everyday life. The problem is left unresolved, for Marie drifts off to sleep during the song. But George II understands and, looking at *La Grande Jatte*, he repeats his great-grandfather's lament when Dot left him: 'Connect' (Sondheim and Lapine, 1990, p. 101).

To connect, George II must go to Paris, in the fourth and final segment of Act II. He has been invited to give a presentation of Chromolume #7 on La Jatte. Marie was to accompany him, but in the meantime she has died. George II sees, too, that the inspiration created by La Jatte is 'dying' (Sondheim and Lapine, 1990, p. 104). Indeed, the park has long disappeared, built over by suburban residences. In a TV programme about Seurat, Waldemar Januszczak commented that, nowadays, La Jatte 'is just a dismal place to walk your dog' (Januszczak, 2020). In 1984, La Jatte, and Paris generally, were no longer the site that so excited American writers of the interwar period. For Bellow, the Paris of Henry James and Scott Fitzgerald 'was already over the hill'; in his words: 'To live *like artists* in Europe's famous capitals isn't possible now' (Bellow, 1981, pp. 181, 185).

The fate of 'The Last Time I Saw Paris' confirms this melancholy assessment of Paris. Kern and Hammerstein's memorial to Paris before the German occupation became the title song of a 1954 film, directed by Richard Brooks. Although it ends with a conventional Hollywood reconciliation, the central section of the film, based on Fitzgerald's short story 'Babylon Revisited' (1931), is a remorseful flashback to the debauchery of an aspiring novelist in interwar Paris, and the whole

FIGURE 17.4 It is a return to Paris which helps the artist in *Sunday in the Park with George* out of his creative crisis. The image shows composer-lyricist Stephen Sondheim discussing how to perform the scene and its pivotal song 'Move On' with Bernadette Peters and Mandy Patinkin.

Source: Photo provided by the editor.

film modifies the celebratory mood of many of the 1950s Hollywood recreations of Paris.

The conclusion of *Sunday in the Park with George* is a little more optimistic. Sondheim's stage-direction states that only one tree remains, but it is enough for George II to recognise that this is the site of the painting. As George II meditates on his loss of inspiration, the vision of Dot reappears and urges him to 'move on', to notice every tree' and 'understand the light', uniting the pair in a duet suggesting that their conflicting demands of art and love can only be reconciled through the magic of a dream (Sondheim, 1984, No. 33; Sondheim and Lapine, 1990, pp. 103–107).

Then, as George II rehearses the formalist words his great-grandfather used to structure his painting, the buildings on the present-day island disappear and the company reassemble to sing a reprise of 'Sunday' and to recreate *La Grande Jatte*. A descending white canvas separates the company from George II, returning the stage to its initial state in Act I. George II recites the final words: 'White. A blank page or canvas. His favourite. So many possibilities' (Sondheim, 1984, No. 34; Sondheim and Lapine, 1990, pp. 108–110).[8] The horn flourish that ended Act I is repeated. It is a triumphant reaffirmation of the continued presence of Paris as a source of artistic imagination, if only in the quality of light, or the endurance of an unfelled tree, or the memory of *la belle époque*.

Acknowledgements

My thanks to Olaf Jubin for offering me the opportunity to write about *Sunday in the Park with George*, for his patience in awaiting the result, and for his sensitive editing. Thanks, as ever, to Jenny Wigram for her advice and constant support.

Notes

1 Colour reproductions are widely available online, including at https://artsandculture. google.com/asset/a-sunday-on-la-grande-jatte/twGyqq52R-lYpA?hl=en.
2 Jubin, 2014, pp. 185–202, examines the function of the doubled roles in *Sunday*.
3 Although my readings of Seurat's and Sondheim's texts have a political and economic cast, I am here using the term bourgeoisie simply to denote the Parisian middle class, including the aspirant petite-bourgeoisie.
4 The case in favour of prostitutes has been put, for instance, by Clark, 1984, p. 266; Smith, 1997, pp. 52–53. That the females are not prostitutes has been argued by House, 1989, pp. 120–22; Herbert et al., 2004, p. 163. Thomson (1989, p. 186) drew on French slang. *Singesse*, or female monkey, was contemporary *argot* for a prostitute, which gives a different status to the woman who apparently owns the animal.
5 They can be seen together in Smith, 1997, pp. 2–3.
6 Hughes, 1980, p. 114, has a good summary of the scientific theory of visual perception.
7 For an excellent analysis of the distinction between tourists and exiles, see Halliwell, 2005, pp. 57–59.
8 There are differences of detail between the productions on Broadway in 1984 and at the Royal National Theatre, 1990, on which my 1990 libretto is based. In the 1984 production the company do not recreate *La Grande Jatte*, but reassemble, with the American tourists, to salute George II before dispersing.

References

Anon. (1940a) 'Reich Tanks Clank in Champs-Elysees,' *The New York Times*, 15 June, p. 1.
———. (1940b) 'Swastika Over Paris,' *The New York Times*, 30 June, p. 96.
Baedeker, K. (1900) *Paris and Environs with Routes from London to Paris: Handbook for Travellers*. Leipsic: Baedeker.
Banfield, S. (1993) *Sondheim's Broadway Musicals*. Ann Arbor: University of Michigan Press.
Banville, J. (1997) *The Untouchable*. London: Picador.
Barnes, J. (2019) *The Man in the Red Coat*. London: Jonathan Cape.
Bellow, S. (1981) *A Writer from Chicago: The Tanner Lectures on Human Values*. Brasenose College, Oxford University, 18, 25 May, https://tannerlectures.utah.edu/_documents/a-to-z/b/bellow82.pdf, accessed 3 July 2020.

Blunt, A. (1965) 'Foreword to R. Fry,' in *Seurat*. London: Phaidon Press, pp. 3–6.

Brettell, R. R. (1986) 'The Bartletts and the *Grande Jatte*: Collecting Modern Painting in the 1920s,' *Art Institute of Chicago Museum Studies*, 12(2), pp. 102–113.

Cachin, F. (1991) 'Georges Seurat,' in *Great French Paintings from the Barnes Foundation*. London: Little, Brown and Company, pp. 174–177.

Clayson, H. (1989) 'The Family and the Father: The *Grande Jatte* and Its Absences,' *Art Institute of Chicago Museum Studies*, 14(2), pp. 154–164, 242–244.

Clark, T. J. (1984) *The Painting of Modern Life: Paris in the Art of Manet and His Followers*. New York: Knopf.

Fenton, J. (2000) *Leonardo's Nephew: Essays on Art and Artists*. Chicago: University of Chicago Press.

Fry, R. (1929) 'Seurat's *La Parade*,' *The Burlington Magazine*, 55, pp. 289–293.

———. (1926/1994) 'The Courtauld Fund,' in J. House (ed.) *Impressionism for England: Samuel Courtauld as Patron and Collector*. London: Courtauld Institute Galleries, pp. 244–245.

Halliwell, M. (2005) 'Tourists or Exiles? American Modernists in Paris in the 1920s and 1950s,' *Nottingham French Studies*, 44(3), pp. 54–68.

Hammerstein II, O. (2020) 'The Last Time I Saw Paris: Lyrics,' https://genius.com/Jerome-kern-the-last-time-i-saw-paris-lyrics, accessed 3 July 2020.

Harison, C. (2020) *Paris in Modern Times: From the Old Regime to the Present Day*. London: Bloomsbury Academic.

Hazan, E. (2010) *The Invention of Paris: A History in Footsteps* (D. Fernbach, trans.). London: Verso.

Herbert, R. L., Harris, N. et al. (2004) *Seurat and the Making of La Grande Jatte*. Chicago: The Art Institute of Chicago in Association with the University of California Press, pp. 22–25, 68–95.

House, J. (1994) *Impressionism for England: Samuel Courtauld as Patron and Collector*. London: Courtauld Institute Galleries.

———. (1989) 'Reading the *Grande Jatte*,' *Art Institute of Chicago Museum Studies*, 14(2), pp. 114–131.

Hughes, R. (1980) *The Shock of the New: Art and the Century of Change*. London: British Broadcasting Corporation.

James, H. (1957) *Parisian Sketches: Letters to the New York Tribune, 1875–76* (L. Edel and I. Desoir Lind, eds.). New York: New York University Press.

Januszczak, W. (2020) 'The Art Mysteries: Georges Seurat,' *BBC4 Television*, 25 March.

Jubin, O. (2014) '"It Takes Two": The Doubling of Actors and Roles in *Sunday in the Park with George*,' in R. Gordon (ed.) *The Oxford Handbook of Sondheim Studies*. New York: Oxford University Press, pp. 185–202.

Leighton, J. and Thomson, R. (1997) *Seurat and the Bathers*. London: National Gallery.

Lipton, J. (1997) 'Stephen Sondheim: The Art of the Musical,' *The Paris Review*, 39, pp. 258–278.

Nochlin, L. (1989) 'Seurat's *Grande Jatte*: An Anti-Utopian Allegory,' *Art Institute of Chicago Museum Studies*, 14(2), pp. 132–153, 241–242.

Rathbone, E. E., Rothkopf, K., Brettell, R. R. and Moffett, C. S. (1996) *Impressionists on the Seine: A Celebration of Renoir's Luncheon of the Boating Party*. Washington, DC: Counterpoint.

Robbins, A. (2017) 'Monet, Pissarro and Fellow French Painters in London 1870–1,' in C. Corbeau-Parsons (ed.) *Impressionists in London: French Artists in Exile 1870–1904*. London: Tate Enterprises.

Sante, L. (2015) *The Other Paris*. London: Faber and Faber.

Secrest, M. (1998) *Stephen Sondheim: A Life*. London: Bloomsbury.

Shattuck, R. (1968) *The Banquet Years: Origins of the Avant-Garde in France, 1885-World War 1*. New York: Vintage Books.

Smith, P. (1997) *Seurat and the Avant-Garde*. New Haven: Yale University Press.

Sondheim, S. (2010) *Finishing the Hat: Collected Lyrics (1954–1981) with Attendant Comments, Principles, Heresies, Grudges, Whines and Anecdotes*. New York: Alfred A. Knopf.

———. (1984) *Sunday in the Park with George*. Vocal Score. New York: Rilting Music.

Sondheim, S. and Lapine, J. (1990). *Sunday in the Park with George*. London: Nick Hern Books.

Stein, G. (1933/1961) *The Autobiography of Alice B. Toklas*. New York: Vintage Books.

Streisand, B. (1985) 'The Broadway Album,' CD Columbia CK 40092, https://www.discogs.com/Barbra-Streisand-The-Broadway-Album/release/13079387.

Thompson, J. A. (2015) 'Durand-Ruel and America,' in S. Patry (ed.) *Inventing Impressionism: Paul Durand-Ruel and the Modern Art Market*. London: National Gallery, p. 134.

Thomson, R. (1989) 'The *Grande Jatte*: Notes on Drawing and Meaning,' *Art Institute of Chicago Museum Studies*, 14(2), pp. 180–197, 245–246.

The Week. (2020) 'Front Cover Illustration: "What's Allowed? The PM's Confused Message",' *The Week*, 16 May, p. 1.

White, E. (2001) *The Flâneur*. London: Bloomsbury.

Zarobell, J. (2015) 'Durand-Ruel and the Market for Modern Art, from 1870 to 1873,' in S. Patry (ed.) *Inventing Impressionism: Paul Durand-Ruel and the Modern Art Market*. London: National Gallery, pp. 76–97.

18

THE PARADOXICAL 'FRENCHNESS' OF AN AUSTRALIAN MUSICAL

Baz Luhrmann's *Moulin Rouge!*

Pierre-Olivier Toulza

Translated from the French by Tresi Murphy

Both the elation and spectacular fervour of Baz Luhrmann's *Moulin Rouge!*, the culmination of the Red Curtain Trilogy that includes *Strictly Ballroom* (1992) and *Romeo + Juliet* (1996), seem tailored to fulfil the aspirations of a director who has on several occasions stated that his intention with this film was to 'reinvent the movie musical' ('A Word from Baz,' 2010) at a time when the genre seemed to be moribund. The surprising success of the film, which took in $185 million at the box office worldwide on a budget of around $52 million and managed to get eight Oscar nominations (and two wins), did lead to a renewed interest in musicals, at least in the press. Even though the film was closely followed by *Chicago* (2002) and by other adaptations of successful Broadway shows, it cannot be said to have truly launched a revival for the genre in the first decade of the 21st century. Steven Cohan (2010, p. 2), for example, points out that the musicals that followed *Moulin Rouge!* did not rival the classic era in terms of quantity or diversity. Nevertheless, the film did stand out from previous musicals by targeting a generation which was 'raised on MTV'. Its repertoire was a 'perfect fit for soundtrack albums, radio play and music vids, which have long ago proven a key promo tool for Hollywood pics', while its 'machine-gun editing . . . lent a cutting-edge, MTV-style aesthetic to the form, departing radically from the cardinal rule of Fred Astaire, who refused to let his directors cut away during a dance number' (Rooney and Bing, 2003).

Luhrmann's wish to reinvent the musical was, in fact, more paradoxical than it seemed, because although *Moulin Rouge!* does indeed dispense with tacit conventions (in particular the long shots in traditional musicals that stay focused on the performers so as to highlight their dancing and singing skills), it still follows the same pattern as big musicals right from the beginning. The opening red curtain creates the theatrical ambience that Luhrmann wanted to project in his trilogy, but it is also a nod to the roadshow exhibition practices of prestige musicals (like *The Sound of Music*, 1965) in the '50s and '60s (Hall, 2002), a time when a number of cinemas still had a curtain that came up just as the film began. Moreover, the Parisian inspiration for *Moulin Rouge!* is derived from '50s musicals, which means the movie stands out from other English-language musicals of the '90s that were also set in Paris but rarely during the *belle époque*.[1] By explicitly referencing the cycle of 'Frenchness films' (Schwartz, 2007) that date from the '50s, from *An American in Paris* (1951) to *Can-Can* (1960) via *Gigi* (1958), *Moulin Rouge* (1952), *Lust for Life* (1956), *Gentlemen Prefer Blondes* (1953) as well as the French film *French Can-Can* (1954), Luhrmann seems to want to 'reinvent' by imitating models through reference, parody and pastiche.

In this chapter, I will explore the paradox of the 'Frenchness film' in the 21st century, and particularly in the context of a movie that had the ambition of dusting off the genre. *Moulin Rouge!* did have a fresh take on the Paris-inspired musical, while at the same time using typical stereotypes of the capital such as the cabaret of the title and the Eiffel Tower, stock *belle époque* characters from the literary and artistic bohemian world, the figure of Toulouse-Lautrec, as well as requisite motifs like the can-can. According to Vanessa Schwartz (2007, p. 21), the '50s films set in *fin de siècle* Paris were not nostalgic 'but rather portrayed the link that helped establish cultural continuity and a historical context for post-war filmmakers and their cultural product' and, in a way, *Moulin Rouge!* does the same thing, by using certain aspects of the Parisian backdrop to affirm its identity, at the crossroads of art and commerce. In doing so, the film creates a continuity as much with *fin de siècle* Paris as it does with the musicals of the '50s.

Bohemian Paris, between art, entertainment and business

Even though the subject matter of *Moulin Rouge!* is unique among musicals in the '90s, the French inspiration behind the film fits in with a decade where Parisian imagery was frequently used. Indeed, Baz Luhrmann himself directed a production of Giacomo Puccini's opera *La Bohème* in 1990, 1993 and 1996. Obviously, *Moulin Rouge!* is not exactly a film adaptation of *La Bohème*, even though the way Paris is depicted as a refuge for starving, bohemian artists in search of fame haunts the film as it does the opera. Certain aspects of the decor of *Moulin Rouge!* owe much to the opera (in particular the illuminated sign on the façade of Christian's hotel that says 'L'Amour' and also featured as part of the stage set of *La Bohème*), but the modernisation of the motif of Bohemia can be attributed, as much if not more so, to the Broadway musical *Rent* that was first performed in 1996. Luhrmann did not choose, as Jonathan Larson did, to relocate Puccini's story in a foreign capital, but both the stage musical and the film bring the music up to date. In both productions, the artistic way of life is lauded and celebrated in big party scenes ('La Vie Bohème' in *Rent*; the closing moments of 'Spectacular Spectacular' in *Moulin Rouge!*, when a character shouts out in French 'Vive la vie de bohème!'), and the characters all belong to the world of entertainment (in *Rent* Mimi is an exotic dancer, while Satine, Nicole Kidman's character in *Moulin Rouge!*, is a cabaret performer) or to the art world: the two main male characters entwine the musical with their own work,

Mark (*Rent*) with his documentary film and Christian (Ewan McGregor) with the book he is writing as early as the opening scenes of *Moulin Rouge!*.

While this renewed interest in 19th century artistic, bohemian life reaches a high point in Luhrmann's musical, a number of films were made about *belle époque* painters before and after *Moulin Rouge!* in the United States (*Vincent & Theo*, 1990) but mostly in France (*Van Gogh*, 1991; *Lautrec*, 1998; *Gauguin*, 2003; *Modigliani*, 2004), and all are set around the turn of the century. Luhrmann's film is obviously not a biopic of Toulouse-Lautrec, but his appearance in the film is far from incongruous in the context of cinema produced between 1990 and 2000.

Indeed, the trend was also marked in the art world as a number of big museums at the time, notably in the United States, highlighted their extensive Lautrec collections with grand exhibitions such as 'Paris – the 1890s' at New York's Museum of Modern Art (MoMA) in 1997. In Australia, Luhrmann's home, the show 'Toulouse-Lautrec: Prints and Posters from the Bibliothèque Nationale' at the Queensland Art Gallery in Brisbane in 1991, confirmed the key position occupied by this particular artist who seems so significant for our current conception of turn-of-the-century Paris. The exhibition catalogue (Bouret et al., 1991, p. 19) states clearly that it constituted 'for Australian audiences, an introduction to France in the era of *La Belle Époque*, an era for which Toulouse-Lautrec might be termed the image-maker'. The motif of the *belle époque* is less of a nostalgic reference to the 1950s cycle of films about Paris, since the 1990s took a very particular interest in the end of the 19th century which was considered almost a reflection of that *fin de siècle* period, mainly for the following three reasons: because of the major artistic figures of the time (their avant-garde ambitions rendering them extremely modern), because culture for the masses expanded around 1900 in France and abroad (as such, it is significant the movie's first title card says 'Paris, 1900', setting it ten years after the opening of the Moulin Rouge and thus a lot later than other films centred around the cabaret), and finally because of the blurring of the line between art and business. Lautrec (in both reality and fiction) could be the emblem of the latter with Luhrmann as the contemporary equivalent.

In fact, Lautrec and his peers worked at a time when living conditions for artists in France were undergoing a sea change. According to Jerrold Seigel,[2] for bohemian artists the new Montmartre cabarets did not constitute a place to

> segregate themselves from the workaday world outside, but to attract and entertain a clientele that was largely respectable and bourgeois. The new establishments testified to a new kind of symbiosis between la Bohème and the bourgeoisie, and to the existence of a broad public seeking a taste of Bohemia.
>
> *(Seigel, 1986, p. 216)*

As a result, 'Bohemia was literally turned into theater, acting out its estrangement from ordinary life but also masking it, channelling its energy to appeal to the bourgeoisie as patrons and consumers of literary and artistic work' (Seigel, 1986, p. 221).

Artists are not only the writers and performers of 'Spectacular Spectacular', they are the very subject of the show, gathered around their guardian, Lautrec (John Leguizamo), and they are evidence not of the precedence of art over entertainment in musicals but the transformation of art into theatrical entertainment, in 'Spectacular Spectacular' as well as in *Moulin Rouge!* itself. Indeed, Zidler (Jim Broadbent) wants to sell Bohemia's effervescence and prestige ('the thrusting, violent, vibrant, wild, Bohemian spirit that the whole production embodies') both to the Duke (Richard Roxburgh) and to the audience at the première ('Vive la vie de bohème!' are, after all, the final words of the show). The artists' need to publicise their work and to become the actual subject of the show is echoed both in the conditions in which Luhrmann himself had to work, as he was under contract with 20th Century-Fox for *Moulin Rouge!*, and in the way artists in the early 21st century have to promote their work to a vast audience. As such, the character of the Duke appears somewhat archaic at a time which saw the 'increasing reliance of writers and artists on the market of cultural products, rather than on direct patronage' (Seigel, 1986, p. 226). Luhrmann, echoing Seigel's thesis and his own film, mentions the 'commercial Bohemianism' (Luhrmann and Martin, 2001, p. 9) of the film's small troupe and underlines the parallels with his own situation:

> CM [Catherine Martin[3]] and I, plus the core collaborators on this film, in some crucial sense live in a kind of Moulin Rouge. We share the Boho's naive belief in Truth, Freedom, Beauty and Love. And like our courtesan and poet lover Satine and Christian, like impresario Zidler and Toulouse's improvisatory band of Bohos, we're constantly dealing with the intersection of our ideals with the harsh reality of time and economics.

Jane Feuer (2010, p. 61) posits that what makes *Moulin Rouge!* different is that it places 'the emphasis on an art form rather than an entertainment form', and it is true that the story is told by Christian and Toulouse, the two artist-narrators. Their narratives open and close the film, and, in the end, take precedence over Satine's point of view. The importance given to art, no doubt inherited from the 'Frenchness films' of the '50s (the figure of Lautrec in John Huston's *Moulin Rouge*; the impressionist paintings brought to life in Jerry's daydream, a painter himself, in *An American in Paris*), must, nevertheless, be put into perspective. In fact, both men – and in particular Toulouse – are jacks-of-all-trades, they are publicists and entertainers as much as they are artists. Christian's 'work of art' that folds into the film itself is, in the end, a fabulous piece of entertainment, and Toulouse is above all the leader of the Bohemians and a willing performer in the show. The fictionalised character of Toulouse allows the film to remind us of the important role Lautrec played in the entertainment culture of the *fin de siècle* period. It does not depict his work as a painter, focusing instead on his more commercial production (in Zidler's office, we catch glimpses of posters inspired by his work as a graphic artist, as well as the murals on the walls near the Moulin) and, above all, his symbolic function as

FIGURE 18.1   The culture of Montmartre filling the frame: Toulouse-Lautrec and the Moulin Rouge; note the sails of the windmill and the stylised representation at the top of the frame.

Source: Screen shot provided by the author.

the 'soul of Montmartre'. When he sings 'Nature Boy' at the start and end of the film, leaning out through the Moulin's skylight, the fiction firmly takes root within the context of commercial entertainment as invented in Montmartre. The *quartier* literally fills the shot [see Figure 18.1]: the sails of the Moulin; the tiny stylised representation at the top of the frame; and the character of Toulouse, about whom we are reminded in the Brisbane exhibition catalogue (Bouret et al., 1991, p. 11) that 'his subjects, for the most part, did not extend beyond the places of entertainment in Montmartre – dance-halls, café-concerts, bars, circuses and theatres'.

From prostitution to theatre and vice versa

The bohemian artists manage to set up an alliance with the courtesan because they become actors themselves. On stage and backstage, she proves to be a particularly talented actress, and she hones her skills with each ordeal she has to face. Backstage, Satine reveals herself to have a knack for impromptu comedy: in her boudoir, she has to improvise with Christian and then with the Duke to avoid a dramatic confrontation between the two men. In a short period of time, she manages to change her tone, come up with lines that hit home, bring characters to life, invent poses, gestures and movements. Satine's second off-stage 'performance' occurs at the end of the film when she goes to Christian's apartment to tell him that she is leaving him. Zidler shows greater cognisance than Christian, and is aware of Satine's talent: 'You're a great actress, Satine. . . . Use your talent to save him.' In Christian's room, Satine is very persuasive in a scene that she might have seen her idol, Sarah Bernhardt, play at the Théâtre de la Renaissance as Marguerite Gautier in the 1896 production of *Camille*, even if this dramatic climax is more reminiscent of George

Cukor's 1936 screen adaptation: Zidler convinces Satine by using almost exactly the same words as M. Duval, played by Lionel Barrymore, to cajole Marguerite to stay away from his son ('Make him believe you don't love him').

The line between the worlds of showbusiness and prostitution is fully blurred, and indeed Christian introduces the Moulin Rouge as 'a nightclub, a dance hall and a bordello', something the real cabaret itself never was. Luhrmann clarifies this specific stylised take in the Blu-ray commentary, where he explains that prostitutes in fact plied their trade in the cabaret's gardens (Luhrmann et al., 2010). It must be said that this representation is faithful to a specific form of Parisian culture of that time and to models such as both Emile Zola's novel *Nana* and Jean Renoir's film adaptation, a source that is often referred to by Luhrmann as well as by Craig Pearce (Luhrmann and Martin, 2001, p. 9). In the novel, Bordenave, who runs the Théâtre des Variétés where Nana works as an actress, likes to refer to the theatre as 'my brothel', and Renoir's film shows him brushing away the suitors lining up at her dressing room door only to let a rich aristocrat in (the title card reads 'Our young star will be very flattered by your visit'). Zidler organises a meeting between the Duke and Satine after the show in a similar way. In both films, the actress/courtesan is almost naked during this meeting, and the theatres' backstage area is particularly sordid. Furthermore, Zidler and Bordenave share the same motive, to refinance a flailing business, and Nana, just like Satine, wants to be recognised for her talent as a dramatic actress: the former has the seemingly ridiculous ambition to act in a serious play, and fails miserably, while the latter dreams of becoming Sarah Bernhardt's equal (an aspiration *Moulin Rouge!* does not really comment on, in contrast to Renoir's film with its misogynistic stance).

In addition to being a source of inspiration, *fin de siècle* Paris thus also provides Luhrmann with a cultural background where showbusiness and prostitution are intertwined. For many writers of the time, Paris was a city of theatre, a huge stage where the show was ongoing; however, the courtesans of the metropolis had a show all of their own. It is this specific theatricality which inspired some of the set design in *Moulin Rouge!*. Firstly, clients during the *belle époque* were no longer satisfied by traditional brothels as it was no longer enough to merely offer the services of submissive prostitutes; in order to fulfil a different kind of demand, prostitution spread to places that were not specifically dedicated to it, like cabarets (Authier, 2015, p. 217). Secondly, the worlds of prostitution and theatre were similar, to the extent that the prostitutes, madams and pimps became more like directors (Authier, 2015, p. 220) in places that were not traditional brothels but 'new sex palaces' (Authier, 2015, p. 219). Here, themed decors tended to erase the distinction between entertainment and prostitution: one famed brothel at that time, the Chabanais, had an oriental-themed room not unlike Satine's boudoir. This context explains Satine's ambition to be taken seriously as an actress because while the stage constituted a real launch pad to love affairs for some, the reverse could also occur since the qualities required of a prostitute were very similar to those required of an actress. Therefore, it is not surprising that Satine longs, in the film's circular system, to become the new Sarah Bernhardt, who most probably started out as a prostitute before becoming an actress (Authier, 2015, p. 220) and one of whose most successful plays, *Camille*, greatly inspired Baz Luhrmann and Craig Pearce.[4]

An immersive tour

The opening shots of the film already declare Baz Luhrmann's intention of making 'audience participation cinema' (Ryan, 2014, p. 74), while at the same time echoing the spectacular strategies of the 'Frenchness' musicals of the '50s. The third image is a vast wide shot which takes in the entire landscape of Paris. It is followed by a very fast immersive tracking shot that sweeps across the capital, before seemingly hesitating in front of a priest who is warning of the dangers of Montmartre, then diving into a stylised door, leading us down a narrow alleyway at great speed into the Paris of another time, where we manage to spot a prostitute and a man who is either high or drunk. The camera then takes to the air again, before eventually slowing down to enter a room where we see a young man sitting on the ground, bottle in hand, surrounded by piles of paper and additional bottles.

In *Moulin Rouge!*, these immersive shots are systematically associated with the French capital and its iconic locations, but they also allow for the depiction of the darker side of Paris, previously shown by John Huston in *Moulin Rouge* (1952). The second immersive tracking shot at the start is launched by Christian's monologue about his arrival the previous year and starts inside the Moulin Rouge, only to quickly leave and travel over the same path as the first shot but backwards, returning back to where we started, overlooking Paris yet again. Then, the camera rapidly swings back across town to a railway station, to a less foreboding part of the city, proven by the use of the song 'La Complainte de la butte', which was written by Jean Renoir for his production of *French Can-Can* (1954). Next comes a fast tracking shot that starts at the Porte de Montmartre, through the narrow street as far as Christian's garret; it confirms a change in tone (the drunkard becomes a jovial musician, the jaded prostitute has disappeared) in favour of a more picturesque vision in line with contemporary representations in both musicals like *Everyone Says I Love You* (1996) and non-musicals like *Amélie* (2001). These immersive shots allow the spectator to experience the mysterious, ambivalent world at the same time as the character and are reminiscent of the descriptive strategies used in classic, Paris-set musicals, that take the viewer on a quick dive into a picture-postcard decor. In *Funny Face* (1957), the spectacular musical number 'Bonjour Paris' offers a guided tour of the capital's iconic locations following the steps of the three main characters. Vanessa Schwartz (2007, p. 26) shows that this scene 'satisfies the touristic urge to see the city, represents it as a series of postcard snapshots made more "cinematic" by virtue of the split-screen triptych that exploited widescreen technology'. The approach is similar in *An American in Paris*, as it starts with a panoramic tour of Parisian highlights narrated by the, as yet, unseen Gene Kelly as Jerry Mulligan. The sequence ends with the camera sliding up a wall, resting on a window of an artist's attic studio, in exactly the same way as Luhrmann's camera does.

In *Moulin Rouge!* as well, what we get is firstly, an accelerated, 'touristic' tour of a city that we only catch glimpses of in the rest of the film, and secondly, a (digitally created) picture-postcard version of the capital.

This vision of Paris from the point of view of a tourist promises an immersive experience in a rich cultural world and is rooted in the late 20th century trend for rediscovering the past – and especially the Parisian past – in both France and elsewhere in the world:

> The past, and more to the point, the recent past, become values of refuge and reassurance. 'Retro' is in fashion and stimulates the increased consumption of cultural nostalgia, that celebrates the landscapes, work and days of France in the olden days.
>
> *(Kalifa, 2017, p. 171)*

The opening title card announcing 'Paris, 1900' heralds a film that will provide a cultivated, enjoyable journey through a world where the ambivalence that contemporary culture associates with the work of Toulouse-Lautrec[5] is now to the fore, unlike in '50s musicals which tended to keep the seedier side of Paris well hidden (except in Huston's *Moulin Rouge*).

Even though not one scene was actually shot in the French capital (while some of the fifties films, like *Funny Face* and *Gigi*, had many scenes shot on location in the streets of Paris), *Moulin Rouge!* nevertheless remains a film for which the city constitutes an ideal backdrop – in particular for the musical numbers – and it shows a level of attention to detail that seems paradoxical for a film that is entirely shot in a studio. The sets and the costumes are, in fact, as faithful to cinematic memories as they are to archive documents. The tie-in book by Bazmark Design that was published to go along with the release of the film, also featuring a number of illustrations from a monograph published almost simultaneously in both France and the United States for the 100th anniversary of the Moulin Rouge (Pessis and Crépineau, 1990), reproduces some of the documents used during the film's preparation and shows the level of concern for historic accuracy in the general design of the sets and the costumes. The set, first of all, is faithful to the cabaret's general layout, if not necessarily to its size, and to the ambience of *fin de siècle* Paris. The Porte de Montmartre which we glimpse at the beginning is a relatively faithful reconstitution of the façade of the Enfer cabaret, itself located close to the Moulin Rouge. The costumes are either interpretations – Toulouse drinks on the roof of his hotel to celebrate the agreement with the Duke dressed in a kimono that is similar to the one he wears in a photograph from 1892 (Luhrmann and Martin, 2001, p. 55) – or, although appearing only fleetingly in the film, are identical reproductions – the elderly men in tutus, tuxedo jackets and top hats are a good example (Luhrmann and Martin, 2001, p. 54).

The Parisian backdrop is mainly showcased in the musical numbers, in particular during 'Your Song', when Satine and Christian fall in love. This scene references a number of classic films with a picture-postcard Parisian backdrop (the lovers

FIGURE 18.2   The bourgeoisie at play in *Moulin Rouge!*. The movie's costume design stays true to *fin de siècle* culture, faithfully reproducing costumes worn in revues at the venue, where people were clad in tutus and top hats.

Source: Screen shot provided by the author.

dance in the air and Christian grabs a model of the Eiffel Tower) that converges with a contemporary tourist vision of the city. For today's tour operators, a good night out in Paris involves a show and a glass of champagne (served by Satine in the film) at the Moulin Rouge, followed by dinner at the top of the Eiffel Tower.[6] This conformist and reassuring vision prevails in the first part of the film and is characterised by the recurring motif of the Eiffel Tower, glimpsed at key moments in the narrative and associated with the image of the 'City of Light'. Lights, be they fixed or mobile, coloured or white, blurred or clear, are particularly present when Christian begins to sing. The city and the Tower light up, and we can see halos of red light from the Moulin and its sails behind him. These effects reference both cabaret culture (the famed poster of the Moulin Rouge by Toulouse-Lautrec puts the emphasis in its top right corner on the lighting that was one of the cabaret's biggest attractions) and more recent changes (since 1999, the Eiffel Tower sparkles at regular intervals after nightfall). Despite the fact that *Moulin Rouge!* is not a travelogue, like other, more recent films such as *French Kiss* (1995) or like the 'Frenchness' '50s musicals, we should not forget that the narrative is filtered through the point of view of a young foreigner (Christian arrives in the city by train at the start of the film, and we are not sure he will stay in Paris after the story ends) and that the film presents Paris and its bohemian lifestyle as one tourist attraction among many, at a time when the World's Fair was attracting millions of visitors from all over the world to the city.

While today the vision of Paris that is systematically highlighted in exhibitions on the period is much less reassuring and diametrically opposed to the picture-postcard ideal (Wye and Isselbacher, 1997, p. 1), *Moulin Rouge!* does not really focus on the city's dark side and rather tends to emphasise the predictable social and sexual transgressive aspect (the cabaret as a place where the middle classes and the bourgeois come to mix with the riff-raff). The can-can feeds into the naughty Paris cliché[7] often associated with Montmartre, while the character of the strictly heterosexual and paradoxically faithful prostitute in love breaks with the usual representations of the period[8] and tends to neutralise the transgressions fleetingly depicted in the musical numbers (same-sex couples spotted in the first cabaret scene), including the more elaborate ones (the camp version of 'Like a Virgin'). The 'Roxane' number, choreographed as a cross between a tango and an Apache Dance, is the only one that is imbued with a more anxious sexuality, as it depicts two sexual assaults.

Paris 1900, the city of 'entertainment with audience-participation'

In addition to the way the film's Parisian backdrop updates the motifs used in classic Hollywood musicals, *Moulin Rouge!* also focuses on audience participation, a feature of *belle époque* culture that Luhrmann evokes by using a number of immersive effects in the cabaret scenes. The audience is swept away by a succession of movements as the camera dashes *into* the space, only for the next shot to seemingly reverse that impulse with characters rushing *out of* the place (in this context, note the way Zidler and his girls stare proudly into the camera and seem to appear from side rooms to invade the entire cabaret). We are then submerged by the profusion of attractions and spectacles on show which are held together by the fact that they are all in the same place and they all take direction from Zidler as MC. In the Blu-ray commentary ('A Word from Baz', 2010), Baz Luhrmann explains that 'we've taken the whole world of Montmartre . . . and we've conjuncted it all in the Moulin Rouge'. Accumulation and profusion are very much part of Luhrmann's visual style and correspond to the type of attractions available in the French capital at the turn of the century, as well as to the reinterpretation they were subjected to in typical party and cabaret scenes in 'Frenchness films'. Jerrold Seigel (1986, p. 225–226) gives a good description of the spectacular, commercial entertainment culture that culminated in the 1900 World's Fair as well as in the cabarets of Montmartre: 'Like the Bon Marché and its imitators, [the cabaret] mixed products of various genres, traded in a mélange of commerce and fantasy, and maintained a policy of entrée libre'. In *An American in Paris*, the art students' masked ball features the same mix of unbridled fantasy and celebration, while Renoir's *French Can-Can* ends with the opening of the Moulin Rouge itself and emphasises the eclecticism of the attractions on offer from light-hearted and serious songs to a belly dancer striptease and a wild can-can.

The can-can is the perfect symbol of this culture of 'audience participation' for which Luhrmann finds precedents in the musicals of the '50s as well as in the Paris shows of the end of the 19th century. The Australian director subverts expectations by putting a spectacular climactic scene at the start of his film, leading the audience to expect even more extraordinary sequences to follow. With the exception of John Huston, who opens *Moulin Rouge* with an elaborate can-can scene, the dance is usually the highlight of the show and comes at the end of the film. In *Can-Can* by Walter Lang, the first can-can is stopped by a police raid at the start of the film, but the big number happens right at the end, just as it does in Jean Renoir's *French Can-Can*. Luhrmann (Luhrmann and Martin, 2001, p. 9) says he wanted to create the same feeling of excitement in the audience of today that the patrons of the Moulin Rouge felt watching the scandalous, sensual dance ('the whole stylistic premise has been to decode what the Moulin Rouge was to the audiences of 1899 and express that same thrill in a way that our contemporary moviegoers can relate to'). The frenetic choreography and editing expertly convey the eccentric, satirical nature of a dance that was originally called the '*chahut*' ('heckling'). It was first and foremost an improvised dance, with moves that defied logic (Maruta, 2014, p. 57) and rejected both the prevailing conventions of dance and the rules of decorum and, in doing so, encouraged the participation of all, performers and audience alike, with no age or social barriers. In Luhrmann's film the unpredictability of the dance scene is also inspired by the way the can-can dancers jump unexpectedly through posters or from the balcony in Renoir's film. Finally, the belligerent nature of the *Moulin Rouge!* choreography, where the dancers seem to line up against one another or to aggressively seduce their partners is inspired as much by a tradition of participation that involves 'faking a confrontation that is not unlike the dance battles of today' (Maruta, 2014, p. 27), as by cinematic models. The can-can at the end of Jean Renoir's *Nana* (1926), for example, expresses Nana's defiance when she is at death's door, and the one in Huston's *Moulin Rouge* depicts a dispute between two dancers.

Finally, the Parisian backdrop provides *Moulin Rouge!* with a wide range of highly original visual effects in order to – in Zidler's words – create 'a sensual ravishment' for the audience ('you'll be dumb with wonderment') while, at the same time, making them react and participate ('so exciting, the audience will stomp and cheer!'). Firstly, Paris allows Luhrmann to use a palette of colours in his film similar to that used in the experimental work of *fin de siècle* painters as well as in Hollywood musicals set in France where the use of colour was ground-breaking. The use of green filters to clearly detach the figures in the foreground in the cabaret scenes is directly inspired by certain pieces by Lautrec – where the greens also highlight the pallid faces of the dancers under artificial lights, for example in *At the Moulin Rouge* – and also by the green filters associated with the character of the painter in Huston's *Moulin Rouge*.

Even though Luhrmann retains the late 19th century omnipresence of colour and the bold primary shades used by Lautrec, the film takes its inspiration mostly from the colour style of MGM's musicals from the '50s that do not limit the expressive use of colour but extend 'the musical's broader palette and techniques for color foregrounding beyond the confines of production numbers' (Higgins, 1998, p. 455). The colours in the early part of the film play on holding back and letting go, as they appear and disappear in order to better dramatise the presentation of the characters and the cabaret and to reinforce the involvement of the audience. The shot of the curtains that highlights the reds and golds is followed by a black and white presentation of 'Paris, 1900' (right after the title card), and then a touch of red reappears with the 'L'Amour' sign on the façade of the hotel. Christian's character brings the next batch of colours to life in the film, where the blue tints (Bosley, 2001, p. 40) contrast with the yellow hues of the candles. When Christian evokes 'The Moulin Rouge', the wide shots of the cabaret and the first shots of Satine at the end of the scene, are both in black and white, alternating with the colours on stage. However, when Zidler's dancers enter, the palette is mainly dominated by reds, of course, but also some unexpected secondary and tertiary shades of green and orange with pink and yellow touches, adding an atmosphere of exoticism and excitement. The way colour is introduced is not unlike the Beaux Arts Ball scene in *An American in Paris*, where the use of black and white renders the colours of the final ballet all the more explosive and spectacular (Schwartz, 2007, p. 43).

Luhrmann uses the Parisian cabaret milieu to confront the spectator with a fast-moving world that prizes the exuberance of improvised movements. These movements bend to tear up the rule book in order to replicate that, back then, 'acrobatic skill, agility and devil-may-care passion were valued over mere prettiness. . . . Most revolutionary of all: the defiant freedom of movement the female dancers enjoyed in an age of intense sartorial restriction' (Luhrmann and Martin, 2001, p. 63). Indeed, the successive musical numbers ('Zidler's Rap' and 'Sparkling Diamonds') in the big cabaret scene are updates of the big numbers which usually end musicals like *An American in Paris*. *Moulin Rouge!* completely reboots the strategy used in *French Can-Can* or *Gigi* of 'literally animating the static visual culture of the bygone French 1890s', so as to update 'the classic *fin de siècle* cultural form of the poster' (Schwartz, 2007, p. 35). Luhrmann uses a wide range of techniques to depict the frenzy of the Moulin dancers: machine-gun editing, blurring techniques, rotation effects on clothing and fragmentation effects on bodies.

The inventiveness of the different techniques is inspired by both the dance scenes in classic musicals and by a certain *fin de siècle* visual culture that was fascinated by speed and movement – see for example Lautrec's work on Loie Fuller's

FIGURE 18.3   The frenzy of the can-can: the dancers' skirts used for rotation effects.

Source: Screen shot provided by the author.

FIGURE 18.4   Henri de Toulouse-Lautrec's *The Wheel. Dancer Loie Fuller Seen from the Backstage* (1893). Oil and tempera on cardboard.

choreography, like *The Wheel* – and that intersected with technology – see the scene in the lithographer's shop in Huston's *Moulin Rouge*, commented upon by Schwartz (2007, p. 41).

Conclusion

Using colour, speed and movement in order to awaken the audience and encourage participation proves the paradoxical nature of a project that aimed to 'reinvent' a genre while using processes that, in fact, remain quite traditional. Jane Feuer (1977, p. 321) tells us that the '50s MGM musicals also wanted to 'give the audience a sense of participation in the performance'. While it was always highly unlikely that one film could reinvent a genre on its own, the hybrid nature of *Moulin Rouge!* is quite unique and makes great use of the landscape, culture and entertainment industry of turn-of-the-century Paris. In this chapter, I have repeatedly referred to *Moulin Rouge!* as a 'Frenchness musical' but there is also much to be said about its status as a Parisian melodrama. Indeed, the narrative, set and costumes are reminiscent of Greta Garbo's cycle of Parisian melodramas – *Camille*, of course, but also *Mata Hari* (1931) or *The Kiss* (1929) – as well as other films, such as Frank Borzage's *7th Heaven* (1927); the latter features an attic room that, similar to Christian's, also gives on to the rooftops of Paris. Finally, the film's hybrid nature means the Paris it depicts references both the contemporary conceptions we have of the *fin de siècle* period and the representations of the city in '50s Hollywood musicals. It refers as much to Montmartre in the 1890s, a very specific culture at a very specific time in a very specific place, as to its transformation into a mass culture thanks to artists like Lautrec in the 19th century and classic musicals in the middle of the 20th century. Since Baz Luhrmann attempts, in his filmmaking, to be both 'local and global' (Cook, 2010, p. 24), no other filmmaker is better placed to so intimately understand all the paradoxes of Parisian culture in the *belle époque* as depicted in the musical genre.

Notes

1 Examples of English-language musicals of the 1990s set in Paris include *Everyone Says I Love You* (1996) and *The Hunchback of Notre Dame* (1996).
2 Jerrold Seigel points out that the renewed interest in the Parisian *fin de siècle* period in the '80s and '90s is also academic. He refutes the idea that Bohemia can only be thought of in opposition to the bourgeoisie, and shows that 'Bohemia was not a realm outside bourgeois life but the expression of a conflict that arose at its very heart' (Seigel, 1986, p. 10), an idea that helps to truly grasp the nature of *fin de siècle* Bohemia in *Moulin Rouge!*.
3 Martin is Luhrmann's wife; she was Associate Producer on *Moulin Rouge!* and also designed its Oscar-winning costumes and its sets.
4 On the mirror in her dressing room, Satine displays pictures of Sarah Bernhardt in two of her other great dramatic roles, *Theodora* by Victorien Sardoux and *Phèdre* by Jean Racine.
5 The MoMA (Museum of Modern Art, 2016) site tells us: 'During his brief artistic career, Henri de Toulouse-Lautrec captured the lively and often sordid atmosphere of Montmartre's late 19th-century dance halls, cabarets, and theaters'.
6 It is not surprising therefore that the film is often cited by official Parisian tourist websites. One description of the Moulin Rouge begins with: 'A legendary **cabaret** and one of the first **music-hall** venues in France, the Moulin Rouge and its **shows** have inspired **artists** since **1889**, from **Toulouse-Lautrec** to **Baz Luhrmann**' (VisitParisRegion n. d.).
7 The final years of the 20th century also saw the growth in popularity of erotic 'French postcards' from the *belle époque*, in France and abroad. Satine's négligée and the way she poses in her boudoir are reminiscent of a number of these pictures (for example Hammond, 1988).

8 Even though Satine evidently owes her name to 'Satin', Nana's mistress in Zola's novel, she has much more in common with the faithful Marguerite in Cukor's film than the flighty heroines of Zola and Dumas.

References

Authier, C. (2015) *Femmes d'exception, femmes d'influence: une histoire des courtisanes au XIXe siècle*. Paris: Armand Colin.
Bosley, R. (2001) 'Bohemian Rhapsody,' *American Cinematographer*, 82(6), June, pp. 38–51.
Bouret, B., Bouret, C. and Sauvage, A.-M. (1991), *Toulouse-Lautrec, Les Estampes et les affiches de la Bibliothèque nationale / Prints and Posters from the Bibliothèque Nationale* (1991). Brisbane: Queensland Art Gallery.
Cohan, S. (2010) 'Introduction: How Do You Solve a Problem Like the Film Musical?,' in S. Cohan (ed.) *The Sound of Musicals*. London: BFI, pp. 1–16.
Cook, P. (2010) 'Transnational Utopias: Baz Luhrmann and Australian Cinema,' *Transnational Cinemas*, 1(1), pp. 23–36. DOI: 10.1386/trac.1.1.23/1.
Feuer, J. (2010) 'The International Art Musical: Defining and Periodising the Post-1980s Musical,' in S. Cohan (ed.) *The Sound of Musicals*. London: BFI, pp. 54–63.
———. (1977) 'The Self-Reflective Musical and the Myth of Entertainment,' *Quarterly Review of Film Studies*, 2(3), pp. 313–326.
Hall, S. (2002) 'Tall Revenue Features: The Genealogy of the Modern Blockbuster,' in S. Neale (ed.) *Genre and Contemporary Hollywood*. London: BFI, pp. 11–26.
Hammond, P. (1988) *French Undressing: Naughty Postcards from 1900–1920*. 2nd edition. London: Bloomsbury Books.
Higgins, S. (1998) 'Color at the Center: Minnelli's Technicolor Style in *Meet Me in St. Louis*,' *Style*, 32(3), pp. 449–470.
Kalifa, D. (2017) *La Véritable Histoire de la Belle Époque*. Paris: Fayard.
Luhrmann, B. and Martin, C. (2001) *Moulin Rouge! A Film Directed by Baz Luhrmann*. London: Palgrave-Macmillan.
Luhrmann, B., Martin, C., McAlpine, D. and Pearce, C. (2010) 'Audio Commentary, *Moulin Rouge!*,' Blu-Ray, Twentieth Century-Fox Entertainment, http://www.dvdbeaver.com/film3/blu-ray_reviews52/moulin_rouge_blu-ray.htm.
Maruta, N. (2014) *L'Incroyable Histoire du cancan: Rebelles et insolentes, les Parisiennes mènent la danse*. Paris: Parigramme.
Museum of Modern Art. (2016) 'Henri de Toulouse-Lautrec,' www.moma.org/artists/5910, accessed 7 November 2019.
Pessis, J. and Crépineau, J. (1990) *The Moulin Rouge*. New York: St Martin's Press.
Rooney, D. and Bing, J. (2003) 'Can Hollywood Carry a Tune? Despite Success of *Chicago*, Studios Still Leery of Musicals,' *Variety*, 10–16 March, p. 1.
Ryan, T. (ed.) (2014) *Baz Luhrmann Interviews*. Jackson: University Press of Mississippi.
Schwartz, V. (2007) *It's So French! Hollywood, Paris, and the Making of Cosmopolitan Film Culture*. Chicago and London: The University of Chicago Press.
Seigel, J. (1986) *Bohemian Paris: Culture, Politics and the Boundaries of Bourgeois Life, 1830–1930*. New York: Penguin Books.
VisitParisRegion. (n.d.). 'Moulin Rouge,' www.visitparisregion.com/en/moulin-rouge/, accessed 7 November 2019.
'A Word from Baz'. (2010) 'Moulin Rouge!,' Blu-Ray, Twentieth Century-Fox Entertainment, https://www.blu-ray.com/movies/Moulin-Rouge-Blu-ray/202/.
Wye, D. and Isselbacher, A. (1997) *Paris: The 1890s*. New York: Museum of Modern Art.

CONCLUSION

Over the centuries Paris has been associated with many things. Patrice Higonnet begins his seminal book on the French capital by enumerating some of the myths linked to the French capital: 'Paris as the capital of modernity, or mystery, or tradition; Paris as the capital of art and fashion; Paris as the capital of world revolution; Paris as the capital of pleasure, crime, sex and science' (Higonnet, 2002, p. 1). Throughout his monograph, the author returns several times to the topic and adds the following characterisations: Paris 'as a prostitute' (p. 21) as well as a place which especially for Americans promised '[p]ublic liberty, private liberty, high culture and untrammelled sexuality' (p. 325). Of course, US mass culture, epitomised by Hollywood and Broadway, made sure that this image was promoted and subsequently shared globally (De Baecque, 2012, p. 13). The list could be further extended by portrayals of Paris 'as a prison, a paradise and a vision of hell. It has also been characterised as a beautiful woman, a sorceress and a demon' (Hussey, 2007, p. xv). Finally, Honoré de Balzac famously described it as 'a monster' (Balzac, 1974, p. 64).

It we take a look which of these myths are most consistently employed by the 33 musicals explored in this volume and how their deployment has changed over the last 115 years (see Table 19.1), the following observations can be made:

No characterisation of Paris is more important for the film and stage musical than the one of the metropolis as a place where people can experience 'personal freedom', where they can go to find themselves or to determine their own fate – this aspect features in practically all of the works under discussion. For the musical, this is far more fascinating than 'public liberty' which only occasionally (quite literally) takes centre stage; after all, what suits a musical better than the protagonist who expresses their self in song and dance?

TABLE 19.1 Myths of Paris associated with the 33 musicals discussed in this volume.

Year	Musical	Paris associated with													
		consumption	fashion/glamour	hedonism	high culture	modernity	personal freedom*	prostitution	public liberty	revolution	romance/love	sexual freedom	tourism	under-world	vitality	war
1905	The Merry Widow	X	X			X	X				X	X				
1905	Mlle Modiste		X			X	X				X				X	
1929	Love Parade					X	X	X			X	X			X	
1932	Love Me Tonight					X	X	X			X	X			X	
1932	One Hour with You					X	X	X			X	X		X	X	
1933	Roberta		X			X	X									
1933	Viktor und Viktoria					X	X								X	
1934	The Merry Widow		X			X	X				X	X			X	
1947	Bless the Bride				X		X				X					X
1949	Miss Liberty						X		X		X		X		X	
1951	An American in Paris			X	X	X	X				X	X	X		X	
1953	Can-Can				X		X		X		X					
1957	Silk Stockings	X	X	X		X	X				X					
1957	Les Girls						X				X	X				
1957	Funny Face		X		X	X	X				X		X			
1958	Gigi	X	X	X			X	X			X	X				
1958	Irma La Douce						X	X				X		X		

1960	Can-Can			X			X				X	X		X		
1962	Gay Purr-ee				X		X				X					
1962	No Strings		X			X	X				X					
1964	Ben Franklin in Paris						X		X	X	X					
1969	Dear World						X		X		X			X		
1970	The Aristocats					X	X							X		
1973	Gigi		X				X	X			X					
1982	Victor/Victoria					X	X				X	X			X	
1984	Sunday in the Park			X	X	X	X				X		X			
1985	Les Misérables						X		X	X	X			X		
1986	The Phantom of the Opera				X	X	X				X			X		
1989	Aspects of Love				X	X	X					X				
2001	Moulin Rouge!		X	X	X	X	X	X			X	X	X	X		
2008	Marguerite	X		X				X			X			X		X
2015	Gigi						X				X					
2015	An American in Paris				X	X	X				X				X	X

★ = also denotes self-determination and self-definition

Nearly as persistent as the trope of individual liberty is the association of the city with love or romance: Paris may love lovers (as Cole Porter put it), but the musical where, as a song in *Aida* (1998) once put it, 'Every Story Is a Love Story' simply loves lovers in Paris. Another strong link is the French capital's association with modernity; the strength of the cultural connection may vary over the decades – it was slightly less pronounced in the 1960s and 1970s – but has never been lost.

However, there are a number of myths whose importance has diminished: it was only in the first half of the 20th century that the 'vitality' of Paris was a major part of its allure, while its notoriety as a place of 'sexual freedom' faded once the sexual revolution swept across the United States and Europe in the 1960s and 1970s. A similar observation can be made about Paris as the capital of 'fashion': as soon as New York, Milan and London stepped up to become important centres of *haute couture* in their own right, the musical became less interested in incorporating this particular trope.

Intriguingly, 'prostitution' as well as the Parisian 'underworld' are only used successfully when both can be given a frivolous spin that avoids revealing their sordid or violent underbelly. Whereas the musical is comfortable with the spirited *fille de la rue*, the elegant *courtesan* and the charismatic *Apache*, it depicts at its own peril the nastiness of forcing yourself to sleep with a man you despise and the brutality of the self-righteous mob, as is proven by the muted reception history of *Marguerite*.

Paris as the 'City of Revolution' plays no great role in the history of the musical, with *Les Misérables* as the one striking exception, but then this blockbuster show is based on a classic French novel and was originated by French artists. Almost as rare is a link between the city and war; such an association is only made by works that were created either immediately after World War II (*Bless the Bride*) or at a safe historical distance from it (*Marguerite*, the stage version of *An American in Paris*).

It may come as no surprise that the musical shows no real interest in exposing Paris as a place of conspicuous 'consumption': as commercial forms neither the stage nor the screen musical appears too keen to draw attention to its own status as a manufactured commodity that is designed to find as large an audience as possible. Indeed it tries to hide the circumstances of its production.[1] It is also not surprising that the musical, so long denigrated as 'only entertainment' regularly strives to benefit from the association with Paris as 'the capital of art', of high culture and sophistication. The city's reputation as a home for art (*An American in Paris* 1951/2015; *Can-Can*, 1953; *Sunday in the Park with George*), literature (*Moulin Rouge!*), acting (*Bless the Bride*), music (*The Phantom of the Opera*), and philosophy (*Funny Face*) is alluded to time and time again, to enhance the musical's own status, even if those allusions occasionally take the form of benign satire.

Summing up how the city has been portrayed in Hollywood films, Antoine De Baecque emphasised: 'The cliché of Paris can take many different forms' – and it certainly does in the works discussed in this volume – 'but nothing prevents it from being beautiful' (De Baecque, 2012, p. 15). The only musical in this volume to emphasise the sinister side of the French capital is *Marguerite*, which tellingly was initiated by French songwriters and was roundly rejected by (British) critics as well as theatregoers. It seems that Anglo-American audiences do not wish to have their idea/ideals of the city undermined, compromised or contradicted.

The Paris depicted in stage and film musicals may function first and foremost as a projection screen for the American, British and French artists depicting it, but tellingly none of them reference the modern metropolis with its myriad problems. Anglo-American entertainment has yet to discover or react to what actually happened to and in the metropolitan area from the mid-1950s onward: the war in Algeria, the student unrests of the late 1960s as well as the ongoing social problems in the *banlieues* – unemployment, poverty, crime and racial tensions as a result of post-war immigration (Abrahamson, 2014, p. 74). Perhaps the musical in its early/ earlier days wasn't ready to address these issues, but the genre certainly should be able to tackle them now.[2]

In the new millennium, the political relationship between the United States and the United Kingdom on the one side and France on the other has deteriorated – the stark disagreements on foreign policy during the Iraq War encouraged contempt for each other's cultures (Schwartz, 2007, p. 2), and in recent years, the presidency of Donald Trump with its calculated rallying cry of 'America First!' as well as the Brexit negotiations – in their own way just as jingoistic – as handled by the successive governments of Theresa May and Boris Johnson, have only exacerbated that friction.

Yet the stage and screen musicals explored here should serve as a reminder of the contribution art and entertainment have made for decades and will continue to make in a post-COVID world to a better understanding between nations: as a fusion of francophone and anglophone culture, the Paris of musical theatre and the film musical regularly combines the best of each to allow all of us – in the United States, the United Kingdom, France and elsewhere – to dream, to swoon, to empathise, to understand and to hope.

In this spirit, a final look back is meant to trigger a look forward; Figure 19.1 is a photograph of Notre Dame de Paris in the 1960s. Right now, the majestic cathedral is undergoing extensive renovations after the devastating fire on 15 April 2019. The French have been reassured by the country's president, Emmanuel Macron, and the city's mayor, Anne Hidalgo, that the landmark will be restored to its former glory, so that it will continue to attract visitors from around the world.

FIGURE 19.1 Notre Dame de Paris, which was built between 1163 and 1345, as seen from the Left Bank quays. This promotional image was used by the French Government Tourist Office in 1963, the year the cathedral celebrated its 800th anniversary.

Source: Photo provided by the editor.

It is to be hoped that the musical on stage and screen will be able to go on contributing its share to the reputation and lustre of Paris for the benefit of lovers everywhere, including lovers of music and other arts, lovers of glorious entertainment and lovers of the 'City of Light'.

Notes

1 Jane Feuer has shown conclusively how this works in the Hollywood musical, see Feuer, 1982, pp. 1–22.
2 In spite of its multiple flaws, the 2020 Netflix series *The Eddy* could be seen as a first step in this direction.

References

Abrahamson, M. (2014) *Urban Sociology: A Global Introduction*. New York: Cambridge University Press.
De Baecque, A. (2012) 'Paris by Hollywood: Introduction,' in A. De Baecque (ed.) *Paris by Hollywood*. Paris: Flammarion, pp. 11–15.
De Balzac, H. (1974) *History of the Thirteen* (H. Hunt, trans.). Harmondsworth: Penguin Books.
Feuer, J. (1982) *The Hollywood Musical*. London and Basingstoke: Palgrave-Macmillan.
Higonnet, P. (2002) *Paris: Capital of the World* (A. Goldhammer, trans.). Cambridge and London: Belknap Press.
Hussey, A. (2007) *Paris: The Secret History*. London and New York: Penguin Books.
Schwartz, V. R. (2007) *It's So French! Hollywood, Paris, and the Making of Cosmopolitan Film Culture*. Chicago and London: University of Chicago Press.

INDEX